QUEEN VICTORIA

QUEEN VICTORIA, PRINCE ALBERT AND THE ROYAL FAMILY.

From the Picture by F. Winterhalter.

QUEEN VICTORIA

BY

LYTTON STRACHEY

NEW YORK
HARCOURT, BRACE AND COMPANY

PRINTED IN THE U S A BY
THE QUINN & BODEN COMPANY
RAHWAY, N. J

TO
VIRGINIA WOOLF

CONTENTS

ILLUSTRATIONS

Authority for every important statement of fact in the following pages will be found in the footnotes. The full titles of the works to which reference is made are given in the Bibliography at the end of the volume.

The author is indebted to the Trustees of the British Museum for their permission to make use of certain unpublished passages in the manuscript of the Greville Memoirs.

QUEEN VICTORIA

CHAPTER I

ANTECEDENTS

I

ON November 6, 1817, died the Princess Charlotte, only child of the Prince Regent, and heir
to the crown of England. Her short life had
hardly been a happy one. By nature impulsive,
capricious, and vehement, she had always longed
for liberty; and she had never possessed it. She
had been brought up among violent family quar-
rels, had been early separated from her disreputable and eccentric mother, and handed over to
the care of her disreputable and selfish father.
When she was seventeen, he decided to marry her
off to the Prince of Orange; she, at first, acquiesced; but, suddenly falling in love with Prince
Augustus of Prussia, she determined to break off
the engagement. This was not her first love affair, for she had previously carried on a clandes-
tine correspondence with a Captain Hess. Prince

Augustus was already married, morganatically, but she did not know it, and he did not tell her. While she was spinning out the negotiations with the Prince of Orange, the allied sovereigns—it was June, 1814—arrived in London to celebrate their victory. Among them, in the suite of the Emperor of Russia, was the young and handsome Prince Leopold of Saxe-Coburg. He made several attempts to attract the notice of the Princess, but she, with her heart elsewhere, paid very little attention. Next month the Prince Regent, discovering that his daughter was having secret meetings with Prince Augustus, suddenly appeared upon the scene and, after dismissing her household, sentenced her to a strict seclusion in Windsor Park. " God Almighty grant me patience! " she exclaimed, falling on her knees in an agony of agitation: then she jumped up, ran down the backstairs and out into the street, hailed a passing cab, and drove to her mother's house in Bayswater. She was discovered, pursued, and at length, yielding to the persuasions of her uncles, the Dukes of York and Sussex, of Brougham, and of the Bishop of Salisbury, she returned to Carlton House at two o'clock in the morning. She was immured at Windsor, but no more was heard of the Prince of Orange. Prince Augustus,

too, disappeared.   The way was at last open to
Prince Leopold of Saxe-Coburg.[1]

This Prince was clever enough to get round the
Regent, to impress the Ministers, and to make
friends with another of the Princess's uncles, the
Duke of Kent.   Through the Duke he was able to
communicate privately with the Princess, who
now declared that he was necessary to her happiness.   When, after Waterloo, he was in Paris,
the Duke's aide-de-camp carried letters backwards
and forwards across the Channel.   In January
1816 he was invited to England, and in May
the marriage took place.[2]

The character of Prince Leopold contrasted
strangely with that of his wife.   The younger
son of a German princeling, he was at this time
twenty-six years of age; he had served with distinction in the war against Napoleon; he had
shown considerable diplomatic skill at the Congress of Vienna;[3] and he was now to try his hand
at the task of taming a tumultuous Princess.
Cold and formal in manner, collected in speech,
careful in action, he soon dominated the wild,
impetuous, generous creature by his side.   There

[1] Greville, II, 326–8; Stockmar, chap. i, 86; Knight, I, chaps.
xv–xviii and Appendix, and II, chap. i.
[2] Grey, 384, 386–8; *Letters*, II, 40.
[3] Grey, 375–86.

was much in her, he found, of which he could not approve. She quizzed, she stamped, she roared with laughter; she had very little of that self-command which is especially required of princes; her manners were abominable. Of the latter he was a good judge, having moved, as he himself explained to his niece many years later, in the best society of Europe, being in fact "what is called in French *de la fleur des pois.*" There was continual friction, but every scene ended in the same way. Standing before him like a rebellious boy in petticoats, her body pushed forward, her hands behind her back, with flaming cheeks and sparkling eyes, she would declare at last that she was ready to do whatever he wanted. "If you wish it, I will do it," she would say. "I want nothing for myself," he invariably answered; "when I press something on you, it is from a conviction that it is for your interest and for your good."[1]

Among the members of the household at Claremont, near Esher, where the royal pair were established, was a young German physician, Christian Friedrich Stockmar. He was the son of a minor magistrate in Coburg, and, after taking part as a medical officer in the war, he had settled

[1] *Letters,* I, 216, 222–3; II, 39–40; Stockmar, 87–90.

down as a doctor in his native town. Here he had met Prince Leopold, who had been struck by his ability, and, on, his marriage, brought him to England as his personal physician. A curious fate awaited this young man; many were the gifts which the future held in store for him—many and various—influence, power, mystery, unhappiness, a broken heart. At Claremont his position was a very humble one; but the Princess took a fancy to him, called him "Stocky," and romped with him along the corridors. Dyspeptic by constitution, melancholic by temperament, he could yet be lively on occasion, and was known as a wit in Coburg. He was virtuous, too, and observed the royal *ménage* with approbation. "My master," he wrote in his diary, "is the best of all husbands in all the five quarters of the globe; and his wife bears him an amount of love, the greatness of which can only be compared with the English national debt." Before long he gave proof of another quality—a quality which was to colour the whole of his life—cautious sagacity. When, in the spring of 1817, it was known that the Princess was expecting a child, the post of one of her physicians-in-ordinary was offered to him, and he had the good sense to refuse it. He perceived that his colleagues would be jealous of him, that his advice would probably not be taken, but that, if anything were to go wrong, it would be certainly the foreign doctor who would be blamed. Very soon, indeed, he came to the opinion that the low diet and constant bleedings, to which the unfortunate Princess was subjected, were an error; he drew the Prince aside, and begged him to communicate this opinion to the English doctors; but it was useless. The fashionable lowering treatment was continued for months. On November 5, at nine o'clock in the evening, after a labour of over fifty hours, the Princess was delivered of a dead boy. At midnight her exhausted strength gave way. Then, at last, Stockmar consented to see her; he went in, and found her obviously dying, while the doctors were plying her with wine. She seized his hand and pressed it. "They have made me tipsy," she said. After a little he left her, and was already in the next room when he heard her call out in her loud voice: "Stocky! Stocky!" As he ran back the death-rattle was in her throat. She tossed herself violently from side to side; then suddenly drew up her legs, and it was over.

The Prince, after hours of watching, had left the room for a few moments' rest; and Stockmar had now to tell him that his wife was dead.

At first he could not be made to realise what had happened. On their way to her room he sank down on a chair while Stockmar knelt beside him: it was all a dream; it was impossible. At last, by the bed, he, too, knelt down and kissed the cold hands. Then rising and exclaiming, " Now I am quite desolate. Promise me never to leave me," he threw himself into Stockmar's arms.[1]

II

The tragedy at Claremont was of a most upsetting kind. The royal kaleidoscope had suddenly shifted, and nobody could tell how the new pattern would arrange itself. The succession to the throne, which had seemed so satisfactorily settled, now became a matter of urgent doubt.

George III was still living, an aged lunatic, at Windsor, completely impervious to the impressions of the outer world. Of his seven sons, the youngest was of more than middle age, and none had legitimate offspring. The outlook, therefore, was ambiguous. It seemed highly improbable that the Prince Regent, who had lately been obliged to abandon his stays, and presented a preposterous figure of debauched

---

[1] Stockmar, *Biographische Skizze,* and cap. iii.

obesity,[1] could ever again, even on the suppo-
sition that he divorced his wife and re-married,
become the father of a family. Besides the Duke
of Kent, who must be noticed separately, the
other brothers, in order of seniority, were the
Dukes of York, Clarence, Cumberland, Sussex,
and Cambridge; their situations and prospects
require a brief description. The Duke of York,
whose escapades in times past with Mrs. Clarke
and the army had brought him into trouble, now
divided his life between London and a large,
extravagantly ordered and extremely uncomfortable country house where he occupied himself
with racing, whist, and improper stories. He was
remarkable among the princes for one reason:
he was the only one of them—so we are informed
by a highly competent observer—who had the
feelings of a gentleman. He had been long
married to the Princess Royal of Prussia, a lady
who rarely went to bed and was perpetually surrounded by vast numbers of dogs, parrots, and
monkeys.[2] They had no children. The Duke
of Clarence had lived for many years in complete
obscurity with Mrs. Jordan, the actress, in Bushey
Park. By her he had had a large family of sons

---

[1] Creevey, I, 264, 272: "Prinny has let loose his belly, which now
reaches his knees; otherwise he is said to be well," 279.

[2] Greville, I, 5-7.

and daughters, and had appeared, in effect, to be married to her, when he suddenly separated from her and offered to marry Miss Wykeham, a crazy woman of large fortune, who, however, would have nothing to say to him. Shortly afterwards Mrs. Jordan died in distressed circumstances in Paris.[1] The Duke of Cumberland was probably the most unpopular man in England. Hideously ugly, with a distorted eye, he was bad-tempered and vindictive in private, a violent reactionary in politics, and was subsequently suspected of murdering his valet and of having carried on an amorous intrigue of an extremely scandalous kind.[2] He had lately married a German Princess, but there were as yet no children by the marriage. The Duke of Sussex had mildly literary tastes and collected books.[3] He had married Lady Augusta Murray, by whom he had two children, but the marriage, under the Royal Marriages Act, was declared void. On Lady Augusta's death, he married Lady Cecilia Buggin; she changed her name to Underwood; but this marriage also was void. Of the Duke of Cambridge, the youngest of the brothers, not very much was known. He lived

[1] Greville, IV, 2.
[2] Stockmar, 95; Creevey, I, 148; Greville, I, 228; Lieven, 183–4.
[3] Crawford, 24.

in Hanover, wore a blonde wig, chattered and fidgeted a great deal, and was unmarried.[1]

Besides his seven sons, George III had five surviving daughters. Of these, two—the Queen of Würtemberg and the Duchess of Gloucester—were married and childless. The three unmarried princesses—Augusta, Elizabeth, and Sophia—were all over forty.

III

The fourth son of George III was Edward, Duke of Kent. He was now fifty years of age—a tall, stout, vigorous man, highly-coloured, with bushy eyebrows, a bald top to his head, and what hair he had carefully dyed a glossy black. His dress was extremely neat, and in his whole appearance there was a rigidity which did not belie his character. He had spent his early life in the army—at Gibraltar, in Canada, in the West Indies—and, under the influence of military training, had become at first a disciplinarian and at last a martinet. In 1802, having been sent to Gibraltar to restore order in a mutinous garrison, he was recalled for undue severity, and his active career had come to an end. Since then he had spent his life regulating his domestic arrange-

[1] Crawford. 80, 113.

ments with great exactitude, busying himself
with the affairs of his numerous dependents,
designing clocks, and struggling to restore order
to his finances, for, in spite of his being, as someone said who knew him well *"reglé comme du
papier à musique,"* and in spite of an income of
£24,000 a year, he was hopelessly in debt. He
had quarrelled with most of his brothers, particularly with the Prince Regent, and it was only
natural that he should have joined the political
Opposition and become a pillar of the Whigs.

What his political opinions may actually have
been is open to doubt; it has often been asserted
that he was a Liberal, or even a Radical; and,
if we are to believe Robert Owen, he was a neces-
sitarian Socialist. His relations with Owen—
the shrewd, gullible, high-minded, wrong-headed,
illustrious and preposterous father of Socialism
and Co-operation—were curious and characteristic. He talked of visiting the Mills at New
Lanark; he did, in fact, preside at one of Owen's
public meetings; he corresponded with him on
confidential terms, and he even (so Owen assures
us) returned, after his death, from "the sphere
of spirits" to give encouragement to the Owenites
on earth. "In an especial manner," says Owen,
"I have to name the very anxious feelings of the

spirit of his Royal Highness the late Duke of
Kent (who early informed me there were no
titles in the spiritual spheres into which he had
entered), to benefit, not a class, a sect, a party,
or any particular country, but the whole of the human race through futurity." "His whole spirit-
proceeding with me has been most beautiful,"
Owen adds, "making his own appointments; and
never in one instance has this spirit not been
punctual to the minute he had named." But Owen
was of a sanguine temperament. He also num-
bered among his proselytes President Jefferson,
Prince Metternich, and Napoleon; so that some
uncertainty must still linger over the Duke of
Kent's views. But there is no uncertainty about
another circumstance: his Royal Highness borrowed from Robert Owen, on various occasions,
various sums of money which were never repaid
and amounted in all to several hundred pounds.[1]

After the death of the Princess Charlotte it
was clearly important, for more than one reason,
that the Duke of Kent should marry. From the
point of view of the nation, the lack of heirs in
the reigning family seemed to make the step
almost obligatory; it was also likely to be highly

[1] Stockmar, 112–3; *Letters,* I, 8; Crawford, 27–30; Owen, 193–4,
197–8, 199, 229.

expedient from the point of view of the Duke. To marry as a public duty, for the sake of the royal succession, would surely deserve some recognition from a grateful country. When the Duke of York had married he had received a settlement of £25,000 a year. Why should not the Duke of Kent look forward to an equal sum? But the situation was not quite simple. There was the Duke of Clarence to be considered; he was the elder brother, and, if *he* married, would clearly have the prior claim. On the other hand, if the Duke of Kent married, it was important to remember that he would be making a serious sacrifice: a lady was involved.

The Duke, reflecting upon all these matters with careful attention, happened, about a month after his niece's death, to visit Brussels, and learnt that Mr. Creevey was staying in the town. Mr. Creevey was a close friend of the leading Whigs and an inveterate gossip; and it occurred to the Duke that there could be no better channel through which to communicate his views upon the situation to political circles at home. Apparently it did not occur to him that Mr. Creevey was malicious and might keep a diary. He therefore sent for him on some trivial pretext, and a remarkable conversation ensued.

After referring to the death of the Princess, to the improbability of the Regent's seeking a divorce, to the childlessness of the Duke of York, and to the possibility of the Duke of Clarence marrying, the Duke adverted to his own position. "Should the Duke of Clarence not marry," he said, "the next prince in succession is myself, and although I trust I shall be at all times ready to obey any call my country may make upon me, God only knows the sacrifice it will be to make, whenever I shall think it my duty to become a married man. It is now seven-and twenty years that Madame St. Laurent and I have lived together: we are of the same age, and have been in all climates, and in all difficulties together, and you may well imagine, Mr. Creevey, the pang it will occasion me to part with her. I put it to your own feelings—in the event of any separation between you and Mrs. Creevey. . . . As for Madame St. Laurent herself, I protest I don't know what is to become of her if a marriage is to be forced upon me; her feelings are already so agitated upon the subject." The Duke went on to describe how, one morning, a day or two after the Princess Charlotte's death, a paragraph had appeared in the *Morning Chronicle,* alluding to the possibility of his marriage. He had

received the newspaper at breakfast together
with his letters, and "I did as is my constant
practice, I threw the newspaper across the table
to Madame St. Laurent, and began to open and
read my letters. I had not done so but a very
short time, when my attention was called to
an extraordinary noise and a strong convulsive
movement in Madame St. Laurent's throat. For
a short time I entertained serious apprehensions
for her safety; and when, upon her recovery, I
enquired into the occasion of this attack, she
pointed to the article in the *Morning Chronicle.*"

The Duke then returned to the subject of
the Duke of Clarence. " My brother the Duke of
Clarence is the elder brother, and has certainly
the right to marry if he chooses, and I would
not interfere with him on any account. If he
wishes to be king—to be married and have
children, poor man—God help him! let him do
so. For myself—I am a man of no ambition, and
wish only to remain as I am. . . . Easter,
you know, falls very early this year—the 22nd
of March. If the Duke of Clarence does not
take any step before that time, I must find some
pretext to reconcile Madame St. Laurent to
my going to England for a short time. When
once there, it will be easy for me to consult with

my friends as to the proper steps to be taken. Should the Duke of Clarence do nothing before that time as to marrying it will become my duty, no doubt, to take some measures upon the subject myself." Two names, the Duke said, had been mentioned in this connection—those of the Princess of Baden and the Princess of Saxe-Coburg. The latter, he thought, would perhaps be the better of the two, from the circumstance of Prince Leopold being so popular with the nation; but before any other steps were taken, he hoped and expected to see justice done to Madame St. Laurent. "She is," he explained, "of very good family, and has never been an actress, and I am the first and only person who ever lived with her. Her disinterestedness, too, has been equal to her fidelity. When she first came to me it was upon £100 a year. That sum was afterwards raised to £400, and finally to £1000; but when my debts made it necessary for me to sacrifice a great part of my income, Madame St. Laurent insisted upon again returning to her income of £400 a year. If Madame St. Laurent is to return to live amongst her friends, it must be in such a state of independence as to command their respect. I shall not require very much, but a certain number of servants and

a carriage are essentials." As to his own settlement, the Duke observed that he would expect
the Duke of York's marriage to be considered
the precedent. " That," he said, " was a marriage
for the succession, and £25,000 for income was
settled, in addition to all his other income,
purely on that account. I shall be contented
with the same arrangement, without making
any demands grounded on the difference of the
value of money in 1792 and at present. As
for the payment of my debts," the Duke concluded, " I don't call them great. The nation,
on the contrary, is greatly my debtor." Here a
clock struck, and seemed to remind the Duke
that he had an appointment; he rose, and Mr.
Creevey left him.

Who could keep such a communication secret?
Certainly not Mr. Creevey. He hurried off to
tell the Duke of Wellington, who was very
much amused, and he wrote a long account of
it to Lord Sefton, who received the letter " very
apropos," while a surgeon was sounding his
bladder to ascertain whether he had a stone. " I
never saw a fellow more astonished than he was,"
wrote Lord Sefton in his reply, " at seeing me
laugh as soon as the operation was over. Nothing
could be more first-rate than the royal Edward's

ingenuousness. One does not know which to
admire most—the delicacy of his attachment to
Madame St. Laurent, the refinement of his sentiments towards the Duke of Clarence, or his own
perfect disinterestedness in pecuniary matters." [1]

As it turned out, both the brothers decided to
marry. The Duke of Kent, selecting the Princess
of Saxe-Coburg in preference to the Princess
of Baden, was united to her on May 29, 1818.
On June 11, the Duke of Clarence followed suit
with a daughter of the Duke of Saxe-Meiningen.
But they were disappointed in their financial
expectations; for though the Government brought
forward proposals to increase their allowances,
together with that of the Duke of Cumberland,
the motions were defeated in the House of
Commons. At this the Duke of Wellington was
not surprised. " By God! " he said, " there is a
great deal to be said about that. They are the
damnedest millstones about the necks of any
Government that can be imagined. They have
insulted—*personally* insulted—two-thirds of the
gentlemen of England, and how can it be won-
dered at that they take their revenge upon them
in the House of Commons? It is their only
opportunity, and I think, by God! they are quite

1 Creevey, I, 267–71.

right to use it." [1] Eventually, however, Parliament increased the Duke of Kent's annuity by
£6000.

The subsequent history of Madame St. Laurent
has not transpired.

IV

The new Duchess of Kent, Victoria Mary
Louisa, was a daughter of Francis, Duke of Saxe-
Coburg-Saalfeld, and a sister of Prince Leopold.
The family was an ancient one, being a branch
of the great House of Wettin, which since the
eleventh century had ruled over the March of
Meissen on the Elbe. In the fifteenth century
the whole possessions of the House had been
divided between the Albertine and Ernestine
branches: from the former descended the electors
and kings of Saxony; the latter, ruling over
Thuringia, became further subdivided into five
branches, of which the duchy of Saxe-Coburg
was one. This principality was very small, containing about 60,000 inhabitants, but it enjoyed
independent and sovereign rights. During the
disturbed years which followed the French Revolution, its affairs became terribly involved. The
Duke was extravagant, and kept open house
for the swarms of refugees, who fled eastward

[1] Creevey, I, 276-7.

over Germany as the French power advanced.
Among these was the Prince of Leiningen, an
elderly beau, whose domains on the Moselle
had been seized by the French, but who was
granted in compensation the territory of Amorbach in Lower Franconia. In 1803 he married
the Princess Victoria, at that time seventeen
years of age. Three years later Duke Francis
died a ruined man. The Napoleonic harrow
passed over Saxe-Coburg. The duchy was seized
by the French, and the ducal family were
reduced to beggary, almost to starvation. At
the same time the little principality of Amorbach
was devastated by the French, Russian, and
Austrian armies, marching and counter-marching
across it. For years there was hardly a cow in
the country, nor enough grass to feed a flock
of geese. Such was the desperate plight of
the family which, a generation later, was to
have gained a foothold in half the reigning
Houses of Europe. The Napoleonic harrow had
indeed done its work; the seed was planted; and
the crop would have surprised Napoleon. Prince
Leopold, thrown upon his own resources at fifteen,
made a career for himself and married the
heiress of England. The Princess of Leiningen,
struggling at Amorbach with poverty, military

requisitions, and a futile husband, developed an
independence of character and a tenacity of
purpose which were to prove useful in very
different circumstances. In 1814, her husband
died, leaving her with two children and the
regency of the principality. After her brother's
marriage with the Princess Charlotte, it was
proposed that she should marry the Duke of
Kent; but she declined, on the ground that the
guardianship of her children and the management of her domains made other ties undesirable.
The Princess Charlotte's death, however, altered
the case; and when the Duke of Kent renewed
his offer, she accepted it. She was thirty-two
years old—short, stout, with brown eyes and
hair, and rosy cheeks, cheerful and voluble, and
gorgeously attired in rustling silks and bright
velvets.[1]

She was certainly fortunate in her contented
disposition; for she was fated, all through her
life, to have much to put up with. Her second
marriage, with its dubious prospects, seemed at
first to be chiefly a source of difficulties and
discomforts. The Duke, declaring that he was
still too poor to live in England, moved about
with uneasy precision through Belgium and

[1] *Letters*, I, 1–3; Grey, 378–81, 389; Crawford, 30–4; Stockmar, 113.

Germany, attending parades and inspecting
barracks in a neat military cap, while the English
notabilities looked askance, and the Duke of
Wellington dubbed him the Corporal. " God
damme!" he exclaimed to Mr. Creevey, " d'ye
know what his sisters call him? By God! they
call him Joseph Surface!" At Valenciennes,
where there was a review and a great dinner,
the Duchess arrived with an old and ugly lady-
in-waiting, and the Duke of Wellington found
himself in a difficulty. " Who the devil is to
take out the maid of honour?" he kept asking;
but at last he thought of a solution. " Damme,
Freemantle, find out the mayor and let him
do it." So the Mayor of Valenciennes was
brought up for the purpose, and—so we learn
from Mr. Creevey—" a capital figure he was."
A few days later, at Brussels, Mr. Creevey
himself had an unfortunate experience. A military school was to be inspected—before breakfast.
The company assembled; everything was highly
satisfactory; but the Duke of Kent continued
for so long examining every detail and asking
meticulous question after meticulous question,
that Mr. Creevey at last could bear it no longer,
and whispered to his neighbour that he was
damned hungry. The Duke of Wellington heard

him, and was delighted. "I recommend you," he said, "whenever you start with the royal family in a morning, and particularly with *the Corporal,* always to breakfast first." He and his staff, it turned out, had taken that precaution, and the great man amused himself, while the stream of royal inquiries poured on, by pointing at Mr. Creevey from time to time with the remark, "Voilà le monsieur qui n'a pas déjeuné!"[1]

Settled down at last at Amorbach, the time hung heavily on the Duke's hands. The establishment was small, the country was impoverished; even clock-making grew tedious at last. He brooded—for in spite of his piety the Duke was not without a vein of superstition—over the prophecy of a gipsy at Gibraltar who told him that he was to have many losses and crosses, that he was to die in happiness, and that his only child was to be a great queen. Before long it became clear that a child was to be expected: the Duke decided that it should be born in England. Funds were lacking for the journey, but his determination was not to be set aside. Come what might, he declared, his child must be English-born. A carriage was hired, and the

[1] Creevey, I, 282–4.

Duke himself mounted the box. Inside were the
Duchess, her daughter Feodora, a girl of fourteen,
with maids, nurses, lap-dogs, and canaries. Off
they drove—through Germany, through France:
bad roads, cheap inns, were nothing to the
rigorous Duke and the equable, abundant Duchess.
The Channel was crossed, London was reached
in safety. The authorities provided a set of
rooms in Kensington Palace; and there, on May
24, 1819, a female infant was born.[1]

[1] Crawford, 25, 37–8.

CHAPTER II

CHILDHOOD

I

THE child who, in these not very impressive circumstances, appeared in the world, received but scant attention. There was small reason to foresee her destiny. The Duchess of Clarence, two months before, had given birth to a daughter; this infant, indeed, had died almost immediately; but it seemed highly probable that the Duchess would again become a mother; and so it actually fell out. More than this, the Duchess of Kent was young, and the Duke was strong; there was every likelihood that before long a brother would follow, to snatch her faint chance of the succession from the little princess.

Nevertheless, the Duke had other views: there were prophecies. . . . At any rate, he would christen the child Elizabeth, a name of happy augury. In this, however, he reckoned without the Regent, who, seeing a chance of annoying his brother, suddenly announced that he himself

would be present at the baptism, and signified
at the same time that one of the godfathers was
to be the Emperor Alexander of Russia. And
so when the ceremony took place, and the Archbishop of Canterbury asked by what name he
was to baptise the child, the Regent replied
" Alexandria."   At this the Duke ventured to
suggest that another name might be added.
" Certainly," said the Regent; " Georgina? " " Or
Elizabeth? " said the Duke.   There was a pause,
during which the Archbishop, with the baby in
his lawn sleeves, looked with some uneasiness
from one Prince to the other.   " Very well,
then," said the Regent at last, " call her after
her mother.   But Alexandrina must come first."
Thus, to the disgust of her father, the child was
christened Alexandrina Victoria.[1]

The Duke had other subjects of disgust. The
meagre grant of the Commons had by no means
put an end to his financial distresses.   It was
to be feared that his services were not appreciated by the nation.   His debts continued to
grow.   For many years he had lived upon £7000
a year; but now his expenses were exactly
doubled; he could make no further reductions;
as it was, there was not a single servant in his

[1] Murray, 62–3; Lee, 11–12.

PRINCESS VICTORIA IN 1836.

From the Portrait by F. Winterhalter.

establishment who was idle for a moment from morning to night. He poured out his griefs in a long letter to Robert Owen, whose sympathy had the great merit of being practical. " I now candidly state," he wrote, " that, after viewing the subject in every possible way, I am satisfied that, to continue to live in England, even in the quiet way in which we are going on, *without splendour,* and *without show, nothing short of doubling the seven thousand pounds will do,* REDUCTION BEING IMPOSSIBLE." It was clear that he would be obliged to sell his house for £51,300: if that failed, he would go and live on the Continent. " If my services are useful to my country, it surely becomes *those who have the power* to support me in substantiating those just claims I have for the very extensive losses and privations I have experienced, during the very long period of my professional servitude in the Colonies; and if this is not attainable, *it is a clear proof to me that they are not appreciated;* and under that impression I shall not scruple, in *due* time, to resume my retirement abroad, when the Duchess and myself shall have fulfilled our duties in establishing the *English* birth of my child, and giving it material nutriment on the soil of Old England; and which we shall certainly repeat, if Providence destines to give us any further increase of family." [1]

In the meantime, he decided to spend the winter at Sidmouth, " in order," he told Owen, " that the Duchess may have the benefit of tepid sea bathing, and our infant that of sea air, on the fine coast of Devonshire, during the months of the year that are so odious in London." [2]   In December the move was made.   With the new year, the Duke remembered another prophecy. In 1820, a fortune-teller had told him, two members of the Royal Family would die. Who would they be?   He speculated on the various possibilities: the King, it was plain, could not live much longer; and the Duchess of York had been attacked by a mortal disease. Probably it would be the King and the Duchess of York; or perhaps the King and the Duke of York; or the King and the Regent.   He himself was one of the healthiest men in England.[3]   " My brothers," he declared, " are not so strong as I am; I have lived a regular life. I shall outlive them all. The crown will come to me and my children." [4] He went out for a walk, and got his feet wet.

[1] Owen, *Journal*, No. 1, February, 1853, 28–9.
[2] *Ibid.*, 31.
[3] Croker, I, 155.
[4] Stockmar, 113.

On coming home, he neglected to change his stockings. He caught cold, inflammation of the lungs set in, and on January 22 he was a dying man. By a curious chance, young Dr. Stockmar was staying in the house at the time; two years before, he had stood by the death-bed of the Princess Charlotte; and now he was watching the Duke of Kent in his agony. On Stockmar's advice, a will was hastily prepared. The Duke's earthly possessions were of a negative character; but it was important that the guardianship of the unwitting child, whose fortunes were now so strangely changing, should be assured to the Duchess. The Duke was just able to understand the document, and to append his signature. Having inquired whether his writing was perfectly clear, he became unconscious, and breathed his last on the following morning.[1] Six days later came the fulfilment of the second half of the gipsy's prophecy. The long, unhappy, and inglorious life of George the Third of England was ended.

II

Such was the confusion of affairs at Sidmouth, that the Duchess found herself without the means of returning to London. Prince Leopold hurried

[1] Stockmar, 114-5.

down, and himself conducted his sister and her
family, by slow and bitter stages, to Kensington.
The widowed lady, in her voluminous blacks,
needed all her equanimity to support her. Her
prospects were more dubious than ever. She had
£6000 a year of her own; but her husband's debts
loomed before her like a mountain. Soon she
learnt that the Duchess of Clarence was once
more expecting a child. What had she to look
forward to in England? Why should she remain
in a foreign country, among strangers, whose
language she could not speak, whose customs
she could not understand? Surely it would be
best to return to Amorbach, and there, among her
own people, bring up her daughters in economical
obscurity. But she was an inveterate optimist;
she had spent her life in struggles, and would
not be daunted now. And besides, she adored
her baby. " C'est mon bonheur, mes délices, mon
existence," she declared; the darling should be
brought up as an English princess, whatever
lot awaited her. Prince Leopold came forward
nobly with an offer of an additional £3000 a year;
and the Duchess remained at Kensington.[1]

The child herself was extremely fat, and bore
a remarkable resemblance to her grandfather.

[1] *Letters*, I, 15, 257–8; Grey, App. A.

" C'est l'image du feu Roi!" exclaimed the Duchess. " C'est le Roi Georges en jupons," echoed the surrounding ladies, as the little creature waddled with difficulty from one to the other.[1]

Before long, the world began to be slightly interested in the nursery at Kensington. When, early in 1821, the Duchess of Clarence's second child, the Princess Elizabeth, died within three months of its birth, the interest increased. Great forces and fierce antagonisms seemed to be moving, obscurely, about the royal cradle. It was a time of faction and anger, of violent repression and profound discontent. A powerful movement, which had for long been checked by adverse circumstances, was now spreading throughout the country. New passions, new desires, were abroad; or rather old passions and old desires, reincarnated with a new potency: love of freedom, hatred of injustice, hope for the future of man. The mighty still sat proudly in their seats, dispensing their ancient tyranny; but a storm was gathering out of the darkness, and already there was lightning in the sky. But the vastest forces must needs operate through frail human instruments; and it seemed for many

[1] Granville, I, 168-9.

years as if the great cause of English liberalism
hung upon the life of the little girl at Kensington.
She alone stood between the country and her
terrible uncle, the Duke of Cumberland, the
hideous embodiment of reaction. Inevitably, the
Duchess of Kent threw in her lot with her
husband's party; Whig leaders, Radical agitators,
rallied round her; she was intimate with the
bold Lord Durham, she was on friendly terms
with the redoubtable O'Connell himself. She
received Wilberforce—though, to be sure, she
did not ask him to sit down.[1] She declared in
public that she put her faith in "the liberties
of the People."[2] It was certain that the young
Princess would be brought up in the way that
she should go; yet there, close behind the throne,
waiting, sinister, was the Duke of Cumberland.
Brougham, looking forward into the future in
his scurrilous fashion, hinted at dreadful possibilities. "I never prayed so heartily for a Prince
before," he wrote, on hearing that George IV
had been attacked by illness. "If he had gone,
all the troubles of these villains [the Tory
Ministers] went with him, and they had Fred. I
[the Duke of York] their own man for his life.
. . . He [Fred. I] won't live long either; that

1 *Wilberforce, William,* V, 71–2.   2 *Letters,* I, 17.

Prince of Blackguards, 'Brother William,' is as bad a life, so we come in the course of nature to be *assassinated* by King Ernest I or Regent Ernest [the Duke of Cumberland]."[1] Such thoughts were not peculiar to Brougham; in the seething state of public feeling, they constantly leapt to the surface; and, even so late as the year previous to her accession, the Radical newspapers were full of suggestions that the Princess Victoria was in danger from the machinations of her wicked uncle.[2]

But no echo of these conflicts and forebodings reached the little Drina—for so she was called in the family circle—as she played with her dolls, or scampered down the passages, or rode on the donkey her uncle York had given her[3] along the avenues of Kensington Gardens. The fair-haired, blue-eyed child was idolised by her nurses, and her mother's ladies, and her sister Feodora; and for a few years there was danger, in spite of her mother's strictness, of her being spoilt. From time to time, she would fly into a violent passion, stamp her little foot, and set everyone at defiance; whatever they might say, she would not learn her letters—no, she *would not;* after-

---

1 Creevey, I, 297–8.   2 Jerrold, *Early Court*, 15–17.   3 *Letters*, I, 10.

wards, she was very sorry, and burst into tears;
but her letters remained unlearnt. When she
was five years old, however, a change came, with
the appearance of Fräulein Lehzen. This lady,
who was the daughter of a Hanoverian clergyman and had previously been the Princess
Feodora's governess, soon succeeded in instilling
a new spirit into her charge. At first, indeed, she
was appalled by the little Princess's outbursts
of temper; never in her life, she declared, had
she seen such a passionate and naughty child.
Then she observed something else; the child was
extraordinarily truthful; whatever punishment
might follow, she never told a lie.[1] Firm, very
firm, the new governess yet had the sense to
see that all the firmness in the world would be
useless, unless she could win her way into little
Drina's heart. She did so, and there were no
more difficulties. Drina learnt her letters like
an angel; and she learnt other things as well. The
Baroness de Späth taught her how to make little
board boxes and decorate them with tinsel and
painted flowers;[2] her mother taught her religion.
Sitting in the pew every Sunday morning, the
child of six was seen listening in rapt attention to the clergyman's endless sermon, for she

---

[1] *Letters*, I, 14; *Girlhood*, I, 280.   [2] Crawford, 6.

was to be examined upon it in the afternoon.[1] The
Duchess was determined that her daughter, from
the earliest possible moment, should be prepared
for her high station in a way that would commend
itself to the most respectable; her good, plain,
thrifty German mind recoiled with horror and
amazement from the shameless junketings at Carlton House; Drina should never be allowed to forget for a moment the virtues of simplicity, regularity, propriety, and devotion. The little girl,
however, was really in small need of such lessons,
for she was naturally simple and orderly, she was
pious without difficulty, and her sense of propriety
was keen. She understood very well the niceties
of her own position. When, a child of six, Lady
Jane Ellice was taken by her grandmother to
Kensington Palace, she was put to play with the
Princess Victoria, who was the same age as herself. The young visitor, ignorant of etiquette, began to make free with the toys on the floor, in a
way which was a little too familiar; but " You
must not touch those," she was quickly told, " they
are mine; and I may call you Jane, but you must
not call me Victoria." [2] The Princess's most constant playmate was Victoire, the daughter of Sir
John Conroy, the Duchess's major-domo. The

two girls were very fond of one another; they would walk hand in hand together in Kensington Gardens. But little Drina was perfectly aware for which of them it was that they were followed, at a respectful distance, by a gigantic scarlet flunkey.[1]

Warm-hearted, responsive, she loved her dear Lehzen, and she loved her dear Feodora, and her dear Victoire, and her dear Madame de Späth. And her dear Mamma . . . of course, she loved her too; it was her duty; and yet—she could not tell why it was—she was always happier when she was staying with her Uncle Leopold at Claremont. There old Mrs. Louis, who, years ago, had waited on her Cousin Charlotte, petted her to her heart's content; and her uncle himself was wonderfully kind to her, talking to her seriously and gently, almost as if she were a grown-up person. She and Feodora invariably wept when the too short visit was over, and they were obliged to return to the dutiful monotony, and the affectionate supervision of Kensington. But sometimes when her mother had to stay at home, she was allowed to go out driving all alone with her dear Feodora and her dear Lehzen, and she could talk and look as she liked, and it was very delightful.[2]

[1] Hunt, II, 257-8.   [2] *Letters*, I, 10, 18.

The visits to Claremont were frequent enough; but one day, on a special occasion, she paid one of a rarer and more exciting kind. When she was seven years old, she and her mother and sister were asked by the King to go down to Windsor. George IV, who had transferred his fraternal ill-temper to his sister-in-law and her family, had at last grown tired of sulking, and decided to be agreeable. The old rip, bewigged and gouty, ornate and enormous, with his jewelled mistress by his side and his flaunting court about him, re-ceived the tiny creature who was one day to hold in those same halls a very different state. " Give me your little paw," he said; and two ages touched. Next morning, driving in his phaeton with the Duchess of Gloucester, he met the Duch-ess of Kent and her child in the Park. " Pop her in," were his orders, which, to the terror of the mother and the delight of the daughter, were im-mediately obeyed. Off they dashed to Virginia Water, where there was a great barge, full of lords and ladies fishing, and another barge with a band; and the King ogled Feodora, and praised her manners, and then turned to his own small niece. " What is your favourite tune? The band shall play it." " God save the King, sir," was the instant answer. The Princess's reply has been

praised as an early example of a tact which was
afterwards famous. But she was a very truthful
child, and perhaps it was her genuine opinion.[1]

III

In 1827 the Duke of York, who had found some
consolation for the loss of his wife in the sympathy of the Duchess of Rutland, died, leaving
behind him the unfinished immensity of Stafford
House and £200,000 worth of debts. Three years
later George IV also disappeared, and the Duke
of Clarence reigned in his stead. The new Queen,
it was now clear, would in all probability never
again be a mother; the Princess Victoria, therefore, was recognised by Parliament as heir-pre-
sumptive; and the Duchess of Kent, whose annuity had been doubled five years previously, was
now given an additional £10,000 for the maintenance of the Princess, and was appointed regent,
in case of the death of the King before the majority of her daughter. At the same time a great
convulsion took place in the constitution of the
State. The power of the Tories, who had dominated England for more than forty years, suddenly began to crumble. In the tremendous
struggle that followed, it seemed for a moment

1 *Letters*, I, 11–12; Lee, 26.

as if the tradition of generations might be snapped, as if the blind tenacity of the reactionaries and the determined fury of their enemies could have no other issue than revolution. But the forces of compromise triumphed: the Reform Bill was passed. The centre of gravity in the constitution was shifted towards the middle classes; the Whigs came into power; and the complexion of the Government assumed a Liberal tinge. One of the results of this new state of affairs was a change in the position of the Duchess of Kent and her daughter. From being the *protégées* of an opposition clique, they became assets of the official majority of the nation. The Princess Victoria was henceforward the living symbol of the victory of the middle classes.

The Duke of Cumberland, on the other hand, suffered a corresponding eclipse: his claws had been pared by the Reform Act. He grew insignificant and almost harmless, though his ugliness remained; he was the wicked uncle still—but only of a story.

The Duchess's own liberalism was not very profound. She followed naturally in the footsteps of her husband, repeating with conviction the catchwords of her husband's clever friends and the generalisations of her clever brother Leopold.

She herself had no pretensions to cleverness; she did not understand very much about the Poor Law and the Slave Trade and Political Economy; but she hoped that she did her duty; and she hoped—she ardently hoped—that the same might be said of Victoria. Her educational conceptions were those of Dr. Arnold, whose views were just then beginning to permeate society. Dr. Arnold's object was, first and foremost, to make his pupils " in the highest and truest sense of the words, Christian gentlemen "; intellectual refinements might follow. The Duchess felt convinced that it was her supreme duty in life to make quite sure that her daughter should grow up into a Christian queen. To this task she bent all her energies; and, as the child developed, she flattered herself that her efforts were not unsuccessful. When the Princess was eleven, she desired the Bishops of London and Lincoln to submit her daughter to an examination, and report upon the progress that had been made. " I feel the time to be now come," the Duchess explained, in a letter obviously drawn up by her own hand, " that what has been done should be put to some test, that if anything has been done in error of judgment it may be corrected, and that the plan for the future should be open to consideration and revision. . . . I attend

almost always myself every lesson, or a part; and
as the lady about the Princess is a competent
person, she assists Her in preparing Her lessons,
for the various masters, as I resolved to act in
that manner so as to be Her Governess myself.
. . . When she was at a proper age she commenced
attending Divine Service regularly with me, and I
have every feeling that she has religion at Her
heart, that she is morally impressed with it to that
degree, that she is less liable to error by its application to her feelings as a Child capable of reflection." " The general bent of Her character," added
the Duchess, " is strength of intellect, capable of
receiving with ease, information, and with a peculiar readiness in coming to a very just and benig-
nant decision on any point Her opinion is asked on.
Her adherence to truth is of so marked a character
that I feel no apprehension of that Bulwark being
broken down by any circumstances." The Bishops attended at the Palace, and the result of their
examination was all that could be wished. " In
answering a great variety of questions proposed
to her," they reported, " the Princess displayed an
accurate knowledge of the most important features of Scripture History, and of the leading
truths and precepts of the Christian Religion as
taught by the Church of England, as well as an

acquaintance with the Chronology and principal facts of English History remarkable in so young a person. To questions in Geography, the use of the Globes, Arithmetic, and Latin Grammar, the answers which the Princess returned were equally satisfactory." They did not believe that the Duchess's plan of education was susceptible of any improvement; and the Archbishop of Canterbury, who was also consulted, came to the same gratifying conclusion.[1]

One important step, however, remained to be taken. So far, as the Duchess explained to the Bishops, the Princess had been kept in ignorance of the station that she was likely to fill. " She is aware of its duties, and that a Sovereign should live for others; so that when Her innocent mind receives the impression of Her future fate, she receives it with a mind formed to be sensible of what is to be expected from Her, and it is to be hoped, she will be too well grounded in Her principles to be dazzled with the station she is to look to." [2] In the following year it was decided that she should be enlightened on this point. The well-known scene followed: the history lesson, the genealogical table of the Kings of England slipped beforehand by the governess into the book, the

[1] *Letters,* I, 14–17.   [2] *Ibid.,* I, 16.

Princess's surprise, her inquiries, her final realisation of the facts. When the child at last understood, she was silent for a moment, and then she spoke: " I will be good," she said. The words were something more than a conventional protestation, something more than the expression of a superimposed desire; they were, in their limitation and their intensity, their egotism and their humility, an instinctive summary of the dominating qualities of a life. " I cried much on learning it," her Majesty noted long afterwards. No doubt, while the others were present, even her dear Lehzen, the little girl kept up her self-command; and then crept away somewhere to ease her heart of an inward, unfamiliar agitation, with a handkerchief, out of her mother's sight.[1]

But her mother's sight was by no means an easy thing to escape. Morning and evening, day and night, there was no relaxation of the maternal vigilance. The child grew into the girl, the girl into the young woman; but still she slept in her mother's bedroom; still she had no place allowed her where she might sit or work by herself.[2] An extraordinary watchfulness surrounded her every step: up to the day of her accession, she never went downstairs without someone beside her hold-

1 Martin, I, 13.   2 Letters, I, 11.

ing her hand.[1] Plainness and regularity ruled the
household. The hours, the days, the years passed
slowly and methodically by. The dolls—the innumerable dolls, each one so neatly dressed, each one
with its name so punctiliously entered in the catalogue—were laid aside, and a little music and a
little dancing took their place. Taglioni came, to
give grace and dignity to the figure,[2] and Lablache, to train the piping treble upon his own
rich bass. The Dean of Chester, the official pre-
ceptor, continued his endless instruction in Scripture history, while the Duchess of Northumber-
land, the official governess, presided over every
lesson with becoming solemnity. Without doubt,
the Princess's main achievement during her school-
days was linguistic. German was naturally the
first language with which she was familiar; but
English and French quickly followed; and she became virtually trilingual, though her mastery of
English grammar remained incomplete. At the
same time, she acquired a working knowledge of
Italian and some smattering of Latin. Nevertheless, she did not read very much. It was not an
occupation that she cared for; partly, perhaps, because the books that were given her were all either
sermons, which were very dull, or poetry, which was

[1] *Girlhood*, I, 42.   [2] Crawford, 87.

incomprehensible. Novels were strictly forbidden. Lord Durham persuaded her mother to get her some of Miss Martineau's tales, illustrating the truths of Political Economy, and they delighted her; but it is to be feared that it was the unaccustomed pleasure of the story that filled her mind, and that she never really mastered the theory of exchanges or the nature of rent.[1]

It was her misfortune that the mental atmosphere which surrounded her during these years of adolescence was almost entirely feminine. No father, no brother, was there to break in upon the gentle monotony of the daily round with impetuosity, with rudeness, with careless laughter and wafts of freedom from the outside world. The Princess was never called by a voice that was loud and growling; never felt, as a matter of course, a hard rough cheek on her own soft one; never climbed a wall with a boy. The visits to Claremont —delicious little escapes into male society—came to an end when she was eleven years old and Prince Leopold left England to be King of the Belgians. She loved him still; he was still " il mio secondo padre—or, rather, *solo* padre, for he is indeed like my real father, as I have none "; but his fatherliness now came to her dimly and indi-

1 Martineau, II, 118-9.

rectly, through the cold channel of correspondence.
Henceforward female duty, female elegance, female enthusiasm, hemmed her completely in; and
her spirit, amid the enclosing folds, was hardly
reached by those two great influences, without
which no growing life can truly prosper—humour
and imagination. The Baroness Lehzen—for she
had been raised to that rank in the Hanoverian
nobility by George IV before he died—was the
real centre of the Princess's world. When Feodora married, when Uncle Leopold went to Belgium, the Baroness was left without a competitor.
The Princess gave her mother her dutiful regards;
but Lehzen had her heart. The voluble, shrewd
daughter of the pastor in Hanover, lavishing her
devotion on her royal charge, had reaped her reward in an unbounded confidence and a passionate
adoration. The girl would have gone through fire
for her *"precious* Lehzen," the " best and truest
friend," she declared, that she had had since her
birth. Her journal, begun when she was thirteen,
where she registered day by day the small succession of her doings and her sentiments, bears on
every page of it the traces of the Baroness and her
circumambient influence. The young creature that
one sees there, self-depicted in ingenuous clarity,
with her sincerity, her simplicity, her quick affec-

tions and pious resolutions, might almost have been the daughter of a German pastor herself. Her enjoyments, her admirations, her *engouements* were of the kind that clothed themselves naturally in underlinings and exclamation marks. "It was a *delightful* ride. We cantered a good deal. SWEET LITTLE ROSY WENT BEAUTIFULLY!! We came home at a ¼ past 1. . . . At 20 minutes to 7 we went out to the Opera. . . . Rubini came on and sang a song out of 'Anna Boulena' *quite beautifully*. We came home at ½ past 11."[1] In her comments on her readings, the mind of the Baroness is clearly revealed. One day, by some mistake, she was allowed to take up a volume of memoirs by Fanny Kemble. "It is certainly very pertly and oddly written. One would imagine by the style that the authoress must be very pert, and not well bred; for there are so many vulgar expressions in it. It is a great pity that a person endowed with so much talent, as Mrs. Butler really is, should turn it to so little account and publish a book which is so full of trash and nonsense which can only do her harm. I stayed up till 20 minutes past 9." Madame de Sévigné's letters, which the Baroness read aloud, met with more approval. "How truly elegant and natural her style is! It

[1] *Girlhood*, I, 66-7.

is so full of *naïveté,* cleverness, and grace." But
her highest admiration was reserved for the Bishop
of Chester's "Exposition of the Gospel of St.
Matthew." "It is a very fine book indeed. Just
the sort of one I like; which is just plain and
comprehensible and full of truth and good feeling.
It is not one of those learned books in which you
have to cavil at almost every paragraph. Lehzen
gave it me on the Sunday that I took the Sacra-
ment." [1] A few weeks previously she had been
confirmed, and she described the event as follows:
"I felt that my confirmation was one of the most
solemn and important events and acts in my life;
and that I trusted that it might have a salutary
effect on my mind. I felt deeply repentant for
all what I had done which was wrong and trusted
in God Almighty to strengthen my heart and
mind; and to forsake all that is bad and follow all
that is virtuous and right. I went with the firm
determination to become a true Christian, to try
and comfort my dear Mamma in all her griefs,
trials, and anxieties, and to become a dutiful and
affectionate daughter to her. Also to be obedient
to *dear* Lehzen, who has done so much for me. I
was dressed in a white lace dress, with a white
crape bonnet with a wreath of white roses round

[1] *Girlhood,* I, 129.

it. I went in the chariot with my dear Mamma
and the others followed in another carriage." [1]
One seems to hold in one's hand a small smooth
crystal pebble, without a flaw and without a scin-
tillation, and so transparent that one can see
through it at a glance.

Yet perhaps, after all, to the discerning eye, the
purity would not be absolute. The careful searcher
might detect, in the virgin soil, the first faint traces
of an unexpected vein. In that conventual existence visits were exciting events; and, as the Duchess had many relatives, they were not infrequent;
aunts and uncles would often appear from Germany, and cousins too. When the Princess was
fourteen she was delighted by the arrival of a
couple of boys from Würtemberg, the Princes
Alexander and Ernst, sons of her mother's sister
and the reigning duke. " They are both *extremely
tall,*" she noted; "Alexander is *very handsome,*
and Ernst has a *very kind expression.* They are
both extremely *amiable.*" And their departure
filled her with corresponding regrets. " We saw
them get into the barge, and watched them sailing
away for some time on the beach. They were so
amiable and so pleasant to have in the house; they
were *always satisfied, always good-humoured;*

[1] *Girlhood,* I, 124–5.

Alexander took such care of me in getting out
of the boat, and rode next to me; so did Ernst." [1]
Two years later, two other cousins arrived, the
Princes Ferdinand and Augustus. "Dear Ferdinand," the Princess wrote, "has elicited universal
admiration from all parties. . . . He is so very
unaffected, and has such a very distinguished appearance and carriage. They are both very dear
and charming young men. Augustus is very amiable, too, and, when known, shows much good
sense." On another occasion, "Dear Ferdinand
came and sat near me and talked so dearly and
sensibly. I do *so* love him. Dear Augustus sat
near me and talked with me, and he is also a dear
good young man, and is very handsome." She
could not quite decide which was the handsomer
of the two. On the whole, she concluded, " I think
Ferdinand handsomer than Augustus, his eyes are
so beautiful, and he has such a lively clever expression; *both* have such a sweet expression; Ferdinand has something *quite beautiful* in his expression when he speaks and smiles, and he is *so* good."
However, it was perhaps best to say that they
were " both very handsome and *very dear*." [2] But
shortly afterwards two more cousins arrived, who
threw all the rest into the shade. These were the

[1] *Girlhood*, I, 78, 82.   [2] *Ibid.*, I, 150-3.

Princes Ernest and Albert, sons of her mother's eldest brother, the Duke of Saxe-Coburg. This time the Princess was more particular in her observations. " Ernest," she remarked, " is as tall as Ferdinand and Augustus; he has dark hair, and fine dark eyes and eyebrows, but the nose and mouth are not good; he has a most kind, honest and intelligent expression in his countenance, and has a very good figure. Albert, who is just as tall as Ernest but stouter, is extremely handsome; his hair is about the same colour as mine; his eyes are large and blue, and he has a beautiful nose and a very sweet mouth with fine teeth; but the charm of his countenance is his expression, which is most delightful; *c'est à la fois* full of goodness and sweetness, and very clever and intelligent." " Both my cousins," she added, " are so kind and good; they are much more *formés* and men of the world than Augustus; they speak English very well, and I speak it with them. Ernest will be 18 years old on the 21st of June, and Albert 17 on the 26th of August. Dear Uncle Ernest made me the present of a most delightful *Lory,* which is so tame that it remains on your hand and you may put your finger into its beak, or do anything with it, without its ever attempting to bite. It is larger than Mamma's grey parrot." A little later, " I

sat between my dear cousins on the sofa and we
looked at drawings. They both draw very well,
particularly Albert, and are both exceedingly
fond of music; they play very nicely on the piano.
The more I see them the more I am delighted with
them, and the more I love them. . . . It is delightful to be with them; they are so fond of being
occupied too; they are quite an example for any
young person." When, after a stay of three weeks,
the time came for the young men and their father
to return to Germany, the moment of parting was
a melancholy one. " It was our last HAPPY HAPPY
breakfast, with this dear Uncle and those *dearest*
beloved cousins, whom I *do* love SO VERY VERY
dearly; *much more dearly* than any other cousins
in the *world*. Dearly as I love Ferdinand, and
also good Augustus, I love Ernest and Albert
more than them, oh yes, MUCH *more*. . . . They
have both learnt a good deal, and are very clever,
naturally clever, particularly Albert, who is the
most reflecting of the two, and they like very much
talking about serious and instructive things and
yet are so *very very* merry and gay and happy,
like young people ought to be; Albert always used
to have some fun and some clever witty answer at
breakfast and everywhere; he used to play and
fondle Dash so funnily too. . . . Dearest Albert

was playing on the piano when I came down. At
11 dear Uncle, my *dearest beloved* cousins, and
Charles, left us, accompanied by Count Kolowrat.
I embraced both my dearest cousins most warmly,
as also my dear Uncle. I cried bitterly, very bitterly." [1] The Princes shared her ecstasies and her
italics between them; but it is clear enough where
her secret preference lay. "Particularly Albert"!
She was just seventeen; and deep was the impression left upon that budding organism by the young
man's charm and goodness and accomplishments,
and his large blue eyes and beautiful nose, and his
sweet mouth and fine teeth.

IV

King William could not away with his sister-in-
law, and the Duchess fully returned his antipathy.
Without considerable tact and considerable forbearance their relative positions were well calculated to cause ill-feeling; and there was very little
tact in the composition of the Duchess, and no
forbearance at all in that of his Majesty. A
bursting, bubbling old gentleman, with quarter-
deck gestures, round rolling eyes, and a head like
a pineapple, his sudden elevation to the throne
after fifty-six years of utter insignificance had al-

[1] *Girlhood*, I, 157–61.

most sent him crazy. His natural exuberance completely got the best of him; he rushed about doing
preposterous things in an extraordinary manner,
spreading amusement and terror in every direction, and talking all the time. His tongue was
decidedly Hanoverian, with its repetitions, its
catchwords—" That's quite another thing! That's
quite another thing!"—its rattling indomitability,
its loud indiscreetness. His speeches, made re-
peatedly at the most inopportune junctures, and
filled pell-mell with all the fancies and furies that
happened at the moment to be whisking about in
his head, were the consternation of Ministers. He
was one part blackguard, people said, and three
parts buffoon; but those who knew him better
could not help liking him—he meant well; and
he was really good-humoured and kind-hearted, if
you took him the right way. If you took him the
wrong way, however, you must look out for
squalls, as the Duchess of Kent discovered.

She had no notion of how to deal with him—
could not understand him in the least. Occupied
with her own position, her own responsibilities, her
duty, and her daughter, she had no attention to
spare for the peppery susceptibilities of a foolish,
disreputable old man. She was the mother of the
heiress of England; and it was for him to recog-

nise the fact—to put her at once upon a proper
footing—to give her the precedence of a dowager
Princess of Wales, with a large annuity from the
privy purse.[1] It did not occur to her that such
pretensions might be galling to a king who had
no legitimate child of his own, and who yet had
not altogether abandoned the hope of having one.
She pressed on, with bulky vigour, along the
course she had laid out. Sir John Conroy, an
Irishman with no judgment and a great deal of
self-importance, was her intimate counsellor, and
egged her on. It was advisable that Victoria
should become acquainted with the various dis-
tricts of England, and through several summers
a succession of tours—in the West, in the Mid-
lands, in Wales—were arranged for her. The
intention of the plan was excellent, but its execution was unfortunate. The journeys, advertised
in the Press, attracting enthusiastic crowds, and
involving official receptions, took on the air of
royal progresses. Addresses were presented by
loyal citizens; the delighted Duchess, swelling in
sweeping feathers and almost obliterating the
diminutive Princess, read aloud, in her German
accent, gracious replies prepared beforehand by
Sir John, who, bustling and ridiculous, seemed to

1 Greville, II, 195–6.

be mingling the rôles of major-domo and Prime
Minister.   Naturally the King fumed over his
newspaper at Windsor.   " That woman is a nuisance! " he exclaimed.   Poor Queen Adelaide,
amiable though disappointed, did her best to
smooth things down, changed the subject, and
wrote affectionate letters to Victoria; but it was
useless. News arrived that the Duchess of Kent,
sailing in the Solent, had insisted that whenever
her yacht appeared it should be received by royal
salutes from all the men-of-war and all the forts.
The King declared that these continual poppings
must cease; the Premier and the First Lord of the
Admiralty were consulted; and they wrote privately to the Duchess, begging her to waive her
rights.   But she would not hear of it; Sir John
Conroy was adamant.   " As her Royal Highness's
confidential adviser," he said, " I cannot recommend her to give way on this point."   Eventually
the King, in a great state of excitement, issued a
special Order in Council, prohibiting the firing of
royal salutes to any ships except those which carried the reigning sovereign or his consort on
board.[1]

When King William quarrelled with his Whig
Ministers the situation grew still more embittered,

[1] Greville, III, 321, 324.

for now the Duchess, in addition to her other short-comings, was the political partisan of his enemies. In 1836 he made an attempt to prepare the ground for a match between the Princess Victoria and one of the sons of the Prince of Orange, and at the same time did his best to prevent the visit of the young Coburg princes to Kensington. He failed in both these objects; and the only result of his efforts was to raise the anger of the King of the Belgians, who, forgetting for a moment his royal reserve, addressed an indignant letter on the subject to his niece. " I am really *astonished,*" he wrote, " at the conduct of your old Uncle the King; this invitation of the Prince of Orange and his sons, this forcing him on others, is very extraordinary. . . . Not later than yesterday I got a half-official communication from England, insinuating that it would be *highly* desirable that the visit of *your* relatives *should not take place this year*—qu'en dites-vous? The relations of the Queen and the King, therefore, to the God-knows-what degree, are to come in shoals and rule the land, when *your relations* are to be *forbidden* the country, and that when, as you know, the whole of your relations have ever been very dutiful and kind to the King. Really and truly I never heard or saw anything like it, and I hope it will a *little rouse your spirit;* now that slavery is even abolished in the British Colonies, I do not comprehend *why your lot alone should be to be kept a white little slavey in England,* for the pleasure of the Court, who never bought you, as I am not aware of their ever having gone to any expense on that head, or the King's ever having *spent a sixpence for your existence.* . . . Oh, consistency and political or *other honesty,* where must one look for you! " [1]

Shortly afterwards King Leopold came to England himself, and his reception was as cold at Windsor as it was warm at Kensington. " To hear dear Uncle speak on any subject," the Princess wrote in her diary, " is like reading a highly instructive book; his conversation is so enlightened, so clear. He is universally admitted to be one of the first politicians now extant. He speaks so mildly, yet firmly and impartially, about politics. Uncle tells me that Belgium is quite a pattern for its organisation, its industry, and prosperity; the finances are in the greatest perfection. Uncle is so beloved and revered by his Belgian subjects, that it must be a great compensation for all his extreme trouble." [2] But her other uncle by no means shared her sentiments. He could not, he

---

[1] *Letters,* I, 47–8.   [2] *Girlhood,* I, 168.

said, put up with a water-drinker; and King Leopold would touch no wine. "What's that you're
drinking, sir?" he asked him one day at dinner.
"Water, sir." "God damn it, sir!" was the re-
joinder. "Why don't you drink wine? I never
allow anybody to drink water at my table."[1]

It was clear that before very long there would
be a great explosion; and in the hot days of August it came. The Duchess and the Princess had
gone down to stay at Windsor for the King's
birthday party, and the King himself, who was in
London for the day to prorogue Parliament, paid
a visit at Kensington Palace in their absence.
There he found that the Duchess had just appro-
priated, against his express orders, a suite of seventeen apartments for her own use. He was extremely angry, and, when he returned to Windsor,
after greeting the Princess with affection, he publicly rebuked the Duchess for what she had done.
But this was little to what followed. On the next
day was the birthday banquet; there were a hundred guests; the Duchess of Kent sat on the
King's right hand, and the Princess Victoria opposite. At the end of the dinner, in reply to the
toast of the King's health, he rose, and, in a long,
loud, passionate speech, poured out the vials of

[1] Greville, III, 377.

his wrath upon the Duchess. She had, he declared,
insulted him—grossly and continually; she had
kept the Princess away from him in the most improper manner; she was surrounded by evil advisers, and was incompetent to act with propriety
in the high station which she filled; but he would
bear it no longer; he would have her to know he
was King; he was determined that his authority
should be respected; henceforward the Princess
should attend at every Court function with the
utmost regularity; and he hoped to God that his
life might be spared for six months longer, so that
the calamity of a regency might be avoided, and
the functions of the Crown pass directly to the
heiress-presumptive instead of into the hands of
the " person now near him," upon whose conduct
and capacity no reliance whatever could be placed.
The flood of vituperation rushed on for what
seemed an interminable period, while the Queen
blushed scarlet, the Princess burst into tears, and
the hundred guests sat aghast. The Duchess said
not a word until the tirade was over and the company had retired; then in a tornado of rage and
mortification, she called for her carriage and announced her immediate return to Kensington. It
was only with the utmost difficulty that some show
of a reconciliation was patched up, and the out-

raged lady was prevailed upon to put off her departure till the morrow.[1]

Her troubles, however, were not over when she
had shaken the dust of Windsor from her feet.
In her own household she was pursued by bitterness and vexation of spirit. The apartments at
Kensington were seething with subdued disaffec-
tion, with jealousies and animosities virulently intensified by long years of propinquity and spite.

There was a deadly feud between Sir John
Conroy and Baroness Lehzen. But that was not
all. The Duchess had grown too fond of her
Major-Domo. There were familiarities, and one
day the Princess Victoria discovered the fact. She
confided what she had seen to the Baroness, and
to the Baroness's beloved ally, Madame de Späth.
Unfortunately, Madame de Späth could not hold
her tongue, and was actually foolish enough to
reprove the Duchess; whereupon she was instantly
dismissed. It was not so easy to get rid of the
Baroness. That lady, prudent and reserved,
maintained an irreproachable demeanour. Her
position was strongly entrenched; she had managed to secure the support of the King; and Sir
John found that he could do nothing against her.
But henceforward the household was divided into

1 Greville, III, 374–6.

two camps.[1] The Duchess supported Sir John
with all the abundance of her authority; but the
Baroness, too, had an adherent who could not be
neglected. The Princess Victoria said nothing,
but she had been much attached to Madame de
Späth, and she adored her Lehzen. The Duchess
knew only too well that in this horrid embroilment
her daughter was against her. Chagrin, annoyance, moral reprobation, tossed her to and fro.
She did her best to console herself with Sir John's
affectionate loquacity, or with the sharp remarks
of Lady Flora Hastings, one of her maids of honour, who had no love for the Baroness. The subject lent itself to satire; for the pastor's daughter,
with all her airs of stiff superiority, had habits
which betrayed her origin. Her passion for carra-
way seeds, for instance, was uncontrollable. Little
bags of them came over to her from Hanover, and
she sprinkled them on her bread and butter, her

[1] Greville, IV, 21; and August 15, 1839 (unpublished). "The
cause of the Queen's alienation from the Duchess and hatred of
Conroy, the Duke [of Wellington] said, was unquestionably owing
to her having witnessed some familiarities between them. What
she had seen she repeated to Baroness Spaeth, and Spaeth not
only did not hold her tongue, but (he thinks) remonstrated with
the Duchess herself on the subject. The consequence was that
they got rid of Spaeth, and they would have got rid of Lehzen,
too, if they had been able, but Lehzen, who knew very well what
was going on, was prudent enough not to commit herself, and
she was, besides, powerfully protected by George IV and
William IV, so that they did not dare to attempt to expel her."

cabbage, and even her roast beef. Lady Flora could not resist a caustic observation; it was repeated to the Baroness, who pursed her lips in fury; and so the mischief grew.[1]

V

The King had prayed that he might live till his niece was of age; and a few days before her eighteenth birthday—the date of her legal majority—a sudden attack of illness very nearly carried him off. He recovered, however, and the Princess was able to go through her birthday festivities—a state ball and a drawing-room—with unperturbed enjoyment. " Count Zichy," she noted in her diary, " is very good-looking in uniform, but not in plain clothes. Count Waldstein looks remarkably well in his pretty Hungarian uniform." [2] With the latter young gentleman she wished to dance, but there was an insurmountable difficulty. " He could not dance quadrilles, and, as in my station I unfortunately cannot valse and gallop, I could not dance with him." [3] Her birthday present from the King was of a pleasing nature, but it led to a painful domestic scene. In spite of the anger of her Belgian uncle, she had remained upon good

1 Greville, IV, 21; Crawford, 128–9.   2 *Girlhood*, I, 192–3.
3 *Ibid.*, I, 191.

terms with her English one. He had always been
very kind to her, and the fact that he had quarrelled with her mother did not appear to be a reason for disliking him. He was, she said, " odd,
very odd and singular," but " his intentions were
often ill interpreted." [1] He now wrote her a letter, offering her an allowance of £10,000 a year,
which he proposed should be at her own disposal,
and independent of her mother. Lord Conyngham, the Lord Chamberlain, was instructed to
deliver the letter into the Princess's own hands.
When he arrived at Kensington, he was ushered
into the presence of the Duchess and the Princess,
and, when he produced the letter, the Duchess put
out her hand to take it. Lord Conyngham begged
her Royal Highness's pardon, and repeated the
King's commands. Thereupon the Duchess drew
back, and the Princess took the letter. She immediately wrote to her uncle, accepting his kind proposal. The Duchess was much displeased; £4000
a year, she said, would be quite enough for Victoria; as for the remaining £6000, it would be only
proper that she should have that herself. [2]

King William had thrown off his illness, and
returned to his normal life. Once more the royal
circle at Windsor—their Majesties, the elder Prin-

[1] *Girlhood*, I, 194.   [2] Greville, III, 407–8.

cesses, and some unfortunate Ambassadress or
Minister's wife—might be seen ranged for hours
round a mahogany table, while the Queen netted
a purse, and the King slept, occasionally waking
from his slumbers to observe " Exactly so, ma'am,
exactly so! " [1] But this recovery was of short dura-
tion. The old man suddenly collapsed; with no
specific symptoms besides an extreme weakness, he
yet showed no power of rallying; and it was clear
to everyone that his death was now close at hand.

All eyes, all thoughts, turned towards the Princess Victoria; but she still remained, shut away in
the seclusion of Kensington, a small, unknown
figure, lost in the large shadow of her mother's
domination. The preceding year had in fact
been an important one in her development. The
soft tendrils of her mind had for the first time begun to stretch out towards unchildish things. In
this King Leopold encouraged her. After his return to Brussels, he had resumed his correspondence in a more serious strain; he discussed the details of foreign politics; he laid down the duties of
kingship; he pointed out the iniquitous foolishness
of the newspaper press. On the latter subject,
indeed, he wrote with some asperity. " If all the
editors," he said, " of the papers in the countries

[1] Creevey, II, 262.

where the liberty of the press exists were to be assembled, we should have a *crew* to which you would *not* confide a dog that you would value, still less your honour and reputation." [1] On the functions of a monarch, his views were unexceptionable. " The business of the highest in a State," he wrote, " is certainly, in my opinion, to act with great impartiality and a spirit of justice for the good of all." [2] At the same time the Princess's tastes were opening out. Though she was still passionately devoted to riding and dancing, she now began to have a genuine love of music as well, and to drink in the roulades and arias of the Italian opera with high enthusiasm. She even enjoyed reading poetry—at any rate, the poetry of Sir Walter Scott.[3]

When King Leopold learnt that King William's death was approaching, he wrote several long letters of excellent advice to his niece. " In every letter I shall write to you," he said, " I mean to repeat to you, as a *fundamental rule, to be courageous, firm, and honest, as you have been till now.*" For the rest, in the crisis that was approaching, she was not to be alarmed, but to trust in her " good natural sense and the *truth* " of her character; she was to do nothing in a hurry; to

1 *Letters,* I, 53.   2 *Letters,* I, 61.   3 *Girlhood,* I, 175.

hurt no one's *amour-propre,* and to continue her confidence in the Whig administration.[1] Not content with letters, however, King Leopold determined that the Princess should not lack personal guidance, and sent over to her aid the trusted friend whom, twenty years before, he had taken to his heart by the death-bed at Claremont. Thus, once again, as if in accordance with some pre-ordained destiny, the figure of Stockmar is discernible—inevitably present at a momentous hour.

On June 18, the King was visibly sinking. The Archbishop of Canterbury was by his side, with all the comforts of the church. Nor did the holy words fall upon a rebellious spirit; for many years his Majesty had been a devout believer. "When I was a young man," he once explained at a public banquet, "as well as I can remember, I believed in nothing but pleasure and folly—nothing at all. But when I went to sea, got into a gale, and saw the wonders of the mighty deep, then I believed; and I have been a sincere Christian ever since." [1] It was the anniversary of the Battle of Waterloo, and the dying man remembered it. He should be glad to live, he said, over that day; he would never see another sunset. "I hope your Majesty may live to see many," said Dr. Chambers. "Oh! that's

---

[1] *Letters,* I, 79-1.　　　　　　[2] Torrens, 419.

quite another thing, that's quite another thing,"
was the answer.[1] One other sunset he did live to
see; and he died in the early hours of the following
morning. It was on June 20, 1837.

When all was over, the Archbishop and the
Lord Chamberlain ordered a carriage, and drove
post-haste from Windsor to Kensington. They
arrived at the Palace at five o'clock, and it was
only with considerable difficulty that they gained
admittance.[2] At six the Duchess woke up her
daughter, and told her that the Archbishop of
Canterbury and Lord Conyngham were there, and
wished to see her. She got out of bed, put on her
dressing-gown, and went, alone, into the room
where the messengers were standing. Lord Conyngham fell on his knees, and officially announced
the death of the King; the Archbishop added some
personal details. Looking at the bending, mur-
muring dignitaries before her, she knew that she
was Queen of England. " Since it has pleased
Providence," she wrote that day in her journal,
" to place me in this station, I shall do my utmost
to fulfil my duty towards my country; I am very
young, and perhaps in many, though not in all
things, inexperienced, but I am sure, that very
few have more real good will and more real desire

[1] Huish, 686.   [2] Wynn, 281.

to do what is fit and right than I have." [1]   But there was scant time for resolutions and reflections. At once, affairs were thick upon her. Stockmar came to breakfast, and gave some good advice. She wrote a letter to her uncle Leopold, and a hurried note to her sister Feodora. A letter came from the Prime Minister, Lord Melbourne, announcing his approaching arrival. He came at nine, in full court dress, and kissed her hand. She saw him alone, and repeated to him the lesson which, no doubt, the faithful Stockmar had taught her at breakfast. "It has long been my intention to retain your Lordship and the rest of the present Ministry at the head of affairs;" whereupon Lord Melbourne again kissed her hand and shortly after left her. She then wrote a letter of condolence to Queen Adelaide. At eleven, Lord Melbourne came again; and at half-past eleven she went downstairs into the red saloon to hold her first Council.[2] The great assembly of lords and notables, bishops, generals, and Ministers of State, saw the doors thrown open and a very short, very slim girl in deep plain mourning come into the room alone and move forward to her seat with extraordinary dignity and grace; they saw a countenance, not beautiful, but prepossessing—fair

---

[1] *Girlhood*, I, 195–6.   [2] *Ibid.*, I, 196–7.

hair, blue prominent eyes, a small curved nose, an open mouth revealing the upper teeth, a tiny chin, a clear complexion, and, over all, the strangely mingled signs of innocence, of gravity, of youth, and of composure; they heard a high unwavering voice reading aloud with perfect clarity; and then, the ceremony was over, they saw the small figure rise and, with the same consummate grace, the same amazing dignity, pass out from among them, as she had come in, alone.[1]

[1] Greville, III, 414–6.

CHAPTER III

LORD MELBOURNE

I

THE new queen was almost entirely unknown to
her subjects. In her public appearances her
mother had invariably dominated the scene. Her
private life had been that of a novice in a convent:
hardly a human being from the outside world had
ever spoken to her; and no human being at all,
except her mother and the Baroness Lehzen, had
ever been alone with her in a room. Thus it was
not only the public at large that was in ignorance
of everything concerning her; the inner circles of
statesmen and officials and high-born ladies were
equally in the dark.[1] When she suddenly emerged
from this deep obscurity, the impression that she
created was immediate and profound. Her bearing at her first Council filled the whole gathering
with astonishment and admiration; the Duke of
Wellington, Sir Robert Peel, even the savage
Croker, even the cold and caustic Greville—all
were completely carried away. Everything that

[1] Greville, III, 411.

was reported of her subsequent proceedings seemed
to be of no less happy augury. Her perceptions
were quick, her decisions were sensible, her language was discreet; she performed her royal duties
with extraordinary facility.[1]   Among the outside
public there was a great wave of enthusiasm.   Sentiment and romance were coming into fashion; and
the spectacle of the little girl-queen, innocent,
modest, with fair hair and pink cheeks, driving
through her capital, filled the hearts of the behold-
ers with raptures of affectionate loyalty.   What,
above all, struck everybody with overwhelming
force was the contrast between Queen Victoria
and her uncles.   The nasty old men, debauched
and selfish, pig-headed and ridiculous, with their
perpetual burden of debts, confusions, and disrep-
utabilities—they had vanished like the snows of
winter, and here at last, crowned and radiant, was
the spring.   Lord John Russell, in an elaborate
oration, gave voice to the general sentiment.   He
hoped that Victoria might prove an Elizabeth
without her tyranny, an Anne without her weakness.   He asked England to pray that the illustrious Princess who had just ascended the throne
with the purest intentions and the justest desires
might see slavery abolished, crime diminished, and

1 Greville, IV, 7, 9, 14–15.

education improved. He trusted that her people would henceforward derive their strength, their conduct, and their loyalty from enlightened religious and moral principles, and that, so fortified, the reign of Victoria might prove celebrated to posterity and to all the nations of the earth.[1]

Very soon, however, there were signs that the future might turn out to be not quite so simple and roseate as a delighted public dreamed. The "illustrious Princess" might perhaps, after all, have something within her which squared ill with the easy vision of a well-conducted heroine in an edifying story-book. The purest intentions and the justest desires? No doubt; but was that all? To those who watched closely, for instance, there might be something ominous in the curious contour of that little mouth. When, after her first Council, she crossed the ante-room and found her mother waiting for her, she said, "And now, Mamma, am I really and truly Queen?" "You see, my dear, that it is so." "Then, dear Mamma, I hope you will grant me the first request I make to you, as Queen. Let me be by myself for an hour."[2] For an hour she remained in solitude. Then she reappeared, and gave a significant order:

[1] Walpole, I, 284.   [2] Crawford, 156-7.

her bed was to be moved out of her mother's room.
It was the doom of the Duchess of Kent. The
long years of waiting were over at last; the moment of a lifetime had come; her daughter was
Queen of England; and that very moment brought
her own annihilation. She found herself, absolutely and irretrievably, shut off from every vestige of influence, of confidence, of power. She
was surrounded, indeed, by all the outward signs
of respect and consideration; but that only made
the inward truth of her position the more intolerable. Through the mingled formalities of Court
etiquette and filial duty, she could never penetrate
to Victoria. She was unable to conceal her disappointment and her rage. " Il n'y a plus d'avenir
pour moi," she exclaimed to Madame de Lieven;
" je ne suis plus rien." For eighteen years, she
said, this child had been the sole object of her existence, of her thoughts, her hopes, and now—no!
she would not be comforted, she had lost everything, she was to the last degree unhappy.[1] Sailing, so gallantly and so pertinaciously, through the
buffeting storms of life, the stately vessel, with
sails still swelling and pennons flying, had put into
harbour at last; to find there nothing—a land of
bleak desolation.

[1] Greville, IV, 16.

Within a month of the accession, the realities of the new situation assumed a visible shape. The whole royal household moved from Kensington to Buckingham Palace, and, in the new abode, the Duchess of Kent was given a suite of apartments entirely separate from the Queen's. By Victoria herself the change was welcomed, though, at the moment of departure, she could afford to be sentimental. "Though I rejoice to *go* into B. P. for many reasons," she wrote in her diary, "it is not without feelings of regret that I shall bid adieu *for ever* to this my birthplace, where I have been born and bred, and to which I am really attached!" Her memory lingered for a moment over visions of the past: her sister's wedding, pleasant balls and *delicious* concerts . . . and there were other recollections. "I have gone through painful and disagreeable scenes here, 'tis true," she concluded, "but still I am fond of the poor old palace." [1]

At the same time she took another decided step. She had determined that she would see no more of Sir John Conroy. She rewarded his past services with liberality: he was given a baronetcy and a pension of £3000 a year; he remained a member of the Duchess's household, but his per-

[1] *Girlhood*, I, 210–1.

sonal intercourse with the Queen came to an abrupt conclusion.[1]

II

It was clear that these interior changes—whatever else they might betoken—marked the triumph of one person—the Baroness Lehzen. The pastor's daughter observed the ruin of her enemies. Discreet and victorious, she remained in possession of the field. More closely than ever did she cleave to the side of her mistress, her pupil, and her friend; and in the recesses of the palace her mysterious figure was at once invisible and omnipresent. When the Queen's Ministers came in at one door, the Baroness went out by another; when they retired, she immediately returned.[2] Nobody knew —nobody ever will know—the precise extent and the precise nature of her influence. She herself declared that she never discussed public affairs with the Queen, that she was concerned with private matters only—with private letters and the details of private life.[3] Certainly her hand is everywhere discernible in Victoria's early correspondence. The Journal is written in the style of a child; the Letters are not so simple; they are the

[1] Greville, IV, 15.   [2] *Ibid.*, IV, 21-2.

[3] Stockmar, 322-3; Maxwell, 159-60.

work of a child, rearranged—with the minimum of alteration, no doubt, and yet perceptibly—by a governess. And the governess was no fool: narrow, jealous, provincial, she might be; but she was an acute and vigorous woman, who had gained by a peculiar insight, a peculiar ascendancy. That ascendancy she meant to keep. No doubt it was true that technically she took no part in public business; but the distinction between what is public and what is private is always a subtle one; and in the case of a reigning sovereign—as the next few years were to show—it is often imaginary. Considering all things—the characters of the persons, and the character of the times—it was something more than a mere matter of private interest that the bedroom of Baroness Lehzen at Buckingham Palace should have been next door to the bedroom of the Queen.

But the influence wielded by the Baroness, supreme as it seemed within its own sphere, was not unlimited; there were other forces at work. For one thing, the faithful Stockmar had taken up his residence in the palace. During the twenty years which had elapsed since the death of the Princess Charlotte, his experiences had been varied and remarkable. The unknown counsellor of a disappointed princeling had gradually risen to a posi-

tion of European importance. His devotion to his
master had been not only whole-hearted but cautious and wise. It was Stockmar's advice that had
kept Prince Leopold in England during the critical years which followed his wife's death, and had
thus secured to him the essential requisite of a
point d'appui in the country of his adoption.[1] It
was Stockmar's discretion which had smoothed
over the embarrassments surrounding the Prince's
acceptance and rejection of the Greek crown. It
was Stockmar who had induced the Prince to become the constitutional Sovereign of Belgium.[2]
Above all, it was Stockmar's tact, honesty, and
diplomatic skill which, through a long series of
arduous and complicated negotiations, had led to
the guarantee of Belgian neutrality by the Great
Powers.[3] His labours had been rewarded by a
German barony and by the complete confidence of
King Leopold. Nor was it only in Brussels that
he was treated with respect and listened to with
attention. The statesmen who governed England
—Lord Grey, Sir Robert Peel, Lord Palmerston,
Lord Melbourne—had learnt to put a high value
upon his probity and his intelligence. "He is
one of the cleverest fellows I ever saw," said Lord

[1] Stockmar, 109-10.   [2] *Ibid.*, 165-6.
[3] *Ibid.*, chaps. viii, ix, x, and xi.

Melbourne—"the most discreet man, the most well-judging, and most cool man." [1] And Lord Palmerston cited Baron Stockmar as the only absolutely disinterested man he had come across in life. [2] At last he was able to retire to Coburg, and to enjoy for a few years the society of the wife and children whom his labours in the service of his master had hitherto only allowed him to visit at long intervals for a month or two at a time. But in 1836 he had been again entrusted with an important negotiation, which he had brought to a successful conclusion in the marriage of Prince Ferdinand of Saxe-Coburg, a nephew of King Leopold's, with Queen Maria II of Portugal. [3] The House of Coburg was beginning to spread over Europe; and the establishment of the Baron at Buckingham Palace in 1837 was to be the prelude of another and a more momentous advance. [4]

King Leopold and his counsellor provide in their careers an example of the curious diversity of human ambitions. The desires of man are wonderfully various; but no less various are the means by which those desires may reach satisfaction: and so the work of the world gets done. The correct mind of Leopold craved for the whole apparatus

[1] *Girlhood*, II, 303.
[2] Stockmar, 324

[3] *Ibid.*, chap. xv, pt. 2.
[4] *Ibid.*, chap. xvii.

of royalty. Mere power would have held no attractions for him; he must be an actual king—the
crowned head of a people. It was not enough to
do; it was essential also to be recognised; anything
else would not be fitting. The greatness that he
dreamt of was surrounded by every appropriate
circumstance. To be a Majesty, to be a cousin of
Sovereigns, to marry a Bourbon for diplomatic
ends, to correspond with the Queen of England, to
be very stiff and very punctual, to found a
dynasty, to bore ambassadresses into fits, to live,
on the highest pinnacle, an exemplary life devoted
to the public service—such were his objects, and
such, in fact, were his achievements. The " Mar-
quis Peu-à-peu," as George IV called him,[1] had
what he wanted. But this would never have been
the case if it had not happened that the ambition
of Stockmar took a form exactly complementary
to his own. The sovereignty that the Baron sought
for was by no means obvious. The satisfaction
of his essential being lay in obscurity, in invisibility
—in passing, unobserved, through a hidden entrance, into the very central chamber of power,
and in sitting there, quietly, pulling the subtle
strings that set the wheels of the whole world in
motion. A very few people, in very high places,

[1] Stein, VI, 932.

and exceptionally well-informed, knew that Baron
Stockmar was a most important person: that was
enough. The fortunes of the master and the servant, intimately interacting, rose together. The
Baron's secret skill had given Leopold his unexceptionable kingdom; and Leopold, in his turn, as
time went on, was able to furnish the Baron with
more and more keys to more and more back doors.

Stockmar took up his abode in the Palace partly
as the emissary of King Leopold, but more particularly as the friend and adviser of a queen who
was almost a child, and who, no doubt, would be
much in need of advice and friendship. For it
would be a mistake to suppose that either of these
two men was actuated by a vulgar selfishness. The
King, indeed, was very well aware on which side
his bread was buttered; during an adventurous and
chequered life he had acquired a shrewd knowledge of the world's workings; and he was ready
enough to use that knowledge to strengthen his
position and to spread his influence. But then,
the firmer his position and the wider his influence,
the better for Europe; of that he was quite certain. And besides, he was a constitutional monarch; and it would be highly indecorous in a constitutional monarch to have any aims that were
low or personal. As for Stockmar, the disinter-

estedness which Palmerston had noted was undoubtedly a basic element in his character. The ordinary schemer is always an optimist; and Stockmar, racked by dyspepsia and haunted by gloomy forebodings, was a constitutionally melancholy man. A schemer, no doubt, he was; but he schemed distrustfully, splenetically, to do good. To do good! What nobler end could a man scheme for? Yet it is perilous to scheme at all.

With Lehzen to supervise every detail of her conduct, with Stockmar in the next room, so full of wisdom and experience of affairs, with her Uncle Leopold's letters, too, pouring out so constantly their stream of encouragements, general reflections, and highly valuable tips, Victoria, even had she been without other guidance, would have stood in no lack of private counsellors. But other guidance she had; for all these influences paled before a new star, of the first magnitude, which, rising suddenly upon her horizon, immediately dominated her life.

III

William Lamb, Viscount Melbourne, was fifty-eight years of age, and had been for the last three years Prime Minister of England. In every outward respect he was one of the most fortunate

LORD MELBOURNE

From the Portrait by Sir Edwin Landseer, R.A.

of mankind. He had been born into the midst of
riches, brilliance, and power. His mother, fascinating and intelligent, had been a great Whig
hostess, and he had been bred up as a member of
that radiant society which, during the last quarter
of the eighteenth century, concentrated within itself the ultimate perfections of a hundred years
of triumphant aristocracy. Nature had given him
beauty and brains; the unexpected death of an
elder brother brought him wealth, a peerage, and
the possibility of high advancement. Within that
charmed circle, whatever one's personal disabili-
ties, it was difficult to fail; and to him, with all
his advantages, success was well-nigh unavoidable.
With little effort, he attained political eminence.
On the triumph of the Whigs he became one of
the leading members of the Government; and
when Lord Grey retired from the premiership he
quietly stepped into the vacant place. Nor was
it only in the visible signs of fortune that Fate
had been kind to him. Bound to succeed, and to
succeed easily, he was gifted with so fine a nature
that his success became him. His mind, at once
supple and copious, his temperament, at once calm
and sensitive, enabled him not merely to work, but
to live with perfect facility and with the grace of
strength. In society he was a notable talker, a

captivating companion, a charming man. If one looked deeper, one saw at once that he was not ordinary, that the piquancies of his conversation and his manner—his free-and-easy vaguenesses, his abrupt questions, his lollings and loungings, his innumerable oaths—were something more than an amusing ornament, were the outward manifestation of an individuality that was fundamental.

The precise nature of this individuality was very difficult to gauge: it was dubious, complex, perhaps self-contradictory. Certainly there was an ironical discordance between the inner history of the man and his apparent fortunes. He owed all he had to his birth, and his birth was shameful; it was known well enough that his mother had passionately loved Lord Egremont, and that Lord Melbourne was not his father.[1] His marriage, which had seemed to be the crown of his youthful ardours, was a long, miserable, desperate failure: the incredible Lady Caroline,

> . . . "with pleasures too refined to please,
> With too much spirit to be e'er at ease,
> With too much quickness to be ever taught,
> With too much thinking to have common thought,"

was very nearly the destruction of his life. When at last he emerged from the anguish and confusion

[1] Greville, VI, 247; Torrens, 14; Hayward, I, 336.

of her folly, her extravagance, her rage, her despair, and her devotion, he was left alone with endless memories of intermingled farce and tragedy, and an only son, who was an imbecile. But there was something else that he owed to Lady Caroline. While she whirled with Byron in a hectic frenzy of love and fashion, he had stayed at home in an indulgence bordering on cynicism, and occupied his solitude with reading. It was thus that he had acquired those habits of study, that love of learning, and that wide and accurate knowledge of ancient and modern literature, which formed so unexpected a part of his mental equipment. His passion for reading never deserted him; even when he was Prime Minister he found time to master every new important book.[1] With an incongruousness that was characteristic, his favourite study was theology. An accomplished classical scholar, he was deeply read in the Fathers of the Church; heavy volumes of commentary and exegesis he examined with scrupulous diligence; and at any odd moment he might be found turning over the pages of the Bible.[2] To the ladies whom he most liked he would lend some learned

[1] Greville, VI, 248.

[2] Greville, III, 331; VI, 254; Haydon, III, 12: "March 1, 1835. Called on Lord Melbourne, and found him reading the Acts, with a quarto Greek Testament that belonged to Samuel Johnson."

work on the Revelation, crammed with marginal
notes in his own hand, or Dr. Lardner's " Observations upon the Jewish Errors with respect to the
Conversion of Mary Magdalene." The more pious
among them had high hopes that these studies
would lead him into the right way; but of this
there were no symptoms in his after-dinner conversations.[1]

The paradox of his political career was no less
curious. By temperament an aristocrat, by conviction a conservative, he came to power as the leader
of the popular party, the party of change. He
had profoundly disliked the Reform Bill, which
he had only accepted at last as a necessary evil;
and the Reform Bill lay at the root of the very
existence, of the very meaning, of his government.
He was far too sceptical to believe in progress of
any kind. Things were best as they were—or
rather, they were least bad. " You'd better try
to do no good," was one of his dictums, " and then
you'll get into no scrapes." Education at best was
futile; education of the poor was positively dangerous. The factory children? " Oh, if you'd only
have the goodness to leave them alone! " Free
Trade was a delusion; the ballot was nonsense;
and there was no such thing as a democracy. Nev-

[1] Greville, III, 142; Torrens, 545.

ertheless, he was not a reactionary; he was simply an opportunist. The whole duty of government, he said, was "to prevent crime and to preserve contracts." All one could really hope to do was to carry on. He himself carried on in a remarkable manner—with perpetual compromises, with fluctuations and contradictions, with every kind of weakness, and yet with shrewdness, with gentleness, even with conscientiousness, and a light and airy mastery of men and of events. He conducted the transactions of business with extraordinary nonchalance. Important persons, ushered up for some grave interview, found him in a towselled bed, littered with books and papers, or vaguely shaving in a dressing-room; but, when they went downstairs again, they would realise that somehow or other they had been pumped. When he had to receive a deputation, he could hardly ever do so with becoming gravity. The worthy delegates of the tallow-chandlers, or the Society for the Abolition of Capital Punishment, were distressed and mortified when, in the midst of their speeches, the Prime Minister became absorbed in blowing a feather, or suddenly cracked an unseemly joke. How could they have guessed that he had spent the night before diligently getting up the details of their case? He hated patronage and the making of appointments—a feeling rare in Ministers. "As for the Bishops," he burst out. " I positively believe they die to vex me." But when at last the appointment was made, it was made with keen discrimination. His colleagues observed another symptom—was it of his irresponsibility or his wisdom? He went to sleep in the Cabinet.[1]

Probably, if he had been born a little earlier, he would have been a simpler and a happier man. As it was, he was a child of the eighteenth century whose lot was cast in a new, difficult, unsympathetic age. He was an autumn rose. With all his gracious amenity, his humour, his happy-go-lucky ways, a deep disquietude possessed him. A sentimental cynic, a sceptical believer, he was restless and melancholy at heart. Above all, he could never harden himself; those sensitive petals shivered in every wind. Whatever else he might be, one thing was certain: Lord Melbourne was always human, supremely human—too human, perhaps.[2]

And now, with old age upon him, his life took a sudden, new, extraordinary turn. He became, in the twinkling of an eye, the intimate adviser and the daily companion of a young girl who had

[1] *Girlhood,* II, 148; Torrens, 278, 431, 517; Greville, IV, 331; VIII, 162.
[2] Greville, VI, 253–4; Torrens, 354.

stepped all at once from a nursery to a throne. His relations with women had been, like everything else about him, ambiguous. Nobody had ever been able quite to gauge the shifting, emotional complexities of his married life; Lady Caroline vanished; but his peculiar susceptibilities remained. Female society of some kind or other was necessary to him, and he did not stint himself; a great part of every day was invariably spent in it. The feminine element in him made it easy, made it natural and inevitable for him to be the friend of a great many women; but the masculine element in him was strong as well. In such circumstances it is also easy, it is even natural, perhaps it is even inevitable, to be something more than a friend. There were rumours and combustions. Lord Melbourne was twice a co-respondent in a divorce action; but on each occasion he won his suit. The lovely Lady Brandon, the unhappy and brilliant Mrs. Norton . . . the law exonerated them both. Beyond that hung an impenetrable veil. But at any rate it was clear that, with such a record, the Prime Minister's position in Buckingham Palace must be a highly delicate one. However, he was used to delicacies, and he met the situation with consummate success. His behaviour was from the first moment impeccable. His manner towards the young Queen mingled, with perfect facility, the watchfulness and the respect of a statesman and a courtier with the tender solicitude of a parent. He was at once reverential and affectionate, at once the servant and the guide. At the same time the habits of his life underwent a surprising change. His comfortable, unpunctual days became subject to the unaltering routine of a palace; no longer did he sprawl on sofas; not a single " damn " escaped his lips. The man of the world who had been the friend of Byron and the regent, the talker whose paradoxes had held Holland House enthralled, the cynic whose ribaldries had' enlivened so many deep potations, the lover whose soft words had captivated such beauty and such passion and such wit, might now be seen, evening after evening, talking with infinite politeness to a schoolgirl, bolt upright, amid the silence and the rigidity of Court etiquette.[1]

IV

On her side, Victoria was instantaneously fascinated by Lord Melbourne. The good report of Stockmar had no doubt prepared the way; Lehzen was wisely propitiated; and the first highly favourable impression was never afterwards belied. She

[1] Greville, IV, 135, 154; *Girlhood*, I, 249.

found him perfect; and perfect in her sight he remained. Her absolute and unconcealed adoration was very natural; what innocent young creature could have resisted, in any circumstances, the charm and the devotion of such a man? But, in her situation, there was a special influence which gave a peculiar glow to all she felt. After years of emptiness and dullness and suppression, she had come suddenly, in the heyday of youth, into freedom and power. She was mistress of herself, of great domains and palaces; she was Queen of England. Responsibilities and difficulties she might have, no doubt, and in heavy measure; but one feeling dominated and absorbed all others— the feeling of joy. Everything pleased her. She was in high spirits from morning till night. Mr. Creevey, grown old now, and very near his end, catching a glimpse of her at Brighton, was much amused, in his sharp fashion, by the ingenuous gaiety of " little Vic."—" A more homely little being you never beheld, *when she is at her ease,* and she is evidently dying to be always more so. She laughs in real earnest, opening her mouth as wide as it can go, showing not very pretty gums. . . . She eats quite as heartily as she laughs, I think I may say she gobbles. . . . She blushes and laughs every instant in so natural a way as

to disarm anybody." [1]   But it was not merely
when she was laughing or gobbling that she enjoyed herself; the performance of her official duties gave her intense satisfaction. " I really have
immensely to do," she wrote in her Journal a few
days after her accession; " I receive so many communications from my Ministers, but I like it very
much." [2]   And again, a week later, " I repeat what
I said before that I have *so many* communications
from the Ministers, and from me to them, and I
get so many papers to sign every day, that I have
always a *very great* deal to do. I *delight* in this
work." [3] Through the girl's immaturity the vigorous predestined tastes of the woman were pushing
themselves into existence with eager velocity, with
delicious force.

One detail of her happy situation deserves particular mention. Apart from the splendour of her
social position and the momentousness of her political one, she was a person of great wealth. As
soon as Parliament met, an annuity of £385,000
was settled upon her. When the expenses of her
household had been discharged, she was left with
£68,000 a year of her own. She enjoyed besides
the revenues of the Duchy of Lancaster, which
amounted annually to over £27,000. The first use

---

[1] Creevey, II, 326.   [2] *Girlhood*, I, 203.   [3] *Ibid.*, I, 206.

to which she put her money was characteristic: she paid off her father's debts. In money matters, no less than in other matters, she was determined to be correct. She had the instincts of a man of business; and she never could have borne to be in a position that was financially unsound.[1]

With youth and happiness gilding every hour, the days passed merrily enough. And each day hinged upon Lord Melbourne. Her diary shows us, with undiminished clarity, the life of the young sovereign during the early months of her reign— a life satisfactorily regular, full of delightful business, a life of simple pleasures, mostly physical— riding, eating, dancing—a quick, easy, highly unsophisticated life, sufficient unto itself. The light of the morning is upon it; and, in the rosy radiance, the figure of " Lord M." emerges, glorified and supreme. If she is the heroine of the story, he is the hero; but indeed they are more than hero and heroine, for there are no other characters at all. Lehzen, the Baron, Uncle Leopold, are unsubstantial shadows—the incidental supers of the piece. Her paradise was peopled by two persons, and surely that was enough. One sees them together still, a curious couple, strangely united in those artless pages, under the magical illumination

[1] Lee, 79–81.

of that dawn of eighty years ago: the polished high fine gentleman with the whitening hair and whiskers and the thick dark eyebrows and the mobile lips and the big expressive eyes; and beside him the tiny Queen—fair, slim, elegant, active, in her plain girl's dress and little tippet, looking up at him earnestly, adoringly, with eyes blue and projecting, and half-open mouth. So they appear upon every page of the Journal; upon every page Lord M. is present, Lord M. is speaking, Lord M. is being amusing, instructive, delightful, and affectionate at once, while Victoria drinks in the honied words, laughs till she shows her gums, tries hard to remember, and runs off, as soon as she is left alone, to put it all down. Their long conversations touched upon a multitude of topics. Lord M. would criticise books, throw out a remark or two on the British Constitution, make some passing reflections on human life, and tell story after story of the great people of the eighteenth century. Then there would be business—a despatch perhaps from Lord Durham in Canada, which Lord M. would read. But first he must explain a little. "He said that I must know that Canada originally belonged to the French, and was only ceded to the English in 1760, when it was taken in an expedition under Wolfe: ' a very daring

enterprise,' he said. Canada was then entirely
French, and the British only came afterwards.
. . . Lord M. explained this very clearly (and
much better than I have done) and said a good
deal more about it. He then read me Durham's
despatch, which is a very long one and took him
more than ½ an hour to read. Lord M. read it
beautifully with that fine soft voice of his, and
with so much expression, so that it is needless to
say I was much interested by it." [1] And then the
talk would take a more personal turn. Lord M.
would describe his boyhood, and she would learn
that " he wore his hair long, as all boys then did,
till he was 17; (*how* handsome he must have
looked!)." [2] Or she would find out about his queer
tastes and habits—how he never carried a watch,
which seemed quite extraordinary. " ' I always
ask the servant what o'clock it is, and then he tells
me what he likes,' said Lord M." [3] Or, as the
rooks wheeled about round the trees, " in a manner which indicated rain," he would say that he
could sit looking at them for an hour, and " was
quite surprised at my disliking them. . . . Lord
M. said, ' The rooks are my delight.' " [4]

The day's routine, whether in London or at

[1] *Girlhood*, II, 3.   [3] *Ibid.*, II, 100.
[2] *Ibid*, II, 29.   [4] *Ibid.*, II, 57, 256.

Windsor, was almost invariable. The morning
was devoted to business and Lord M. In the
afternoon the whole Court went out riding. The
Queen, in her velvet riding-habit and a top-hat
with a veil draped about the brim, headed the cav-
alcade; and Lord M. rode beside her. The lively
troupe went fast and far, to the extreme exhilaration of Her Majesty. Back in the Palace again,
there was still time for a little more fun before
dinner—a game of battledore and shuttlecock perhaps, or a romp along the galleries with some children.[1] Dinner came, and the ceremonial decidedly
tightened. The gentleman of highest rank sat on
the right hand of the Queen; on her left—it soon
became an established rule—sat Lord Melbourne.
After the ladies had left the dining-room, the gentlemen were not permitted to remain behind for
very long; indeed, the short time allowed them for
their wine-drinking formed the subject—so it was
rumoured—of one of the very few disputes between the Queen and her Prime Minister;[2] but her

[1] Lee, 71.

[2] The Duke of Bedford told Greville he was "sure there was a
battle between her and Melbourne. . . . He is sure there was
one about the men's sitting after dinner, for he heard her say to him
rather angrily, 'it is a horrid custom'—but when the ladies left
the room (he dined there) directions were given that the men
should remain *five minutes* longer." Greville *Memoirs*, February 26,
1840 (unpublished).

QUEEN VICTORIA IN 1838.

From the Painting by E. Corbould.

determination carried the day, and from that moment after-dinner drunkenness began to go out of
fashion. When the company was reassembled in
the drawing-room the etiquette was stiff. For a
few moments the Queen spoke in turn to each one
of her guests; and during these short uneasy collo-
quies the aridity of royalty was apt to become
painfully evident. One night Mr. Greville, the
Clerk of the Privy Council, was present; his turn
soon came; the middle-aged, hard-faced *viveur* was
addressed by his young hostess. " Have you been
riding to-day, Mr. Greville? " asked the Queen.
" No, Madam, I have not," replied Mr. Greville.
" It was a fine day," continued the Queen. " Yes,
Madam, a very fine day," said Mr. Greville. " It
was rather cold, though," said the Queen. " It
was rather cold, Madam," said Mr. Greville.
" Your sister, Lady Frances Egerton, rides, I
think, doesn't she? " said the Queen. " She does
ride sometimes, Madam," said Mr. Greville. There
was a pause, after which Mr. Greville ventured to
take the lead, though he did not venture to change
the subject. " Has your Majesty been riding today? " asked Mr. Greville. " Oh yes, a very long
ride," answered the Queen with animation. " Has
your Majesty got a nice horse? " said Mr. Greville. " Oh, a very nice horse," said the Queen.

It was over. Her Majesty gave a smile and an inclination of the head, Mr. Greville a profound bow, and the next conversation began with the next gentleman.[1] When all the guests had been disposed of, the Duchess of Kent sat down to her whist, while everybody else was ranged about the round table. Lord Melbourne sat beside the Queen, and talked pertinaciously—very often *à propos* to the contents of one of the large albums of engravings with which the round table was covered—until it was half-past eleven and time to go to bed.[2]

Occasionally, there were little diversions: the evening might be spent at the opera or at the play. Next morning the royal critic was careful to note down her impressions. " It was Shakespeare's tragedy of *Hamlet,* and we came in at the beginning of it. Mr. Charles Kean (son of old Kean) acted the part of Hamlet, and I must say beautifully. His conception of this very difficult, and I may almost say incomprehensible, character is admirable; his delivery of all the fine long speeches quite beautiful; he is excessively graceful and all his actions and attitudes are good, though not at all good-looking in face. . . . I came away just

[1] Greville, March 11, 1838 (unpublished).
[2] Greville, IV, 152–3.

as *Hamlet* was over." [1]   Later on, she went to
see Macready in *King Lear*. The story was new
to her; she knew nothing about it, and at first she
took very little interest in what was passing on
the stage; she preferred to chatter and laugh with
the Lord Chamberlain. But, as the play went on,
her mood changed; her attention was fixed, and
then she laughed no more. Yet she was puzzled;
it seemed a strange, a horrible business. What did
Lord M. think? Lord M. thought it was a very
fine play, but to be sure, " a rough, coarse play,
written for those times, with exaggerated characters." " I'm glad you've seen it," he added. [2] But,
undoubtedly, the evenings which she enjoyed most
were those on which there was dancing. She was
always ready enough to seize any excuse—the arrival of cousins—a birthday—a gathering of young
people—to give the command for that. Then,
when the band played, and the figures of the dan-
cers swayed to the music, and she felt her own
figure swaying too, with youthful spirits so close
on every side—then her happiness reached its
height, her eyes sparkled, she must go on and on
into the small hours of the morning. For a moment Lord M. himself was forgotten.

[1] *Girlhood*, I, 265–6.
[2] Martineau, II, 119–20; *Girlhood*, II, 121–2.

V

The months flew past. The summer was over:
" the pleasantest summer I EVER passed in *my life,*
and I shall never forget this first summer of my
reign." [1] With surprising rapidity, another summer was upon her. The coronation came and
went—a curious dream. The antique, intricate,
endless ceremonial worked itself out as best it
could, like some machine of gigantic complexity
which was a little out of order. The small central
figure went through her gyrations. She sat; she
walked; she prayed; she carried about an orb that
was almost too heavy to hold; the Archbishop of
Canterbury came and crushed a ring upon the
wrong finger, so that she was ready to cry out
with the pain; old Lord Rolle tripped up in his
mantle and fell down the steps as he was doing
homage; she was taken into a side chapel, where
the altar was covered with a table-cloth, sand-
wiches, and bottles of wine; she perceived Lehzen
in an upper box and exchanged a smile with her
as she sat, robed and crowned, on the Confessor's
throne. " I shall ever remember this day as the
proudest of my life," she noted. But the pride
was soon merged once more in youth and simplicity. When she returned to Buckingham Pal-

[1] *Girlhood,* I, 229.

ace at last she was not tired; she ran up to her
private rooms, doffed her splendours, and gave
her dog Dash its evening bath.[1]

Life flowed on again with its accustomed smoothness—though, of course, the smoothness was occasionally disturbed. For one thing, there was the
distressing behaviour of Uncle Leopold. The King
of the Belgians had not been able to resist attempting to make use of his family position to further
his diplomatic ends. But, indeed, why should there
be any question of resisting? Was not such a
course of conduct, far from being a temptation,
simply *selon les règles?* What were royal marriages for, if they did not enable sovereigns, in
spite of the hindrances of constitutions, to control
foreign politics? For the highest purposes, of
course; that was understood. The Queen of England was his niece—more than that—almost his
daughter; his confidential agent was living, in a
position of intimate favour, at her court. Surely,
in such circumstances, it would be preposterous,
it would be positively incorrect, to lose the opportunity of bending to his wishes by means of personal influence, behind the backs of the English
Ministers, the foreign policy of England.

He set about the task with becoming precau-

[1] *Girlhood,* I, 356–64; Leslie, II, 239.

tions. He continued in his letters his admirable advice. Within a few days of her accession, he recommended the young Queen to lay emphasis, on every possible occasion, upon her English birth; to praise the English nation; " the Established Church I also recommend strongly; you cannot, without *pledging* yourself to anything *particular, say too much on the subject."* And then " before you decide on anything important I should be glad if you would consult me; this would also have the advantage of giving you time "; nothing was more injurious than to be hurried into wrong decisions unawares. His niece replied at once with all the accustomed warmth of her affection; but she wrote hurriedly—and, perhaps, a trifle vaguely too. *" Your* advice is always of the *greatest importance* to me," she said.[1]

Had he, possibly, gone too far? He could not be certain; perhaps Victoria *had* been hurried. In any case, he would be careful; he would draw back—*pour mieux sauter,* he added to himself with a smile. In his next letters he made no reference to his suggestion of consultations with himself; he merely pointed out the wisdom, in general, of refusing to decide upon important questions off-hand. So far, his advice was taken; and it

[1] *Letters,* I, 79.

was noticed that the Queen, when applications were made to her, rarely gave an immediate answer. Even with Lord Melbourne, it was the same; when he asked for her opinion upon any subject, she would reply that she would think it over, and tell him her conclusions next day.[1]

King Leopold's counsels continued. The Princess de Lieven, he said, was a dangerous woman; there was reason to think that she would make attempts to pry into what did not concern her; let Victoria beware. " A rule which I cannot sufficiently recommend is *never to permit* people to speak on subjects concerning yourself or your affairs, without you having yourself desired them to do so." Should such a thing occur, " change the conversation, and make the individual feel that he has made a mistake." This piece of advice was also taken; for it fell out as the King had predicted. Madame de Lieven sought an audience, and appeared to be verging towards confidential topics; whereupon the Queen, becoming slightly embarrassed, talked of nothing but commonplaces. The individual felt that she had made a mistake.[2]

The King's next warning was remarkable. Letters, he pointed out, are almost invariably read in

---

[1] *Letters*, I, 80; Greville, IV, 22.
[2] Greville, I, 85–6; Greville, IV, 16.

the post. This was inconvenient, no doubt; but the fact, once properly grasped, was not without its advantages. "I will give you an example: we are still plagued by Prussia concerning those fortresses; now to tell the Prussian Government many things, which we *should not like* to tell them officially, the Minister is going to write a despatch to our man at Berlin, sending it *by post;* the Prussians *are sure* to read it, and to learn in this way what we wish them to hear." Analogous circumstances might very probably occur in England. "I tell you the *trick,*" wrote His Majesty, "that you should be able to guard against it." Such were the subtleties of constitutional sovereignty.[1]

It seemed that the time had come for another step. The King's next letter was full of foreign politics—the situation in Spain and Portugal, the character of Louis Philippe; and he received a favourable answer. Victoria, it is true, began by saying that she had shown the *political part* of his letter to Lord Melbourne; but she proceeded to a discussion of foreign affairs. It appeared that she was not unwilling to exchange observations on such matters with her uncle.[2] So far so good. But King Leopold was still cautious; though a crisis was impending in his diplomacy, he still hung back; at last, however, he could keep silence no longer. It was of the utmost importance to him that, in his manœuvrings with France and Holland, he should have, or at any rate appear to have, English support. But the English Government appeared to adopt a neutral attitude; it was too bad; not to be for him was to be against him—could they not see that? Yet, perhaps, they were only wavering, and a little pressure upon them from Victoria might still save all. He determined to put the case before her, delicately yet forcibly—just as he saw it himself. " All I want from your kind Majesty," he wrote, " is, that you will *occasionally* express to your Ministers, and particularly to good Lord Melbourne, that, as far as it is *compatible* with the interests *of your own* dominions, you do *not* wish that your Government should take the lead in such measures as might in a short time bring on the *destruction* of this country, as well as that of your uncle and his family." [1] The result of this appeal was unexpected; there was dead silence for more than a week. When Victoria at last wrote, she was prodigal of her affection—" it would, indeed, my dearest Uncle, be *very wrong* of you, if you thought my feelings of warm and devoted attachment to you, and of great

[1] *Letters,* I, 116.

affection for you, could be changed—*nothing* can ever change them "—but her references to foreign politics, though they were lengthy and elaborate, were non-committal in the extreme; they were almost cast in an official and diplomatic form. Her Ministers, she said, entirely shared her views upon the subject; she understood and sympathised with the difficulties of her beloved uncle's position; and he might rest assured " that both Lord Melbourne and Lord Palmerston are most anxious at all times for the prosperity and welfare of Belgium." That was all. The King in his reply declared himself delighted, and re-echoed the affectionate protestations of his niece. " My dearest and most beloved Victoria," he said, " you have written me a *very dear* and long letter, which has given me *great pleasure and satisfaction.*" He would not admit that he had had a rebuff.[1]

A few months later the crisis came. King Leopold determined to make a bold push, and to carry Victoria with him, this time, by a display of royal vigour and avuncular authority. In an abrupt, an almost peremptory letter, he laid his case, once more, before his niece. " You know from experience," he wrote, " that I *never ask anything of you.* . . . But, as I said before, if we are not

[1] *Letters*, I, 117–20.

careful we may see serious consequences which may affect more or less everybody, and *this* ought to be the object of our most anxious attention. I remain, my dear Victoria, your affectionate uncle, Leopold R." [1] The Queen immediately despatched this letter to Lord Melbourne, who replied with a carefully thought-out form of words, signifying nothing whatever, which, he suggested, she should send to her uncle. She did so, copying out the elaborate formula, with a liberal scattering of "dear Uncles" interspersed; and she concluded her letter with a message of "affectionate love to Aunt Louise and the children." Then at last King Leopold was obliged to recognise the facts. His next letter contained no reference at all to politics. "I am glad," he wrote, "to find that you like Brighton better than last year. I think Brighton very agreeable at this time of the year, till the east winds set in. The pavilion, besides, is comfortable; that cannot be denied. Before my marriage, it was there that I met the Regent. Charlotte afterwards came with old Queen Charlotte. How distant all this already, but still how present to one's memory." Like poor Madame de Lieven, His Majesty felt that he had made a mistake.[2]

[1] *Letters*, I, 134.   [2] *Ibid.*, I, 134–6, 140.

Nevertheless, he could not quite give up all hope. Another opportunity offered, and he made another effort—but there was not very much conviction in it, and it was immediately crushed. " My dear Uncle," the Queen wrote, " I have to thank you for your last letter which I received on Sunday. Though you seem not to dislike my political sparks, I think it is better not to increase them, as they might finally take fire, particularly as I see with regret that upon this one subject we cannot agree. I shall, therefore, limit myself to my expressions of very sincere wishes for the welfare and prosperity of Belgium." [1] After that, it was clear that there was no more to be said. Henceforward there is audible in the King's letters a curiously elegiac note. " My dearest Victoria, your *delightful* little letter has just arrived and went like *an arrow to my heart*. Yes, my beloved Victoria! I *do love you tenderly* . . . I love you *for yourself,* and I love in you the dear child whose welfare I tenderly watched." He had gone through much; yet, if life had its disappointments, it had its satisfactions too. " I have all the honours that can be given, and I am, politically speaking, very solidly established." But there were other things besides politics; there were romantic yearnings in

[1] *Letters*, I, 154.

his heart. " The only longing I still have is for the Orient, where I perhaps shall once end my life, rising in the west and setting in the east." As for his devotion to his niece, that could never end. " I never press my services on you, nor my councils, though I may say with some truth that from the extraordinary fate which the higher powers had ordained for me, my experience, both political and of private life, is great. I am *always ready* to be useful to you *when and where* it may be, and I repeat it, *all I want in return is some little sincere affection from you.*" [1]

VI

The correspondence with King Leopold was significant of much that still lay partly hidden in the character of Victoria. Her attitude towards her uncle had never wavered for a moment. To all his advances she had presented an absolutely unyielding front. The foreign policy of England was not his province; it was hers and her Ministers'; his insinuations, his entreaties, his struggles—all were quite useless; and he must understand that this was so. The rigidity of her position was the more striking owing to the respectfulness and the affection with which it was accompanied. From

[1] *Letters,* I, 185.

start to finish the unmoved Queen remained the
devoted niece. Leopold himself must have envied
such perfect correctitude; but what may be admirable in an elderly statesman is alarming in a
maiden of nineteen. And privileged observers
were not without their fears. The strange mixture of ingenuous light-heartedness and fixed determination, of frankness and reticence, of child-
ishness and pride, seemed to augur a future that
was perplexed and full of dangers. As time
passed the less pleasant qualities in this curious
composition revealed themselves more often and
more seriously. There were signs of an imperious,
a peremptory temper, an egotism that was strong
and hard. It was noticed that the palace etiquette,
far from relaxing, grew ever more and more inflexible. By some, this was attributed to Lehzen's
influence; but, if that was so, Lehzen had a willing
pupil; for the slightest infringements of the freez-
ing rules of regularity and deference were invariably and immediately visited by the sharp and
haughty glances of the Queen.[1] Yet Her Majesty's eyes, crushing as they could be, were less
crushing than her mouth. The self-will depicted
in those small projecting teeth and that small re-
ceding chin was of a more dismaying kind than

[1] Greville, IV, 16–17; Crawford, 163–4.

that which a powerful jaw betokens; it was a self-will imperturbable, impenetrable, unintelligent; a self-will dangerously akin to obstinacy. And the obstinacy of monarchs is not as that of other men.

Within two years of her accession, the storm-clouds which, from the first, had been dimly visible on the horizon, gathered and burst. Victoria's relations with her mother had not improved. The Duchess of Kent, still surrounded by all the galling appearances of filial consideration, remained in Buckingham Palace a discarded figure, powerless and inconsolable. Sir John Conroy, banished from the presence of the Queen, still presided over the Duchess's household, and the hostilities of Kensington continued unabated in the new surroundings. Lady Flora Hastings still cracked her malicious jokes; the animosity of the Baroness was still unappeased. One day, Lady Flora found the joke was turned against her. Early in 1839, travelling in the suite of the Duchess, she had returned from Scotland in the same carriage with Sir John. A change in her figure became the subject of an unseemly jest; tongues wagged; and the jest grew serious. It was whispered that Lady Flora was with child.[1] The state of her health seemed to confirm the suspicion; she con-

[1] Greville, IV, 178, and August 15, 1839 (unpublished).

sulted Sir James Clark, the royal physician, and, after the consultation, Sir James let his tongue wag, too. On this, the scandal flared up sky-high. Everyone was talking; the Baroness was not surprised; the Duchess rallied tumultuously to the support of her lady; the Queen was informed. At last the extraordinary expedient of a medical examination was resorted to, during which Sir James, according to Lady Flora, behaved with brutal rudeness, while a second doctor was extremely polite. Finally, both physicians signed a certificate entirely exculpating the lady. But this was by no means the end of the business. The Hastings family, socially a very powerful one, threw itself into the fray with all the fury of outraged pride and injured innocence; Lord Hastings insisted upon an audience of the Queen, wrote to the papers, and demanded the dismissal of Sir James Clark. The Queen expressed her regret to Lady Flora, but Sir James Clark was not dismissed. The tide of opinion turned violently against the Queen and her advisers; high society was disgusted by all this washing of dirty linen in Buckingham Palace; the public at large was indignant at the ill-treatment of Lady Flora. By the end of March, the popularity, so radiant and so abundant, with which the young

Sovereign had begun her reign, had entirely disappeared.[1]

There can be no doubt that a great lack of discretion had been shown by the Court. Ill-natured tittle-tattle, which should have been instantly nipped in the bud, had been allowed to assume disgraceful proportions; and the Throne itself had become involved in the personal malignities of the palace. A particularly awkward question had been raised by the position of Sir James Clark. The Duke of Wellington, upon whom it was customary to fall back, in cases of great difficulty in high places, had been consulted upon this question, and he had given it as his opinion that, as it would be impossible to remove Sir James without a public enquiry, Sir James must certainly stay where he was.[2] Probably the Duke was right; but the fact that the peccant doctor continued in the Queen's service made the Hastings family irreconcilable and produced an unpleasant impression of unrepentant error upon the public mind. As for Victoria, she was very young and quite inexperienced; and she can hardly be blamed for having failed to control an extremely difficult situation. That

[1] " Nobody cares for the Queen, her popularity has sunk to zero, and loyalty is a dead letter." Greville, March 25, 1839; *Morning Post*, September 14, 1839.

[2] Greville, August 15, 1839 (unpublished).

was clearly Lord Melbourne's task; he was a man
of the world, and, with vigilance and circumspec-
tion, he might have quietly put out the ugly flames
while they were still smouldering. He did not do
so; he was lazy and easy-going; the Baroness was
persistent, and he let things slide. But doubtless
his position was not an easy one; passions ran high
in the palace; and Victoria was not only very
young, she was very headstrong, too. Did he possess the magic bridle which would curb that fiery
steed? He could not be certain. And then, suddenly, another violent crisis revealed more unmis-
takably than ever the nature of the mind with
which he had to deal.

VII

The Queen had for long been haunted by a
terror that the day might come when she would
be obliged to part with her Minister. Ever since
the passage of the Reform Bill, the power of the
Whig Government had steadily declined. The
General Election of 1837 had left them with a
very small majority in the House of Commons;
since then, they had been in constant difficulties—
abroad, at home, in Ireland; the Radical group
had grown hostile; it became highly doubtful how
much longer they could survive. The Queen

watched the development of events in great anxiety. She was a Whig by birth, by upbringing, by every association, public and private; and, even if those ties had never existed, the mere fact that Lord M. was the head of the Whigs would have amply sufficed to determine her politics. The fall of the Whigs would mean a sad upset for Lord M. But it would have a still more terrible consequence: Lord M. would have to leave her; and the daily, the hourly, presence of Lord M. had become an integral part of her life. Six months after her accession she had noted in her diary " I shall be very sorry to lose him *even* for *one* night ";[1] and this feeling of personal dependence on her Minister steadily increased. In these circumstances it was natural that she should have become a Whig partisan. Of the wider significance of political questions she knew nothing; all she saw was that her friends were in office and about her, and that it would be dreadful if they ceased to be so. " I cannot say," she wrote when a critical division was impending, "(though I feel *confident* of *our success*) HOW *low*, HOW *sad* I feel, when I think of the POSSIBILITY of this excellent and truly kind man not *remaining* my Minister! Yet I trust fervently that *He* who has so wonderfully pro-

[1] *Girlhood,* I, 254.

tected me through such manifold difficulties will
not *now* desert me! I should have liked to have
expressed to Lord M. my anxiety, but the tears
were nearer than words throughout the time I saw
him, and I felt I should have choked, had I attempted to say anything." [1]   Lord Melbourne
realised clearly enough how undesirable was such a
state of mind in a constitutional sovereign who
might be called upon at any moment to receive as
her Ministers the leaders of the opposite party;
he did what he could to cool her ardour; but in
vain.

With considerable lack of foresight, too, he had
himself helped to bring about this unfortunate
condition of affairs.   From the moment of her
accession, he had surrounded the Queen with ladies
of his own party; the Mistress of the Robes and
all the Ladies of the Bedchamber were Whigs.   In
the ordinary course, the Queen never saw a Tory:
eventually she took pains never to see one in any
circumstances.   She disliked the whole tribe; and
she did not conceal the fact.   She particularly disliked Sir Robert Peel, who would almost certainly
be the next Prime Minister.   His manners were
detestable, and he wanted to turn out Lord M.
His supporters, without exception, were equally

[1] *Girlhood,* I, 324.

bad; and as for Sir James Graham, she could not bear the sight of him; he was exactly like Sir John Conroy.[1]

The affair of Lady Flora intensified these party rumours still further. The Hastings were Tories, and Lord Melbourne and the Court were attacked by the Tory press in unmeasured language. The Queen's sectarian zeal proportionately increased. But the dreaded hour was now fast approaching. Early in May the Ministers were visibly tottering; on a vital point of policy they could only secure a majority of five in the House of Commons; they determined to resign. When Victoria heard the news she burst into tears. Was it possible, then, that all was over? Was she, indeed, about to see Lord M. for the last time? Lord M. came; and it is a curious fact that, even in this crowning moment of misery and agitation, the precise girl noted, to the minute, the exact time of the arrival and the departure of her beloved Minister. The conversation was touching and prolonged; but it could only end in one way—the Queen must send for the Duke of Wellington. When, next morning, the Duke came, he advised her Majesty to send for Sir Robert Peel. She was in " a state of dreadful grief," but she swallowed down her tears, and

[1] Greville, August 4, 1841 (unpublished); *Girlhood*, II, 154, 162.

braced herself, with royal resolution, for the odious, odious interview.

Peel was by nature reserved, proud, and shy. His manners were not perfect, and he knew it; he was easily embarrassed, and, at such moments, he grew even more stiff and formal than before, while his feet mechanically performed upon the carpet a dancing-master's measure. Anxious as he now was to win the Queen's good graces, his very anxiety to do so made the attainment of his object the more difficult. He entirely failed to make any headway whatever with the haughty hostile girl before him. She coldly noted that he appeared to be unhappy and " put out," and, while he stood in painful fixity, with an occasional uneasy pointing of the toe, her heart sank within her at the sight of that manner, " Oh! how different, how dreadfully different, to the frank, open, natural, and most kind warm manner of Lord Melbourne." Nevertheless, the audience passed without disaster. Only at one point had there been some slight hint of a disagreement. Peel had decided that a change would be necessary in the composition of the royal Household: the Queen must no longer be entirely surrounded by the wives and sisters of his opponents; some, at any rate, of the Ladies of the Bedchamber should be friendly to his Government. When this matter was touched upon, the Queen had intimated that she wished her Household to remain unchanged; to which Sir Robert had replied that the question could be settled later, and shortly afterwards withdrew to arrange the details of his Cabinet. While he was present, Victoria had remained, as she herself said, " very much collected, civil and high, and betrayed no agitation "; but as soon as she was alone she completely broke down. Then she pulled herself together to write to Lord Melbourne an account of all that had happened, and of her own wretchedness. " She feels," she said, " Lord Melbourne will understand it, amongst enemies to those she most relied on and most esteemed; but what is worst of all is the being deprived of seeing Lord Melbourne as she used to do."

Lord Melbourne replied with a very wise letter. He attempted to calm the Queen and to induce her to accept the new position gracefully; and he had nothing but good words for the Tory leaders. As for the question of the Ladies of the Household, the Queen, he said, should strongly urge what she desired, as it was a matter which concerned her personally, " but," he added, " if Sir Robert is unable to concede it, it will not do to refuse and to put off the negotiation upon it."

On this point there can be little doubt that Lord
Melbourne was right. The question was a complicated and subtle one, and it had never arisen
before; but subsequent constitutional practice has
determined that a Queen Regnant must accede to
the wishes of her Prime Minister as to the *personnel* of the female part of her Household. Lord
Melbourne's wisdom, however, was wasted. The
Queen would not be soothed, and still less would
she take advice. It was outrageous of the Tories
to want to deprive her of her Ladies, and that
night she made up her mind that, whatever Sir
Robert might say, she would refuse to consent to
the removal of a single one of them. Accordingly,
when, next morning, Peel appeared again, she
was ready for action. He began by detailing the
Cabinet appointments, and then he added " Now,
ma'am, about the Ladies "—when the Queen
sharply interrupted him. " I cannot give up *any*
of my Ladies," she said. " What, ma'am! " said
Sir Robert, " does your Majesty mean to retain
them *all?* " " *All*," said the Queen. Sir Robert's
face worked strangely; he could not conceal his
agitation. " The Mistress of the Robes and the
Ladies of the Bedchamber? " he brought out at
last. " *All*," replied once more her Majesty. It
was in vain that Peel pleaded and argued; in vain

that he spoke, growing every moment more pompous and uneasy, of the constitution, and Queens Regnant, and the public interest; in vain that he danced his pathetic minuet. She was adamant; but he, too, through all his embarrassment, showed no sign of yielding; and when at last he left her nothing had been decided—the whole formation of the Government was hanging in the wind. A frenzy of excitement now seized upon Victoria. Sir Robert, she believed in her fury, had tried to outwit her, to take her friends from her, to impose his will upon her own; but that was not all: she had suddenly perceived, while the poor man was moving so uneasily before her, the one thing that she was desperately longing for—a loop-hole of escape. She seized a pen and dashed off a note to Lord Melbourne.

" Sir Robert has behaved very ill," she wrote, " he insisted on my giving up my Ladies, to which I replied that I *never* would consent, and I never saw a man so frightened. . . . I was calm but very decided, and I think you would have been pleased to see my composure and great firmness; the Queen of England will not submit to such trickery. Keep yourself in readiness, for you may soon be wanted." Hardly had she finished when the Duke of Wellington was announced. "Well,

Ma'am," he said as he entered, " I am very sorry to find there is a difficulty." " Oh! " she instantly replied, " *he* began it, not me." She felt that only one thing now was needed: she must be firm. And firm she was. The venerable conqueror of Napoleon was outfaced by the relentless equanimity of a girl in her teens. He could not move the Queen one inch. At last, she even ventured to rally him. " Is Sir Robert so weak," she asked, " that even the Ladies must be of his opinion? " On which the Duke made a brief and humble expostulation, bowed low, and departed.

Had she won? Time would show; and in the meantime she scribbled down another letter. " Lord Melbourne must not think the Queen rash in her conduct. . . . The Queen felt this was an attempt to see whether she could be led and managed like a child." The Tories were not only wicked but ridiculous. Peel, having, as she understood, expressed a wish to remove only those members of the Household who were in Parliament, now objected to her Ladies. " I should like to know," she exclaimed in triumphant scorn, " if they mean to give the *Ladies* seats in Parliament? "

The end of the crisis was now fast approaching. Sir Robert returned, and told her that if she in-

sisted upon retaining all her Ladies he could not
form a Government. She replied that she would
send him her final decision in writing. Next morning the late Whig Cabinet met. Lord Melbourne
read to them the Queen's letters, and the group of
elderly politicians were overcome by an extraordinary wave of enthusiasm. They knew very well
that, to say the least, it was highly doubtful
whether the Queen had acted in strict accordance
with the constitution; that in doing what she had
done she had brushed aside Lord Melbourne's advice; that, in reality, there was no public reason
whatever why they should go back upon their decision to resign. But such considerations vanished
before the passionate urgency of Victoria. The
intensity of her determination swept them head-
long down the stream of her desire. They unanimously felt that "it was impossible to abandon
such a Queen and such a woman." Forgetting
that they were no longer her Majesty's Ministers,
they took the unprecedented course of advising the
Queen by letter to put an end to her negotiation
with Sir Robert Peel. She did so; all was over;
she had triumphed. That evening there was a ball
at the Palace. Everyone was present. "Peel and
the Duke of Wellington came by looking very
much put out." She was perfectly happy; Lord

M. was Prime Minister once more, and he was by her side.[1]

VIII

Happiness had returned with Lord M., but it was happiness in the midst of agitation. The domestic imbroglio continued unabated, until at last the Duke, rejected as a Minister, was called in once again in his old capacity as moral physician to the family. Something was accomplished when, at last, he induced Sir John Conroy to resign his place about the Duchess of Kent and leave the Palace for ever; something more when he persuaded the Queen to write an affectionate letter to her mother. The way seemed open for a reconciliation, but the Duchess was stormy still. She didn't believe that Victoria had written that letter; it was not in her handwriting; and she sent for the Duke to tell him so. The Duke, assuring her that the letter was genuine, begged her to forget the

1 *Letters*, I, 154–72; *Girlhood*, II, 163–75; Greville, IV, 206–217, and unpublished passages; Broughton, V, 195; Clarendon, I, 165. The exclamation "They wished to treat me like a girl, but I will show them that I am Queen of England!" often quoted as the Queen's, is apocryphal. It is merely part of Greville's summary of the two letters to Melbourne, printed in *Letters*, 162 and 163. It may be noted that the phrase "the Queen of England will not submit to such trickery" is omitted in *Girlhood*, 169; and in general there are numerous verbal discrepancies between the versions of the journal and the letters in the two books.

past. But that was not so easy. "What am I to do if Lord Melbourne comes up to me?" "Do, ma'am? Why, receive him with civility." Well, she would make an effort. . . . "But what am I to do if Victoria asks me to shake hands with Lehzen?" "Do, ma'am? Why, take her in your arms and kiss her." "What!" The Duchess bristled in every feather, and then she burst into a hearty laugh. "No, ma'am, no," said the Duke, laughing too. "I don't mean you are to take *Lehzen* in your arms and kiss *her*, but the Queen." [1]

The Duke might perhaps have succeeded, had not all attempts at conciliation been rendered hopeless by a tragical event. Lady Flora, it was discovered, had been suffering from a terrible internal malady, which now grew rapidly worse. There could be little doubt that she was dying. The Queen's unpopularity reached an extraordinary height. More than once she was publicly insulted. "Mrs. Melbourne," was shouted at her when she appeared at her balcony; and, at Ascot, she was hissed by the Duchess of Montrose and Lady Sarah Ingestre as she passed. Lady Flora died. The whole scandal burst out again with redoubled vehemence; while, in the Palace, the two parties

[1] Greville, June 7, June 10, June 15, August 15, 1839 (unpublished).

were henceforth divided by an impassable, a Stygian, gulf.[1]

Nevertheless, Lord M. was back, and every trouble faded under the enchantment of his presence and his conversation. He, on his side, had gone through much; and his distresses were intensified by a consciousness of his own shortcomings. He realised clearly enough that, if he had intervened at the right moment, the Hastings scandal might have been averted; and, in the bedchamber crisis, he knew that he had allowed his judgment to be overruled and his conduct to be swayed by private feelings and the impetuosity of Victoria.[2] But he was not one to suffer too acutely from the pangs of conscience. In spite of the dullness and the formality of the Court, his relationship with the Queen had come to be the dominating interest in his life; to have been deprived of it would have been heartrending; that dread eventuality had been—somehow—avoided; he was installed once more, in a kind of triumph; let him enjoy the fleeting hours to the full! And so, cherished by the favour of a sovereign and warmed by the adoration of a girl, the autumn rose, in those autumn months of 1839, came to a wondrous

1 Greville, June 24 and July 7, 1839 (unpublished); Crawford, 222.
2 Greville, VI, 251-2.

blooming. The petals expanded, beautifully, for the last time. For the last time in this unlooked-for, this incongruous, this almost incredible intercourse, the old epicure tasted the exquisiteness of romance. To watch, to teach, to restrain, to encourage the royal young creature beside him—that was much; to feel with such a constant intimacy the impact of her quick affection, her radiant vitality—that was more; most of all, perhaps, was it good to linger vaguely in humorous contemplation, in idle apostrophe, to talk disconnectedly, to make a little joke about an apple or a furbelow, to dream. The springs of his sensibility, hidden deep within him, were overflowing. Often, as he bent over her hand and kissed it, he found himself in tears.[1]

Upon Victoria, with all her impermeability, it was inevitable that such a companionship should have produced, eventually, an effect. She was no longer the simple schoolgirl of two years since. The change was visible even in her public demeanour. Her expression, once " ingenuous and serene," now appeared to a shrewd observer to be " bold and discontented." [2] She had learnt something of the pleasures of power and the pains

[1] Greville, VI, 251; *Girlhood,* I, 236, 238; II, 267.
[2] Martineau, II, 120.

of it; but that was not all. Lord Melbourne with
his gentle instruction had sought to lead her into
the paths of wisdom and moderation, but the whole
unconscious movement of his character had swayed
her in a very different direction. The hard clear
pebble, subjected for so long and so constantly to
that encircling and insidious fluidity, had suffered
a curious corrosion; it seemed to be actually growing a little soft and a little clouded. Humanity
and fallibility are infectious things; was it possible
that Lehzen's prim pupil had caught them? That
she was beginning to listen to siren voices? That
the secret impulses of self-expression, of self-
indulgence even, were mastering her life? For a
moment the child of a new age looked back, and
wavered towards the eighteenth century. It was
the most critical moment of her career. Had those
influences lasted, the development of her character,
the history of her life, would have been completely
changed.

And why should they not last? She, for one,
was very anxious that they should. Let them last
for ever! She was surrounded by Whigs, she was
free to do whatever she wanted, she had Lord M.;
she could not believe that she could ever be happier. Any change would be for the worse; and
the worst change of all . . . no, she would not

hear of it; it would be quite intolerable, it would
upset everything, if she were to marry. And yet
everyone seemed to want her to—the general public, the Ministers, her Saxe-Coburg relations—it
was always the same story. Of course, she knew
very well that there were excellent reasons for it.
For one thing, if she remained childless, and were
to die, her uncle Cumberland, who was now the
King of Hanover, would succeed to the Throne
of England. That, no doubt, would be a most
unpleasant event; and she entirely sympathised
with everybody who wished to avoid it. But there
was no hurry; naturally, she would marry in the
end—but not just yet—not for three or four years.
What was tiresome was that her uncle Leopold
had apparently determined, not only that she
ought to marry, but that her cousin Albert ought
to be her husband. That was very like her uncle
Leopold, who wanted to have a finger in every
pie; and it was true that long ago, in far-off days,
before her accession even, she had written to him in
a way which might well have encouraged him in
such a notion. She had told him then that Albert
possessed " every quality that could be desired to
render her perfectly happy," and had begged her
" dearest uncle to take care of the health of one,
now *so dear* to me, and to take him under *your*

special protection," adding, " I hope and trust all will go on prosperously and well on this subject of so much importance to me." [1] But that had been years ago, when she was a mere child; perhaps, indeed, to judge from the language, the letter had been dictated by Lehzen; at any rate, her feelings, and all the circumstances, had now entirely changed. Albert hardly interested her at all.

In later life the Queen declared that she had never for a moment dreamt of marrying anyone but her cousin; [2] her letters and diaries tell a very different story. On August 26, 1837, she wrote in her journal: " To-day is my *dearest* cousin Albert's 18th birthday, and I pray Heaven to pour its choicest blessings on his beloved head!" In the subsequent years, however, the date passes unnoticed. It had been arranged that Stockmar should accompany the Prince to Italy, and the faithful Baron left her side for that purpose. He wrote to her more than once with sympathetic descriptions of his young companion; but her mind was by this time made up. She liked and admired Albert very much, but she did not want to marry him. " At present," she told Lord Melbourne in April, 1839, " *my* feeling is quite against ever

marrying." [1] When her cousin's Italian tour
came to an end, she began to grow nervous; she
knew that, according to a long-standing engagement, his next journey would be to England. He
would probably arrive in the autumn, and by July
her uneasiness was intense. She determined to
write to her uncle, in order to make her position
clear. It must be understood she said, that " there
is *no engagement* between us." If she should like
Albert, she could "make *no final promise this
year,* for, at the *very earliest,* any such event could
not take place till *two or three years hence.*" She
had, she said, " a *great* repugnance " to change her
present position; and, if she should not like him,
she was "*very* anxious that it should be understood that she would *not* be guilty of any breach
of promise, for she *never gave any.*" [2] To Lord
Melbourne she was more explicit. She told him
that she " had no great wish to see Albert, as the
whole subject was an odious one "; she hated to
have to decide about it; and she repeated once
again that seeing Albert would be " a disagreeable
thing." [3] But there was no escaping the horrid
business; the visit must be made, and she must
see him. The summer slipped by and was over;

[1] *Girlhood,* II, 153.   [2] *Letters,* I, 177–8.
[3] *Girlhood,* II, 215–6.

it was the autumn already; on the evening of
October 10 Albert, accompanied by his brother
Ernest, arrived at Windsor.

Albert arrived; and the whole structure of her
existence crumbled into nothingness like a house
of cards. He was beautiful—she gasped—she
knew no more. Then, in a flash, a thousand mysteries were revealed to her; the past, the present,
rushed upon her with a new significance; the delu-
sions of years were abolished, and an extraordinary,
an irresistible certitude leapt into being in the
light of those blue eyes, the smile of that lovely
mouth. The succeeding hours passed in a rapture.
She was able to observe a few more details—the
" exquisite nose," the " delicate moustachios and
slight but very slight whiskers," the " beautiful
figure, broad in the shoulders and a fine waist."
She rode with him, danced with him, talked with
him, and it was all perfection. She had no shadow
of a doubt. He had come on a Thursday evening,
and on the following Sunday morning she told
Lord Melbourne that she had " a good deal
changed her opinion as to marrying." Next morning, she told him that she had made up her mind
to marry Albert. The morning after that, she
sent for her cousin. She received him alone, and
" after a few minutes I said to him that I thought

he must be aware *why* I wished them to come here—and that it would make me *too happy* if he would consent to what I wished (to marry me)." Then "we embraced each other, and he was *so* kind, *so* affectionate." She said that she was quite unworthy of him, while he murmured that he would be very happy "Das Leben mit dir zu zubringen." They parted, and she felt "the happiest of human beings," when Lord M. came in. At first she beat about the bush, and talked of the weather, and indifferent subjects. Somehow or other she felt a little nervous with her old friend. At last, summoning up her courage, she said, "I have got well through this with Albert." "Oh! you have," said Lord M.[1]

[1] *Girlhood*, II, 262–9. Greville's statement (Nov. 27, 1839) that "the Queen settled everything about her marriage herself, and without consulting Melbourne at all on the subject, not even communicating to him her intention," has no foundation in fact. The Queen's journal proves that she consulted Melbourne at every point.

CHAPTER IV

MARRIAGE

I

IT was decidedly a family match. Prince Francis Charles Augustus Albert Emmanuel of Saxe-Coburg-Gotha—for such was his full title—had been born just three months after his cousin Victoria, and the same midwife had assisted at the two births. The children's grandmother, the Dowager Duchess of Coburg, had from the first looked forward to their marriage; as they grew up, the Duke, the Duchess of Kent, and King Leopold came equally to desire it. The Prince, ever since the time when, as a child of three, his nurse had told him that some day "the little English May flower" would be his wife, had never thought of marrying anyone else. When eventually Baron Stockmar himself signified his assent, the affair seemed as good as settled.[1]

The Duke had one other child—Prince Ernest, Albert's senior by one year, and heir to the principality. The Duchess was a sprightly and beau-

[1] Martin, I, 1–2; Grey, 213–4.

PRINCE ALBERT IN 1840.

From the Portrait by John Partridge.

tiful woman, with fair hair and blue eyes; Albert
was very like her and was her declared favourite.
But in his fifth year he was parted from her for
ever. The ducal court was not noted for the
strictness of its morals; the Duke was a man of
gallantry, and it was rumoured that the Duchess
followed her husband's example. There were
scandals: one of the Court Chamberlains, a charming and cultivated man of Jewish extraction, was
talked of; at last there was a separation, followed
by a divorce. The Duchess retired to Paris, and
died unhappily in 1831. Her memory was always
very dear to Albert.[1]

He grew up a pretty, clever, and high-spirited
boy. Usually well-behaved, he was, however, sometimes violent. He had a will of his own, and asserted it; his elder brother was less passionate, less
purposeful, and, in their wrangles, it was Albert
who came out top. The two boys, living for the
most part in one or other of the Duke's country
houses, among pretty hills and woods and streams,
had been at a very early age—Albert was less than
four—separated from their nurses and put under
a tutor, in whose charge they remained until they
went to the University. They were brought up
in a simple and unostentatious manner, for the

[1] Grey, 7–9; Crawford, 245–6; Panam, 256–7.

Duke was poor and the duchy very small and very insignificant.   Before long it became evident that Albert was a model lad.   Intelligent and pains-taking, he had been touched by the moral earnest-ness of his generation; at the age of eleven he sur-prised his father by telling him that he hoped to make himself " a good and useful man."   And yet he was not over-serious; though, perhaps, he had little humour, he was full of fun—of practical jokes and mimicry.   He was no milksop; he rode, and shot, and fenced; above all did he delight in being out of doors, and never was he happier than in his long rambles with his brother through the wild country round his beloved Rosenau—stalking the deer, admiring the scenery, and returning laden with specimens for his natural history collection. He was, besides, passionately fond of music.   In one particular it was observed that he did not take after his father: owing either to his peculiar up-bringing or to a more fundamental idiosyncrasy he had a marked distaste for the opposite sex.   At the age of five, at a children's dance, he screamed with disgust and anger when a little girl was led up to him for a partner; and though, later on, he grew more successful in disguising such feelings, the feelings remained.[1]

[1] Grey, chaps. i to vi; Ernest, I, 18–23.

The brothers were very popular in Coburg, and, when the time came for them to be confirmed, the preliminary examination which, according to ancient custom, was held in public in the " Giants' Hall " of the Castle, was attended by an enthusiastic crowd of functionaries, clergy, delegates from the villages of the duchy, and miscellaneous onlookers. There were also present, besides the Duke and the Dowager Duchess, their Serene Highnesses the Princes Alexander and Ernest of Würtemberg, Prince Leiningen, Princess Hohenlohe-Langenburg, and Princess Hohenlohe-Schillingsfürst. Dr. Jacobi, the Court chaplain, presided at an altar, simply but appropriately decorated, which had been placed at the end of the hall; and the proceedings began by the choir singing the first verse of the hymn, " Come, Holy Ghost." After some introductory remarks, Dr. Jacobi began the examination. " The dignified and decorous bearing of the Princes," we are told in a contemporary account, " their strict attention to the questions, the frankness, decision, and correctness of their answers, produced a deep impression on the numerous assembly. Nothing was more striking in their answers than the evidence they gave of deep feeling and of inward strength of conviction. The questions put by the examiner

were not such as to be met by a simple " yes " or
" no." They were carefully considered in order
to give the audience a clear insight into the views
and feelings of the young princes. One of the
most touching moments was when the examiner
asked the hereditary prince whether he intended
steadfastly to hold to the Evangelical Church, and
the Prince answered not only " Yes! " but added
in a clear and decided tone: " I and my brother
are firmly resolved ever to remain faithful to the
acknowledged truth." The examination having
lasted an hour, Dr. Jacobi made some concluding
observations, followed by a short prayer; the second and third verses of the opening hymn were
sung; and the ceremony was over. The Princes,
stepping down from the altar, were embraced by
the Duke and the Dowager Duchess; after which
the loyal inhabitants of Coburg dispersed, well
satisfied with their entertainment.[1]

Albert's mental development now proceeded
apace. In his seventeenth year he began a careful
study of German literature and German philosophy. He set about, he told his tutor, " to follow
the thoughts of the great Klopstock into their
depths—though in this, for the most part," he
modestly added, " I do not succeed." He wrote

[1] Grey, App. B.

an essay on the " Mode of Thought of the Germans, and a Sketch of the History of German
Civilisation," " making use," he said, " in its general outlines, of the divisions which the treatment
of the subject itself demands," and concluding with
" a retrospect of the shortcomings of our time,
with an appeal to every one to correct those short-
comings in his own case, and thus set a good example to others." [1] Placed for some months under
the care of King Leopold at Brussels, he came
under the influence of Adolphe Quetelet, a math-
ematical professor, who was particularly interested in the application of the laws of probability
to political and moral phenomena; this line of
inquiry attracted the Prince, and the friendship
thus begun continued till the end of his life. [2] From
Brussels he went to the University of Bonn, where
he was speedily distinguished both by his intellectual and his social activities; his energies were
absorbed in metaphysics, law, political economy,
music, fencing, and amateur theatricals. Thirty
years later his fellow-students recalled with delight
the fits of laughter into which they had been sent
by Prince Albert's mimicry. The *verve* with which
his Serene Highness reproduced the tones and
gestures of one of the professors who used to point

[1] Grey, 124–7.   [2] Gossart; Ernest, I, 72–3.

to a picture of a row of houses in Venice with the remark, " That is the Ponte Realte," and of another who fell down in a race and was obliged to look for his spectacles, was especially appreciated.[1]

After a year at Bonn, the time had come for a foreign tour, and Baron Stockmar arrived from England to accompany the Prince on an expedition to Italy.   The Baron had been already, two years previously, consulted by King Leopold as to his views upon the proposed marriage of Albert and Victoria.   His reply had been remarkable. With a characteristic foresight, a characteristic absence of optimism, a characteristic sense of the moral elements in the situation, Stockmar had pointed out what were, in his opinion, the conditions essential to make the marriage a success. Albert, he wrote, was a fine young fellow, well grown for his age, with agreeable and valuable qualities; and it was probable that in a few years he would turn out a strong handsome man, of a kindly, simple, yet dignified demeanour.   " Thus, externally, he possesses all that pleases the sex, and at all times and in all countries must please." Supposing, therefore, that Victoria herself was in favour of the marriage, the further question arose

[1] Grey, 169-73.

as to whether Albert's mental qualities were such as to fit him for the position of husband of the Queen of England. On this point, continued the Baron, one heard much to his credit; the Prince was said to be discreet and intelligent; but all such judgments were necessarily partial, and the Baron preferred to reserve his opinion until he could come to a trustworthy conclusion from personal observation. And then he added: " But all this is not enough. The young man ought to have not merely great ability, but a *right* ambition, and great force of will as well. To pursue for a lifetime a political career so arduous demands more than energy and inclination—it demands also that earnest frame of mind which is ready of its own accord to sacrifice mere pleasure to real usefulness. If he is not satisfied hereafter with the consciousness of having achieved one of the most influential positions in Europe, how often will he feel tempted to repent his adventure! If he does not from the very outset accept it as a vocation of grave responsibility, on the efficient performance of which his honour and happiness depend, there is small likelihood of his succeeding." [1]

Such were the views of Stockmar on the qualifications necessary for the due fulfilment of that

[1] Stockmar, 310.

destiny which Albert's family had marked out for him; and he hoped, during the tour in Italy, to come to some conclusion as to how far the Prince possessed them. Albert on his side was much impressed by the Baron, whom he had previously seen but rarely; he also became acquainted, for the first time in his life, with a young Englishman, Lieut. Francis Seymour, who had been engaged to accompany him, whom he found *sehr liebenswürdig,* and with whom he struck up a warm friendship. He delighted in the galleries and scenery of Florence, though with Rome he was less impressed. "But for some beautiful palaces," he said, "it might just as well be any town in Germany." In an interview with Pope Gregory XVI, he took the opportunity of displaying his erudition. When the Pope observed that the Greeks had taken their art from the Etruscans, Albert replied that, on the contrary, in his opinion, they had borrowed from the Egyptians: his Holiness politely acquiesced. Wherever he went he was eager to increase his knowledge, and, at a ball in Florence, he was observed paying no attention whatever to the ladies, and deep in conversation with the learned Signor Capponi. "Voilà un prince dont nous pouvons être fiers," said the Grand Duke of Tuscany, who was standing by: "la belle danseuse l'attend, le savant l'occupe." [1]

On his return to Germany, Stockmar's observations, imparted to King Leopold, were still critical. Albert, he said, was intelligent, kind, and amiable; he was full of the best intentions and the noblest resolutions, and his judgment was in many things beyond his years. But great exertion was repugnant to him; he seemed to be too willing to spare himself, and his good resolutions too often came to nothing. It was particularly unfortunate that he took not the slightest interest in politics, and never read a newspaper. In his manners, too, there was still room for improvement. "He will always," said the Baron, "have more success with men than with women, in whose society he shows too little *empressement,* and is too indifferent and retiring." One other feature of the case was noted by the keen eye of the old physician: the Prince's constitution was not a strong one.[2] Yet, on the whole, he was favourable to the projected marriage. But by now the chief obstacle seemed to lie in another quarter, Victoria was apparently determined to commit herself to nothing. And so it happened that when Albert went to England he had made up his mind to withdraw entirely

1 Grey, 133, 415, 416, 419.   2 Stockmar, 331-2.

from the affair. Nothing would induce him, he confessed to a friend, to be kept vaguely waiting; he would break it all off at once. His reception at Windsor threw an entirely new light upon the situation. The wheel of fortune turned with a sudden rapidity; and he found, in the arms of Victoria, the irrevocable assurance of his overwhelming fate.[1]

II

He was not in love with her. Affection, gratitude, the natural reactions to the unqualified devotion of a lively young cousin who was also a queen—such feelings possessed him, but the ardours of reciprocal passion were not his. Though he found that he liked Victoria very much, what immediately interested him in his curious position was less her than himself. Dazzled and delighted, riding, dancing, singing, laughing, amid the splendours of Windsor, he was aware of a new sensation—the stirrings of ambition in his breast. His place would indeed be a high, an enviable one! And then, on the instant, came another thought. The teaching of religion, the admonitions of Stockmar, his own inmost convictions, all spoke with the same utterance. He would not be there to

[1] Grey, 425.

please himself, but for a very different purpose—
to do good. He must be "noble, manly, and
princely in all things," he would have "to live
and to sacrifice himself for the benefit of his new
country"; to "use his powers and endeavours
for a great object—that of promoting the welfare
of multitudes of his fellowmen." One serious
thought led on to another. The wealth and the
bustle of the English Court might be delightful
for the moment, but, after all, it was Coburg that
had his heart. "While I shall be untiring," he
wrote to his grandmother, "in my efforts and
labours for the country to which I shall in future
belong, and where I am called to so high a position, I shall never cease *ein treuer Deutscher, Co-
burger, Gothaner zu sein.*" And now he must
part from Coburg for ever! Sobered and sad,
he sought relief in his brother Ernest's company;
the two young men would shut themselves up together, and, sitting down at the pianoforte, would
escape from the present and the future in the
sweet familiar gaiety of a Haydn duet.[1]

They returned to Germany; and while Albert,
for a few farewell months, enjoyed, for the last
time, the happiness of home, Victoria, for the last
time, resumed her old life in London and Wind-

[1] Grey, 421-5; *Letters,* I, 188.

sor. She corresponded daily with her future husband in a mingled flow of German and English;
but the accustomed routine reasserted itself; the
business and the pleasures of the day would brook
no interruption; Lord M. was once more constantly
beside her; and the Tories were as intolerable as
ever. Indeed, they were more so. For now, in
these final moments, the old feud burst out with
redoubled fury.[1] The impetuous sovereign found,
to her chagrin, that there might be disadvantages
in being the declared enemy of one of the great
parties in the State. On two occasions, the Tories
directly thwarted her in a matter on which she had
set her heart. She wished her husband's rank to
be fixed by statute, and their opposition prevented
it. She wished her husband to receive a settlement
from the nation of £50,000 a year; and, again
owing to the Tories, he was only allowed £30,000.
It was too bad. When the question was discussed
in Parliament, it had been pointed out that the
bulk of the population was suffering from great

[1] "I had much talk with Lady Cowper about the Court. She
lamented the obstinate character of the Queen, from which she
thought that hereafter great evils might be apprehended. She said
that her prejudices and antipathies were deep and strong, and
her disposition very inflexible. Her hatred of Peel and her resentment against the Duke for having sided with him rather than with
her in the old quarrel are unabated." Greville, November 3, 1839
(unpublished).

poverty, and that £30,000 was the whole revenue of Coburg; but her uncle Leopold had been given £50,000, and it would be monstrous to give Albert less. Sir Robert Peel—it might have been expected—had had the effrontery to speak and vote for the smaller sum. She was very angry; and determined to revenge herself by omitting to invite a single Tory to her wedding. She would make an exception in favour of old Lord Liverpool, but even the Duke of Wellington she refused to ask. When it was represented to her that it would amount to a national scandal if the Duke were absent from her wedding, she was angrier than ever. "What! That old rebel! I won't have him," she was reported to have said. Eventually she was induced to send him an invitation; but she made no attempt to conceal the bitterness of her feelings, and the Duke himself was only too well aware of all that had passed.[1]

Nor was it only against the Tories that her irritation rose. As the time for her wedding approached, her temper grew steadily sharper and more arbitrary. Queen Adelaide annoyed her. King Leopold, too, was "ungracious" in his correspondence; "Dear Uncle," she told Albert, "is given to believe that he must rule the roost every-

---

[1] Greville, January 29, February 15, 1840 (unpublished).

where. However," she added with asperity, " that
is not a necessity." [1] Even Albert himself was
not impeccable. Engulfed in Coburgs, he failed
to appreciate the complexity of English affairs.
There were difficulties about his household. He
had a notion that he ought not to be surrounded
by violent Whigs; very likely, but he would not
understand that the only alternatives to violent
Whigs were violent Tories; and it would be preposterous if his Lords and Gentlemen were to be
found voting against the Queen's. He wanted to
appoint his own Private Secretary. But how
could he choose the right person? Lord M. was
obviously best qualified to make the appointment;
and Lord M. had decided that the Prince should
take over his own Private Secretary—George
Anson, a staunch Whig. Albert protested, but it
was useless; Victoria simply announced that Anson
was appointed, and instructed Lehzen to send the
Prince an explanation of the details of the case.
Then, again, he had written anxiously upon the
necessity of maintaining unspotted the moral
purity of the Court. Lord M.'s pupil considered
that dear Albert was strait-laced, and, in a brisk
Anglo-German missive, set forth her own views.
" I like Lady A. very much," she told him, " only

[1] *Letters*, I, 201.

she is a little *strict and particular,* and too severe
towards others, which is not right; for I think one
ought always to be indulgent towards other people, as I always think, if we had not been well
taken care of, we might also have gone astray.
That is always my feeling. Yet it is always right
to show that one does not like to see what is obviously wrong; but it is very dangerous to be *too*
severe, and I am certain that as a rule such people
always greatly regret that in their youth they
have not been so careful as they ought to have
been. I have explained this so badly and written
it so badly, that I fear you will hardly be able to
make it out." [1]

On one other matter she was insistent. Since
the affair of Lady Flora Hastings, a sad fate had
overtaken Sir James Clark. His flourishing practice had quite collapsed; nobody would go to him
any more. But the Queen remained faithful. She
would show the world how little she cared for
their disapproval, and she desired Albert to make
" poor Clark " his physician in ordinary. He did
as he was told; but, as it turned out, the appointment was not a happy one.[2]

The wedding-day was fixed, and it was time

[1] *Letters,* I, 200–8; *Girlhood,* II, 287.
[2] *Dictionary of National Biography,* Art. Sir James Clark;
Letters, I, 202.

for Albert to tear himself away from his family and the scenes of his childhood. With an aching heart, he had revisited his beloved haunts—the woods and the valleys where he had spent so many happy hours shooting rabbits and collecting botanical specimens; in deep depression, he had sat through the farewell banquets in the Palace and listened to the *Freischutz* performed by the State band. It was time to go. The streets were packed as he drove through them; for a short space his eyes were gladdened by a sea of friendly German faces, and his ears by a gathering volume of good guttural sounds. He stopped to bid a last adieu to his grandmother. It was a heartrending moment. "Albert! Albert!" she shrieked, and fell fainting into the arms of her attendants as his carriage drove away. He was whirled rapidly to his destiny. At Calais a steamboat awaited him, and, together with his father and his brother, he stepped, dejected, on board. A little later, he was more dejected still. The crossing was a very rough one; the Duke went hurriedly below; while the two Princes, we are told, lay on either side of the cabin staircase "in an almost helpless state." At Dover a large crowd was collected on the pier, and "it was by no common effort that Prince Albert, who had continued to suffer up to the last

moment, got up to bow to the people." His sense
of duty triumphed. It was a curious omen: his
whole life in England was foreshadowed as he
landed on English ground.[1]

Meanwhile Victoria, in growing agitation, was
a prey to temper and to nerves. She grew feverish, and at last Sir James Clark pronounced that
she was going to have the measles. But, once
again, Sir James's diagnosis was incorrect. It was
not the measles that were attacking her, but a
very different malady; she was suddenly pros-
trated by alarm, regret, and doubt. For two years
she had been her own mistress—the two happiest
years, by far, of her life. And now it was all
to end! She was to come under an alien domination—she would have to promise that she would
honour and obey . . . someone, who might, after
all, thwart her, oppose her—and how dreadful that
would be! Why had she embarked on this hazardous experiment? Why had she not been contented with Lord M.? No doubt, she loved Albert;
but she loved power too. At any rate, one thing
was certain: she might be Albert's wife, but she
would always be Queen of England.[2] He reappeared, in an exquisite uniform, and her hesita-

1 Grey, 292–303.
2 Greville, February 15, 1840 (unpublished).

tions melted in his presence like mist before the
sun.   On February 10, 1840, the marriage took
place.   The wedded pair drove down to Windsor;
but they were not, of course, entirely alone.   They
were accompanied by their suites, and, in particular, by two persons—the Baron Stockmar and the
Baroness Lehzen.

III

Albert had foreseen that his married life would
not be all plain sailing; but he had by no means
realised the gravity and the complication of the
difficulties which he would have to face.   Politically, he was a cipher.   Lord Melbourne was not
only Prime Minister, he was in effect the Private
Secretary of the Queen, and thus controlled the
whole of the political existence of the sovereign.
A queen's husband was an entity unknown to the
British Constitution. In State affairs there seemed
to be no place for him; nor was Victoria herself at
all unwilling that this should be so.   " The English," she had told the Prince when, during their
engagement, a proposal had been made to give
him a peerage, " are very jealous of any foreigner
interfering in the government of this country, and
have already in some of the papers expressed a

hope that you would not interfere. Now, though
I know you never would, still, if you were a Peer,
they would all say, the Prince meant to play a
political part."[1] "I know you never would!" In
reality, she was not quite so certain; but she wished
Albert to understand her views. He would, she
hoped, make a perfect husband; but, as for gov-
erning the country, he would see that she and
Lord M. between them could manage that very
well, without his help.

But it was not only in politics that the Prince
discovered that the part cut out for him was a
negligible one. Even as a husband, he found, his
functions were to be of an extremely limited kind.
Over the whole of Victoria's private life the Baroness reigned supreme; and she had not the slightest intention of allowing that supremacy to be
diminished by one iota. Since the accession, her
power had greatly increased. Besides the undefined and enormous influence which she exercised
through her management of the Queen's private
correspondence, she was now the superintendent
of the royal establishment and controlled the important office of Privy Purse.[2] Albert very soon
perceived that he was not master in his own house.[3]
Every detail of his own and his wife's existence

---

[1] *Letters,* I, 199.   [2] Martin, I, 71, 153.   [3] Grey, 319–20.

was supervised by a third person: nothing could be done until the consent of Lehzen had first been obtained. And Victoria, who adored Lehzen with unabated intensity, saw nothing in all this that was wrong.

Nor was the Prince happier in his social surroundings. A shy young foreigner, awkward in ladies' company, unexpansive and self-opinionated, it was improbable that, in any circumstances, he would have been a society success. His appearance, too, was against him. Though in the eyes of Victoria he was the mirror of manly beauty, her subjects, whose eyes were of a less Teutonic cast, did not agree with her. To them—and particularly to the high-born ladies and gentlemen who naturally saw him most—what was immediately and distressingly striking in Albert's face and figure and whole demeanour was his un-English look. His features were regular, no doubt, but there was something smooth and smug about them; he was tall, but he was clumsily put together, and he walked with a slight slouch. Really, they thought, this youth was more like some kind of foreign tenor than anything else. These were serious disadvantages; but the line of conduct which the Prince adopted from the first moment of his arrival was far from calculated to dispel

them. Owing partly to a natural awkwardness,
partly to a fear of undue familiarity, and partly
to a desire to be absolutely correct, his manners
were infused with an extraordinary stiffness and
formality. Whenever he appeared in company,
he seemed to be surrounded by a thick hedge of
prickly etiquette. He never went out into ordinary society; he never walked in the streets of
London; he was invariably accompanied by an
equerry when he rode or drove. He wanted to be
irreproachable and, if that involved friendlessness,
it could not be helped. Besides, he had no very
high opinion of the English. So far as he could
see, they cared for nothing but fox-hunting and
Sunday observances; they oscillated between an
undue frivolity and an undue gloom; if you spoke
to them of friendly joyousness they stared; and
they did not understand either the Laws of
Thought or the wit of a German University.
Since it was clear that with such people he could
have very little in common, there was no reason
whatever for relaxing in their favour the rules of
etiquette. In strict privacy, he could be natural
and charming; Seymour and Anson were devoted
to him, and he returned their affection; but they
were subordinates—the receivers of his confidences
and the agents of his will. From the support and

the solace of true companionship he was utterly
cut off.[1]

A friend, indeed, he had—or rather, a mentor.
The Baron, established once more in the royal
residence, was determined to work with as whole-
hearted a detachment for the Prince's benefit as,
more than twenty years before, he had worked for
his uncle's. The situations then and now, similar
in many respects, were yet full of differences.
Perhaps in either case the difficulties to be encountered were equally great; but the present problem was the more complex and the more interesting. The young doctor who, unknown and insignificant, had nothing at the back of him but his
own wits and the friendship of an unimportant
Prince, had been replaced by the accomplished
confidant of kings and ministers, ripe in years, in
reputation, and in the wisdom of a vast experience. It was possible for him to treat Albert with
something of the affectionate authority of a father;
but, on the other hand, Albert was no Leopold.
As the Baron was very well aware, he had none
of his uncle's rigidity of ambition, none of his overweening impulse to be personally great. He was
virtuous and well-intentioned; he was clever and

---

[1] Greville, April 3, 1840 (unpublished); Grey, 353–4; Ernest,
I, 93–4.

well-informed; but he took no interest in politics, and there were no signs that he possessed any commanding force of character. Left to himself, he would almost certainly have subsided into a high-minded nonentity, an aimless dilettante busy over culture, a palace appendage without influence or power. But he was not left to himself: Stockmar saw to that. For ever at his pupil's elbow, the hidden Baron pushed him forward, with tireless pressure, along the path which had been trod by Leopold so many years ago. But, this time, the goal at the end of it was something more than the mediocre royalty that Leopold had reached. The prize which Stockmar, with all the energy of disinterested devotion, had determined should be Albert's was a tremendous prize indeed.

The beginning of the undertaking proved to be the most arduous part of it. Albert was easily dispirited: what was the use of struggling to perform in a rôle which bored him and which, it was quite clear, nobody but the dear good Baron had any desire that he should take up? It was simpler, and it saved a great deal of trouble, to let things slide. But Stockmar would not have it.[1] Incessantly, he harped upon two strings—Albert's sense of duty and his personal pride. Had the

[1] Stockmar, 351.

Prince forgotten the noble aims to which his life
was to be devoted? And was he going to allow
himself, his wife, his family, his whole existence,
to be governed by Baroness Lehzen? The latter
consideration was a potent one. Albert had never
been accustomed to giving way; and now, more
than ever before, it would be humiliating to do
so. Not only was he constantly exasperated by
the position of the Baroness in the royal household; there was another and a still more serious
cause of complaint. He was, he knew very well,
his wife's intellectual superior, and yet he found,
to his intense annoyance, that there were parts of
her mind over which he exercised no influence.
When, urged on by the Baron, he attempted to
discuss politics with Victoria, she eluded the subject, drifted into generalities, and then began to
talk of something else. She was treating him as
she had once treated their uncle Leopold. When
at last he protested, she replied that her conduct
was merely the result of indolence; that when she
was with *him* she could not bear to bother her
head with anything so dull as politics. The excuse was worse than the fault: was he the wife
and she the husband? It almost seemed so. But
the Baron declared that the root of the mischief
was Lehzen: that it was she who encouraged the

Queen to have secrets; who did worse—under-
mined the natural ingenuousness of Victoria, and
induced her to give, unconsciously no doubt, false
reasons to explain away her conduct.[1]

Minor disagreements made matters worse. The
royal couple differed in their tastes. Albert,
brought up in a régime of Spartan simplicity
and early hours, found the great Court functions
intolerably wearisome, and was invariably observed to be nodding on the sofa at half-past ten;
while the Queen's favourite form of enjoyment
was to dance through the night, and then, going
out into the portico of the Palace, watch the sun
rise behind St. Paul's and the towers of Westminster.[2] She loved London and he detested it.
It was only in Windsor that he felt he could really
breathe; but Windsor too had its terrors: though
during the day there he could paint and walk and
play on the piano, after dinner black tedium descended like a pall. He would have liked to summon distinguished scientific and literary men to his
presence, and after ascertaining their views upon
various points of art and learning, to set forth his
own; but unfortunately Victoria " had no fancy to
encourage such people "; knowing that she was
unequal to taking a part in their conversation,

[1] *Letters*, I, 224.   [2] Bloomfield, I, 19.

she insisted that the evening routine should remain unaltered; the regulation interchange of platitudes with official persons was followed as usual by the round table and the books of engravings, while the Prince, with one of his attendants, played game after game of double chess.[1]

It was only natural that in so peculiar a situation, in which the elements of power, passion, and pride were so strangely apportioned, there should have been occasionally something more than mere irritation—a struggle of angry wills. Victoria, no more than Albert, was in the habit of playing second fiddle. Her arbitrary temper flashed out. Her vitality, her obstinacy, her overweening sense of her own position, might well have beaten down before them his superiorities and his rights. But she fought at a disadvantage; she was, in very truth, no longer her own mistress; a profound preoccupation dominated her, seizing upon her inmost purposes for its own extraordinary ends. She was madly in love. The details of those curious battles are unknown to us; but Prince Ernest, who remained in England with his brother for some months, noted them with a friendly and startled eye.[2] One story, indeed, survives, ill-authenticated and perhaps mythical, yet summing

[1] Grey, 340; *Letters*, I, 256.   [2] Ernest, I, 93.

up, as such stories often do, the central facts of
the case. When, in wrath, the Prince one day
had locked himself into his room, Victoria, no less
furious, knocked on the door to be admitted.
" Who is there? " he asked. " The Queen of England " was the answer. He did not move, and
again there was a hail of knocks. The question
and the answer were repeated many times; but at
last there was a pause, and then a gentler knock-
ing. " Who is there? " came once more the relentless question. But this time the reply was different. " Your wife, Albert." And the door was
immediately opened.[1]

Very gradually the Prince's position changed.
He began to find the study of politics less uninter-
esting than he had supposed; he read Blackstone,
and took lessons in English Law; he was occasionally present when the Queen interviewed her Ministers; and at Lord Melbourne's suggestion he was
shown all the despatches relating to Foreign Affairs. Sometimes he would commit his views to
paper, and read them aloud to the Prime Minister, who, infinitely kind and courteous, listened
with attention, but seldom made any reply.[2] An
important step was taken when, before the birth
of the Princess Royal, the Prince, without any

[1] Jerrold, *Married Life*, 56.   [2] Grey 320-1, 361-2.

opposition in Parliament, was appointed Regent in case of the death of the Queen.[1] Stockmar, owing to whose intervention with the Tories this happy result had been brought about, now felt himself at liberty to take a holiday with his family in Coburg; but his solicitude, poured out in innumerable letters, still watched over his pupil from afar. "Dear Prince," he wrote, "I am satisfied with the news you have sent me. Mistakes, misunderstandings, obstructions, which come in vexatious opposition to one's views, are always to be taken for just what they are—namely, natural phenomena of life, which represent one of its sides, and that the shady one. In overcoming them with dignity, your mind has to exercise, to train, to enlighten itself; and your character to gain force, endurance, and the necessary hardness." The Prince had done well so far; but he must continue in the right path; above all, he was "never to relax."—"Never to relax in putting your magnanimity to the proof; never to relax in logical separation of what is great and essential from what is trivial and of no moment; never to relax in keeping yourself up to a high standard—in the determination, daily renewed, to be consistent, patient, courageous." It was a hard programme,

[1] Stockmar, 352–7.

perhaps, for a young man of twenty-one; and yet
there was something in it which touched the very
depths of Albert's soul. He sighed, but he listened—listened as to the voice of a spiritual direc-
tor inspired with divine truth. " The stars which
are needful to you now," the voice continued,
" and perhaps for some time to come, are *Love,
Honesty, Truth*. All those whose minds are
warped, or who are destitute of true feeling, will
be apt to mistake you," and to persuade themselves and the world that you are not the man
you are—or, at least, may become. . . . Do you,
therefore, be on the alert betimes, with your eyes
open in every direction. . . . I wish for my Prince
a great, noble, warm, and true heart, such as shall
serve as the richest and surest basis for the noblest
views of human nature, and the firmest resolve to
give them development." [1]

Before long, the decisive moment came. There
was a General Election, and it became certain that
the Tories, at last, must come into power. The
Queen disliked them as much as ever; but, with a
large majority in the House of Commons, they
would now be in a position to insist upon their
wishes being attended to. Lord Melbourne himself was the first to realise the importance of car-

[1] Martin, I, 90–2.

rying out the inevitable transition with as little friction as possible; and with his consent, the Prince, following up the *rapprochement* which had begun over the Regency Act, opened, through Anson, a negotiation with Sir Robert Peel. In a series of secret interviews, a complete understanding was reached upon the difficult and complex question of the Bedchamber. It was agreed that the constitutional point should not be raised, but that on the formation of the Tory Government, the principal Whig ladies should retire, and their places be filled by others appointed by Sir Robert.[1] Thus, in effect, though not in form, the Crown abandoned the claims of 1839, and they have never been subsequently put forward. The transaction was a turning point in the Prince's career. He had conducted an important negotiation with skill and tact; he had been brought into close and friendly relations with the new Prime Minister; it was obvious that a great political future lay before him. Victoria was much impressed and deeply grateful. " My dearest Angel," she told King Leopold, " is indeed a great comfort to me. He takes the greatest interest in what goes on, feeling with and for me, and yet abstaining as he ought from biasing me either

[1] *Letters.* I, 271–4, 284–6.

way, though we talk much on the subject, and
his judgment is, as you say, good and mild." [1]
She was in need of all the comfort and assistance
he could give her. Lord M. was going; and she
could hardly bring herself to speak to Peel. Yes;
she would discuss everything with Albert now!

Stockmar, who had returned to England,
watched the departure of Lord Melbourne with
satisfaction. If all went well, the Prince should
now wield a supreme political influence over Victoria. But would all go well? An unexpected
development put the Baron into a serious fright.
When the dreadful moment finally came, and the
Queen, in anguish, bade adieu to her beloved Minister, it was settled between them that, though it
would be inadvisable to meet very often, they
could continue to correspond. Never were the
inconsistencies of Lord Melbourne's character
shown more clearly than in what followed. So
long as he was in office, his attitude towards Peel
had been irreproachable; he had done all he could
to facilitate the change of government; he had
even, through more than one channel, transmitted
privately to his successful rival advice as to the
best means of winning the Queen's good graces. [2]
Yet, no sooner was he in opposition than his heart

---

[1] *Letters,* I, 280.   [2] *Letters,* I, 305; Greville, V, 39–40.

failed him. He could not bear the thought of sur-
rendering altogether the privilege and the pleasure
of giving counsel to Victoria—of being cut off
completely from the power and the intimacy which
had been his for so long and in such abundant
measure. Though he had declared that he would
be perfectly discreet in his letters, he could not
resist taking advantage of the opening they afforded. He discussed in detail various public
questions, and, in particular, gave the Queen a
great deal of advice in the matter of appointments.
This advice was followed. Lord Melbourne recommended that Lord Heytesbury, who, he said,
was an able man, should be made Ambassador at
Vienna; and a week later the Queen wrote to the
Foreign Secretary urging that Lord Heytesbury,
whom she believed to be a very able man, should
be employed " on some important mission." Stockmar was very much alarmed. He wrote a memorandum, pointing out the unconstitutional nature
of Lord Melbourne's proceedings and the unpleasant position in which the Queen might find herself
if they were discovered by Peel; and he instructed
Anson to take this memorandum to the ex-Min-
ister. Lord Melbourne, lounging on a sofa, read
it through with compressed lips. " This is quite
an apple-pie opinion," he said. When Anson ven-

tured to expostulate further, suggesting that it was unseemly in the leader of the Opposition to maintain an intimate relationship with the Sovereign, the old man lost his temper. " God eternally damn it! " he exclaimed, leaping up from his sofa, and dashing about the room. " Flesh and blood cannot stand this! " He continued to write to the Queen, as before; and two more violent bombardments from the Baron were needed before he was brought to reason. Then, gradually, his letters grew less and less frequent, with fewer and fewer references to public concerns; at last, they were entirely innocuous. The Baron smiled; Lord M. had accepted the inevitable.[1]

The Whig Ministry resigned in September, 1841; but more than a year was to elapse before another and an equally momentous change was effected—the removal of Lehzen. For, in the end, the mysterious governess was conquered. The steps are unknown by which Victoria was at last led to accept her withdrawal with composure —perhaps with relief; but it is clear that Albert's domestic position must have been greatly strengthened by the appearance of children. The birth of the Princess Royal had been followed in November, 1841, by that of the Prince of Wales; and

[1] *Letters,* I, 325–6, 329, 330–1, 339–42, 352–4, 360–3, 368.

before very long another baby was expected. The Baroness, with all her affection, could have but a remote share in such family delights. She lost ground perceptibly. It was noticed as a phenomenon that, once or twice, when the Court travelled, she was left behind at Windsor.[1] The Prince was very cautious; at the change of Ministry, Lord Melbourne had advised him to choose that moment for decisive action; but he judged it wiser to wait.[2] Time and the pressure of inevitable circumstances were for him; every day his predominance grew more assured—and every night. At length he perceived that he need hesitate no longer—that every wish, every velleity of his had only to be expressed to be at once Victoria's. He spoke, and Lehzen vanished for ever. No more would she reign in that royal heart and those royal halls. No more, watching from a window at Windsor, would she follow her pupil and her sovereign walking on the terrace among the obsequious multitude, with the eye of triumphant love.[3] Returning to her native Hanover she established herself at Bückeburg in a small but comfortable house, the walls of which were entirely covered by portraits of Her Majesty.[4] The Baron, in spite of his dyspepsia, smiled again: Albert was supreme.

[1] *Letters.*, I, 291, 295.
[2] *Ibid.*, I, 303.
[3] Lyttelton, 282–3.
[4] Bloomfield, I, 215.

IV

The early discords had passed away completely —resolved into the absolute harmony of married life. Victoria, overcome by a new, an unimagined revelation, had surrendered her whole soul to her husband. The beauty and the charm which so suddenly had made her his at first were, she now saw, no more than but the outward manifestation of the true Albert. There was an inward beauty, an inward glory which, blind that she was, she had then but dimly apprehended, but of which now she was aware in every fibre of her being—he was good—he was great! How could she ever have dreamt of setting up her will against his wisdom, her ignorance against his knowledge, her fancies against his perfect taste? Had she really once loved London and late hours and dissipation? She who now was only happy in the country, she who jumped out of bed every morning—oh, so early! —with Albert, to take a walk, before breakfast, with Albert alone! How wonderful it was to be taught by him! To be told by him which trees were which; and to learn all about the bees! And then to sit doing cross-stitch while he read aloud to her Hallam's Constitutional History of England! Or to listen to him playing on his new organ (" The organ is the first of instruments," he said); or to sing to him a song by Mendelssohn, with a great deal of care over the time and the breathing, and only a very occasional false note! And, after dinner, too—oh, how good of him! He had given up his double chess! And so there could be round games at the round table, or everyone could spend the evening in the most amusing way imaginable—spinning counters and rings.[1] When the babies came it was still more wonderful. Pussy was such a clever little girl ("I am not Pussy! I am the Princess Royal!" she had angrily exclaimed on one occasion); and Bertie—well, she could only pray *most* fervently that the little Prince of Wales would grow up to "resemble his angelic dearest Father in *every, every* respect, both in body and mind."[2] Her dear Mamma, too, had been drawn once more into the family circle, for Albert had brought about a reconciliation, and the departure of Lehzen had helped to obliterate the past.[3] In Victoria's eyes, life had become an idyll, and, if the essential elements of an idyll are happiness, love and simplicity, an idyll it was; though, indeed, it was of a kind that might have disconcerted Theocritus. "Albert brought in

---

[1] Grey 338–9; Bloomfield, I, 28, 123; Lyttelton, 300, 303, 305–6, 312, 334–5; Martin, I, 488; *Letters*, I, 369.

[2] *Letters*, I, 366.

[3] *Ibid.*, III, 439.

dearest little Pussy," wrote Her Majesty in her journal, " in such a smart white merino dress trimmed with blue, which Mamma had given her, and a pretty cap, and placed her on my bed, seating himself next to her, and she was very dear and good. And, as my precious, invaluable Albert sat there, and our little Love between us, I felt quite moved with happiness and gratitude to God." [1]

The past—the past of only three years since— when she looked back upon it, seemed a thing so remote and alien that she could explain it to herself in no other way than as some kind of delusion —an unfortunate mistake. Turning over an old volume of her diary, she came upon this sentence —" As for 'the confidence of the Crown,' God knows! No *Minister, no friend* EVER possessed it so entirely as this truly excellent Lord Melbourne possesses mine!" A pang shot through her—she seized a pen, and wrote upon the margin—" Reading this again, I cannot forbear remarking what an artificial sort of happiness *mine* was *then,* and what a blessing it is I have now in my beloved Husband *real* and solid happiness, which no Politics, no worldly reverses *can* change; it could not have lasted long as it was then, for after all, kind

[1] Martin, I, 125.

and excellent as Lord M. is, and kind as he was
to me, it was but in Society that I had amusement,
and I was only living on that superficial resource,
which I *then fancied* was happiness! Thank God!
for *me* and others, this is changed, and I *know
what* REAL *happiness* is—V. R." [1] How did she
know? What is the distinction between happiness
that is real and happiness that is felt? So a philosopher—Lord M. himself perhaps—might have
inquired. But she was no philosopher, and Lord
M. was a phantom, and Albert was beside her,
and that was enough.

Happy, certainly, she was; and she wanted
everyone to know it. Her letters to King Leopold
are sprinkled thick with raptures. " Oh! my dearest uncle, I am sure if you knew *how* happy, how
blessed I feel, and how *proud* I feel in possessing
such a perfect being as my husband . . ." such
ecstasies seemed to gush from her pen unceasingly
and almost of their own accord.[2] When, one day,
without thinking, Lady Lyttelton described someone to her as being " as happy as a queen," and
then grew a little confused, " Don't correct yourself, Lady Lyttelton," said Her Majesty. " A
queen *is* a very happy woman." [3]

[1] *Girlhood,* II, 135.   [2] *Letters,* I, 366, 464–5, 475, etc.
[3] Lyttelton, 306.

But this new happiness was no lotus dream. On the contrary, it was bracing, rather than relaxing. Never before had she felt so acutely the necessity for doing her duty. She worked more methodically than ever at the business of State; she watched over her children with untiring vigilance. She carried on a large correspondence; she was occupied with her farm—her dairy—a whole multitude of household avocations—from morning till night. Her active, eager little body hurrying with quick steps after the long strides of Albert down the corridors and avenues of Windsor,[1] seemed the very expression of her spirit. Amid all the softness, the deliciousness of unmixed joy, all the liquescence, the overflowings of inexhaustible sentiment, her native rigidity remained. "A vein of iron," said Lady Lyttelton, who, as royal governess, had good means of observation, "runs through her most extraordinary character."[2]

Sometimes the delightful routine of domestic existence had to be interrupted. It was necessary to exchange Windsor for Buckingham Palace, to open Parliament, or to interview official personages, or, occasionally, to entertain foreign visitors at the Castle. Then the quiet Court put on a sudden magnificence, and sovereigns from over the

[1] Crawford, 243.   [2] Lyttelton, 348.

seas—Louis Philippe, or the King of Prussia, or
the King of Saxony—found at Windsor an entertainment that was indeed a royal one. Few spectacles in Europe, it was agreed, produced an effect
so imposing as the great Waterloo banqueting hall,
crowded with guests in sparkling diamonds and
blazing uniforms, the long walls hung with the
stately portraits of heroes, and the tables loaded
with the gorgeous gold plate of the kings of England.[1] But, in that wealth of splendour, the most
imposing spectacle of all was the Queen. The
little *hausfrau,* who had spent the day before
walking out with her children, inspecting her livestock, practising shakes at the piano, and filling up
her journal with adoring descriptions of her husband, suddenly shone forth, without art, without
effort, by a spontaneous and natural transition, the
very culmination of Majesty. The Tsar of Russia himself was deeply impressed. Victoria on her
side viewed with secret awe the tremendous Nich-
olas. " A great event and a great compliment *his*
visit certainly is," she told her uncle, " and the
people *here* are extremely flattered at it. He is
certainly a *very striking* man; still very handsome.
His profile is *beautiful,* and his manners *most*
dignified and graceful; extremely civil—quite

[1] *Letters,* II, 13; Bunsen, II, 6; Bloomfield, I, 53–4.

alarmingly so, as he is so full of attentions and *politeness*. But the expression of the *eyes* is *formidable*, and unlike anything I ever saw before." [1] She and Albert and " the good King of Saxony," who happened to be there at the same time, and whom, she said, " we like much—he is *so* unassuming "—drew together like tame villatic fowl in the presence of that awful eagle. When he was gone, they compared notes about his face, his unhappiness, and his despotic power over millions. Well! She for her part could not help pitying him, and she thanked God she was Queen of England. [2]

When the time came for returning some of these visits, the royal pair set forth in their yacht, much to Victoria's satisfaction. " I do love a ship! " she exclaimed, ran up and down ladders with the greatest agility, and cracked jokes with the sailors. [3] The Prince was more aloof. They visited Louis Philippe at the Château d'Eu; they visited King Leopold in Brussels. It happened that a still more remarkable Englishwoman was in the Belgian capital, but she was not remarked; and Queen Victoria passed unknowing before the steady gaze of one of the mistresses in M. Héger's *pensionnat*. " A little stout, vivacious lady, very plainly dressed

---

[1] *Letters*, II, 12–16. [2] Martin, I, 224.
[3] Lyttelton. 292; Bloomfield, I, 76–7.

—not much dignity or pretension about her," was
Charlotte Brontë's comment as the royal carriage
and six flashed by her, making her wait on the
pavement for a moment, and interrupting the
train of her reflections.[1] Victoria was in high
spirits, and even succeeded in instilling a little
cheerfulness into her uncle's sombre Court. King
Leopold, indeed, was perfectly contented. His
dearest hopes had been fulfilled; all his ambitions
were satisfied; and for the rest of his life he had
only to enjoy, in undisturbed decorum, his throne,
his respectability, the table of precedence, and the
punctual discharge of his irksome duties. But
unfortunately the felicity of those who surrounded
him was less complete. His Court, it was murmured, was as gloomy as a conventicle, and the
most dismal of all the sufferers was his wife. " Pas
de plaisanteries, madame!" he had exclaimed to
the unfortunate successor of the Princess Charlotte, when, in the early days of their marriage,
she had attempted a feeble joke. Did she not understand that the consort of a constitutional sovereign must not be frivolous? She understood,
at last, only too well; and when the startled walls
of the state apartments re-echoed to the chatter-
ing and the laughter of Victoria, the poor lady

[1] Gaskell, I, 313.

found that she had almost forgotten how to smile.

Another year, Germany was visited, and Albert displayed the beauties of his home. When Victoria crossed the frontier, she was much excited— and she was astonished as well. "To hear the people speak German," she noted in her diary, "and to see the German soldiers, etc., seemed to me so singular." Having recovered from this slight shock, she found the country charming. She was fêted everywhere, crowds of the surrounding royalties swooped down to welcome her, and the prettiest groups of peasant children, dressed in their best clothes, presented her with bunches of flowers. The principality of Coburg, with its romantic scenery and its well-behaved inhabitants, particularly delighted her; and when she woke up one morning to find herself in "dear Rosenau, my Albert's birthplace," it was "like a beautiful dream." On her return home, she expatiated, in a letter to King Leopold, upon the pleasures of the trip, dwelling especially upon the intensity of her affection for Albert's native land. "I have a feeling," she said, "for our dear little Germany, which I cannot describe. I felt it at Rosenau so much. It is a something which touches me, and which goes to my heart, and makes me inclined to

cry. I never felt at any other place that sort of
pensive pleasure and peace which I felt there. I
fear I almost like it too much." [1]

V

The husband was not so happy as the wife. In
spite of the great improvement in his situation, in
spite of a growing family and the adoration of
Victoria, Albert was still a stranger in a strange
land, and the serenity of spiritual satisfaction was
denied him. It was something, no doubt, to have
dominated his immediate environment; but it was
not enough; and, besides, in the very completeness
of his success, there was a bitterness. Victoria
idolised him; but it was understanding that he
craved for, not idolatry; and how much did Victoria, filled to the brim though she was with him,
understand him? How much does the bucket understand the well? He was lonely. He went to
his organ and improvised with learned modulations
until the sounds, swelling and subsiding through
elaborate cadences, brought some solace to his
heart. Then, with the elasticity of youth, he hurried off to play with the babies, or to design a new
pigsty, or to read aloud the " Church History of
Scotland " to Victoria, or to pirouette before her

[1] Martin, I, 275, 306.

on one toe, like a ballet-dancer, with a fixed smile,
to show her how she ought to behave when she
appeared in public places.[1] Thus did he amuse
himself; but there was one distraction in which
he did not indulge. He never flirted—no, not
with the prettiest ladies of the Court. When, during their engagement, the Queen had remarked
with pride to Lord Melbourne that the Prince paid
no attention to any other woman, the cynic had
answered, " No, that sort of thing is apt to come
later "; upon which she had scolded him severely,
and then hurried off to Stockmar to repeat what
Lord M. had said. But the Baron had reassured
her; though in other cases, he had replied, that
might happen, he did not think it would in Albert's. And the Baron was right. Throughout
their married life no rival female charms ever had
cause to give Victoria one moment's pang of jealousy.[1]

What more and more absorbed him—bringing
with it a curious comfort of its own—was his work.
With the advent of Peel, he began to intervene
actively in the affairs of the State. In more ways
than one—in the cast of their intelligence, in their
moral earnestness, even in the uneasy formalism of

[1] Lyttelton, 303, 354, 402.
[2] Clarendon, I, 181–2; *Girlhood,* II, 299, 306.

their manners—the two men resembled each other; there was a sympathy between them; and thus Peel was ready enough to listen to the advice of Stockmar, and to urge the Prince forward into public life. A royal commission was about to be formed to enquire whether advantage might not be taken of the rebuilding of the Houses of Parliament to encourage the Fine Arts in the United Kingdom; and Peel, with great perspicacity, asked the Prince to preside over it. The work was of a kind which precisely suited Albert: his love of art, his love of method, his love of coming into contact—close yet dignified—with distinguished men—it satisfied them all; and he threw himself into it *con amore*. Some of the members of the commission were somewhat alarmed when, in his opening speech, he pointed out the necessity of dividing the subjects to be considered into " categories "—the word, they thought, smacked dangerously of German metaphysics; but their confidence returned when they observed His Royal Highness's extraordinary technical acquaintance with the processes of fresco painting. When the question arose as to whether the decorations upon the walls of the new buildings should, or should not, have a moral purpose, the Prince spoke strongly for the affirmative. Although many, he

observed, would give but a passing glance to the
works, the painter was not therefore to forget
that others might view them with more thoughtful
eyes. This argument convinced the commission,
and it was decided that the subjects to be depicted
should be of an improving nature. The frescoes
were carried out in accordance with the commission's instructions, but unfortunately before very
long they had become, even to the most thoughtful eyes, totally invisible. It seems that His
Royal Highness's technical acquaintance with the
processes of fresco painting was incomplete.[1]

The next task upon which the Prince embarked
was a more arduous one: he determined to reform
the organisation of the royal household. This
reform had been long overdue. For years past
the confusion, discomfort, and extravagance in
the royal residences, and in Buckingham Palace
particularly, had been scandalous; no reform had
been practicable under the rule of the Baroness;
but her functions had now devolved upon the
Prince, and in 1844, he boldly attacked the problem. Three years earlier, Stockmar, after careful enquiry, had revealed in an elaborate memorandum an extraordinary state of affairs. The
control of the household, it appeared, was divided

[1] Martin, I, 119–25, 167; Stockmar, 660.

in the strangest manner between a number of authorities, each independent of the other, each possessed of vague and fluctuating powers, without responsibility, and without co-ordination. Of these authorities, the most prominent were the Lord Steward and the Lord Chamberlain—noblemen of high rank and political importance, who changed office with every administration, who did not reside with the Court, and had no effective representatives attached to it. The distribution of their respective functions was uncertain and peculiar. In Buckingham Palace, it was believed that the Lord Chamberlain had charge of the whole of the rooms, with the exception of the kitchen, sculleries, and pantries, which were claimed by the Lord Steward. At the same time, the outside of the Palace was under the control of neither of these functionaries—but of the Office of Woods and Forests; and thus, while the insides of the windows were cleaned by the Department of the Lord Chamberlain—or possibly, in certain cases, of the Lord Steward—the Office of Woods and Forests cleaned their outsides. Of the servants, the housekeepers, the pages, and the housemaids were under the authority of the Lord Chamberlain; the clerk of the kitchen, the cooks, and the porters were under that of the Lord Steward; but the footmen, the livery-porters, and the under-butlers took their orders from yet another official—the Master of the Horse. Naturally, in these circumstances the service was extremely defective and the lack of discipline among the servants disgraceful. They absented themselves for as long as they pleased and whenever the fancy took them; " and if," as the Baron put it, " smoking, drinking, and other irregularities occur in the dormitories, where footmen, etc., sleep ten and twelve in each room, no one can help it." As for Her Majesty's guests, there was nobody to show them to their rooms, and they were often left, having utterly lost their way in the complicated passages, to wander helpless by the hour. The strange divisions of authority extended not only to persons but to things. The Queen observed that there was never a fire in the dining-room. She enquired why. The answer was " the Lord Steward lays the fire, and the Lord Chamberlain lights it "; the underlings of those two great noblemen having failed to come to an accommodation, there was no help for it— the Queen must eat in the cold.[1]

A surprising incident opened everyone's eyes to the confusion and negligence that reigned in the Palace. A fortnight after the birth of the

[1] Stockmar, 404–10; Martin, I, 156–60.

Princess Royal the nurse heard a suspicious noise in the room next to the Queen's bedroom. She called to one of the pages, who, looking under a large sofa, perceived there a crouching figure " with a most repulsive appearance." It was " the boy Jones." This enigmatical personage, whose escapades dominated the newspapers for several ensuing months, and whose motives and character remained to the end ambiguous, was an undersized lad of 17, the son of a tailor, who had apparently gained admittance to the Palace by climbing over the garden wall and walking in through an open window. Two years before he had paid a similar visit in the guise of a chimney-sweep. He now declared that he had spent three days in the Palace, hiding under various beds, that he had " helped himself to soup and other eatables," and that he had " sat upon the throne, seen the Queen, and heard the Princess Royal squall." Every detail of the strange affair was eagerly canvassed. *The Times* reported that the boy Jones had " from his infancy been fond of reading," but that " his countenance is exceedingly sullen." It added: " The sofa under which the boy Jones was discovered, we understand, is one of the most costly and magnificent material and workmanship, and ordered expressly for the accommodation of the

royal and illustrious visitors who call to pay their
respects to Her Majesty." The culprit was sent
for three months to the "House of Correction."
When he emerged, he immediately returned to
Buckingham Palace. He was discovered, and sent
back to the "House of Correction" for another
three months, after which he was offered £4 a
week by a music hall to appear upon the stage.
He refused this offer, and shortly afterwards was
found by the police loitering round Buckingham
Palace. The authorities acted vigorously, and,
without any trial or process of law, shipped the
boy Jones off to sea. A year later his ship put
into Portsmouth to refit, and he at once disem-
barked and walked to London. He was re-arrested
before he reached the Palace, and sent back to
his ship, the *Warspite*. On this occasion it was
noticed that he had "much improved in personal
appearance and grown quite corpulent"; and so
the boy Jones passed out of history, though we
catch one last glimpse of him in 1844 falling over-
board in the night between Tunis and Algiers. He
was fished up again; but it was conjectured—as
one of the *Warspite's* officers explained in a letter
to *The Times*—that his fall had not been accidental, but that he had deliberately jumped into
the Mediterranean in order to "see the life-buoy

light burning." Of a boy with such a record, what else could be supposed?[1]

But discomfort and alarm were not the only results of the mismanagement of the household; the waste, extravagance, and peculation that also flowed from it were immeasurable. There were preposterous perquisites and malpractices of every kind. It was, for instance, an ancient and immutable rule that a candle that had once been lighted should never be lighted again; what happened to the old candles, nobody knew. Again, the Prince, examining the accounts, was puzzled by a weekly expenditure of thirty-five shillings on " Red Room Wine." He enquired into the matter, and after great difficulty discovered that in the time of George III a room in Windsor Castle with red hangings had once been used as a guard-room, and that five shillings a day had been allowed to provide wine for the officers. The guard had long since been moved elsewhere, but the payment for wine in the Red Room continued, the money being received by a half-pay officer who held the sinecure position of under-butler.[2]

After much laborious investigation, and a stiff struggle with the multitude of vested interests

[1] *The Times*, December, 1840; March, July, December, 1841; February, October, 1842; July, 1844.
[2] *The Times*, " Life," 45.

which had been brought into being by long years of neglect, the Prince succeeded in effecting a complete reform. The various conflicting authorities were induced to resign their powers into the hands of a single official, the Master of the Household, who became responsible for the entire management of the royal palaces. Great economies were made, and the whole crowd of venerable abuses was swept away. Among others, the unlucky half-pay officer of the Red Room was, much to his surprise, given the choice of relinquishing his weekly emolument or of performing the duties of an under-butler. Even the irregularities among the footmen, etc., were greatly diminished. There were outcries and complaints; the Prince was accused of meddling, of injustice, and of saving candle-ends; but he held on his course, and before long the admirable administration of the royal household was recognised as a convincing proof of his perseverance and capacity.[1]

At the same time his activity was increasing enormously in a more important sphere. He had become the Queen's Private Secretary, her confidential adviser, her second self. He was now always present at her interviews with Ministers.[2] He took, like the Queen, a special interest in for-

[1] Stockmar, 409–10; Martin, I, 161.　　[2] Greville, VII, 132.

eign policy; but there was no public question in
which his influence was not felt. A double process
was at work; while Victoria fell more and more
absolutely under his intellectual predominance, he,
simultaneously, grew more and more completely
absorbed by the machinery of high politics—the
incessant and multifarious business of a great
State. Nobody any more could call him a dilettante; he was a worker, a public personage, a man
of affairs. Stockmar noted the change with exultation. " The Prince," he wrote, " has improved
very much lately. He has evidently a head for
politics. He has become, too, far more independent. His mental activity is constantly on the increase, and he gives the greater part of his time
to business, without complaining." " The relations
between husband and wife," added the Baron,
" are all one could desire." [1]

Long before Peel's ministry came to an end,
there had been a complete change in Victoria's
attitude towards him. His appreciation of the
Prince had softened her heart; the sincerity and
warmth of his nature, which, in private intercourse
with those whom he wished to please, had the
power of gradually dissipating the awkwardness
of his manners, did the rest.[2] She came in time

[1] Stockmar, 466–7.   [2] Disraeli, 311; Greville, VI, 367–8.

to regard him with intense feelings of respect and
attachment. She spoke of " our worthy Peel," for
whom, she said, she had " an *extreme* admiration "
and who had shown himself " a man of unbounded
loyalty, courage, patriotism, and *high-mindedness,*
and his conduct towards me has been *chivalrous*
almost, I might say." [1] She dreaded his removal
from office almost as frantically as she had once
dreaded that of Lord M. It would be, she declared, a *great calamity.* Six years before, what
would she have said, if a prophet had told her that
the day would come when she would be horrified
by the triumph of the Whigs? Yet there was no
escaping it; she had to face the return of her old
friends. In the ministerial crises of 1845 and
1846, the Prince played a dominating part. Everybody recognised that he was the real centre of the
negotiations—the actual controller of the forces
and the functions of the Crown. The process by
which this result was reached had been so gradual
as to be almost imperceptible; but it may be said
with certainty that, by the close of Peel's administration, Albert had become, in effect, the King of
England.[2]

[1] *Letters,* II, 64.   [2] Greville, V, 329-30.

VI

With the final emergence of the Prince came the final extinction of Lord Melbourne. A year after his loss of office, he had been struck down by a paralytic seizure; he had apparently recovered, but his old elasticity had gone for ever. Moody, restless, and unhappy, he wandered like a ghost about the town, bursting into soliloquies in public places, or asking odd questions, suddenly, *à propos de bottes.* "I'll be hanged if I'll do it for you, my Lord," he was heard to say in the hall at Brooks's, standing by himself, and addressing the air after much thought. "Don't you consider," he abruptly asked a fellow-guest at Lady Holland's, leaning across the dinner-table in a pause of the conversation, "that it was a most damnable act of Henri Quatre to change his religion with a view to securing the Crown?" He sat at home, brooding for hours in miserable solitude. He turned over his books—his classics and his Testaments—but they brought him no comfort at all. He longed for the return of the past, for the impossible, for he knew not what, for the devilries of Caro, for the happy platitudes of Windsor. His friends had left him, and no wonder, he said in bitterness—the fire was out. He secretly hoped for a return to power, scanning the newspapers with solicitude,

and occasionally making a speech in the House of
Lords. His correspondence with the Queen continued, and he appeared from time to time at
Court; but he was a mere simulacrum of his former self; " the dream," wrote Victoria, " is *past.*"
As for his political views, they could no longer be
tolerated. The Prince was an ardent Free Trader,
and so, of course, was the Queen; and when, din-
ing at Windsor at the time of the repeal of the
Corn Laws, Lord Melbourne suddenly exclaimed,
" Ma'am, it's a damned dishonest act! " everyone
was extremely embarrassed. Her Majesty laughed
and tried to change the conversation, but without
avail; Lord Melbourne returned to the charge
again and again with—" I say, Ma'am, it's damned
dishonest! "—until the Queen said " Lord Melbourne, I must beg you not to say anything more
on this subject now "; and then he held his
tongue. She was kind to him, writing him long
letters, and always remembering his birthday; but
it was kindness at a distance, and he knew it. He
had become " poor Lord Melbourne." A profound disquietude devoured him. He tried to fix
his mind on the condition of Agriculture and the
Oxford Movement. He wrote long memoranda
in utterly undecipherable handwriting. He was
convinced that he had lost all his money, and could

not possibly afford to be a Knight of the Garter.
He had run through everything, and yet—if Peel
went out, he might be sent for—why not? He was
never sent for. The Whigs ignored him in their
consultations, and the leadership of the party
passed to Lord John Russell. When Lord John
became Prime Minister, there was much politeness,
but Lord Melbourne was not asked to join the
Cabinet. He bore the blow with perfect amenity;
but he understood, at last, that that was the end.[1]

For two years more he lingered, sinking slowly
into unconsciousness and imbecility. Sometimes,
propped up in his chair, he would be heard to murmur, with unexpected appositeness, the words of
Samson:—

> "So much I feel my general spirit droop,
> My hopes all flat, nature within me seems
> In all her functions weary of herself,
> My race of glory run, and race of shame,
> And I shall shortly be with them that rest." [2]

A few days before his death, Victoria, learning
that there was no hope of his recovery, turned
her mind for a little towards that which had once
been Lord M. " You will grieve to hear," she told
King Leopold, " that our good, dear, old friend

[1] Torrens, 502, chap. xxxiii; *Letters,* I, 451; II, 140; Greville,
V, 359; VI, 125.
[2] Greville, VI, 255.

Melbourne is dying. . . . One cannot forget how good and kind and amiable he was, and it brings back so many recollections to my mind, though, God knows! I never wish that time back again." [1]

She was in little danger. The tide of circumstance was flowing now with irresistible fullness towards a very different consummation. The seriousness of Albert, the claims of her children, her own inmost inclinations, and the movement of the whole surrounding world, combined to urge her forward along the narrow way of public and domestic duty. Her family steadily increased. Within eighteen months of the birth of the Prince of Wales the Princess Alice appeared, and a year later the Prince Alfred, and then the Princess Helena, and, two years afterwards, the Princess Louise; and still there were signs that the pretty row of royal infants was not complete. The parents, more and more involved in family cares and family happiness, found the pomp of Windsor galling, and longed for some more intimate and remote retreat. On the advice of Peel they purchased the estate of Osborne, in the Isle of Wight. Their skill and economy in financial matters had enabled them to lay aside a substantial sum of

[1] *Letters*, II, 203.

money; and they could afford, out of their savings, not merely to buy the property but to build
a new house for themselves and to furnish it at
a cost of £200,000.[1] At Osborne, by the sea-shore,
and among the woods, which Albert, with memories of Rosenau in his mind, had so carefully
planted, the royal family spent every hour that
could be snatched from Windsor and London—
delightful hours of deep retirement and peaceful
work.[2] The public looked on with approval. A
few aristocrats might sniff or titter; but with the
nation at large the Queen was now once more extremely popular. The middle-classes, in particular, were pleased. They liked a love-match; they
liked a household which combined the advantages
of royalty and virtue, and in which they seemed
to see, reflected as in some resplendent looking-
glass, the ideal image of the very lives they led
themselves. Their own existences, less exalted,
but oh! so soothingly similar, acquired an added
excellence, an added succulence, from the early
hours, the regularity, the plain tuckers, the round
games, the roast beef and Yorkshire pudding of
Osborne. It was indeed a model Court. Not only
were its central personages the patterns of propriety, but no breath of scandal, no shadow of in-

[1] Greville, VI, 68–9.   [2] Martin, I, 247–9; Grey, 113.

decorum, might approach its utmost boundaries.[1]
For Victoria, with all the zeal of a convert, upheld
now the standard of moral purity with an inflexi-
bility surpassing, if that were possible, Albert's
own. She blushed to think how she had once believed—how she had once actually told *him*—that
one might be too strict and particular in such matters, and that one ought to be indulgent towards
other people's dreadful sins. But she was no
longer Lord M.'s pupil: she was Albert's wife.
She was more—the embodiment, the living apex
of a new era in the generations of mankind. The
last vestige of the eighteenth century had disappeared; cynicism and subtlety were shrivelled into
powder; and duty, industry, morality, and domes-
ticity triumphed over them. Even the very chairs
and tables had assumed, with a singular respon-
siveness, the forms of prim solidity. The Victorian Age was in full swing.

VII

Only one thing more was needed: material expression must be given to the new ideals and the
new forces so that they might stand revealed, in
visible glory, before the eyes of an astonished

[1] Stockmar, 363; Martin, I, 316.

world. It was for Albert to supply this want.
He mused, and was inspired: the Great Exhibition
came into his head.

Without consulting anyone, he thought out the
details of his conception with the minutest care.
There had been exhibitions before in the world,
but this should surpass them all. It should con-
tain specimens of what every country could produce in raw materials, in machinery and mechanical inventions, in manufactures, and in the applied
and plastic arts. It should not be merely useful
and ornamental; it should teach a high moral lesson. It should be an international monument to
those supreme blessings of civilisation—peace,
progress, and prosperity. For some time past the
Prince had been devoting much of his attention to
the problems of commerce and industry. He had
a taste for machinery of every kind, and his sharp
eye had more than once detected, with the precision
of an expert, a missing cog-wheel in some vast
and complicated engine.[1] A visit to Liverpool,
where he opened the Albert Dock, impressed upon
his mind the immensity of modern industrial
forces, though in a letter to Victoria describing
his experiences, he was careful to retain his customary lightness of touch. "As I write," he play-

[1] Martin, II, 87.

fully remarked, " you will be making your evening
toilette, and not be ready in time for dinner. I
must set about the same task, and not, let me hope,
with the same result. . . . The loyalty and enthusiasm of the inhabitants are great; but the heat
is greater still. I am satisfied that if the population of Liverpool had been weighed this morning,
and were to be weighed again now, they would
be found many degrees lighter. The docks are
wonderful, and the mass of shipping incredible." [1]
In art and science he had been deeply interested
since boyhood; his reform of the household had put
his talent for organisation beyond a doubt; and
thus from every point of view the Prince was well
qualified for his task. Having matured his plans,
he summoned a small committee and laid an outline of his scheme before it. The committee approved, and the great undertaking was set on foot
without delay.[2]

Two years, however, passed before it was completed. For two years the Prince laboured with
extraordinary and incessant energy. At first all
went smoothly. The leading manufacturers warmly
took up the idea; the colonies and the East India
Company were sympathetic; the great foreign nations were eager to send in their contributions;

[1] Martin, I, 334.   [2] *Ibid.,* II, 224–5.

the powerful support of Sir Robert Peel was obtained, and the use of a site in Hyde Park, selected by the Prince, was sanctioned by the Government. Out of 234 plans for the exhibition
building, the Prince chose that of Joseph Paxton,
famous as a designer of gigantic conservatories;
and the work was on the point of being put in
hand when a series of unexpected difficulties arose.
Opposition to the whole scheme, which had long
been smouldering in various quarters, suddenly
burst forth. There was an outcry, headed by *The
Times,* against the use of the park for the exhibition; for a moment it seemed as if the building
would be relegated to a suburb; but, after a fierce
debate in the House, the supporters of the site
in the Park won the day. Then it appeared that
the project lacked a sufficient financial backing;
but this obstacle, too, was surmounted, and eventually £200,000 was subscribed as a guarantee fund.
The enormous glass edifice rose higher and higher,
covering acres and enclosing towering elm trees
beneath its roof: and then the fury of its enemies
reached a climax. The fashionable, the cautious,
the Protectionists, the pious, all joined in the hue
and cry. It was pointed out that the Exhibition
would serve as a rallying point for all the ruffians
in England, for all the malcontents in Europe;

and that on the day of its opening there would certainly be a riot and probably a revolution. It
was asserted that the glass roof was porous, and
that the droppings of fifty million sparrows would
utterly destroy every object beneath it. Agitated
nonconformists declared that the Exhibition was
an arrogant and wicked enterprise which would infallibly bring down God's punishment upon the
nation. Colonel Sibthorpe, in the debate on the
Address, prayed that hail and lightning might descend from heaven on the accursed thing. The
Prince, with unyielding perseverance and infinite
patience, pressed on to his goal. His health was
seriously affected; he suffered from constant sleeplessness; his strength was almost worn out. But
he remembered the injunctions of Stockmar and
never relaxed. The volume of his labours grew
more prodigious every day; he toiled at committees, presided over public meetings, made speeches,
and carried on communications with every corner
of the civilised world—and his efforts were rewarded. On May 1, 1851, the Great Exhibition
was opened by the Queen before an enormous
concourse of persons, amid scenes of dazzling bril-
liancy and triumphant enthusiasm.[1]

[1] Martin, II, 225, 243–51, 289, 297–9, 358–9; *Dictionary of National
Biography*, Art. " Joseph Paxton "; Bloomfield, II, 3–4.

Victoria herself was in a state of excitement which bordered on delirium. She performed her duties in a trance of joy, gratitude, and amazement, and, when it was all over, her feelings poured themselves out into her journal in a torrential flood. The day had been nothing but an endless succession of glories—or rather one vast glory— one vast radiation of Albert. Everything she had seen, everything she had felt or heard, had been so beautiful, so wonderful that even the royal underlinings broke down under the burden of emphasis, while her remembering pen rushed on, regardless, from splendour to splendour—the huge crowds, so well-behaved and loyal—flags of all the nations floating—the inside of the building, so immense, with myriads of people and the sun shining through the roof—a little side room, where we left our shawls—palm-trees and machinery—dear Albert—the place so big that we could hardly hear the organ—thankfulness to God—a curious assemblage of political and distinguished men—the March from Athalie—God bless my dearest Albert, God bless my dearest country!—a glass fountain—the Duke and Lord Anglesey walking arm in arm—a beautiful Amazon, in bronze, by Kiss—Mr. Paxton, who might be justly proud, and rose from being a common gardener's boy—

Sir George Grey in tears, and everybody astonished and delighted.[1]

A striking incident occurred when, after a short prayer by the Archbishop of Canterbury, the choir of 600 voices burst into the " Hallelujah Chorus." At that moment a Chinaman, dressed in full national costume, stepped out into the middle of the central nave, and, advancing slowly towards the royal group, did obeisance to Her Majesty. The Queen, much impressed, had no doubt that he was an eminent mandarin; and, when the final procession was formed, orders were given that, as no representative of the Celestial Empire was present, he should be included in the diplomatic cortège. He accordingly, with the utmost gravity, followed immediately behind the Ambassadors. He subsequently disappeared, and it was rumoured, among ill-natured people, that, far from being a mandarin, the fellow was a mere impostor. But nobody ever really discovered the nature of the comments that had been lurking behind the matchless impassivity of that yellow face.[2]

A few days later Victoria poured out her heart to her uncle. The first of May, she said, was " the *greatest* day in our history, the most *beautiful* and *imposing* and *touching* spectacle ever seen, and

----

[1] Martin, II, 364–8.   [2] Martin, II, 367 and note.

the triumph of my beloved Albert. . . . It was the *happiest, proudest* day in my life, and I can think of nothing else. Albert's dearest name is immortalised with this *great* conception, *his* own, and my *own* dear country *showed* she was *worthy* of it. The triumph is *immense.*" [1]

It was. The enthusiasm was universal; even the bitterest scoffers were converted, and joined in the chorus of praise.[2] Congratulations from public bodies poured in; the City of Paris gave a great *fête* to the Exhibition committee; and the Queen and the Prince made a triumphal progress through the North of England. The financial results were equally remarkable. The total profit made by the Exhibition amounted to a sum of £165,000, which was employed in the purchase of land for the erection of a permanent National Museum in South Kensington. During the six months of its existence in Hyde Park over six million persons visited it, and not a single accident occurred. But there is an end to all things; and the time had come for the Crystal Palace to be removed to the salubrious seclusion of Sydenham. Victoria, sad but resigned, paid her final visit. "It looked so beautiful," she said. "I could not believe it was the last time I was to see it. An organ, accompa-

1 *Letters*, II, 317–8.   2 Greville, VI, 413.

nied by a fine and powerful wind instrument called
the sommerophone, was being played, and it nearly
upset me. The canvas is very dirty, the red curtains are faded and many things are very much
soiled, still the effect is fresh and new as ever and
most beautiful. The glass fountain was already
removed . . . and the sappers and miners were
rolling about the little boxes just as they did at
the beginning. It made us all very melancholy."
But more cheerful thoughts followed. When all
was over, she expressed her boundless satisfaction
in a dithyrambic letter to the Prime Minister. Her
beloved husband's name, she said, was for ever
immortalised, and that this was universally recognised by the country was a source to her of immense happiness and gratitude. " She feels grateful to Providence," Her Majesty concluded, " to
have permitted her to be united to so great, so
noble, so excellent a Prince, and this year will ever
remain the proudest and happiest of her life. The
day of the closing of the Exhibition (which the
Queen regretted much she could not witness), was
the twelfth anniversary of her betrothal to the
Prince, which is a curious coincidence." [1]

[1] Martin, II, 369–72, 386–92, 403–5.

CHAPTER V

LORD PALMERSTON

I

IN 1851 the Prince's fortunes reached their high-water mark. The success of the Great Exhibition enormously increased his reputation and seemed to assure him henceforward a leading place in the national life. But before the year was out another triumph, in a very different sphere of action, was also his. This triumph, big with fateful consequences, was itself the outcome of a series of complicated circumstances which had been gathering to a climax for many years.

The unpopularity of Albert in high society had not diminished with time. Aristocratic persons continued to regard him with disfavour; and he on his side, withdrew further and further into a contemptuous reserve. For a moment, indeed, it appeared as if the dislike of the upper classes was about to be suddenly converted into cordiality; for they learnt with amazement that the Prince, during a country visit, had ridden to hounds and acquitted himself remarkably well. They had al-

ways taken it for granted that his horsemanship
was of some second-rate foreign quality, and here
he was jumping five-barred gates and tearing
after the fox as if he had been born and bred in
Leicestershire. They could hardly believe it; was
it possible that they had made a mistake, and that
Albert was a good fellow after all? Had he
wished to be thought so he would certainly have
seized this opportunity, purchased several hunters,
and used them constantly. But he had no such
desire; hunting bored him, and made Victoria
nervous. He continued, as before, to ride, as he
himself put it, for exercise or convenience, not for
amusement; and it was agreed that though the
Prince, no doubt, could keep in his saddle well
enough, he was no sportsman.[1]

This was a serious matter. It was not merely
that Albert was laughed at by fine ladies and
sneered at by fine gentlemen; it was not merely
that Victoria, who before her marriage had cut
some figure in society, had, under her husband's
influence, almost completely given it up. Since
Charles the Second the sovereigns of England
had, with a single exception, always been unfash-
ionable; and the fact that the exception was George
the Fourth seemed to give an added significance

[1] Martin, I, 194–6; *Letters*, I, 510–11.

to the rule. What was grave was not the lack of
fashion, but the lack of other and more important
qualities. The hostility of the upper classes was
symptomatic of an antagonism more profound
than one of manners or even of tastes. The Prince,
in a word, was un-English. What that word precisely meant it was difficult to say; but the fact
was patent to every eye. Lord Palmerston, also,
was not fashionable; the great Whig aristocrats
looked askance at him, and only tolerated him as
an unpleasant necessity thrust upon them by fate.
But Lord Palmerston was English through and
through; there was something in him that expressed, with extraordinary vigour, the fundamental qualities of the English race. And he was the
very antithesis of the Prince. By a curious chance
it so happened that this typical Englishman was
brought into closer contact than any other of his
countrymen with the alien from over the sea. It
thus fell out that differences which, in more fortunate circumstances, might have been smoothed
away and obliterated, became accentuated to the
highest pitch. All the mysterious forces in Albert's soul leapt out to do battle with his adversary, and, in the long and violent conflict that
followed, it almost seemed as if he was struggling
with England herself.

Palmerston's whole life had been spent in the government of the country. At twenty-two he had been a Minister; at twenty-five he had been offered the Chancellorship of the Exchequer, which, with that prudence which formed so unexpected a part of his character, he had declined to accept. His first spell of office had lasted uninterruptedly for twenty-one years. When Lord Grey came into power he received the Foreign Secretaryship, a post which he continued to occupy, with two intervals, for another twenty-one years. Throughout this period his reputation with the public had steadily grown, and when, in 1846, he became Foreign Secretary for the third time, his position in the country was almost, if not quite, on an equality with that of the Prime Minister, Lord John Russell. He was a tall, big man of sixty-two, with a jaunty air, a large face, dyed whiskers, and a long sardonic upper lip. His private life was far from respectable, but he had greatly strengthened his position in society by marrying, late in life, Lady Cowper, the sister of Lord Melbourne, and one of the most influential of the Whig hostesses. Powerful, experienced, and supremely self-confident, he naturally paid very little attention to Albert. Why should he? The Prince was interested in foreign affairs? Very

well, then; let the Prince pay attention to *him*—
to him, who had been a Cabinet Minister when
Albert was in the cradle, who was the chosen
leader of a great nation, and who had never failed
in anything he had undertaken in the whole course
of his life. Not that he wanted the Prince's attention—far from it: so far as he could see, Albert
was merely a young foreigner, who suffered from
having no vices, and whose only claim to distinction was that he had happened to marry the Queen
of England. This estimate, as he found out to
his cost, was a mistaken one. Albert was by no
means insignificant, and, behind Albert, there was
another figure by no means insignificant either—
there was Stockmar.

But Palmerston, busy with his plans, his ambitions, and the management of a great department,
brushed all such considerations on one side; it was
his favourite method of action. He lived by instinct—by a quick eye and a strong hand, a dex-
terous management of every crisis as it arose, a
half-unconscious sense of the vital elements in a
situation. He was very bold; and nothing gave
him more exhilaration than to steer the ship of
state in a high wind, on a rough sea, with every
stitch of canvas on her that she could carry. But
there is a point beyond which boldness becomes

rashness—a point perceptible only to intuition and not to reason; and beyond that point Palmerston never went. When he saw that the case demanded it, he could go slow—very slow indeed; in fact, his whole career, so full of vigorous adventure, was nevertheless a masterly example of the proverb, "tout vient à point à qui sait attendre." But when he decided to go quick, nobody went quicker. One day, returning from Osborne, he found that he had missed the train to London; he ordered a special, but the station-master told him that to put a special train upon the line at that time of day would be dangerous, and he could not allow it. Palmerston insisted, declaring that he had important business in London, which could not wait. The station-master, supported by all the officials, continued to demur; the company, he said, could not possibly take the responsibility. "On *my* responsibility, then!" said Palmerston, in his off-hand, peremptory way; whereupon the station-master ordered up the train, and the Foreign Secretary reached London in time for his work, without an accident.[1] The story is typical of the happy valiance with which he conducted both his own affairs and those of the nation. "England," he used to say, "is strong

[1] Bunsen, II, 152.

enough to brave consequences."[1] Apparently, under Palmerston's guidance, she was. While the officials protested and shook in their shoes, he would wave them away with his airy "*My* responsibility!" and carry the country swiftly along the line of his choice, to a triumphant destination,— without an accident. His immense popularity was the result partly of his diplomatic successes, partly of his extraordinary personal affability, but chiefly of the genuine intensity with which he responded to the feelings and supported the interests of his countrymen. The public knew that it had in Lord Palmerston not only a high-mettled master, but also a devoted servant—that he was, in every sense of the word, a public man. When he was Prime Minister, he noticed that iron hurdles had been put up on the grass in the Green Park; he immediately wrote to the Minister responsible, ordering, in the severest language, their instant removal, declaring that they were "an intolerable nuisance," and that the purpose of the grass was "to be walked upon freely and without restraint by the people, old and young, for whose enjoyment the parks are maintained."[2] It was in this spirit that, as Foreign Secretary, he watched over the interests of Englishmen abroad. Noth-

[1] Dalling, I, 346.   [2] Dalling, III, 413-5.

ing could be more agreeable for Englishmen; but
foreign governments were less pleased. They
found Lord Palmerston interfering, exasperating,
and alarming. In Paris they spoke with bated
breath of " ce terrible milord Palmerston "; and
in Germany they made a little song about him—

"Hat der Teufel einen Sohn,
So ist er sicher Palmerston." [1]

But their complaints, their threats, and their agitations were all in vain. Palmerston, with his
upper lip sardonically curving, braved consequences, and held on his course.

The first diplomatic crisis which arose after his
return to office, though the Prince and the Queen
were closely concerned with it, passed off without
serious disagreement between the Court and the
Minister. For some years past a curious problem
had been perplexing the chanceries of Europe.
Spain, ever since the time of Napoleon a prey
to civil convulsions, had settled down for a short
interval to a state of comparative quiet under the
rule of Christina, the Queen Mother, and her
daughter Isabella, the young Queen. In 1846,
the question of Isabella's marriage, which had for
long been the subject of diplomatic speculations,

[1] Ashley, II, 213.

suddenly became acute. Various candidates for her hand were proposed—among others, two cousins of her own, another Spanish prince, and Prince Leopold of Saxe-Coburg, a first cousin of Victoria's and Albert's; for different reasons, however, none of these young men seemed altogether satisfactory. Isabella was not yet sixteen; and it might have been supposed that her marriage could be put off for a few years more; but this was considered to be out of the question. " Vous ne savez pas," said a high authority, " ce que c'est que ces princesses espagnoles; elles ont le diable au corps, et on a toujours dit que si nous ne nous hâtions pas, l'héritier viendrait avant le mari." [1] It might also have been supposed that the young Queen's marriage was a matter to be settled by herself, her mother, and the Spanish Government; but this again was far from being the case. It had become, by one of those periodical reversions to the ways of the eighteenth century, which, it is rumoured, are still not unknown in diplomacy, a question of dominating importance in the foreign policies both of France and England. For several years, Louis Philippe and his Prime Minister Guizot had been privately maturing a very subtle plan. It was the object of the French King to repeat

[1] Greville, VI, 33.

the glorious *coup* of Louis XIV, and to abolish
the Pyrenees by placing one of his grandsons on
the throne of Spain. In order to bring this about,
he did not venture to suggest that his younger
son, the Duc de Montpensier, should marry Isabella; that would have been too obvious a move,
which would have raised immediate and insurmountable opposition. He therefore proposed
that Isabella should marry her cousin, the Duke
of Cadiz, while Montpensier married Isabella's
younger sister, the Infanta Fernanda; and pray,
what possible objection could there be to that?
The wily old King whispered into the chaste ears
of Guizot the key to the secret; he had good reason to believe that the Duke of Cadiz was incapable of having children, and therefore the offspring
of Fernanda would inherit the Spanish crown.
Guizot rubbed his hands, and began at once to
set the necessary springs in motion; but, of course,
the whole scheme was very soon divulged and
understood. The English Government took an
extremely serious view of the matter; the balance
of power was clearly at stake, and the French intrigue must be frustrated at all hazards. A diplomatic struggle of great intensity followed; and
it occasionally appeared that a second War of the
Spanish Succession was about to break out. This

was avoided, but the consequences of this strange imbroglio were far-reaching and completely different from what any of the parties concerned could have guessed.

In the course of the long and intricate negotiations there was one point upon which Louis Philippe laid a special stress—the candidature of Prince Leopold of Saxe-Coburg. The prospect of a marriage between a Coburg Prince and the Queen of Spain was, he declared, at least as threatening to the balance of power in Europe as that of a marriage between the Duc de Montpensier and the Infanta; and, indeed, there was much to be said for this contention. The ruin which had fallen upon the House of Coburg during the Napoleonic wars had apparently only served to multiply its vitality, for that princely family had by now extended itself over Europe in an extraordinary manner. King Leopold was firmly fixed in Belgium; his niece was Queen of England; one of his nephews was the husband of the Queen of England, and another the husband of the Queen of Portugal; yet another was Duke of Würtemberg. Where was this to end? There seemed to be a Coburg Trust ready to send out one of its members at any moment to fill up any vacant place among the ruling families of Europe. And even beyond Europe there were signs of this infection spreading. An American who had arrived in Brussels had assured King Leopold that there was a strong feeling in the United States in favour of monarchy instead of the misrule of mobs, and had suggested, to the delight of His Majesty, that some branch of the Coburg family might be available for the position.[1] That danger might, perhaps, be remote; but the Spanish danger was close at hand; and if Prince Leopold were to marry Queen Isabella the position of France would be one of humiliation, if not of positive danger. Such were the asseverations of Louis Philippe. The English Government had no wish to support Prince Leopold, and though Albert and Victoria had some hankerings for the match, the wisdom of Stockmar had induced them to give up all thoughts of it. The way thus seemed open for a settlement: England would be reasonable about Leopold, if France would be reasonable about Montpensier. At the Château d'Eu, the agreement was made, in a series of conversations between the King and Guizot on the one side, and the Queen, the Prince, and Lord Aberdeen on the other. Aberdeen, as Foreign Minister, declared that England would neither recognise nor support

[1] *Letters*, I, 511.

Prince Leopold as a candidate for the hand of the
Queen of Spain; while Louis Philippe solemnly
promised, both to Aberdeen and to Victoria, that
the Duc de Montpensier should not marry the
Infanta Fernanda until after the Queen was married and had issue. All went well, and the crisis
seemed to be over, when the whole question was
suddenly re-opened by Palmerston, who had succeeded Aberdeen at the Foreign Office. In a
despatch to the English Minister at Madrid, he
mentioned, in a list of possible candidates for
Queen Isabella's hand, Prince Leopold of Coburg;
and at the same time he took occasion to denounce
in violent language the tyranny and incompetence
of the Spanish Government. This despatch, in-
discreet in any case, was rendered infinitely more
so by being communicated to Guizot. Louis
Philippe saw his opportunity and pounced on it.
Though there was nothing in Palmerston's language to show that he either recognised or supported Prince Leopold, the King at once assumed
that the English had broken their engagement,
and that he was therefore free to do likewise. He
then sent the despatch to the Queen Mother, declared that the English were intriguing for the
Coburg marriage, bade her mark the animosity
of Palmerston against the Spanish Government,

and urged her to escape from her difficulties and
ensure the friendship of France by marrying Isabella to the Duke of Cadiz and Fernanda to Montpensier. The Queen Mother, alarmed and furious, was easily convinced. There was only one
difficulty: Isabella loathed the very sight of her
cousin. But this was soon surmounted; there was
a wild supper-party at the Palace, and in the
course of it the young girl was induced to consent
to anything that was asked of her. Shortly after,
and on the same day, both the marriages took
place.

The news burst like a bomb on the English
Government, who saw with rage and mortification
that they had been completely outmanœuvred by
the crafty King. Victoria, in particular, was outraged. Not only had she been the personal recipient of Louis Philippe's pledge, but he had won
his way to her heart by presenting the Prince of
Wales with a box of soldiers and sending the Princess Royal a beautiful Parisian doll with eyes that
opened and shut. And now insult was added to
injury. The Queen of the French wrote her a
formal letter, calmly announcing, as a family
event in which she was sure Victoria would be interested, the marriage of her son, Montpensier—
" qui ajoutera à notre bonheur intérieur, le seul

vrai dans ce monde, et que vous, madame, savez
si bien apprécier." [1] But the English Queen had
not long to wait for her revenge. Within eighteen
months the monarchy of Louis Philippe, discredited, unpopular, and fatally weakened by the withdrawal of English support, was swept into limbo,
while he and his family threw themselves as sup-
pliant fugitives at the feet of Victoria. [2]

II

In this affair both the Queen and the Prince had
been too much occupied with the delinquencies of
Louis Philippe to have any wrath to spare for
those of Palmerston; and, indeed, on the main
issue, Palmerston's attitude and their own had
been in complete agreement. But in this the case
was unique. In every other foreign complication
—and they were many and serious—during the
ensuing years, the differences between the royal
couple and the Foreign Secretary were constant
and profound. There was a sharp quarrel over
Portugal, where violently hostile parties were flying at each other's throats. The royal sympathy
was naturally enlisted on behalf of the Queen and
her Coburg husband, while Palmerston gave his

[1] *Letters*, II, 100–1.
[2] Dalling, III, chaps. vii and viii; Stockmar, chap. xxi.

support to the progressive elements in the country. It was not until 1848, however, that the
strain became really serious. In that year of revo-
lutions, when, in all directions and with alarming
frequency, crowns kept rolling off royal heads,
Albert and Victoria were appalled to find that the
policy of England was persistently directed—in
Germany, in Switzerland, in Austria, in Italy, in
Sicily—so as to favour the insurgent forces. The
situation, indeed, was just such an one as the soul
of Palmerston loved. There was danger and excitement, the necessity of decision, the opportunity
for action, on every hand. A disciple of Canning,
with an English gentleman's contempt and dislike of foreign potentates deep in his heart, the
spectacle of the popular uprisings, and of the
oppressors bundled ignominiously out of the palaces they had disgraced, gave him unbounded
pleasure, and he was determined that there should
be no doubt whatever, all over the Continent, on
which side in the great struggle England stood.
It was not that he had the slightest tincture in
him of philosophical radicalism; he had no philosophical tinctures of any kind; he was quite content to be inconsistent—to be a Conservative at
home and a Liberal abroad. There were very good
reasons for keeping the Irish in their places; but

what had that to do with it? The point was this
—when any decent man read an account of the
political prisons in Naples his gorge rose. He did
not want war; but he saw that without war a skilful and determined use of England's power might
do much to further the cause of the Liberals in
Europe. It was a difficult and a hazardous game
to play, but he set about playing it with delighted
alacrity. And then, to his intense annoyance, just
as he needed all his nerve and all possible freedom
of action, he found himself being hampered and
distracted at every turn by . . . those people at
Osborne. He saw what it was; the opposition was
systematic and informed, and the Queen alone
would have been incapable of it; the Prince was
at the bottom of the whole thing. It was exceedingly vexatious; but Palmerston was in a hurry,
and could not wait; the Prince, if he would insist
upon interfering, must be brushed on one side.

Albert was very angry. He highly disapproved
both of Palmerston's policy and of his methods of
action. He was opposed to absolutism; but in his
opinion Palmerston's proceedings were simply calculated to substitute for absolutism, all over Europe, something no better and very possibly worse
—the anarchy of faction and mob violence. The
dangers of this revolutionary ferment were grave;

even in England Chartism was rampant—a sinister movement, which might at any moment upset the Constitution and abolish the Monarchy.
Surely, with such dangers at home, this was a very
bad time to choose for encouraging lawlessness
abroad. He naturally took a particular interest
in Germany. His instincts, his affections, his prepossessions, were ineradicably German; Stockmar
was deeply involved in German politics; and he
had a multitude of relatives among the ruling
German families, who, from the midst of the
hurly-burly of revolution, wrote him long and agitated letters once a week. Having considered the
question of Germany's future from every point of
view, he came to the conclusion, under Stockmar's
guidance, that the great aim for every lover of
Germany should be her unification under the sovereignty of Prussia. The intricacy of the situation
was extreme, and the possibilities of good or evil
which every hour might bring forth were incalcu-
lable; yet he saw with horror that Palmerston
neither understood nor cared to understand the
niceties of this momentous problem, but rushed on
blindly, dealing blows to right and left, quite—so
far as he could see—without system, and even
without motive—except, indeed, a totally unreasonable distrust of the Prussian State.

But his disagreement with the details of Palmerston's policy was in reality merely a symptom of the fundamental differences between the characters of the two men. In Albert's eyes Palmerston was a coarse, reckless egotist, whose combined arrogance and ignorance must inevitably have their issue in folly and disaster. Nothing could be more antipathetic to him than a mind so strangely lacking in patience, in reflection, in principle, and in the habits of ratiocination. For to him it was intolerable to think in a hurry, to jump to slapdash decisions, to act on instincts that could not be explained. Everything must be done in due order, with careful premeditation; the premises of the position must first be firmly established; and he must reach the correct conclusion by a regular series of rational steps. In complicated questions—and what questions, rightly looked at, were not complicated?—to commit one's thoughts to paper was the wisest course, and it was the course which Albert, laborious though it might be, invariably adopted. It was as well, too, to draw up a reasoned statement after an event, as well as before it; and accordingly, whatever happened, it was always found that the Prince had made a memorandum. On one occasion he reduced to six pages of foolscap the substance of a confidential

conversation with Sir Robert Peel, and, having
read them aloud to him, asked him to append his
signature; Sir Robert, who never liked to commit
himself, became extremely uneasy; upon which the
Prince, understanding that it was necessary to
humour the singular susceptibilities of Englishmen, with great tact dropped that particular memorandum into the fire. But as for Palmerston, he
never even gave one so much as a chance to read
him a memorandum; he positively seemed to dislike discussion; and, before one knew where one
was, without any warning whatever, he would
plunge into some hare-brained, violent project,
which, as likely as not, would logically involve a
European war. Closely connected, too, with this
cautious, painstaking reasonableness of Albert's,
was his desire to examine questions thoroughly
from every point of view, to go down to the roots
of things, and to act in strict accordance with
some well-defined principle. Under Stockmar's
tutelage he was constantly engaged in enlarging
his outlook and in endeavouring to envisage vital
problems both theoretically and practically—both
with precision and with depth. To one whose
mind was thus habitually occupied, the empirical
activities of Palmerston, who had no notion what
a principle meant, resembled the incoherent vaga-

ries of a tiresome child. What did Palmerston know of economics, of science, of history? What did he care for morality and education? How much consideration had he devoted in the whole course of his life to the improvement of the condition of the working-classes and to the general amelioration of the human race? The answers to such questions were all too obvious; and yet it is easy to imagine, also, what might have been Palmerston's jaunty comment. "Ah! your Royal Highness is busy with fine schemes and beneficent calculations—exactly! Well, as for me, I must say I'm quite satisfied with my morning's work— I've had the iron hurdles taken out of the Green Park."

The exasperating man, however, preferred to make no comment, and to proceed in smiling silence on his inexcusable way. The process of " brushing on one side " very soon came into operation. Important Foreign Office despatches were either submitted to the Queen so late that there was no time to correct them, or they were not submitted to her at all; or, having been submitted, and some passage in them being objected to and an alteration suggested, they were after all sent off in their original form. The Queen complained; the Prince complained; both complained together.

It was quite useless. Palmerston was most apologetic—could not understand how it had occurred —must give the clerks a wigging—certainly Her Majesty's wishes should be attended to, and such a thing should never happen again. But, of course, it very soon happened again, and the royal remonstrances redoubled. Victoria, her partisan passions thoroughly aroused, imported into her protests a personal vehemence which those of Albert lacked. Did Lord Palmerston forget that she was Queen of England? How could she tolerate a state of affairs in which despatches written in her name were sent abroad without her approval or even her knowledge? What could be more derogatory to her position than to be obliged to receive indignant letters from the crowned heads to whom those despatches were addressed—letters which she did not know how to answer, since she so thoroughly agreed with them? She addressed herself to the Prime Minister. "No remonstrance has any effect with Lord Palmerston," she said.[1] "Lord Palmerston," she told him on another occasion, "has as usual pretended not to have had time to submit the draft to the Queen before he had sent it off."[2] She summoned Lord John to her presence, poured out her indignation, and after-

[1] *Letters*, II, 181.   [2] *Ibid.*, II, 194.

wards, on the advice of Albert, noted down what had passed in a memorandum: "I said that I thought that Lord Palmerston often endangered the honour of England by taking a very prejudiced and one-sided view of a question; that his writings were always as bitter as gall and did great harm, which Lord John entirely assented to, and that I often felt quite ill from anxiety." [1] Then she turned to her uncle. "The state of Germany," she wrote in a comprehensive and despairing review of the European situation, "is dreadful, and one does feel quite ashamed about that once really so peaceful and happy country. That there are still good people there I am sure, but they allow themselves to be worked upon in a frightful and shameful way. In France a crisis seems at hand. *What* a very bad figure we cut in this mediation! Really it is quite immoral, with Ireland quivering in our grasp and ready to throw off her allegiance at any moment, for us to force Austria to give up her lawful possessions.[2] What shall we say if Canada, Malta, etc., begin to trouble us? It hurts me terribly." [3] But what did Lord Palmerston care?

Lord John's position grew more and more irksome. He did not approve of his colleague's treat-

[1] *Letters*, II, 195. [2] Venice and Lombardy.
[3] *Letters*, 11, 199.

ment of the Queen. When he begged him to be
more careful, he was met with the reply that
28,000 despatches passed through the Foreign
Office in a single year, that, if every one of these
were to be subjected to the royal criticism, the delay would be most serious, that, as it was, the waste
of time and the worry involved in submitting
drafts to the meticulous examination of Prince
Albert was almost too much for an overworked
Minister, and that, as a matter of fact, the post-
ponement of important decisions owing to this
cause had already produced very unpleasant diplomatic consequences.[1] These excuses would have
impressed Lord John more favourably if he had
not himself had to suffer from a similar neglect.
As often as not Palmerston failed to communicate
even to him the most important despatches. The
Foreign Secretary was becoming an almost independent power, acting on his own initiative, and
swaying the policy of England on his own responsibility. On one occasion, in 1847, he had actually
been upon the point of threatening to break off
diplomatic relations with France without consulting either the Cabinet or the Prime Minister.[2] And
such incidents were constantly recurring. When
this became known to the Prince, he saw that his

[1] *Letters*, II, 221; Ashley, II, 195–6.   [2] Greville, VI, 63–4.

opportunity had come. If he could only drive in to the utmost the wedge between the two statesmen, if he could only secure the alliance of Lord John, then the suppression or the removal of Lord Palmerston would be almost certain to follow. He set about the business with all the pertinacity of his nature. Both he and the Queen put every kind of pressure upon the Prime Minister. They wrote, they harangued, they relapsed into awful silence. It occurred to them that Lord Clarendon, an important member of the Cabinet, would be a useful channel for their griefs. They commanded him to dine at the Palace, and, directly the meal was over, " the Queen," as he described it afterwards, " exploded, and went with the utmost vehemence and bitterness into the whole of Palmerston's conduct, all the effects produced all over the world, and all her own feelings and sentiments about it." When she had finished, the Prince took up the tale, with less excitement, but with equal force. Lord Clarendon found himself in an awkward situation; he disliked Palmerston's policy, but he was his colleague, and he disapproved of the attitude of his royal hosts. In his opinion, they were " wrong in wishing that courtiers rather than Ministers should conduct the affairs of the country," and he thought that they " laboured

under the curious mistake that the Foreign Office
was their peculiar department, and that they had
the right to control, if not to direct, the foreign
policy of England." He, therefore, with extreme
politeness, gave it to be understood that he would
not commit himself in any way.[1] But Lord John,
in reality, needed no pressure. Attacked by his
Sovereign, ignored by his Foreign Secretary, he
led a miserable life.[2] With the advent of the
dreadful Schleswig-Holstein question—the most
complex in the whole diplomatic history of Europe
—his position, crushed between the upper and the
nether mill-stones, grew positively unbearable. He
became anxious above all things to get Palmerston
out of the Foreign Office. But then—supposing
Palmerston refused to go?

In a memorandum made by the Prince, at about
this time, of an interview between himself, the
Queen, and the Prime Minister, we catch a curious
glimpse of the states of mind of those three high
personages—the anxiety and irritation of Lord
John, the vehement acrimony of Victoria, and the
reasonable animosity of Albert—drawn together,
as it were, under the shadow of an unseen Presence, the cause of that celestial anger—the gay,

1 Greville, VI, 324–6; Clarendon, I, 341.
2 Clarendon, I, 337, 342.

portentous Palmerston. At one point in the conversation Lord John observed that he believed the Foreign Secretary would consent to a change of offices; Lord Palmerston, he said, realised that he had lost the Queen's confidence—though only on public, and not on personal, grounds. But on that, the Prince noted, " the Queen interrupted Lord John by remarking that she distrusted him on *personal* grounds also, but I remarked that Lord Palmerston had so far at least seen rightly; that he had become disagreeable to the Queen, not on account of his person, but of his political doings—to which the Queen assented." Then the Prince suggested that there was a danger of the Cabinet breaking up, and of Lord Palmerston returning to office as Prime Minister. But on that point Lord John was reassuring: he " thought Lord Palmerston too old to do much in the future (having passed his sixty-fifth year)." Eventually it was decided that nothing could be done for the present, but that the *utmost secrecy* must be observed; and so the conclave ended.[1]

At last, in 1850, deliverance seemed to be at hand. There were signs that the public were growing weary of the alarums and excursions of Palmerston's diplomacy; and when his support of

1 *Letters,* II, 235-7.

Don Pacifico, a British subject, in a quarrel with
the Greek Government, seemed to be upon the
point of involving the country in a war not only
with Greece but also with France, and possibly
with Russia into the bargain, a heavy cloud of
distrust and displeasure appeared to be gathering
and about to burst over his head. A motion directed against him in the House of Lords was
passed by a substantial majority. The question
was next to be discussed in the House of Commons, where another adverse vote was not improbable, and would seal the doom of the Minister.
Palmerston received the attack with complete nonchalance, and then, at the last possible moment, he
struck. In a speech of over four hours, in which
exposition, invective, argument, declamation, plain
talk and resounding eloquence were mingled together with consummate art and extraordinary
felicity, he annihilated his enemies. The hostile
motion was defeated, and Palmerston was once
more the hero of the hour. Simultaneously, Atro-
pos herself conspired to favour him. Sir Robert
Peel was thrown from his horse and killed. By
this tragic chance, Palmerston saw the one rival
great enough to cope with him removed from his
path. He judged—and judged rightly—that he
was the most popular man in England; and when

Lord John revived the project of his exchanging
the Foreign Office for some other position in the
Cabinet, he absolutely refused to stir.[1]

Great was the disappointment of Albert; great
was the indignation of Victoria. " The House of
Commons," she wrote, " is becoming very unman-
ageable and troublesome." [2] The Prince, perceiving that Palmerston was more firmly fixed in the
saddle than ever, decided that something drastic
must be done. Five months before, the prescient
Baron had drawn up, in case of emergency, a
memorandum, which had been carefully docketed,
and placed in a pigeon-hole ready to hand. The
emergency had now arisen, and the memorandum
must be used. The Queen copied out the words
of Stockmar, and sent them to the Prime Minister, requesting him to show her letter to Palmerston. " She thinks it right," she wrote, " in order
to prevent any mistake for the *future,* shortly to
explain *what it is she expects from her Foreign
Secretary.* She requires: (1) That he will distinctly state what he proposes in a given case, in
order that the Queen may know as distinctly to
what she has given her Royal sanction; (2) Having *once given* her sanction to a measure, that it
be not arbitrarily altered or modified by the Min-

[1] *Letters,* II, 261–4.   [2] *Ibid.,* II, 253.

ister; such an act she must consider as failing in sincerity towards the Crown, and justly to be visited by the exercise of her Constitutional right of dismissing that Minister." [1] Lord John Russell did as he was bid, and forwarded the Queen's letter to Lord Palmerston. This transaction, which was of grave constitutional significance, was entirely unknown to the outside world.

If Palmerston had been a sensitive man, he would probably have resigned on the receipt of the Queen's missive. But he was far from sensitive; he loved power, and his power was greater than ever; an unerring instinct told him that this was not the time to go. Nevertheless, he was seriously perturbed. He understood at last that he was struggling with a formidable adversary, whose skill and strength, unless they were mollified, might do irreparable injury to his career. He therefore wrote to Lord John, briefly acquiescing in the Queen's requirements—"I have taken a copy of this memorandum of the Queen and will not fail to attend to the directions which it contains"—and at the same time, he asked for an interview with the Prince. Albert at once summoned him to the Palace, and was astonished to observe, as he noted in a memorandum, that when

[1] *Letters*, II, 238 and 264.

Palmerston entered the room " he was very much agitated, shook, and had tears in his eyes, so as quite to move me, who never under any circumstances had known him otherwise than with a bland smile on his face." The old statesman was profuse in protestations and excuses; the young one was coldly polite. At last, after a long and inconclusive conversation, the Prince, drawing himself up, said that, in order to give Lord Palmerston " an example of what the Queen wanted," he would " ask him a question point-blank." Lord Palmerston waited in respectful silence, while the Prince proceeded as follows:—" You are aware that the Queen has objected to the Protocol about Schleswig, and of the grounds on which she has done so. Her opinion has been overruled, the Protocol stating the desire of the Great Powers to see the integrity of the Danish monarchy preserved has been signed, and upon this the King of Denmark has invaded Schleswig, where the war is raging. If Holstein is attacked also, which is likely, the Germans will not be restrained from flying to her assistance; Russia has menaced to interfere with arms, if the Schleswigers are successful. What will you do, if this emergency arises (provoking most likely an European war), and which will arise very probably when we shall be at Bal-

moral and Lord John in another part of Scotland?
The Queen expects from your foresight that you
have contemplated this possibility, and requires a
categorical answer as to what you would do in the
event supposed." Strangely enough, to this point-
blank question, the Foreign Secretary appeared to
be unable to reply. The whole matter, he said,
was extremely complicated, and the contingencies
mentioned by His Royal Highness were very unlikely to arise. The Prince persisted; but it was
useless; for a full hour he struggled to extract a
categorical answer, until at length Palmerston
bowed himself out of the room. Albert threw up
his hands in shocked amazement: what could one
do with such a man?[1]

What indeed? For, in spite of all his apologies
and all his promises, within a few weeks the incorrigible reprobate was at his tricks again. The
Austrian General Haynau, notorious as a rigorous suppressor of rebellion in Hungary and Italy,
and in particular as a flogger of women, came to
England and took it into his head to pay a visit
to Messrs. Barclay and Perkins's brewery. The
features of " General Hyæna," as he was everywhere called—his grim thin face, his enormous
pepper-and-salt moustaches—had gained a horrid

<hr>

[1] Martin, II, 307–10.

celebrity; and it so happened that among the clerks at the brewery there was a refugee from Vienna, who had given his fellow-workers a first-hand account of the General's characteristics. The Austrian Ambassador, scenting danger, begged his friend not to appear in public, or, if he must do so, to cut off his moustaches first. But the General would take no advice. He went to the brewery, was immediately recognised, surrounded by a crowd of angry draymen, pushed about, shouted at, punched in the ribs, and pulled by the moustaches until, bolting down an alley with the mob at his heels brandishing brooms and roaring "Hyæna!" he managed to take refuge in a public house, whence he was removed under the protection of several policemen. The Austrian Government was angry and demanded explanations. Palmerston, who, of course, was privately delighted by the incident, replied regretting what had occurred, but adding that in his opinion the General had "evinced a want of propriety in coming to England at the present moment"; and he delivered his note to the Ambassador without having previously submitted it to the Queen or to the Prime Minister. Naturally, when this was discovered, there was a serious storm. The Prince was especially indignant; the conduct of the draymen

he regarded, with disgust and alarm, as " a slight
foretaste of what an unregulated mass of illiterate
people is capable "; and Palmerston was requested
by Lord John to withdraw his note, and to substitute for it another from which all censure of the
General had been omitted. On this the Foreign
Secretary threatened resignation, but the Prime
Minister was firm. For a moment the royal hopes
rose high, only to be dashed to the ground again
by the cruel compliance of the enemy. Palmerston, suddenly lamblike, agreed to everything; the
note was withdrawn and altered, and peace was
patched up once more.[1]

It lasted for a year, and then, in October, 1851,
the arrival of Kossuth in England brought on
another crisis. Palmerston's desire to receive the
Hungarian patriot at his house in London was
vetoed by Lord John; once more there was a sharp
struggle; once more Palmerston, after threatening resignation, yielded. But still the insubordi-
nate man could not keep quiet. A few weeks later
a deputation of Radicals from Finsbury and
Islington waited on him at the Foreign Office and
presented him with an address, in which the Emperors of Austria and Russia were stigmatised as
" odious and detestable assassins " and " merciless

[1] *Letters*, II, 267–70; Martin, II, 324–7; Ashley, II, 169–70.

tyrants and despots." The Foreign Secretary in his reply, while mildly deprecating these expressions, allowed his real sentiments to appear with a most undiplomatic *insouciance*. There was an immediate scandal, and the Court flowed over with rage and vituperation. " I think," said the Baron, " the man has been for some time insane." Victoria, in an agitated letter, urged Lord John to assert his authority. But Lord John perceived that on this matter the Foreign Secretary had the support of public opinion, and he judged it wiser to bide his time.[1]

He had not long to wait. The culmination of the long series of conflicts, threats, and exacerbations came before the year was out. On December 2, Louis Napoleon's *coup d'état* took place in Paris; and on the following day Palmerston, without consulting anybody, expressed in a conversation with the French Ambassador his approval of Napoleon's act. Two days later, he was instructed by the Prime Minister, in accordance with a letter from the Queen, that it was the policy of the English Government to maintain an attitude of strict neutrality towards the affairs of France. Nevertheless, in an official despatch to the British Am-

---

[1] *Letters,* II, 324–31; Martin, II, 406–11; Spencer Walpole, II, 33–7; Stockmar, 642; Greville, VI, 421–4.

bassador in Paris, he repeated the approval of the *coup d'état* which he had already given verbally to the French Ambassador in London. This despatch was submitted neither to the Queen nor to the Prime Minister. Lord John's patience, as he himself said, "was drained to the last drop." He dismissed Lord Palmerston.[1]

Victoria was in ecstasies; and Albert knew that the triumph was his even more than Lord John's. It was his wish that Lord Granville, a young man whom he believed to be pliant to his influence, should be Palmerston's successor; and Lord Granville was appointed. Henceforward, it seemed that the Prince would have his way in foreign affairs. After years of struggle and mortification, success greeted him on every hand. In his family, he was an adored master; in the country, the Great Exhibition had brought him respect and glory; and now in the secret seats of power he had gained a new supremacy. He had wrestled with the terrible Lord Palmerston, the embodiment of all that was most hostile to him in the spirit of England, and his redoubtable opponent had been overthrown.[2] Was England herself at his feet? It might be so; and yet . . . it is said that the sons

[1] *Letters*, II, 334–43; Martin, II, 411–18; Ashley, II, 200–12; Walpole, II, 138–42; Clarendon, I, 338.

[2] Ernest, III, 14.

of England have a certain tiresome quality: they never know when they are beaten. It was odd, but Palmerston was positively still jaunty. Was it possible? Could he believe, in his blind arrogance, that even his ignominious dismissal from office was something that could be brushed aside?

III

The Prince's triumph was short-lived. A few weeks later, owing to Palmerston's influence, the Government was defeated in the House, and Lord John resigned. Then, after a short interval, a coalition between the Whigs and the followers of Peel came into power, under the premiership of Lord Aberdeen. Once more, Palmerston was in the Cabinet. It was true that he did not return to the Foreign Office; that was something to the good; in the Home Department it might be hoped that his activities would be less dangerous and disagreeable. But the Foreign Secretary was no longer the complacent Granville; and in Lord Clarendon the Prince knew that he had a Minister to deal with, who, discreet and courteous as he was, had a mind of his own.

These changes, however, were merely the preliminaries of a far more serious development. Events, on every side, were moving towards a catastrophe. Suddenly the nation found itself under the awful shadow of imminent war. For several months, amid the shifting mysteries of diplomacy and the perplexed agitations of politics, the issue grew more doubtful and more dark, while the national temper was strained to the breaking-point. At the very crisis of the long and ominous negotiations, it was announced that Lord Palmerston had resigned. Then the pent-up fury of the people burst forth. They had felt that in the terrible complexity of events they were being guided by weak and embarrassed counsels; but they had been reassured by the knowledge that at the centre of power there was one man with strength, with courage, with determination, in whom they could put their trust. They now learnt that that man was no longer among their leaders. Why? In their rage, anxiety, and nervous exhaustion, they looked round desperately for some hidden and horrible explanation of what had occurred. They suspected plots, they smelt treachery in the air. It was easy to guess the object upon which their frenzy would vent itself. Was there not a foreigner in the highest of high places, a foreigner whose hostility to their own adored champion was unrelenting and unconcealed? The moment that Palmerston's resignation was known, there was a universal outcry and an extraordinary tempest of anger and hatred burst, with unparalleled violence, upon the head of the Prince.

It was everywhere asserted and believed that the Queen's husband was a traitor to the country, that he was a tool of the Russian Court, that in obedience to Russian influences he had forced Palmerston out of the Government, and that he was directing the foreign policy of England in the interests of England's enemies. For many weeks these accusations filled the whole of the press; repeated at public meetings, elaborated in private talk, they flew over the country, growing every moment more extreme and more improbable. While respectable newspapers thundered out their grave invectives, halfpenny broadsides, hawked through the streets of London, re-echoed in doggerel vulgarity the same sentiments and the same suspicions.[1] At last the wildest rumours began to spread.

[1] "The Turkish war both far and near
    Has played the very deuce then,
And little Al, the royal pal,
    They say has turned a Russian;
Old Aberdeen, as may be seen,
    Looks woeful pale and yellow,
And Old John Bull had his belly full
    Of dirty Russian tallow.

In January, 1854, it was whispered that the
Prince had been seized, that he had been found
guilty of high treason, that he was to be committed
to the Tower. The Queen herself, some declared,
had been arrested, and large crowds actually collected round the Tower to watch the incarceration
of the royal miscreants.[1]

These fantastic hallucinations, the result of the
fevered atmosphere of approaching war, were de-
void of any basis in actual fact. Palmerston's res-

Chorus.

" We'll send him home and make him groan,
    Oh, Al! you've played the deuce then;
The German lad has acted sad
    And turned tail with the Russians.

    .   .   .   .

" Last Monday night, all in a fright,
    Al out of bed did tumble.
The German lad was raving mad,
    How he did groan and grumble!
He cried to Vic, ' I've cut my stick:
    To St. Petersburg go right slap.'
When Vic, 'tis said, jumped out of bed,
    And wopped him with her night-cap."

From *Lovely Albert!* a broadside preserved at the British
Museum; Martin, II, 539–41; Greville, VII, 127–9.
[1] Martin, II, 540, 562.

        " You Jolly Turks, now go to work,
            And show the Bear your power.
        It is rumoured over Britain's isle
            That A——— is in the Tower;
        The postmen some suspicion had,
            And opened the two letters,
        'Twas a pity sad the German lad
            Should not have known much better! "

                        Lovely Albert!

ignation had been in all probability totally disconnected with foreign policy; it had certainly been
entirely spontaneous, and had surprised the Court
as much as the nation. Nor had Albert's influence
been used in any way to favour the interests of
Russia. As often happens in such cases, the Government had been swinging backwards and forwards between two incompatible policies—that of
non-interference and that of threats supported by
force—either of which, if consistently followed,
might well have had a successful and peaceful issue,
but which, mingled together, could only lead to war.
Albert, with characteristic scrupulosity, attempted
to thread his way through the complicated labyrinth
of European diplomacy, and eventually was lost
in the maze. But so was the whole of the Cabinet;
and, when war came, his anti-Russian feelings were
quite as vehement as those of the most bellicose of
Englishmen.

Nevertheless, though the specific charges levelled
against the Prince were without foundation, there
were underlying elements in the situation which explained, if they did not justify, the popular state of
mind. It was true that the Queen's husband was a
foreigner, who had been brought up in a foreign
Court, was impregnated with foreign ideas, and
was closely related to a multitude of foreign

princes. Clearly this, though perhaps an unavoidable, was an undesirable, state of affairs; nor were
the objections to it merely theoretical; it had in fact
produced unpleasant consequences of a serious
kind. The Prince's German proclivities were perpetually lamented by English Ministers; Lord
Palmerston, Lord Clarendon, Lord Aberdeen,[1] all
told the same tale; and it was constantly necessary,
in grave questions of national policy, to combat the
prepossessions of a Court in which German views
and German sentiments held a disproportionate
place. As for Palmerston, his language on this
topic was apt to be unbridled. At the height of
his annoyance over his resignation, he roundly declared that he had been made a victim to foreign
intrigue.[2] He afterwards toned down this accusation; but the mere fact that such a suggestion
from such a quarter was possible at all showed to
what unfortunate consequences Albert's foreign
birth and foreign upbringing might lead.

But this was not all. A constitutional question
of the most profound importance was raised by
the position of the Prince in England. His pres-

[1] " Aberdeen spoke much of the Queen and Prince, of course
with great praise. He said the Prince's views were generally sound
and wise, with one exception, which was his violent and incorrigible
German unionism. He goes all lengths with Prussia."—Greville,
VI, 305.

[2] Ashley, II, 218.

ence gave a new prominence to an old problem—
the precise definition of the functions and the
powers of the Crown. Those functions and powers had become, in effect, his; and what sort of use
was he making of them? His views as to the
place of the Crown in the Constitution are easily
ascertainable; for they were Stockmar's; and it
happens that we possess a detailed account of
Stockmar's opinions upon the subject in a long
letter addressed by him to the Prince at the time
of this very crisis, just before the outbreak of the
Crimean War. Constitutional Monarchy, according to the Baron, had suffered an eclipse since the
passing of the Reform Bill. It was now " constantly in danger of becoming a pure Ministerial
Government." The old race of Tories, who " had
a direct interest in upholding the prerogatives of
the Crown," had died out; and the Whigs were
" nothing but partly conscious, partly unconscious
Republicans, who stand in the same relation to the
Throne as the wolf does to the lamb." There was
a rule that it was unconstitutional to introduce
" the name and person of the irresponsible Sovereign " into parliamentary debates on constitutional matters; this was " a constitutional fiction,
which, although undoubtedly of old standing, was
fraught with danger "; and the Baron warned

the Prince that " if the English Crown permit a
Whig Ministry to follow this rule in practice,
without exception, you must not wonder if in a
little time you find the majority of the people
impressed with the belief that the King, in the
view of the law, is nothing but a mandarin figure,
which has to nod its head in assent, or shake it in
denial, as his Minister pleases." To prevent this
from happening, it was of extreme importance,
said the Baron, " that no opportunity should be
let slip of vindicating the legitimate position of the
Crown." " And this is not hard to do," he added,
" and can never embarrass a Minister where such
straightforward loyal personages as the Queen
and the Prince are concerned." In his opinion,
the very lowest claim of the Royal Prerogative
should include " a right on the part of the King to
be the permanent President of his Ministerial
Council." The Sovereign ought to be " in the
position of a permanent Premier, who takes rank
above the temporary head of the Cabinet, and in
matters of discipline exercises supreme authority."
The Sovereign " may even take a part in the initi-
ation and the maturing of the Government measures; for it would be unreasonable to expect that
a king, himself as able, as accomplished, and as
patriotic as the best of his Ministers, should be

prevented from making use of these qualities at the deliberations of his Council." " The judicious exercise of this right," concluded the Baron, " which certainly requires a master mind, would not only be the best guarantee for Constitutional Monarchy, but would raise it to a height of power, stability, and symmetry, which has never been attained." [1]

Now it may be that this reading of the Constitution is a possible one, though indeed it is hard to see how it can be made compatible with the fundamental doctrine of ministerial responsibility. William III presided over his Council, and he was a constitutional monarch; and it seems that Stockmar had in his mind a conception of the Crown which would have given it a place in the Constitution analogous to that which it filled at the time of William III. But it is clear that such a theory, which would invest the Crown with more power than it possessed even under George III, runs counter to the whole development of English public life since the Revolution; and the fact that it was held by Stockmar, and instilled by him into Albert, was of very serious importance. For there was good reason to believe not only that these doctrines were held by Albert in theory, but that he

[1] Martin, II, 545–57.

was making a deliberate and sustained attempt to give them practical validity. The history of the struggle between the Crown and Palmerston provided startling evidence that this was the case. That struggle reached its culmination when, in Stockmar's memorandum of 1850, the Queen asserted her " constitutional right " to dismiss the Foreign Secretary if he altered a despatch which had received her sanction. The memorandum was, in fact, a plain declaration that the Crown intended to act independently of the Prime Minister. Lord John Russell, anxious at all costs to strengthen himself against Palmerston, accepted the memorandum, and thereby implicitly allowed the claim of the Crown. More than that; after the dismissal of Palmerston, among the grounds on which Lord John justified that dismissal in the House of Commons he gave a prominent place to the memorandum of 1850. It became apparent that the displeasure of the Sovereign might be a reason for the removal of a powerful and popular Minister. It seemed indeed as if, under the guidance of Stockmar and Albert, the " Constitutional Monarchy " might in very truth be rising " to a height of power, stability, and symmetry, which had never been attained."

But this new development in the position of the

Crown, grave as it was in itself, was rendered
peculiarly disquieting by the unusual circumstances which surrounded it. For the functions of
the Crown were now, in effect, being exercised by
a person unknown to the Constitution, who
wielded over the Sovereign an undefined and unbounded influence. The fact that this person was
the Sovereign's husband, while it explained his
influence and even made it inevitable, by no means
diminished its strange and momentous import. An
ambiguous, prepotent figure had come to disturb
the ancient, subtle, and jealously guarded balance
of the English Constitution. Such had been the
unexpected outcome of the tentative and faint-
hearted opening of Albert's political life. He
himself made no attempt to minimise either the
multiplicity or the significance of the functions he
performed. He considered that it was his duty, he
told the Duke of Wellington in 1850, to " sink his
own individual existence in that of his wife . . .
—assume no separate responsibility before the
public, but make his position entirely a part of
hers—fill up every gap which, as a woman, she
would naturally leave in the exercise of her regal
functions—continually and anxiously watch every
part of the public business, in order to be able to
advise and assist her at any moment in any of the

multifarious and difficult questions or duties brought before her, sometimes international, sometimes political, or social, or personal. As the natural head of her family, superintendent of her household, manager of her private affairs, sole *confidential* adviser in politics, and only assistant in her communications with the officers of the Government, he is, besides, the husband of the Queen, the tutor of the royal children, the private secretary of the Sovereign, and her permanent minister." [1] Stockmar's pupil had assuredly gone far and learnt well. Stockmar's pupil!—precisely; the public, painfully aware of Albert's predominance, had grown, too, uneasily conscious that Victoria's master had a master of his own. Deep in the darkness the Baron loomed. Another foreigner! Decidedly, there were elements in the situation which went far to justify the popular alarm. A foreign Baron controlled a foreign Prince, and the foreign Prince controlled the Crown of England. And the Crown itself was creeping forward ominously; and when, from under its shadow, the Baron and the Prince had frowned, a great Minister, beloved of the people, had fallen. Where was all this to end?

Within a few weeks Palmerston withdrew his

[1] Martin, II, 259–60.

resignation, and the public frenzy subsided as
quickly as it had arisen. When Parliament met,
the leaders of both the parties in both the Houses
made speeches in favour of the Prince, asserting
his unimpeachable loyalty to the country and vindicating his right to advise the Sovereign in all
matters of State. Victoria was delighted. " The
position of my beloved lord and master," she told
the Baron, " has been defined for *once and all* and
his merits have been acknowledged on all sides
most duly. There was an immense concourse of
people assembled when we went to the House of
Lords, and the people were very friendly." [1] Immediately afterwards, the country finally plunged
into the Crimean War. In the struggle that followed, Albert's patriotism was put beyond a
doubt, and the animosities of the past were forgotten. But the war had another consequence,
less gratifying to the royal couple: it crowned the
ambition of Lord Palmerston. In 1855, the man
who five years before had been pronounced by
Lord John Russell to be " too old to do much in
the future," became Prime Minister of England,
and, with one short interval, remained in that position for ten years.

[1] Martin, II, 563–4.

CHAPTER VI

LAST YEARS OF PRINCE CONSORT

I

THE weak-willed youth who took no interest in politics and never read a newspaper had grown into a man of unbending determination whose tireless energies were incessantly concentrated upon the laborious business of government and the highest questions of State. He was busy now from morning till night. In the winter, before the dawn, he was to be seen, seated at his writing-table, working by the light of the green reading-lamp which he had brought over with him from Germany, and the construction of which he had much improved by an ingenious device. Victoria was early too, but she was not so early as Albert; and when, in the chill darkness, she took her seat at her own writing-table, placed side by side with his, she invariably found upon it a neat pile of papers arranged for her inspection and her signature.[1] The day, thus begun, continued in unremitting industry. At breakfast, the newspapers—

---

[1] Martin, II, 161.

the once hated newspapers—made their appearance, and the Prince, absorbed in their perusal, would answer no questions, or, if an article struck him, would read it aloud. After that there were ministers and secretaries to interview; there was a vast correspondence to be carried on; there were numerous memoranda to be made. Victoria, treasuring every word, preserving every letter, was all breathless attention and eager obedience. Sometimes Albert would actually ask her advice. He consulted her about his English: " Lese recht aufmerksam, und sage wenn irgend ein Fehler ist," [1] he would say; or, as he handed her a draft for her signature, he would observe, " Ich hab' Dir hier ein Draft gemacht, lese es mal! Ich dächte es wäre recht so." [2] Thus the diligent, scrupulous, absorbing hours passed by. Fewer and fewer grew the moments of recreation and of exercise. The demands of society were narrowed down to the smallest limits, and even then but grudgingly attended to. It was no longer a mere pleasure, it was a positive necessity, to go to bed as early as possible in order to be up and at work on the morrow betimes. [3]

[1] " Read this carefully, and tell me if there are any mistakes in it."
[2] " Here is a draft I have made for you. Read it. I should think this would do."
[3] Martin, V, 273–5.

QUEEN VICTORIA AND THE PRINCE CONSORT IN 1860.

The important and exacting business of government, which became at last the dominating preoccupation in Albert's mind, still left unimpaired his old tastes and interests; he remained devoted to art, to science, to philosophy; and a multitude of subsidiary activities showed how his energies increased as the demands upon them grew. For whenever duty called, the Prince was all alertness. With indefatigable perseverance he opened museums, laid the foundation stones of hospitals, made speeches to the Royal Agricultural Society, and attended meetings of the British Association.[1] The National Gallery particularly interested him: he drew up careful regulations for the arrangement of the pictures according to schools; and he attempted —though in vain—to have the whole collection transported to South Kensington.[2] Feodora, now the Princess Hohenlohe, after a visit to England, expressed in a letter to Victoria her admiration of Albert both as a private and a public character. Nor did she rely only on her own opinion. " I must just copy out," she said, " what Mr. Klumpp wrote to me some little time ago, and which is quite true—'Prince Albert is one of the few Royal personages who can sacrifice to any principle (as soon as it has become evident to them to

[1] Martin, II, 379.   [2] Martin, IV, 14–15, 60.

be good and noble) all those notions (or sentiments) to which others, owing to their narrow-
mindedness, or to the prejudices of their rank, are
so thoroughly inclined strongly to cling.'—There
is something so truly religious in this," the Princess added, " as well as humane and just, most
soothing to my feelings which are so often hurt
and disturbed by what I hear and see." [1]

Victoria, from the depth of her heart, subscribed
to all the eulogies of Feodora and Mr. Klumpp.
She only found that they were insufficient. As
she watched her beloved Albert, after toiling with
state documents and public functions, devoting
every spare moment of his time to domestic duties, to artistic appreciation, and to intellectual
improvements; as she listened to him cracking his
jokes at the luncheon table, or playing Mendelssohn on the organ, or pointing out the merits of Sir
Edwin Landseer's pictures; as she followed him
round while he gave instructions about the breed-
ing of cattle, or decided that the Gainsboroughs
must be hung higher up so that the Winterhalters
might be properly seen—she felt perfectly certain
that no other wife had ever had such a husband.
His mind was apparently capable of everything,
and she was hardly surprised to learn that he had

[1] Martin, II, 479.

made an important discovery for the conversion of sewage into agricultural manure. Filtration from below upwards, he explained, through some appropriate medium, which retained the solids and set free the fluid sewage for irrigation, was the principle of the scheme. " All previous plans," he said, " would have cost millions; mine costs next to nothing." Unfortunately, owing to a slight miscalculation, the invention proved to be impracticable; but Albert's intelligence was unrebuffed, and he passed on, to plunge with all his accustomed ardour into a prolonged study of the rudiments of lithography.[1]

But naturally it was upon his children that his private interests and those of Victoria were concentrated most vigorously. The royal nurseries showed no sign of emptying. The birth of the Prince Arthur in 1850 was followed, three years later, by that of the Prince Leopold; and in 1857 the Princess Beatrice was born. A family of nine must be, in any circumstances, a grave responsibility; and the Prince realised to the full how much the high destinies of his offspring intensified the need of parental care. It was inevitable that he should believe profoundly in the importance of education; he himself had been the product of

[1] Martin, II, 251–2; Bloomfield, II, 110.

education; Stockmar had made him what he was;
it was for him, in his turn, to be a Stockmar—to
be even more than a Stockmar—to the young creatures he had brought into the world. Victoria
would assist him; a Stockmar, no doubt, she could
hardly be; but she could be perpetually vigilant,
she could mingle strictness with her affection, and
she could always set a good example. These considerations, of course, applied pre-eminently to
the education of the Prince of Wales. How tremendous was the significance of every particle of
influence which went to the making of the future
King of England! Albert set to work with a will.
But, watching with Victoria the minutest details
of the physical, intellectual, and moral training of
his children, he soon perceived, to his distress, that
there was something unsatisfactory in the development of his eldest son. The Princess Royal was
an extremely intelligent child; but Bertie, though
he was good-humoured and gentle, seemed to display a deep-seated repugnance to every form of
mental exertion. This was most regrettable, but
the remedy was obvious: the parental efforts must
be redoubled; instruction must be multiplied; not
for a single instant must the educational pressure
be allowed to relax. Accordingly, more tutors
were selected, the curriculum was revised, the

time-table of studies was rearranged, elaborate
memoranda dealing with every possible contin-
gency were drawn up. It was above all essential
that there should be no slackness: " work," said
the Prince, " must be work." And work indeed it
was. The boy grew up amid a ceaseless round of
paradigms, syntactical exercises, dates, genealogical tables, and lists of capes. Constant notes flew
backwards and forwards between the Prince, the
Queen, and the tutors, with inquiries, with reports
of progress, with detailed recommendations; and
these notes were all carefully preserved for future
reference. It was, besides, vital that the heir to
the throne should be protected from the slightest
possibility of contamination from the outside
world. The Prince of Wales was not as other
boys; he might, occasionally, be allowed to invite
some sons of the nobility, boys of good character,
to play with him in the garden of Buckingham
Palace; but his father presided, with alarming precision, over their sports. In short, every possible
precaution was taken, every conceivable effort was
made. Yet, strange to say, the object of all this
vigilance and solicitude continued to be unsatisfactory—appeared, in fact, to be positively growing worse. It was certainly very odd: the more
lessons that Bertie had to do, the less he did them;

and the more carefully he was guarded against excitements and frivolities, the more desirous of mere amusement he seemed to become. Albert was deeply grieved and Victoria was sometimes very angry; but grief and anger produced no more effect than supervision and time-tables. The Prince of Wales, in spite of everything, grew up into manhood without the faintest sign of " adherence to and perseverance in the plan both of studies and life "—as one of the Royal memoranda put it—which had been laid down with such extraordinary forethought by his father.[1]

II

Against the insidious worries of politics, the boredom of society functions, and the pompous publicity of state ceremonies, Osborne had afforded a welcome refuge; but it soon appeared that even Osborne was too little removed from the world. After all, the Solent was a feeble barrier. Oh, for some distant, some almost inaccessible sanctuary, where, in true domestic privacy, one could make happy holiday, just as if—or at least very, very, nearly—one were anybody else! Victoria, ever since, together with Albert, she had visited Scot-

[1] *D.N.B.*, Second Supplement, Art. " Edward VII "; *Quarterly Review*, ccxiii, 4–7, 16

land in the early years of her marriage, had felt
that her heart was in the Highlands. She had
returned to them a few years later, and her passion had grown. How romantic they were! And
how Albert enjoyed them too! His spirits rose
quite wonderfully as soon as he found himself
among the hills and the conifers. " It is a happiness to see him," she wrote. " Oh! What can
equal the beauties of nature! " she exclaimed in
her journal, during one of these visits. " What
enjoyment there is in them! Albert enjoys it so
much; he is in ecstasies here." " Albert said,"
she noted next day, " that the chief beauty of
mountain scenery consists in its frequent changes.
We came home at six o'clock." Then she went
on a longer expedition—up to the very top of a
high hill. " It was quite romantic. Here we were
with only this Highlander behind us holding the
ponies (for we got off twice and walked about).
. . . We came home at half-past eleven,—the
most delightful, most romantic ride and walk I
ever had. I had never been up such a mountain,
and then the day was so fine." The Highlanders,
too, were such astonishing people. They " never
make difficulties," she noted, " but are cheerful,
and happy, and merry, and ready to walk, and
run, and do anything." As for Albert he " highly

appreciated the good-breeding, simplicity, and intelligence, which make it so pleasant and even instructive to talk to them." "We were always in the habit," wrote Her Majesty, "of conversing with the Highlanders—with whom one comes so much in contact in the Highlands." She loved everything about them—their customs, their dress, their dances, even their musical instruments. "There were nine pipers at the castle," she wrote, after staying with Lord Breadalbane; "sometimes one and sometimes three played. They always played about breakfast-time, again during the morning, at luncheon, and also whenever we went in and out; again before dinner, and during most of dinner-time. We both have become quite fond of the bag-pipes." [1]

It was quite impossible not to wish to return to such pleasures again and again; and in 1848 the Queen took a lease of Balmoral House, a small residence near Braemar in the wilds of Aberdeenshire. Four years later she bought the place outright. Now she could be really happy every summer; now she could be simple and at her ease; now she could be romantic every evening, and dote upon Albert, without a single distraction, all day long. The diminutive scale of the house was in

[1] *Leaves*, 18, 33, 34, 36, 127–8, 132n.

itself a charm. Nothing was more amusing than
to find oneself living in two or three little sitting-
rooms, with the children crammed away upstairs,
and the minister in attendance with only a tiny
bedroom to do all his work in. And then to be
able to run in and out of doors as one liked, and
to sketch, and to walk, and to watch the red deer
coming so surprisingly close, and to pay visits to
the cottagers! And occasionally one could be
more adventurous still—one could go and stay for
a night or two at the Bothie at Alt-na-giuthasach
—a mere couple of huts with " a wooden addition "—and only eleven people in the whole party!
And there were mountains to be climbed and
cairns to be built in solemn pomp. " At last, when
the cairn, which is, I think, seven or eight feet
high, was nearly completed, Albert climbed up to
the top of it, and placed the last stone; after which
three cheers were given. It was a gay, pretty,
and touching sight; and I felt almost inclined to
cry. The view was so beautiful over the dear hills;
the day so fine; the whole so *gemüthlich*." [1] And
in the evening there were sword-dances and reels.

But Albert had determined to pull down the
little old house, and to build in its place a castle
of his own designing. With great ceremony, in

[1] *Leaves*, 73–4, 95–6; Greville, VI, 303–4.

accordance with a memorandum drawn up by the Prince for the occasion, the foundation-stone of the new edifice was laid,[1] and by 1855 it was habitable. Spacious, built of granite in the Scotch baronial style, with a tower 100 feet high, and minor turrets and castellated gables, the castle was skilfully arranged to command the finest views of the surrounding mountains and of the neighbouring river Dee. Upon the interior decorations Albert and Victoria lavished all their care. The wall and the floors were of pitch-pine, and covered with specially manufactured tartans. The Balmoral tartan, in red and grey, designed by the Prince, and the Victoria tartan, with a white stripe, designed by the Queen, were to be seen in every room: there were tartan curtains, and tartan chair-covers, and even tartan linoleums. Occasionally the Royal Stuart tartan appeared, for Her Majesty always maintained that she was an ardent Jacobite. Water-colour sketches by Victoria hung upon the walls, together with innumerable stags' antlers, and the head of a boar, which had been shot by Albert in Germany. In an alcove in the hall, stood a life-sized statue of Albert in Highland dress.[2]

[1] *Leaves*, 99–100.
[2] *Private Life*, 209–11; *Quarterly Review*, cxciii, 335.

Victoria declared that it was perfection. " Every year," she wrote, " my heart becomes more fixed in this dear paradise, and so much more so now, that *all* has become my dear Albert's *own* creation, own work, own building, own lay-out; . . . and his great taste, and the impress of his dear hand, have been stamped everywhere." [1]

And here, in very truth, her happiest days were passed. In after years, when she looked back upon them, a kind of glory, a radiance as of an unearthly holiness, seemed to glow about these golden hours. Each hallowed moment stood out clear, beautiful, eternally significant. For, at the time, every experience there, sentimental, or grave, or trivial, had come upon her with a peculiar vividness, like a flashing of marvellous lights. Albert's stalkings—an evening walk when she lost her way—Vicky sitting down on a wasps' nest—a torchlight dance—with what intensity such things, and ten thousand like them, impressed themselves upon her eager consciousness! And how she flew to her journal to note them down! The news of the Duke's death! What a moment!—when, as she sat sketching after a picnic by a loch in the lonely hills, Lord Derby's letter had been brought to her, and she had learnt that " *England's,* or

[1] *Leaves*, 103, 111.

rather *Britain's* pride, her glory, her hero, the greatest man she had ever produced, was no more!" For such were here reflections upon the "old rebel" of former days. But that past had been utterly obliterated—no faintest memory of it remained. For years she had looked up to the Duke as a figure almost superhuman. Had he not been a supporter of good Sir Robert? Had he not asked Albert to succeed him as commander-in-chief? And what a proud moment it had been when he stood as sponsor to her son Arthur, who was born on his eighty-first birthday! So now she filled a whole page of her diary with pane-gyrical regrets. "His position was the highest a subject ever had—above party,—looked up to by all,—revered by the whole nation,—the friend of the Sovereign . . . The Crown never pos-sessed,—and I fear never *will*—so *devoted,* loyal, and faithful a subject, so staunch a supporter! To *us* his loss is *irreparable* . . . To Albert he showed the greatest kindness and the utmost con-fidence . . . Not an eye will be dry in the whole country."[1] These were serious thoughts; but they were soon succeeded by others hardly less moving —by events as impossible to forget—by Mr. Mac-Leod's sermon on Nicodemus,—by the gift of a

[1] *Leaves,* 92–4.

red flannel petticoat to Mrs. P. Farquharson, and another to old Kitty Kear.[1]

But, without doubt, most memorable, most delightful of all were the expeditions—the rare, exciting expeditions up distant mountains, across broad rivers, through strange country, and lasting several days. With only two gillies—Grant and Brown—for servants, and with assumed names . . . it was more like something in a story than real life. " We had decided to call ourselves *Lord and Lady Churchill and party*—Lady Churchill passing as *Miss Spencer* and General Grey as *Dr. Grey!* Brown once forgot this and called me ' Your Majesty ' as I was getting into the carriage, and Grant on the box once called Albert ' Your Royal Highness,' which set us off laughing, but no one observed it." Strong, vigorous, enthusiastic, bringing, so it seemed, good fortune with her—the Highlanders declared she had " a lucky foot "—she relished everything—the scrambles and the views and the contretemps and the rough inns with their coarse fare and Brown and Grant waiting at table. She could have gone on for ever and ever, absolutely happy with Albert beside her and Brown at her pony's head. But the time came for turning homewards; alas! the

[1] *Leaves,* 102, 113–4.

time came for going back to England. She could hardly bear it; she sat disconsolate in her room and watched the snow falling. The last day! Oh! If only she could be snowed up! [1]

III

The Crimean War brought new experiences, and most of them were pleasant ones. It was pleasant to be patriotic and pugnacious, to look out appropriate prayers to be read in the churches, to have news of glorious victories, and to know oneself, more proudly than ever, the representative of England. With that spontaneity of feeling which was so peculiarly her own, Victoria poured out her emotion, her admiration, her pity, her love, upon her " dear soldiers." When she gave them their medals her exultation knew no bounds. " Noble fellows! " she wrote to the King of the Belgians. " I own I feel as if these were *my own children;* my heart beats for *them* as for my *nearest and dearest.* They were so touched, so pleased; many, I hear, cried—and they won't hear of giving up their medals to have their names engraved upon them for fear they should *not* receive the *identical one* put into *their hands by me,* which is quite touching. Several came by in a

1 *Leaves,* 72, 117, 137.

sadly mutilated state." [1] She and they were at
one. They felt that she had done them a splendid
honour, and she, with perfect genuineness, shared
their feeling. Albert's attitude towards such
things was different; there was an austerity in
him which quite prohibited the expansions of emotion. When General Williams returned from the
heroic defence of Kars and was presented at
Court, the quick, stiff, distant bow with which the
Prince received him struck like ice upon the be-
holders. [2] He was a stranger still.

But he had other things to occupy him, more
important, surely, than the personal impressions
of military officers and people who went to Court.
He was at work—ceaselessly at work—on the tremendous task of carrying through the war to a
successful conclusion. State papers, despatches,
memoranda, poured from him in an overwhelming
stream. Between 1853 and 1857 fifty folio volumes were filled with the comments of his pen
upon the Eastern question. [3] Nothing would induce him to stop. Weary ministers staggered
under the load of his advice; but his advice continued, piling itself up over their writing-tables,
and flowing out upon them from red box after red

---

[1] *Letters*, III, 127.   [2] Private information.

[3] Martin, III, v.

box. Nor was it advice to be ignored. The talent for administration which had reorganised the royal palaces and planned the Great Exhibition asserted itself no less in the confused complexities of war. Again and again the Prince's suggestions, rejected or unheeded at first, were adopted under the stress of circumstances and found to be full of value. The enrolment of a foreign legion, the establishment of a depôt for troops at Malta, the institution of periodical reports and tabulated returns as to the condition of the army at Sebastopol—such were the contrivances and the achievements of his indefatigable brain. He went further: in a lengthy minute he laid down the lines for a radical reform in the entire administration of the army. This was premature, but his proposal that " a camp of evolution " should be created, in which troops should be concentrated and drilled, proved to be the germ of Aldershot.[1]

Meanwhile Victoria had made a new friend: she had suddenly been captivated by Napoleon III. Her dislike of him had been strong at first. She considered that he was a disreputable adventurer who had usurped the throne of poor old Louis Philippe; and besides he was hand-in-glove with Lord Palmerston. For a long time, although

[1] Martin, III, 146-7, 168-9, 177-9, 190n.

he was her ally, she was unwilling to meet him; but at last a visit of the Emperor and Empress to England was arranged. Directly he appeared at Windsor her heart began to soften. She found that she was charmed by his quiet manners, his low, soft voice, and by the soothing simplicity of his conversation. The good-will of England was essential to the Emperor's position in Europe, and he had determined to fascinate the Queen. He succeeded. There was something deep within her which responded immediately and vehemently to natures that offered a romantic contrast with her own. Her adoration of Lord Melbourne was intimately interwoven with her half-unconscious appreciation of the exciting unlikeness between herself and that sophisticated, subtle, aristocratical old man. Very different was the quality of her unlikeness to Napoleon; but its quantity was at least as great. From behind the vast solidity of her respectability, her conventionality, her established happiness, she peered out with a strange delicious pleasure at that unfamiliar, darkly-glittering foreign object, moving so meteorically before her, an ambiguous creature of wilfulness and Destiny. And, to her surprise, where she had dreaded antagonisms, she discovered only sympathies. He was, she said, " so quiet, so simple, *naïf* even, so pleased to be informed about things he does not know, so gentle, so full of tact, dignity, and modesty, so full of kind attention towards us, never saying a word, or doing a thing, which could put me out . . . There is something fascinating, melancholy, and engaging, which draws you to him, in spite of any *prévention* you may have against him, and certainly without the assistance of any outward appearance, though I like his face." She observed that he rode " extremely well, and looks well on horseback, as he sits high." And he danced " with great dignity and spirit." Above all, he listened to Albert; listened with the most respectful attention; showed, in fact, how pleased he was " to be informed about things he did not know "; and afterwards was heard to declare that he had never met the Prince's equal. On one occasion, indeed—but only on one—he had seemed to grow slightly restive. In a diplomatic conversation, " I expatiated a little on the Holstein question," wrote the Prince in a memorandum, " which appeared to bore the Emperor as ' *très-compliquée.*' " [1]

Victoria, too, became much attached to the Empress, whose looks and graces she admired without a touch of jealousy. Eugénie, indeed, in the plen-

[1] Martin, III, 242, 245, 351; IV, 111.

itude of her beauty, exquisitely dressed in wonderful Parisian crinolines which set off to perfection
her tall and willowy figure, might well have caused
some heartburning in the breast of her hostess,
who, very short, rather stout, quite plain, in garish
middle-class garments, could hardly be expected
to feel at her best in such company. But Victoria
had no misgivings. To her it mattered nothing
that her face turned red in the heat and that her
purple pork-pie hat was of last year's fashion,
while Eugénie, cool and modish, floated in an infinitude of flounces by her side. She was Queen
of England, and was not that enough? It certainly seemed to be; true majesty was hers, and
she knew it. More than once, when the two were
together in public, it was the woman to whom, as
it seemed, nature and art had given so little, who,
by the sheer force of an inherent grandeur, completely threw her adorned and beautiful companion into the shade.[1]

There were tears when the moment came for
parting, and Victoria felt " quite *wehmüthig,*" as
her guests went away from Windsor. But before long she and Albert paid a return visit to
France, where everything was very delightful, and
she drove incognito through the streets of Paris

[1] *Quarterly Review,* cxciii, 313–4; *Spinster Lady,* 7.

in a "common bonnet," and saw a play in the theatre at St. Cloud, and, one evening, at a great party given by the Emperor in her honour at the Château of Versailles, talked a little to a distinguished-looking Prussian gentleman, whose name was Bismarck. Her rooms were furnished so much to her taste that she declared they gave her quite a home feeling—that, if her little dog were there, she should really imagine herself at home. Nothing was said, but three days later her little dog barked a welcome to her as she entered the apartments. The Emperor himself, sparing neither trouble nor expense, had personally arranged the charming surprise.[1] Such were his attentions. She returned to England more enchanted than ever. "Strange indeed," she exclaimed, " are the dispensations and ways of Providence! "[2]

The alliance prospered, and the war drew towards a conclusion. Both the Queen and the Prince, it is true, were most anxious that there should not be a premature peace. When Lord Aberdeen wished to open negotiations Albert attacked him in a *" geharnischten "* letter, while Victoria rode about on horseback reviewing the troops. At last, however, Sebastopol was cap-

1 Crawford, 311-2.   2 Martin, III, 350.

tured. The news reached Balmoral late at night, and " in a few minutes Albert and all the gentle-men in every species of attire sallied forth, fol-lowed by all the servants, and gradually by all the population of the village—keepers, gillies, work-men—up to the top of the cairn." A bonfire was lighted, the pipes were played, and guns were shot off. " About three-quarters of an hour after Albert came down and said the scene had been wild and exciting beyond everything. The people had been drinking healths in whisky and were in great ecstasy." [1] The " great ecstasy," perhaps, would be replaced by other feelings next morning; but at any rate the war was over—though, to be sure, its end seemed as difficult to account for as its beginning. The dispensations and ways of Providence continued to be strange.

IV

An unexpected consequence of the war was a complete change in the relations between the royal pair and Palmerston. The Prince and the Minis-ter drew together over their hostility to Russia, and thus it came about that when Victoria found it necessary to summon her old enemy to form an administration she did so without reluctance. The

[1] *Leaves,* 105–6.

premiership, too, had a sobering effect upon Palmerston; he grew less impatient and dictatorial; considered with attention the suggestions of the Crown, and was, besides, genuinely impressed by the Prince's ability and knowledge.[1] Friction, no doubt, there still occasionally was, for, while the Queen and the Prince devoted themselves to foreign politics as much as ever, their views, when the war was over, became once more antagonistic to those of the Prime Minister. This was especially the case with regard to Italy. Albert, theoretically the friend of constitutional government, distrusted Cavour, was horrified by Garibaldi, and dreaded the danger of England being drawn into war with Austria. Palmerston, on the other hand, was eager for Italian independence; but he was no longer at the Foreign Office, and the brunt of the royal displeasure had now to be borne by Lord John Russell. In a few years the situation had curiously altered. It was Lord John who now filled the subordinate and the ungrateful rôle; but the Foreign Secretary, in his struggle with the Crown, was supported, instead of opposed, by the Prime Minister. Nevertheless the struggle was fierce, and the policy, by which the vigorous sympathy of England became one of the decisive fac-

[1] Martin, II, 429.

tors in the final achievement of Italian unity, was only carried through in face of the violent opposition of the Court.[1]

Towards the other European storm-centre, also, the Prince's attitude continued to be very different to that of Palmerston. Albert's great wish was for a united Germany under the leadership of a constitutional and virtuous Prussia; Palmerston did not think that there was much to be said for the scheme, but he took no particular interest in German politics, and was ready enough to agree to a proposal which was warmly supported by both the Prince and the Queen—that the royal Houses of England and Prussia should be united by the marriage of the Princess Royal with the Prussian Crown Prince. Accordingly, when the Princess was not yet fifteen, the Prince, a young man of twenty-four, came over on a visit to Balmoral, and the betrothal took place.[2] Two years later, in 1857, the marriage was celebrated. At the last moment, however, it seemed that there might be a hitch. It was pointed out in Prussia that it was customary for Princes of the blood royal to be married in Berlin, and it was suggested that there was no reason why the present case

[1] Letters, III, especially July-December, 1859; Martin, IV, 488–91; V, 189.
[2] Leaves, 107.

should be treated as an exception. When this reached the ears of Victoria, she was speechless with indignation. In a note, emphatic even for Her Majesty, she instructed the Foreign Secretary to tell the Prussian Ambassador "not to *entertain* the *possibility* of such a question. . . . The Queen *never* could consent to it, both for public and for private reasons, and the assumption of its being *too much* for a Prince Royal of Prussia to *come* over to marry *the Princess Royal of Great Britain in* England is too *absurd* to say the least. . . . Whatever may be the usual practice of Prussian princes, it is not *every* day that one marries the eldest daughter of the Queen of England. The question must therefore be considered as settled and closed."[1] It was, and the wedding took place in St. James's Chapel. There were great festivities—illuminations, state concerts, immense crowds, and general rejoicings. At Windsor a magnificent banquet was given to the bride and bridegroom in the Waterloo room, at which, Victoria noted in her diary, "everybody was most friendly and kind about Vicky and full of the universal enthusiasm, of which the Duke of Buccleuch gave us most pleasing instances, he having been in the very thick of the crowd and among the lowest of

[1] *Letters,* III, 253.

the low." Her feelings during several days had been growing more and more emotional, and when the time came for the young couple to depart she very nearly broke down—but not quite. " Poor dear child!" she wrote afterwards. "I clasped her in my arms and blessed her, and knew not what to say. I kissed good Fritz and pressed his hand again and again. He was unable to speak and the tears were in his eyes. I embraced them both again at the carriage door, and Albert got into the carriage, an open one, with them and Bertie. . . . The band struck up. I wished good-bye to the good Perponchers. General Schreckenstein was much affected. I pressed his hand, and the good Dean's, and then went quickly upstairs."[1]

Albert, as well as General Schreckenstein, was much affected. He was losing his favourite child, whose opening intelligence had already begun to display a marked resemblance to his own—an adoring pupil, who, in a few years, might have become an almost adequate companion. An ironic fate had determined that the daughter who was taken from him should be sympathetic, clever, interested in the arts and sciences, and endowed with a strong taste for memoranda, while not a single one of these qualities could be discovered in the

[1] Martin, IV, 160-9.

son who remained. For certainly the Prince of
Wales did not take after his father. Victoria's
prayer had been unanswered, and with each succeeding year it became more obvious that Bertie
was a true scion of the House of Brunswick. But
these evidences of innate characteristics only served
to redouble the efforts of his parents; it still might
not be too late to incline the young branch, by
ceaseless pressure and careful fastenings, to grow
in the proper direction. Everything was tried.
The boy was sent on a continental tour with a
picked body of tutors, but the results were unsatisfactory. At his father's request he kept a diary
which, on his return, was inspected by the Prince.
It was found to be distressingly meagre: what a
multitude of highly interesting reflections might
have been arranged under the heading: " The First
Prince of Wales visiting the Pope!" But there
was not a single one. " Le jeune prince plaisit à
tout le monde," old Metternich reported to Guizot,
" mais avait l'air embarrassé et très triste." On
his seventeenth birthday a memorandum was
drawn up over the names of the Queen and the
Prince informing their eldest son that he was
now entering upon the period of manhood, and
directing him henceforward to perform the duties
of a Christian gentleman. " Life is composed of

duties," said the memorandum, " and in the due, punctual and cheerful performance of them the true Christian, true soldier, and true gentleman is recognised. . . . A new sphere of life will open for you in which you will have to be taught what to do and what not to do, a subject requiring study more important than any in which you have hitherto been engaged." On receipt of the memorandum Bertie burst into tears. At the same time another memorandum was drawn up, headed " confidential: for the guidance of the gentlemen appointed to attend on the Prince of Wales." This long and elaborate document laid down " certain principles " by which the " conduct and demeanour " of the gentlemen were to be regulated " and which it is thought may conduce to the benefit of the Prince of Wales." " The qualities which distinguish a gentleman in society," continued this remarkable paper, " are:—

(1) His appearance, his deportment and dress.

(2) The character of his relations with, and treatment of, others.

(3) His desire and power to acquit himself creditably in conversation or whatever is the occupation of the society with which he mixes."

A minute and detailed analysis of these subheadings followed, filling several pages, and the

memorandum ended with a final exhortation to
the gentlemen: " If they will duly appreciate the
responsibility of their position, and taking the
points above laid down as the outline, will exercise their own good sense in acting *upon all occasions* upon these principles, thinking no point of
detail too minute to be important, but maintaining
one steady consistent line of conduct they may
render essential service to the young Prince and
justify the flattering selection made by the royal
parents." A year later the young Prince was sent
to Oxford, where the greatest care was taken that
he should not mix with the undergraduates. Yes,
everything had been tried—everything . . . with
one single exception. The experiment had never
been made of letting Bertie enjoy himself. But
why should it have been? " Life is composed of
duties." What possible place could there be for
enjoyment in the existence of a Prince of Wales? [1]

The same year which deprived Albert of the
Princess Royal brought him another and a still
more serious loss. The Baron had paid his last
visit to England. For twenty years, as he himself
said in a letter to the King of the Belgians, he had
performed " the laborious and exhausting office of

---

[1] *D.N.B.*, Second Supplement, 551; *Quarterly Review*, ccxiii,
9–20, 24; Greville, VIII, 217.

a paternal friend and trusted adviser " to the Prince and the Queen. He was seventy; he was tired, physically and mentally; it was time to go. He returned to his home in Coburg, exchanging, once for all, the momentous secrecies of European statecraft for the tittle-tattle of a provincial capital and the gossip of family life. In his stiff chair by the fire he nodded now over old stories—not of emperors and generals—but of neighbours and relatives and the domestic adventures of long ago —the burning of his father's library—and the goat that ran upstairs to his sister's room and ran twice round the table and then ran down again. Dyspepsia and depression still attacked him; but, looking back over his life, he was not dissatisfied. His conscience was clear. " I have worked as long as I had strength to work," he said, " and for a purpose no one can impugn. The consciousness of this is my reward—the only one which I desired to earn." [1]

Apparently, indeed, his " purpose " had been accomplished. By his wisdom, his patience, and his example he had brought about, in the fullness of time, the miraculous metamorphosis of which he had dreamed. The Prince was his creation. An indefatigable toiler, presiding, for the highest

---

[1] Stockmar, 4, 44.

ends, over a great nation—that was his achievement; and he looked upon his work and it was good. But had the Baron no misgivings? Did he never wonder whether, perhaps, he might have accomplished not too little but too much? How subtle and how dangerous are the snares which fate lays for the wariest of men! Albert, certainly, seemed to be everything that Stockmar could have wished—virtuous, industrious, persevering, intelligent. And yet—why was it?—all was not well with him. He was sick at heart.

For in spite of everything he had never reached to happiness. His work, for which at last he came to crave with an almost morbid appetite, was a solace and not a cure; the dragon of his dissatisfaction devoured with dark relish that ever-growing tribute of laborious days and nights; but it was hungry still. The causes of his melancholy were hidden, mysterious, unanalysable perhaps—too deeply rooted in the innermost recesses of his temperament for the eye of reason to apprehend. There were contradictions in his nature, which, to some of those who knew him best, made him seem an inexplicable enigma: he was severe and gentle; he was modest and scornful; he longed for affection and he was cold.[1] He was lonely, not merely

[1] Ernest, I, 140-1.

with the loneliness of exile but with the loneliness
of conscious and unrecognised superiority. He
had the pride, at once resigned and overweening,
of a doctrinaire. And yet to say that he was simply a doctrinaire would be a false description; for
the pure doctrinaire rejoices always in an internal
contentment, and Albert was very far from doing
that. There was something that he wanted and
that he could never get. What was it? Some absolute, some ineffable sympathy? Some extraordinary, some sublime success? Possibly, it was a
mixture of both. To dominate and to be understood! To conquer, by the same triumphant influence, the submission and the appreciation of men—
that would be worth while indeed! But, to such
imaginations, he saw too clearly how faint were
the responses of his actual environment. Who
was there who appreciated him, really and truly?
Who *could* appreciate him in England? And, if
the gentle virtue of an inward excellence availed
so little, could he expect more from the hard ways
of skill and force? The terrible land of his exile
loomed before him a frigid, an impregnable mass.
Doubtless he had made some slight impression:
it was true that he had gained the respect of his
fellow workers, that his probity, his industry, his
exactitude, had been recognised, that he was a

highly influential, an extremely important man. But how far, how very far, was all this from the goal of his ambitions! How feeble and futile his efforts seemed against the enormous coagulation of dullness, of folly, of slackness, of ignorance, of confusion that confronted him! He might have the strength or the ingenuity to make some small change for the better here or there—to rearrange some detail, to abolish some anomaly, to insist upon some obvious reform; but the heart of the appalling organism remained untouched. England lumbered on, impervious and self-satisfied, in her old intolerable course. He threw himself across the path of the monster with rigid purpose and set teeth, but he was brushed aside. Yes! even Palmerston was still unconquered—was still there to afflict him with his jauntiness, his muddle-headedness, his utter lack of principle. It was too much. Neither nature nor the Baron had given him a sanguine spirit; the seeds of pessimism, once lodged within him, flourished in a propitious soil. He

> "questioned things, and did not find
> One that would answer to his mind;
> And all the world appeared unkind."

He believed that he was a failure and he began to despair.

Yet Stockmar had told him that he must " never relax," and he never would. He would go on, working to the utmost and striving for the highest, to the bitter end. His industry grew almost maniacal. Earlier and earlier was the green lamp lighted; more vast grew the correspondence; more searching the examination of the newspapers; the interminable memoranda more punctilious, analytical, and precise. His very recreations became duties. He enjoyed himself by time-table, went deer-stalking with meticulous gusto, and made puns at lunch—it was the right thing to do. The mechanism worked with astonishing efficiency, but it never rested and it was never oiled. In dry exactitude the innumerable cog-wheels perpetually revolved. No, whatever happened, the Prince would not relax; he had absorbed the doctrines of Stockmar too thoroughly. He knew what was right, and, at all costs, he would pursue it. That was certain. But alas! in this our life what are the certainties? " In nothing be over-zealous! " says an old Greek. " The due measure in all the works of man is best. For often one who zealously pushes towards some excellence, though he be pursuing a gain, is really being led utterly astray by the will of some Power, which makes those things that are evil seem to him good, and those things seem to him evil that are for his advantage." [1]   Surely, both the Prince and the Baron might have learnt something from the frigid wisdom of Theognis.

Victoria noticed that her husband sometimes seemed to be depressed and overworked. She tried to cheer him up. Realising uneasily that he was still regarded as a foreigner, she hoped that by conferring upon him the title of Prince Consort (1857) she would improve his position in the country. "The Queen has a right to claim that her husband should be an Englishman," she wrote. [2] But unfortunately, in spite of the Royal Letters Patent, Albert remained as foreign as before; and as the years passed his dejection deepened. She worked with him, she watched over him, she walked with him through the woods at Osborne, while he whistled to the nightingales, as he had whistled once at Rosenau so long ago. [3] When his birthday came round, she took the greatest pains to choose him presents that he would really like. In 1858, when he was thirty-nine, she gave him " a picture of Beatrice, life-size, in oil, by Horsley, a complete collection of photographic views of Gotha and the country round, which I had taken by Bedford, and a paper-weight of Balmoral granite and

[1] *Theognis*, 401 ff.   [2] *Letters*, III, 194.   [3] Grey, 195*n*.

deers' teeth, designed by Vicky." [1] Albert was of course delighted, and his merriment at the family gathering was more pronounced than ever: and yet . . . what was there that was wrong?

No doubt it was his health. He was wearing himself out in the service of the country; and certainly his constitution, as Stockmar had perceived from the first, was ill-adapted to meet a serious strain. He was easily upset; he constantly suffered from minor ailments. His appearance in itself was enough to indicate the infirmity of his physical powers. The handsome youth of twenty years since with the flashing eyes and the soft complexion had grown into a sallow, tired-looking man, whose body, in its stoop and its loose fleshiness, betrayed the sedentary labourer, and whose head was quite bald on the top. Unkind critics, who had once compared Albert to an operatic tenor, might have remarked that there was something of the butler about him now. Beside Victoria, he presented a painful contrast. She, too, was stout, but it was with the plumpness of a vigorous matron; and an eager vitality was everywhere visible—in her energetic bearing, her protruding, enquiring glances, her small, fat, capable, and commanding hands. If only, by some sympa-

[1] Martin, IV, 298.

thetic magic, she could have conveyed into that portly, flabby figure, that desiccated and discouraged brain, a measure of the stamina and the self-assurance which were so pre-eminently hers!

But suddenly she was reminded that there were other perils besides those of ill-health. During a visit to Coburg in 1860, the Prince was very nearly killed in a carriage accident. He escaped with a few cuts and bruises; but Victoria's alarm was extreme, though she concealed it. " It is when the Queen feels most deeply," she wrote afterwards, " that she always appears calmest, and she could not and dared not allow herself to speak of what might have been, or even to admit to herself (and she cannot and dare not now) the entire danger, for her head would turn! " Her agitation, in fact, was only surpassed by her thankfulness to God. She felt, she said, that she could not rest " without doing something to mark permanently her feelings," and she decided that she would endow a charity in Coburg. " £1,000, or even £2,000, given either at once, or in instalments yearly, would not, in the Queen's opinion, be too much." Eventually, the smaller sum having been fixed upon, it was invested in a trust, called the " Victoria-Stift," in the name of the Burgomaster and chief clergyman of Coburg, who were directed to distribute the interest yearly among a certain number of young men and women of exemplary character belonging to the humbler ranks of life.[1]

Shortly afterwards the Queen underwent, for the first time in her life, the actual experience of close personal loss. Early in 1861 the Duchess of Kent was taken seriously ill, and in March she died. The event overwhelmed Victoria. With a morbid intensity, she filled her diary for pages with minute descriptions of her mother's last hours, her dissolution, and her corpse, interspersed with vehement apostrophes, and the agitated outpourings of emotional reflection. In the grief of the present the disagreements of the past were totally forgotten. It was the horror and the mystery of Death—Death, present and actual—that seized upon the imagination of the Queen. Her whole being, so instinct with vitality, recoiled in agony from the grim spectacle of the triumph of that awful power. Her own mother, with whom she had lived so closely and so long that she had become a part almost of her existence, had fallen into nothingness before her very eyes! She tried to forget, but she could not. Her lamentations continued with a strange abundance, a strange persistency. It was almost as if, by some mysterious

[1] Martin, V, 202-4, 217-9.

and unconscious precognition, she realised that
for her, in an especial manner, that grisly Majesty
had a dreadful dart in store.

For indeed, before the year was out, a far more
terrible blow was to fall upon her. Albert, who
had for long been suffering from sleeplessness,
went, on a cold and drenching day towards the end
of November, to inspect the buildings for the new
Military Academy at Sandhurst. On his return,
it was clear that the fatigue and exposure to which
he had been subjected had seriously affected his
health. He was attacked by rheumatism, his sleeplessness continued, and he complained that he felt
thoroughly unwell. Three days later a painful
duty obliged him to visit Cambridge. The Prince
of Wales, who had been placed at that University
in the previous year, was behaving in such a manner that a parental visit and a parental admonition
had become necessary. The disappointed father,
suffering in mind and body, carried through his
task; but, on his return journey to Windsor, he
caught a fatal chill.[1] During the next week he
gradually grew weaker and more miserable. Yet,
depressed and enfeebled as he was, he continued
to work. It so happened that at that very moment a grave diplomatic crisis had arisen. Civil

[1] *D.N.B.*, Second Supplement, 557.

war had broken out in America, and it seemed as if England, owing to a violent quarrel with the Northern States, was upon the point of being drawn into the conflict. A severe despatch by Lord John Russell was submitted to the Queen; and the Prince perceived that, if it was sent off unaltered, war would be the almost inevitable consequence. At seven o'clock on the morning of December 1, he rose from his bed, and with a quavering hand wrote a series of suggestions for the alteration of the draft, by which its language might be softened, and a way left open for a peaceful solution of the question. These changes were accepted by the Government, and war was averted. It was the Prince's last memorandum.[1]

He had always declared that he viewed the prospect of death with equanimity. " I do not cling to life," he had once said to Victoria. " You do; but I set no store by it." And then he had added: " I am sure, if I had a severe illness, I should give up at once, I should not struggle for life. I have no tenacity of life." [2]   He had judged correctly. Before he had been ill many days, he told a friend that he was convinced he would not recover.[3]   He sank and sank. Nevertheless, if his case had been

1 Martin, V, 416–27.   2 Martin, V, 415.
3 Bloomfield, II, 155.

properly understood and skilfully treated from the
first, he might conceivably have been saved; but
the doctors failed to diagnose his symptoms; and
it is noteworthy that his principal physician was
Sir James Clark. When it was suggested that
other advice should be taken, Sir James pooh-
poohed the idea: " there was no cause for alarm,"
he said. But the strange illness grew worse. At
last, after a letter of fierce remonstrance from
Palmerston, Dr. Watson was sent for; and Dr.
Watson saw at once that he had come too late.
The Prince was in the grip of typhoid fever. " I
think that everything so far is satisfactory," said
Sir James Clark.[1]

The restlessness and the acute suffering of the
earlier days gave place to a settled torpor and an
ever-deepening gloom. Once the failing patient
asked for music—" a fine chorale at a distance ";
and a piano having been placed in the adjoining
room, Princess Alice played on it some of
Luther's hymns, after which the Prince repeated
" The Rock of Ages." Sometimes his mind wandered; sometimes the distant past came rushing

[1] Martin, V, 427–35; Clarendon, II, 253–4: "One cannot speak
with certainty; but it is horrible to think that such a life *may* have
been sacrificed to Sir J. Clark's selfish jealousy of every member
of his profession."—The Earl of Clarendon to the Duchess of
Manchester, December 17, 1861.

upon him; he heard the birds in the early morning, and was at Rosenau again, a boy. Or Victoria would come and read to him " Peveril of
the Peak," and he showed that he could follow
the story, and then she would bend over him, and
he would murmur " liebes Frauchen " and " gutes
Weibchen," stroking her cheek. Her distress and
her agitation were great, but she was not seriously
frightened. Buoyed up by her own abundant
energies, she would not believe that Albert's might
prove unequal to the strain. She refused to face
such a hideous possibility. She declined to see Dr.
Watson. Why should she? Had not Sir James
Clark assured her that all would be well? Only
two days before the end, which was seen now to
be almost inevitable by everyone about her, she
wrote, full of apparent confidence, to the King of
the Belgians: " I do not sit up with him at night,"
she said, " as I could be of no use; and there is
nothing to cause alarm." [1] The Princess Alice
tried to tell her the truth, but her hopefulness
would not be daunted. On the morning of December 14, Albert, just as she had expected,
seemed to be better; perhaps the crisis was
over. But in the course of the day there was
a serious relapse. Then at last she allowed her-

[1] *Letters*, III, 472–3.

self to see that she was standing on the edge of an appalling gulf. The whole family was summoned, and, one after another, the children took a silent farewell of their father. " It was a terrible moment," Victoria wrote in her diary, " but, thank God! I was able to command myself, and to be perfectly calm, and remained sitting by his side." He murmured something, but she could not hear what it was; she thought he was speaking in French. Then all at once he began to arrange his hair, " just as he used to do when well and he was dressing." " Es ist kleines Fräuchen," she whispered to him; and he seemed to understand. For a moment, towards the evening, she went into another room, but was immediately called back; she saw at a glance that a ghastly change had taken place. As she knelt by the bed, he breathed deeply, breathed gently, breathed at last no more. His features became perfectly rigid; she shrieked one long wild shriek that rang through the terror-stricken castle—and understood that she had lost him for ever.[1]

[1] Martin, V, 435–42; Hare, II, 286–8; *Spinster Lady*, 176–7.

CHAPTER VII

WIDOWHOOD

I

The death of the Prince Consort was the central turning-point in the history of Queen Victoria. She herself felt that her true life had ceased with her husband's, and that the remainder of her days upon earth was of a twilight nature—an epilogue to a drama that was done. Nor is it possible that her biographer should escape a similar impression. For him, too, there is a darkness over the latter half of that long career. The first forty-two years of the Queen's life are illuminated by a great and varied quantity of authentic information. With Albert's death a veil descends. Only occasionally, at fitful and disconnected intervals, does it lift for a moment or two; a few main outlines, a few remarkable details may be discerned; the rest is all conjecture and ambiguity. Thus, though the Queen survived her great bereavement for almost as many years as she had lived before it, the chronicle of those years can bear no proportion to the tale of her earlier life. We must be content in our ignorance with a brief and summary relation.

The sudden removal of the Prince was not merely a matter of overwhelming personal concern to Victoria; it was an event of national, of European importance. He was only forty-two, and in the ordinary course of nature he might have been expected to live at least thirty years longer. Had he done so it can hardly be doubted that the whole development of the English polity would have been changed. Already at the time of his death he filled a unique place in English public life; already among the inner circle of politicians he was accepted as a necessary and useful part of the mechanism of the State. Lord Clarendon, for instance, spoke of his death as " a national calamity of far greater importance than the public dream of," and lamented the loss of his " sagacity and foresight," which, he declared, would have been " more than ever valuable " in the event of an American war.[1] And, as time went on, the Prince's influence must have enormously increased. For, in addition to his intellectual and moral qualities, he enjoyed, by virtue of his position, one supreme advantage which every other holder of high office in the country was without: he was permanent.

[1] Clarendon, II, 251.

QUEEN VICTORIA IN 1863.

Politicians came and went, but the Prince was perpetually installed at the centre of affairs. Who can doubt that, towards the end of the century, such a man, grown grey in the service of the nation, virtuous, intelligent, and with the unexampled experience of a whole life-time of government, would have acquired an extraordinary prestige? If, in his youth, he had been able to pit the Crown against the mighty Palmerston and to come off with equal honours from the contest, of what might he not have been capable in his old age? What Minister, however able, however popular, could have withstood the wisdom, the irreproachability, the vast prescriptive authority, of the venerable Prince? It is easy to imagine how, under such a ruler, an attempt might have been made to convert England into a State as exactly organised, as elaborately trained, as efficiently equipped, and as autocratically controlled, as Prussia herself. Then perhaps, eventually, under some powerful leader—a Gladstone or a Bright—the democratic forces in the country might have rallied together, and a struggle might have followed in which the Monarchy would have been shaken to its foundations. Or, on the other hand, Disraeli's hypothetical prophecy might have come true. "With Prince Albert," he said, "we have buried our sovereign. This German Prince has governed England for twenty-one years with a wisdom and energy such as none of our kings have ever shown. . . . If he had outlived some of our " old stagers " he would have given us the blessings of absolute government." [1]

The English Constitution—that indescribable entity—is a living thing, growing with the growth of men, and assuming ever-varying forms in accordance with the subtle and complex laws of human character. It is the child of wisdom and chance. The wise men of 1688 moulded it into the shape we know; but the chance that George I could not speak English gave it one of its essential peculiarities—the system of a Cabinet independent of the Crown and subordinate to the Prime Minister. The wisdom of Lord Grey saved it from petrifaction and destruction, and set it upon the path of Democracy. Then chance intervened once more; a female sovereign happened to marry an able and pertinacious man; and it seemed likely that an element which had been quiescent within it for years—the element of irresponsible administrative power—was about to become its predominant characteristic and to change completely the direction of its growth. But what

[1] Vitzthum, II, 161.

chance gave chance took away. The Consort perished in his prime; and the English Constitution, dropping the dead limb with hardly a tremor, continued its mysterious life as if he had never been.

One human being, and one alone, felt the full force of what had happened. The Baron, by his fireside at Coburg, suddenly saw the tremendous fabric of his creation crash down into sheer and irremediable ruin. Albert was gone, and he had lived in vain. Even his blackest hypochondria had never envisioned quite so miserable a catastrophe. Victoria wrote to him, visited him, tried to console him by declaring with passionate conviction that she would carry on her husband's work. He smiled a sad smile and looked into the fire. Then he murmured that he was going where Albert was— that he would not be long.[1] He shrank into himself. His children clustered round him and did their best to comfort him, but it was useless: the Baron's heart was broken. He lingered for eighteen months, and then, with his pupil, explored the shadow and the dust.

II

With appalling suddenness Victoria had exchanged the serene radiance of happiness for the

[1] Stockmar, 49; Ernest, IV, 71.

utter darkness of woe. In the first dreadful moments those about her had feared that she might lose her reason, but the iron strain within her held firm, and in the intervals between the intense paroxysms of grief it was observed that the Queen was calm. She remembered, too, that Albert had always disapproved of exaggerated manifestations of feeling, and her one remaining desire was to do nothing but what he would have wished. Yet there were moments when her royal anguish would brook no restraints. One day she sent for the Duchess of Sutherland, and, leading her to the Prince's room, fell prostrate before his clothes in a flood of weeping, while she adjured the Duchess to tell her whether the beauty of Albert's character had ever been surpassed.[1] At other times a feeling akin to indignation swept over her. " The poor fatherless baby of eight months," she wrote to the King of the Belgians, " is now the utterly heartbroken and crushed widow of forty-two! My *life* as a *happy* one is *ended!* The world is gone for *me!* . . . Oh! to be cut off in the prime of life— to see our pure, happy, quiet, domestic life, which *alone* enabled me to bear my *much* disliked position, CUT OFF at forty-two—when I *had* hoped with such instinctive certainty that God never

---

[1] Clarendon, II, 251, 253.

would part us, and would let us grow old together (though *he* always talked of the shortness of life) —is *too awful,* too cruel! " [1] The tone of outraged Majesty seems to be discernible. Did she wonder in her heart of hearts how the Deity could have dared?

But all other emotions gave way before her overmastering determination to continue, absolutely unchanged, and for the rest of her life on earth, her reverence, her obedience, her idolatry. " I am anxious to repeat *one* thing," she told her uncle, " and *that one* is *my firm* resolve, *my irrevocable decision,* viz., that *his* wishes—*his* plans— about everything, *his* views about *every* thing are to be *my law!* And *no human power* will make me swerve from *what he* decided and wished." She grew fierce, she grew furious, at the thought of any possible intrusion between her and her desire. Her uncle was coming to visit her, and it flashed upon her that *he* might try to interfere with her and seek to " rule the roast " as of old. She would give him a hint. " I am *also determined,"* she wrote, " that *no one* person— may *he* be ever so good, ever so devoted among my servants—is to lead or guide or dictate *to me.* I know *how he* would disapprove it . . . Though

[1] *Letters,* III, 474–5.

miserably weak and utterly shattered, my spirit rises when I think *any* wish or plan of his is to be touched or changed, or I am to be *made to do* anything." She ended her letter in grief and affection. She was, she said, his " ever wretched but devoted child, Victoria R." And then she looked at the date: it was the 24th of December. An agonising pang assailed her, and she dashed down a postcript.—" What a Xmas! I won't think of it." [1]

At first, in the tumult of her distresses, she declared that she could not see her Ministers, and the Princess Alice, assisted by Sir Charles Phipps, the keeper of the Privy Purse, performed, to the best of her ability, the functions of an intermediary. After a few weeks, however, the Cabinet, through Lord John Russell, ventured to warn the Queen that this could not continue. [2] She realised that they were right: Albert would have agreed with them; and so she sent for the Prime Minister. But when Lord Palmerston arrived at Osborne, in the pink of health, brisk, with his whiskers freshly dyed, and dressed in a brown overcoat, light grey trousers, green gloves, and blue studs, he did not create a very good impression. [3]

[1] *Letters,* III, 476.　　　　[2] Lee, 322–3; Crawford, 368.
[3] Clarendon, II, 257.

Nevertheless, she had grown attached to her old enemy, and the thought of a political change filled her with agitated apprehensions. The Government, she knew, might fall at any moment; she felt she could not face such an eventuality; and therefore, six months after the death of the Prince, she took the unprecedented step of sending a private message to Lord Derby, the leader of the Opposition, to tell him that she was not in a fit state of mind or body to undergo the anxiety of a change of Government, and that if he turned the present Ministers out of office it would be at the risk of sacrificing her life—or her reason. When this message reached Lord Derby he was considerably surprised. " Dear me! " was his cynical comment. " I didn't think she was so fond of them as *that.*" [1]

Though the violence of her perturbations gradually subsided, her cheerfulness did not return. For months, for years, she continued in settled gloom. Her life became one of almost complete seclusion. Arrayed in thickest *crêpe,* she passed dolefully from Windsor to Osborne, from Osborne to Balmoral. Rarely visiting the capital, refusing to take any part in the ceremonies of state, shutting herself off from the slightest intercourse with

[1] Clarendon, II, 261–2.

society, she became almost as unknown to her subjects as some potentate of the East. They might murmur, but they did not understand. What had she to do with empty shows and vain enjoyments? No! She was absorbed by very different preoccupations. She was the devoted guardian of a sacred trust. Her place was in the inmost shrine of the house of mourning—where she alone had the right to enter, where she could feel the effluence of a mysterious presence, and interpret, however faintly and feebly, the promptings of a still living soul. That, and that only was her glorious, her terrible duty. For terrible indeed it was. As the years passed her depression seemed to deepen and her loneliness to grow more intense. "I am on a dreary sad pinnacle of solitary grandeur," she said.[1] Again and again she felt that she could bear her situation no longer—that she would sink under the strain. And then, instantly, that Voice spoke: and she braced herself once more to perform, with minute conscientiousness, her grim and holy task.

Above all else, what she had to do was to make her own the master-impulse of Albert's life—she must work, as he had worked, in the service of the country. That vast burden of toil which he

[1] Martin, *Queen Victoria*, 155.

had taken upon his shoulders it was now for her
to bear. She assumed the gigantic load; and naturally she staggered under it. While he had lived,
she had worked, indeed, with regularity and conscientiousness; but it was work made easy, made
delicious, by his care, his forethought, his advice,
and his infallibility. The mere sound of his voice,
asking her to sign a paper, had thrilled her; in
such a presence she could have laboured gladly for
ever. But now there was a hideous change. Now
there were no neat piles and docketings under the
green lamp; now there were no simple explanations of difficult matters; now there was nobody
to tell her what was right and what was wrong.
She had her secretaries, no doubt: there were Sir
Charles Phipps, and General Grey, and Sir
Thomas Biddulph; and they did their best. But
they were mere subordinates: the whole weight of
initiative and responsibility rested upon her alone.
For so it had to be. "I am *determined*"—had
she not declared it?—"that *no one* person is to
lead or guide or dictate to *me*"; anything else
would be a betrayal of her trust. She would follow the Prince in all things. He had refused to
delegate authority; he had examined into every
detail with his own eyes; he had made it a rule
never to sign a paper without having first, not

merely read it, but made notes on it too. She would do the same. She sat from morning till night surrounded by huge heaps of despatch-boxes, reading and writing at her desk—at her desk, alas! which stood alone now in the room.[1]

Within two years of Albert's death a violent disturbance in foreign politics put Victoria's faithfulness to a crucial test. The fearful Schleswig-Holstein dispute, which had been smouldering for more than a decade, showed signs of bursting out into conflagration. The complexity of the questions at issue was indescribable. "Only three people," said Palmerston, "have ever really understood the Schleswig-Holstein business—the Prince Consort, who is dead—a German professor, who has gone mad—and I, who have forgotten all about it."[2] But, though the Prince might be dead, had he not left a vicegerent behind him? Victoria threw herself into the seething embroilment with the vigour of inspiration. She devoted hours daily to the study of the affair in all its windings; but she had a clue through the labyrinth: whenever the question had been discussed, Albert, she recollected it perfectly, had always taken the side of Prussia. Her course was clear. She became an ardent cham-

---

[1] Clarendon, II, 261; Lee, 327; Martin, *Queen Victoria*, 30.
[2] Grant Robertson, *Bismarck*, 156.

pion of the Prussian point of view. It was a legacy from the Prince, she said.[1] She did not realise
that the Prussia of the Prince's day was dead, and
that a new Prussia, the Prussia of Bismarck, was
born. Perhaps Palmerston, with his queer prescience, instinctively apprehended the new danger;
at any rate, he and Lord John were agreed upon
the necessity of supporting Denmark against Prussia's claims. But opinion was sharply divided, not
only in the country but in the Cabinet. For eighteen months the controversy raged; while the
Queen, with persistent vehemence, opposed the
Prime Minister and the Foreign Secretary. When
at last the final crisis arose—when it seemed possible that England would join forces with Denmark in a war against Prussia—Victoria's agitation grew febrile in its intensity. Towards her
German relatives she preserved a discreet appearance of impartiality; but she poured out upon her
Ministers a flood of appeals, protests, and expos-
tulations. She invoked the sacred cause of Peace.
" The only chance of preserving peace for Europe," she wrote, " is by not assisting Denmark,
who has brought this entirely upon herself. . . .

[1] Morley, II, 102; Ernest, IV, 133: " I know that our dear angel
Albert, always regarded a strong Prussia as a necessity, for which,
therefore, it is a sacred duty for *me* to work."—Queen Victoria
to the Duke of Saxe-Coburg-Gotha, August 29, 1863.

The Queen suffers much, and her nerves are more and more totally shattered. . . . But though all this anxiety is wearing her out, it will not shake her firm purpose of resisting any attempt to involve this country in a mad and useless combat." She was, she declared, " prepared to make a stand," even if the resignation of the Foreign Secretary should follow.[1]   " The Queen," she told Lord Granville, " is completely exhausted by the anxiety and suspense, and misses her beloved husband's help, advice, support, and love in an overwhelming manner." She was so worn out by her efforts for peace that she could " hardly hold up her head or hold her pen." [2]   England did not go to war, and Denmark was left to her fate; but how far the attitude of the Queen contributed to this result it is impossible, with our present knowledge, to say. On the whole, however, it seems probable that the determining factor in the situation was the powerful peace party in the Cabinet rather than the imperious and pathetic pressure of Victoria.

It is, at any rate, certain that the Queen's enthusiasm for the sacred cause of peace was shortlived. Within a few months her mind had completely altered. Her eyes were opened to the true

[1] Fitzmaurice, I, 459, 460.   [2] *Ibid.*, I, 472-3.

nature of Prussia, whose designs upon Austria were about to culminate in the Seven Weeks' War. Veering precipitately from one extreme to the other, she now urged her Ministers to interfere by force of arms in support of Austria. But she urged in vain.[1]

Her political activity, no more than her social seclusion, was approved by the public. As the years passed, and the royal mourning remained as unrelieved as ever, the animadversions grew more general and more severe. It was observed that the Queen's protracted privacy not only cast a gloom over high society, not only deprived the populace of its pageantry, but also exercised a highly deleterious effect upon the dressmaking, millinery, and hosiery trades. This latter consideration carried great weight. At last, early in 1864, the rumour spread that Her Majesty was about to go out of mourning, and there was much rejoicing in the newspapers; but unfortunately it turned out that the rumour was quite without foundation. Victoria, with her own hand, wrote a letter to *The Times* to say so. " This idea," she declared, " cannot be too explicitly contradicted. " The Queen," the letter continued, " heartily appreciates the desire of her subjects to see her, and

[1] Clarendon, II, 310–1.

whatever she *can* do to gratify them in this loyal and affectionate wish, she *will* do. . . . But there are other and higher duties than those of mere representation which are now thrown upon the Queen, alone and unassisted—duties which she cannot neglect without injury to the public service, which weigh unceasingly upon her, overwhelming her with work and anxiety." [1] The justification might have been considered more cogent had it not been known that those " other and higher duties " emphasised by the Queen consisted for the most part of an attempt to counteract the foreign policy of Lord Palmerston and Lord John Russell. A large section—perhaps a majority—of the nation were violent partisans of Denmark in the Schleswig-Holstein quarrel; and Victoria's support of Prussia was widely denounced. A wave of unpopularity, which reminded old observers of the period preceding the Queen's marriage more than twenty-five years before, was beginning to rise. The press was rude; Lord Ellenborough attacked the Queen in the House of Lords; there were curious whispers in high quarters that she had had thoughts of abdicating—whispers followed by regrets that she had not done so. [2] Victoria, out-

[1] *The Times,* April 6, 1864; Clarendon, II, 290.
[2] Clarendon, II, 292–3.

raged and injured, felt that she was misunderstood. She was profoundly unhappy. After Lord
Ellenborough's speech, General Grey declared
that he "had never seen the Queen so completely
upset." "Oh, how fearful it is," she herself wrote
to Lord Granville, "to be suspected—uncheered—
unguided and unadvised—and how alone the poor
Queen feels!" [1] Nevertheless, suffer as she might,
she was as resolute as ever; she would not move by
a hair's breadth from the course that a supreme
obligation marked out for her; she would be faithful to the end.

And so, when Schleswig-Holstein was forgotten, and even the image of the Prince had begun
to grow dim in the fickle memories of men, the
solitary watcher remained immutably concentrated
at her peculiar task. The world's hostility, steadily
increasing, was confronted and outfaced by the impenetrable weeds of Victoria. Would the world
never understand? It was not mere sorrow that
kept her so strangely sequestered; it was devotion,
it was self-immolation; it was the laborious legacy
of love. Unceasingly the pen moved over the
black-edged paper. The flesh might be weak, but
that vast burden must be borne. And fortunately,
if the world would not understand, there were

[1] Fitzmaurice, I, 466, 469.

faithful friends who did. There was Lord Granville, and there was kind Mr. Theodore Martin. Perhaps Mr. Martin, who was so clever, would find means to make people realise the facts. She would send him a letter, pointing out her arduous labours and the difficulties under which she struggled, and then he might write an article for one of the magazines. It is not, she told him in 1863, " the Queen's *sorrow* that keeps her secluded. . . . It is her *overwhelming work* and her health, which is greatly shaken by her sorrow, and the totally overwhelming amount of work and responsibility—work which she feels really wears her out. Alice Helps was wonderfully struck at the Queen's room; and if Mrs. Martin will look at it, she can tell Mr. Martin what surrounds her. From the hour she gets out of bed till she gets into it again there is work, work, work,—letter-boxes, questions, &c., which are dreadfully exhausting—and if she had not comparative rest and quiet in the evening she would most likely not be *alive*. Her brain is constantly overtaxed." [1] It was too true.

III

To carry on Albert's work—that was her first duty; but there was another, second only to that,

[1] Martin, *Queen Victoria*, 28–9.

and yet nearer, if possible, to her heart—to impress
the true nature of his genius and character upon
the minds of her subjects. She realised that during his life he had not been properly appreciated;
the full extent of his powers, the supreme quality
of his goodness, had been necessarily concealed;
but death had removed the need of barriers, and
now her husband, in his magnificent entirety,
should stand revealed to all. She set to work
methodically. She directed Sir Arthur Helps to
bring out a collection of the Prince's speeches and
addresses, and the weighty tome appeared in 1862.
Then she commanded General Grey to write an
account of the Prince's early years—from his birth
to his marriage; she herself laid down the design
of the book, contributed a number of confidential
documents, and added numerous notes; General
Grey obeyed, and the work was completed in 1866.
But the principal part of the story was still untold,
and Mr. Martin was forthwith instructed to write
a complete biography of the Prince Consort. Mr.
Martin laboured for fourteen years. The mass
of material with which he had to deal was almost
incredible, but he was extremely industrious, and
he enjoyed throughout the gracious assistance of
Her Majesty. The first bulky volume was published in 1874; four others slowly followed; so

that it was not until 1880 that the monumental work was finished.[1]

Mr. Martin was rewarded by a knighthood; and yet it was sadly evident that neither Sir Theodore nor his predecessors had achieved the purpose which the Queen had in view. Perhaps she was unfortunate in her coadjutors, but, in reality, the responsibility for the failure must lie with Victoria herself. Sir Theodore and the others faithfully carried out the task which she had set them—faithfully put before the public the very image of Albert that filled her own mind. The fatal drawback was that the public did not find that image attractive. Victoria's emotional nature, far more remarkable for vigour than for subtlety, rejecting utterly the qualifications which perspicuity, or humour, might suggest, could be satisfied with nothing but the absolute and the categorical. When she disliked she did so with an unequivocal emphasis which swept the object of her repugnance at once and finally outside the pale of consideration; and her feelings of affection were equally unmitigated. In the case of Albert her passion for superlatives reached its height. To have conceived of him as anything short of perfect—perfect in virtue, in wisdom, in beauty, in all the glories and

[1] Martin, *Queen Victoria*, 97–106.

graces of man—would have been an unthinkable blasphemy: perfect he was, and perfect he must be shown to have been. And so, Sir Arthur, Sir Theodore, and the General painted him. In the circumstances, and under such supervision, to have done anything else would have required talents considerably more distinguished than any that those gentlemen possessed. But that was not all. By a curious mischance Victoria was also able to press into her service another writer, the distinction of whose talents was this time beyond a doubt. The Poet Laureate, adopting, either from complaisance or conviction, the tone of his sovereign, joined in the chorus, and endowed the royal formula with the magical resonance of verse. This settled the matter. Henceforward it was impossible to forget that Albert had worn the white flower of a blameless life.

The result was doubly unfortunate. Victoria, disappointed and chagrined, bore a grudge against her people for their refusal, in spite of all her efforts, to rate her husband at his true worth. She did not understand that the picture of an embodied perfection is distasteful to the majority of mankind. The cause of this is not so much an envy of the perfect being as a suspicion that he must be inhuman; and thus it happened that the public, when it saw displayed for its admiration a figure resembling the sugary hero of a moral story-book rather than a fellow man of flesh and blood, turned away with a shrug, a smile, and a flippant ejaculation. But in this the public was the loser as well as Victoria. For in truth Albert was a far more interesting personage than the public dreamed. By a curious irony an impeccable waxwork had been fixed by the Queen's love in the popular imagination, while the creature whom it represented—the real creature, so full of energy and stress and torment, so mysterious and so unhappy, and so fallible and so very human—had altogether disappeared.

IV

Words and books may be ambiguous memorials; but who can misinterpret the visible solidity of bronze and stone? At Frogmore, near Windsor, where her mother was buried, Victoria constructed, at the cost of £200,000, a vast and elaborate mausoleum for herself and her husband.[1] But that was a private and domestic monument, and the Queen desired that wherever her subjects might be gathered together they should be reminded of the Prince. Her desire was gratified;

[1] Lee, 390.

all over the country—at Aberdeen, at Perth, and
at Wolverhampton—statues of the Prince were
erected; and the Queen, making an exception to
her rule of retirement, unveiled them herself. Nor
did the capital lag behind. A month after the
Prince's death a meeting was called together at
the Mansion House to discuss schemes for honour-
ing his memory. Opinions, however, were divided
upon the subject. Was a statue or an institution
to be preferred? Meanwhile a subscription was
opened; an influential committee was appointed,
and the Queen was consulted as to her wishes in
the matter. Her Majesty replied that she would
prefer a granite obelisk, with sculptures at the
base, to an institution. But the committee hesi-
tated: an obelisk, to be worthy of the name, must
clearly be a monolith; and where was the quarry
in England capable of furnishing a granite block
of the required size? It was true that there was
granite in Russian Finland; but the committee
were advised that it was not adapted to resist exposure to the open air. On the whole, therefore,
they suggested that a Memorial Hall should be
erected, together with a statue of the Prince. Her
Majesty assented; but then another difficulty arose.
It was found that not more than £60,000 had been
subscribed—a sum insufficient to defray the dou-

ble expense. The Hall, therefore, was abandoned; a statue alone was to be erected; and certain eminent architects were asked to prepare designs. Eventually the committee had at their disposal a total sum of £120,000, since the public subscribed another £10,000, while £50,000 was voted by Parliament. Some years later a joint stock company was formed and built, as a private speculation, the Albert Hall.[1]

The architect whose design was selected, both by the committee and by the Queen, was Mr. Gilbert Scott, whose industry, conscientiousness, and genuine piety had brought him to the head of his profession. His lifelong zeal for the Gothic style having given him a special prominence, his handiwork was strikingly visible, not only in a multitude of original buildings, but in most of the cathedrals of England. Protests, indeed, were occasionally raised against his renovations; but Mr. Scott replied with such vigour and unction in articles and pamphlets that not a Dean was unconvinced, and he was permitted to continue his labours without interruption. On one occasion, however, his devotion to Gothic had placed him in an unpleasant situation. The Government offices in Whitehall were to be rebuilt; Mr. Scott com-

[1] *National Memorial.*

peted, and his designs were successful. Naturally, they were in the Gothic style, combining " a certain squareness and horizontality of outline " with pillar-mullions, gables, high-pitched roofs, and dormers; and the drawings, as Mr. Scott himself observed, " were, perhaps, the best ever sent in to a competition, or nearly so." After the usual difficulties and delays the work was at last to be put in hand, when there was a change of Government and Lord Palmerston became Prime Minister. Lord Palmerston at once sent for Mr. Scott. "Well, Mr. Scott," he said, in his jaunty way, "I can't have anything to do with this Gothic style. I must insist on your making a design in the Italian manner, which I am sure you can do very cleverly." Mr. Scott was appalled; the style of the Italian renaissance was not only unsightly, it was positively immoral, and he sternly refused to have anything to do with it. Thereupon Lord Palmerston assumed a fatherly tone. " Quite true; a Gothic architect can't be expected to put up a Classical building; I must find someone else." This was intolerable, and Mr. Scott, on his return home, addressed to the Prime Minister a strongly-worded letter, in which he dwelt upon his position as an architect, upon his having won two European competitions, his being an A.R.A., a gold

medallist of the Institute, and a lecturer on archi-
tecture at the Royal Academy; but it was useless
—Lord Palmerston did not even reply. It then
occurred to Mr. Scott that, by a judicious mixture, he might, while preserving the essential character of the Gothic, produce a design which would
give a superficial impression of the Classical style.
He did so, but no effect was produced upon Lord
Palmerston. The new design, he said, was " neither
one thing nor 'tother—a regular mongrel affair—
and he would have nothing to do with it either."
After that Mr. Scott found it necessary to recruit
for two months at Scarborough, " with a course of
quinine." He recovered his tone at last, but only
at the cost of his convictions. For the sake of his
family he felt that it was his unfortunate duty to
obey the Prime Minister; and, shuddering with
horror, he constructed the Government offices in
a strictly Renaissance style.

Shortly afterwards Mr. Scott found some consolation in building the St. Pancras Hotel in a
style of his own.[1]

And now another and yet more satisfactory task
was his. " My idea in designing the Memorial,"
he wrote, " was to erect a kind of ciborium to protect a statue of the Prince; and its special charac-

[1] Scott, 177–201, 271.

teristic was that the ciborium was designed in some degree on the principles of the ancient shrines. These shrines were models of imaginary buildings, such as had never in reality been erected; and my idea was to realise one of these imaginary structures with its precious materials, its inlaying, its enamels, &c. &c." [1] His idea was particularly appropriate since it chanced that a similar conception, though in the reverse order of magnitude, had occurred to the Prince himself, who had designed and executed several silver cruet-stands upon the same model. At the Queen's request a site was chosen in Kensington Gardens as near as possible to that of the Great Exhibition; and in May, 1864, the first sod was turned. The work was long, complicated, and difficult; a great number of workmen were employed, besides several subsidiary sculptors and metal-workers under Mr. Scott's direction, while at every stage sketches and models were submitted to Her Majesty, who criticised all the details with minute care, and constantly suggested improvements. The frieze, which encircled the base of the monument, was in itself a very serious piece of work. " This," said Mr. Scott, " taken as a whole, is perhaps one of the most laborious works of sculpture ever under-

[1] Scott, 225.

taken, consisting, as it does, of a continuous range of figure-sculpture of the most elaborate description, in the highest *alto-relievo* of life-size, of more than 200 feet in length, containing about 170 figures, and executed in the hardest marble which could be procured." After three years of toil the memorial was still far from completion, and Mr. Scott thought it advisable to give a dinner to the workmen, " as a substantial recognition of his appreciation of their skill and energy." " Two long tables," we are told, " constructed of scaffold planks, were arranged in the workshops, and covered with newspapers, for want of table-cloths. Upwards of eighty men sat down. Beef and mutton, plum pudding and cheese were supplied in abundance, and each man who desired it had three pints of beer, gingerbeer and lemonade being provided for the teetotalers, who formed a very considerable proportion. . . . Several toasts were given and many of the workmen spoke, almost all of them commencing by " Thanking God that they enjoyed good health "; some alluded to the temperance that prevailed amongst them, others observed how little swearing was ever heard, whilst all said how pleased and proud they were to be engaged on so great a work."

Gradually the edifice approached completion.

The one hundred and seventieth life-size figure in the frieze was chiselled, the granite pillars arose, the mosaics were inserted in the allegorical pediments, the four colossal statues representing the greater Christian virtues, the four other colossal statues representing the greater moral virtues, were hoisted into their positions, the eight bronzes representing the greater sciences—Astronomy, Chemistry, Geology, Geometry, Rhetoric, Medicine, Philosophy, and Physiology—were fixed on their glittering pinnacles, high in air. The statue of Physiology was particularly admired. " On her left arm," the official description informs us, " she bears a new-born infant, as a representation of the development of the highest and most perfect of physiological forms; her hand points towards a microscope, the instrument which lends its assistance for the investigation of the minuter forms of animal and vegetable organisms." At last the gilded cross crowned the dwindling galaxies of superimposed angels, the four continents in white marble stood at the four corners of the base, and, seven years after its inception, in July, 1872, the monument was thrown open to the public.

But four more years were to elapse before the central figure was ready to be placed under its starry canopy. It was designed by Mr. Foley, though in one particular the sculptor's freedom was restricted by Mr. Scott. " I have chosen the sitting posture," Mr. Scott said, " as best conveying the idea of dignity befitting a royal personage." Mr. Foley ably carried out the conception of his principal. " In the attitude and expression," he said, " the aim has been, with the individuality of portraiture, to embody rank, character, and enlightenment, and to convey a sense of that responsive intelligence indicating an active, rather than a passive, interest in those pursuits of civilisation illustrated in the surrounding figures, groups, and relievos. . . . To identify the figure with one of the most memorable undertakings of the public life of the Prince—the International Exhibition of 1851—a catalogue of the works collected in that first gathering of the industry of all nations, is placed in the right hand." The statue was of bronze gilt and weighed nearly ten tons. It was rightly supposed that the simple word " Albert," cast on the base, would be a sufficient means of identification.[1]

[1] *National Memorial;* Dafforne, 43–4.

CHAPTER VIII

MR. GLADSTONE AND LORD BEA-
CONSFIELD

I

LORD PALMERSTON'S laugh—a queer metallic
" Ha! ha! ha! " with reverberations in it from the
days of Pitt and the Congress of Vienna—was
heard no more in Piccadilly;[1] Lord John Russell
dwindled into senility; Lord Derby tottered from
the stage. A new scene opened; and new protagonists—Mr. Gladstone and Mr. Disraeli—
struggled together in the limelight. Victoria, from
her post of vantage, watched these developments
with that passionate and personal interest which
she invariably imported into politics. Her prepossessions were of an unexpected kind. Mr.
Gladstone had been the disciple of her revered
Peel, and had won the approval of Albert; Mr.
Disraeli had hounded Sir Robert to his fall with
hideous virulence, and the Prince had pronounced
that he " had not one single element of a gentleman in his composition."[2] Yet she regarded Mr.
Gladstone with a distrust and dislike which

---

[1] Adams, 135.   [2] Clarendon, II, 342.

steadily deepened, while upon his rival she lavished an abundance of confidence, esteem, and
affection such as Lord Melbourne himself had
hardly known.

Her attitude towards the Tory Minister had
suddenly changed when she found that he alone
among public men had divined her feelings at Albert's death. Of the others she might have said
" they pity me and not my grief "; but Mr. Disraeli had understood; and all his condolences had
taken the form of reverential eulogies of the departed. The Queen declared that he was " the
only person who appreciated the Prince." [1] She
began to show him special favour; gave him and
his wife two of the coveted seats in St. George's
Chapel at the Prince of Wales's wedding, and invited him to stay a night at Windsor. When the
grant for the Albert Memorial came before the
House of Commons, Disraeli, as leader of the
Opposition, eloquently supported the project. He
was rewarded by a copy of the Prince's speeches,
bound in white morocco, with an inscription in the
royal hand. In his letter of thanks he " ventured
to touch upon a sacred theme," and, in a strain
which re-echoed with masterly fidelity the sentiments of his correspondent, dwelt at length upon

[1] Buckle, IV, 385.

QUEEN VICTORIA IN 1876.

From the Portrait by Von Angeli.

the absolute perfection of Albert. " The Prince," he said, " is the only person whom Mr. Disraeli has ever known who realised the Ideal. None with whom he is acquainted have ever approached it. There was in him an union of the manly grace and sublime simplicity, of chivalry with the intellectual splendour of the Attic Academe. The only character in English history that would, in some respects, draw near to him is Sir Philip Sidney: the same high tone, the same universal accomplishments, the same blended tenderness and vigour, the same rare combination of romantic energy and classic repose." As for his own acquaintance with the Prince, it had been, he said, " one of the most satisfactory incidents of his life: full of refined and beautiful memories, and exercising, as he hopes, over his remaining existence, a soothing and exalting influence." Victoria was much affected by " the depth and delicacy of these touches," and henceforward Disraeli's place in her affections was assured.[1] When, in 1866, the Conservatives came into office, Disraeli's position as Chancellor of the Exchequer and leader of the House necessarily brought him into a closer relation with the Sovereign. Two years later Lord Derby resigned, and Victoria, with intense delight and peculiar

[1] Buckle, IV, 382-95.

graciousness, welcomed Disraeli as her First Minister.[1]

But only for nine agitated months did he remain in power. The Ministry, in a minority in the Commons, was swept out of existence by a general election. Yet by the end of that short period the ties which bound together the Queen and her Premier had grown far stronger than ever before; the relationship between them was now no longer merely that between a grateful mistress and a devoted servant: they were friends. His official letters, in which the personal element had always been perceptible, developed into racy records of political news and social gossip, written, as Lord Clarendon said, "in his best novel style." Victoria was delighted; she had never, she declared, had such letters in her life, and had never before known *everything*.[2] In return, she sent him, when the spring came, several bunches of flowers, picked by her own hands. He despatched to her a set of his novels, for which, she said, she was "most grateful, and which she values much." She herself had lately published her "Leaves from the Journal of our Life in the Highlands," and it was observed that the Prime Minister, in conversing with Her Majesty at this period, constantly used

1 Buckle, IV, 592.   2 Clarendon, II, 346.

the words " we authors, ma'am." [1] Upon political questions, she was his staunch supporter. " Really there never was such conduct as that of the Opposition," she wrote. And when the Government was defeated in the House she was " really shocked at the way in which the House of Commons go on; they really bring discredit on Constitutional Government." [2] She dreaded the prospect of a change; she feared that if the Liberals insisted upon disestablishing the Irish Church, her Coronation Oath might stand in the way. [1] But a change there had to be, and Victoria vainly tried to console herself for the loss of her favourite Minister by bestowing a peerage upon Mrs. Disraeli.

Mr. Gladstone was in his shirt-sleeves at Hawarden, cutting down a tree, when the royal message was brought to him. " Very significant," he remarked, when he had read the letter, and went on cutting down his tree. His secret thoughts on the occasion were more explicit, and were committed to his diary. " The Almighty," he wrote, " seems to sustain and spare me for some purpose of His own, deeply unworthy as I know myself to be. Glory be to His name." [4]

[1] Buckle, V, 49.
[2] Ibid., V, 48.
[3] Ibid., V, 28.
[4] Morley, II, 252, 256.

The Queen, however, did not share her new Minister's view of the Almighty's intentions. She could not believe that there was any divine purpose to be detected in the programme of sweeping changes which Mr. Gladstone was determined to carry out. But what could she do? Mr. Gladstone, with his daemonic energy and his powerful majority in the House of Commons, was irresistible; and for five years (1869-74) Victoria found herself condemned to live in an agitating atmosphere of interminable reform—reform in the Irish Church and the Irish land system, reform in education, reform in parliamentary elections, reform in the organisation of the Army and the Navy, reform in the administration of justice. She disapproved, she struggled, she grew very angry; she felt that if Albert had been living things would never have happened so; but her protests and her complaints were alike unavailing. The mere effort of grappling with the mass of documents which poured in upon her in an ever-growing flood was terribly exhausting. When the draft of the lengthy and intricate Irish Church Bill came before her, accompanied by an explanatory letter from Mr. Gladstone covering a dozen closely-written quarto pages, she almost despaired. She turned from the Bill to the explanation, and

from the explanation back again to the Bill, and
she could not decide which was the most confusing.
But she had to do her duty: she had not only to
read, but to make notes. At last she handed the
whole heap of papers to Mr. Martin, who happened to be staying at Osborne, and requested
him to make a précis of them.[1] When he had done
so, her disapproval of the measure became more
marked than ever; but, such was the strength of
the Government, she actually found herself obliged
to urge moderation upon the Opposition, lest
worse should ensue.[2]

In the midst of this crisis, when the future of
the Irish Church was hanging in the balance,
Victoria's attention was drawn to another proposed reform. It was suggested that the sailors
in the Navy should henceforward be allowed to
wear beards. "Has Mr. Childers ascertained
anything on the subject of the beards?" the Queen
wrote anxiously to the First Lord of the Admiralty. On the whole, Her Majesty was in favour
of the change. "Her own personal feeling," she
wrote, "would be for the beards without the moustaches, as the latter have rather a soldierlike appearance; but then the object in view would not
be obtained, viz. to prevent the necessity of shav-

[1] Martin, *Queen Victoria*, 50–1. [2] Tait, II, chap. i.

ing. Therefore it had better be as proposed, the entire beard, only it should be kept short and very clean." After thinking over the question for another week, the Queen wrote a final letter. She wished, she said, " to make one additional observation respecting the beards, viz. that on no account should moustaches be allowed without beards. That must be clearly understood." [1]

Changes in the Navy might be tolerated; to lay hands upon the Army was a more serious matter. From time immemorial there had been a particularly close connection between the Army and the Crown; and Albert had devoted even more time and attention to the details of military business than to the processes of fresco-painting or the planning of sanitary cottages for the deserving poor. But now there was to be a great alteration: Mr. Gladstone's fiat had gone forth, and the Commander-in-Chief was to be removed from his direct dependence upon the Sovereign, and made subordinate to Parliament and the Secretary of State for War. Of all the liberal reforms this was the one which aroused the bitterest resentment in Victoria. She considered that the change was an attack upon her personal position—almost an attack upon the personal position of Albert. But

[1] Childers, I, 175–7.

she was helpless, and the Prime Minister had his way. When she heard that the dreadful man had yet another reform in contemplation—that he was about to abolish the purchase of military commissions—she could only feel that it was just what might have been expected. For a moment she hoped that the House of Lords would come to the rescue; the Peers opposed the change with unexpected vigour; but Mr. Gladstone, more conscious than ever of the support of the Almighty, was ready with an ingenious device. The purchase of commissions had been originally allowed by Royal Warrant; it should now be disallowed by the same agency. Victoria was faced by a curious dilemma: she abominated the abolition of purchase; but she was asked to abolish it by an exercise of sovereign power which was very much to her taste. She did not hesitate for long; and when the Cabinet, in a formal minute, advised her to sign the Warrant, she did so with a good grace.[1]

Unacceptable as Mr. Gladstone's policy was, there was something else about him which was even more displeasing to Victoria. She disliked his personal demeanour towards herself. It was not that Mr. Gladstone, in his intercourse with her, was in any degree lacking in courtesy or respect.

[1] Morley, II, 360-5.

On the contrary, an extraordinary reverence impregnated his manner, both in his conversation and his correspondence with the Sovereign. Indeed, with that deep and passionate conservatism which, to the very end of his incredible career, gave such an unexpected colouring to his inexplicable character, Mr. Gladstone viewed Victoria through a haze of awe which was almost religious—as a sacrosanct embodiment of venerable traditions—a vital element in the British Constitution—a Queen by Act of Parliament. But unfortunately the lady did not appreciate the compliment. The well-known complaint—" He speaks to me as if I were a public meeting "—whether authentic or no—and the turn of the sentence is surely a little too epigrammatic to be genuinely Victorian—undoubtedly expresses the essential element of her antipathy. She had no objection to being considered as an institution; she was one, and she knew it. But she was a woman too, and to be considered *only* as an institution—that was unbearable. And thus all Mr. Gladstone's zeal and devotion, his ceremonious phrases, his low bows, his punctilious correctitudes, were utterly wasted; and when, in the excess of his loyalty, he went further, and imputed to the object of his veneration, with obsequious blindness, the subtlety of intellect, the wide reading, the grave enthusiasm, which he himself possessed, the misunderstanding became complete. The discordance between the actual Victoria and this strange Divinity made in Mr. Gladstone's image produced disastrous results. Her discomfort and dislike turned at last into positive animosity, and, though her manners continued to be perfect, she never for a moment unbent; while he on his side was overcome with disappointment, perplexity, and mortification.[1]

Yet his fidelity remained unshaken. When the Cabinet met, the Prime Minister, filled with his beatific vision, would open the proceedings by reading aloud the letters which he had received from the Queen upon the questions of the hour. The assembly sat in absolute silence while, one after another, the royal missives, with their emphases, their ejaculations, and their grammatical peculiarities, boomed forth in all the deep solemnity of Mr. Gladstone's utterance. Not a single comment, of any kind, was ever hazarded; and, after a fitting pause, the Cabinet proceeded with the business of the day.[2]

[1] Morley, II, 423–8; Crawford, 356, 370–1.
[2] Private information.

II

Little as Victoria appreciated her Prime Minister's attitude towards her, she found that it had its uses. The popular discontent at her uninterrupted seclusion had been gathering force for many years, and now burst out in a new and alarming shape. Republicanism was in the air. Radical opinion in England, stimulated by the fall of Napoleon III and the establishment of a republican government in France, suddenly grew more extreme than it ever had been since 1848. It also became for the first time almost respectable. Chartism had been entirely an affair of the lower classes; but now Members of Parliament, learned professors, and ladies of title openly avowed the most subversive views. The monarchy was attacked both in theory and in practice. And it was attacked at a vital point: it was declared to be too expensive. What benefits, it was asked, did the nation reap to counterbalance the enormous sums which were expended upon the Sovereign? Victoria's retirement gave an unpleasant handle to the argument. It was pointed out that the ceremonial functions of the Crown had virtually lapsed; and the awkward question remained whether any of the other functions which it did continue to perform were really worth £385,000 per annum. The royal balance-sheet was curiously examined. An anonymous pamphlet entitled "What does she do with it?" appeared, setting forth the financial position with malicious clarity. The Queen, it stated, was granted by the Civil List £60,000 a year for her private use; but the rest of her vast annuity was given, as the Act declared, to enable her " to defray the expenses of her royal household and to support the honour and dignity of the Crown." Now it was obvious that, since the death of the Prince, the expenditure for both these purposes must have been very considerably diminished, and it was difficult to resist the conclusion that a large sum of money was diverted annually from the uses for which it had been designed by Parliament, to swell the private fortune of Victoria. The precise amount of that private fortune it was impossible to discover; but there was reason to suppose that it was gigantic; perhaps it reached a total of five million pounds. The pamphlet protested against such a state of affairs, and its protests were repeated vigorously in newspapers and at public meetings. Though it is certain that the estimate of Victoria's riches was much exaggerated, it is equally certain that she was an exceedingly wealthy woman. She probably saved £20,000 a year from the Civil List, the revenues of the Duchy of Lancaster were steadily increasing, she had inherited a considerable property from the Prince Consort, and she had been left, in 1852, an estate of half a million by Mr. John Neild, an eccentric miser. In these circumstances it was not surprising that when, in 1871, Parliament was asked to vote a dowry of £30,000 to the Princess Louise on her marriage with the eldest son of the Duke of Argyle, together with an annuity of £6,000, there should have been a serious outcry.[1]

In order to conciliate public opinion, the Queen opened Parliament in person, and the vote was passed almost unanimously. But a few months later another demand was made: the Prince Arthur had come of age, and the nation was asked to grant him an annuity of £15,000. The outcry was redoubled. The newspapers were filled with angry articles; Bradlaugh thundered against " princely paupers " to one of the largest crowds that had ever been seen in Trafalgar Square; and Sir Charles Dilke expounded the case for a re-

[1] In 1889 it was officially stated that the Queen's total savings from the Civil List amounted to £824,025, but that out of this sum much had been spent on special entertainments to foreign visitors (Lee, 499). Taking into consideration the proceeds from the Duchy of Lancaster, which were more than £60,000 a year (Lee, 79), the savings of the Prince Consort, and Mr. Neild's legacy, it seems probable that, at the time of her death, Victoria's private fortune approached two million pounds.

public in a speech to his constituents at Newcastle. The Prince's annuity was ultimately sanctioned in the House of Commons by a large majority; but a minority of fifty members voted in favour of reducing the sum to £10,000.

Towards every aspect of this distasteful question, Mr. Gladstone presented an iron front. He absolutely discountenanced the extreme section of his followers. He declared that the whole of the Queen's income was justly at her personal disposal, argued that to complain of royal savings was merely to encourage royal extravagance, and successfully convoyed through Parliament the unpopular annuities, which, he pointed out, were strictly in accordance with precedent. When, in 1872, Sir Charles Dilke once more returned to the charge in the House of Commons, introducing a motion for a full enquiry into the Queen's expenditure with a view to a root and branch reform of the Civil List, the Prime Minister brought all the resources of his powerful and ingenious eloquence to the support of the Crown. He was completely successful; and amid a scene of great disorder the motion was ignominiously dismissed. Victoria was relieved; but she grew no fonder of Mr. Gladstone.[1]

[1] Morley, II, 425-6; Lee, 410-2, 415-8; Jerrold, *Widowhood*, 153-7, 162-3, 169-71.

It was perhaps the most miserable moment of
her life. The Ministers, the press, the public, all
conspired to vex her, to blame her, to misinterpret
her actions, to be unsympathetic and disrespectful
in every way. She was " a cruelly misunderstood
woman," she told Mr. Martin, complaining to him
bitterly of the unjust attacks which were made
upon her, and declaring that " the great worry and
anxiety and hard work for ten years, alone, un-
aided, with increasing age and never very strong
health " were breaking her down, and " almost
drove her to despair." [1] The situation was indeed
deplorable. It seemed as if her whole existence
had gone awry; as if an irremediable antagonism
had grown up between the Queen and the nation.
If Victoria had died in the early seventies, there
can be little doubt that the voice of the world
would have pronounced her a failure.

III

But she was reserved for a very different fate.
The outburst of republicanism had been in fact
the last flicker of an expiring cause. The liberal
tide, which had been flowing steadily ever since
the Reform Bill, reached its height with Mr. Gladstone's first administration; and towards the end

[1] Martin, *Queen Victoria*, 41–2.

of that administration the inevitable ebb began.
The reaction, when it came, was sudden and complete. The General Election of 1874 changed the
whole face of politics. Mr. Gladstone and the
Liberals were routed; and the Tory party, for the
first time for over forty years, attained an unquestioned supremacy in England. It was obvious
that their surprising triumph was pre-eminently
due to the skill and vigour of Disraeli. He returned to office, no longer the dubious commander
of an insufficient host, but with drums beating and
flags flying, a conquering hero. And as a conquering hero Victoria welcomed her new Prime
Minister.

Then there followed six years of excitement,
of enchantment, of felicity, of glory, of romance.
The amazing being, who now at last, at the age
of seventy, after a lifetime of extraordinary struggles, had turned into reality the absurdest of his
boyhood's dreams, knew well enough how to make
his own, with absolute completeness, the heart of the
Sovereign Lady whose servant, and whose master, he had so miraculously become. In women's
hearts he had always read as in an open book. His
whole career had turned upon those curious enti-
ties; and the more curious they were, the more
intimately at home with them he seemed to be.

But Lady Beaconsfield, with her cracked idolatry, and Mrs. Brydges-Williams, with her clogs, her corpulence, and her legacy, were gone: an even more remarkable phenomenon stood in their place. He surveyed what was before him with the eye of a past-master; and he was not for a moment at a loss. He realised everything—the interacting complexities of circumstance and character, the pride of place mingled so inextricably with personal arrogance, the superabundant emotionalism, the ingenuousness of outlook, the solid, the laborious respectability, shot through so incongruously by temperamental cravings for the coloured and the strange, the singular intellectual limitations, and the mysteriously essential female elements impregnating every particle of the whole. A smile hovered over his impassive features, and he dubbed Victoria " the Faery." The name delighted him, for, with that epigrammatic ambiguity so dear to his heart, it precisely expressed his vision of the Queen. The Spenserian allusion was very pleasant—the elegant evocations of Gloriana; but there was more in it than that: there was the suggestion of a diminutive creature, endowed with magical— and mythical—properties, and a portentousness almost ridiculously out of keeping with the rest of her make-up. The Faery, he determined, should henceforward wave her wand for him alone. Detachment is always a rare quality, and rarest of all, perhaps, among politicians; but that veteran egotist possessed it in a supreme degree. Not only did he know what he had to do, not only did he do it; he was in the audience as well as on the stage; and he took in with the rich relish of a connoisseur every feature of the entertaining situation, every phase of the delicate drama, and every detail of his own consummate performance.

The smile hovered and vanished, and, bowing low with Oriental gravity and Oriental submissiveness, he set himself to his task. He had understood from the first that in dealing with the Faery the appropriate method of approach was the very antithesis of the Gladstonian; and such a method was naturally his. It was not his habit to harangue and exhort and expatiate in official conscientiousness; he liked to scatter flowers along the path of business, to compress a weighty argument into a happy phrase, to insinuate what was in his mind with an air of friendship and confidential courtesy. He was nothing if not personal; and he had perceived that personality was the key that opened the Faery's heart. Accordingly, he never for a moment allowed his intercourse with her to lose the personal tone; he invested all the transactions of State with the charms of familiar conversation; she was always the royal lady, the adored and revered mistress, he the devoted and respectful friend. When once the personal relation was firmly established, every difficulty disappeared. But to maintain that relation uninterruptedly in a smooth and even course a particular care was necessary: the bearings had to be most assiduously oiled. Nor was Disraeli in any doubt as to the nature of the lubricant. "You have heard me called a flatterer," he said to Matthew Arnold, "and it is true. Everyone likes flattery; and when you come to royalty you should lay it on with a trowel." [1] He practised what he preached. His adulation was incessant, and he applied it in the very thickest slabs. "There is no honor and no reward," he declared, "that with him can ever equal the possession of your Majesty's kind thoughts. All his own thoughts and feelings and duties and affections are now concentrated in your Majesty, and he desires nothing more for his remaining years than to serve your Majesty, or, if that service ceases, to live still on its memory as a period of his existence most interesting and fascinating." [2] "In life," he told her, "one must have for one's thoughts a sacred depository, and

[1] Buckle, VI, 463.   [2] *Ibid.*, VI, 226.

Lord Beaconsfield ever presumes to seek that in his Sovereign Mistress." [1] She was not only his own solitary support; she was the one prop of the State. " If your Majesty is ill," he wrote during a grave political crisis, " he is sure he will himself break down. All, really, depends upon your Majesty." " He lives only for Her," he asseverated, " and works only for Her, and without Her all is lost." [2] When her birthday came he produced an elaborate confection of hyperbolic compliment. " To-day Lord Beaconsfield ought fitly, perhaps, to congratulate a powerful Sovereign on her imperial sway, the vastness of her Empire, and the success and strength of her fleets and armies. But he cannot, his mind is in another mood. He can only think of the strangeness of his destiny that it has come to pass that he should be the servant of one so great, and whose infinite kindness, the brightness of whose intelligence and the firmness of whose will, have enabled him to undertake labours to which he otherwise would be quite unequal, and supported him in all things by a condescending sympathy, which in the hour of difficulty alike charms and inspires. Upon the Sovereign of many lands and many hearts may an omnipotent Providence shed every blessing that the wise can

---

[1] Buckle, VI, 445m.   [2] *Ibid.*, VI, 254-5.

desire and the virtuous deserve!"[1] In those expert hands the trowel seemed to assume the qualities of some lofty masonic symbol—to be the ornate and glittering vehicle of verities unrealised by the profane.

Such tributes were delightful, but they remained in the nebulous region of words, and Disraeli had determined to give his blandishments a more significant solidity. He deliberately encouraged those high views of her own position which had always been native to Victoria's mind and had been reinforced by the principles of Albert and the doctrines of Stockmar. He professed to a belief in a theory of the Constitution which gave the Sovereign a leading place in the councils of government; but his pronouncements upon the subject were indistinct; and when he emphatically declared that there ought to be " a real Throne," it was probably with the mental addition that that throne would be a very unreal one indeed whose occupant was unamenable to his cajoleries. But the vagueness of his language was in itself an added stimulant to Victoria. Skilfully confusing the woman and the Queen, he threw, with a grandiose gesture, the government of England at her feet, as if in doing so he were performing an act

[1] Buckle, VI, 430.

of personal homage. In his first audience after returning to power, he assured her that " whatever she wished should be done." [1] When the intricate Public Worship Regulation Bill was being discussed by the Cabinet, he told the Faery that his " only object " was " to further your Majesty's wishes in this matter." [2] When he brought off his great *coup* over the Suez Canal, he used expressions which implied that the only gainer by the transaction was Victoria. " It is just settled," he wrote in triumph; " you have it, Madam . . . Four millions sterling! and almost immediately. There was only one firm that could do it—Rothschilds. They behaved admirably; advanced the money at a low rate, and the entire interest of the Khedive is now yours, Madam." [3] Nor did he limit himself to highly-spiced insinuations. Writing with all the authority of his office, he advised the Queen that she had the constitutional right to dismiss a Ministry which was supported by a large majority in the House of Commons; he even urged her to do so, if, in her opinion, " your Majesty's Government have from wilfulness, or even from weakness, deceived your Majesty." [4] To the horror of Mr. Gladstone, he not only kept the Queen in-

[1] Buckle, V, 286.
[2] *Ibid.*, V, 321.
[3] *Ibid.*, V, 448–9.
[4] *Ibid.*, II, 246.

formed as to the general course of business in the
Cabinet, but revealed to her the part taken in its
discussions by individual members of it.[1] Lord
Derby, the son of the late Prime Minister and
Disraeli's Foreign Secretary, viewed these developments with grave mistrust. " Is there not," he
ventured to write to his Chief, " just a risk of
encouraging her in too large ideas of her personal
power, and too great indifference to what the
public expects? I only ask; it is for you to
judge." [2]

As for Victoria, she accepted everything—compliments, flatteries, Elizabethan prerogatives—
without a single qualm. After the long gloom of
her bereavement, after the chill of the Gladstonian discipline, she expanded to the rays of Disraeli's devotion like a flower in the sun. The
change in her situation was indeed miraculous.
No longer was she obliged to puzzle for hours
over the complicated details of business, for now
she had only to ask Mr. Disraeli for an explanation, and he would give it her in the most concise,
in the most amusing, way. No longer was she
worried by alarming novelties; no longer was she
put out at finding herself treated, by a reverential
gentleman in high collars, as if she were some em-

1 Morley, II, 574–5.   2 Buckle, V, 414.

bodied precedent, with a recondite knowledge of Greek. And her deliverer was surely the most fascinating of men. The strain of charlatanism, which had unconsciously captivated her in Napoleon III, exercised the same enchanting effect in the case of Disraeli. Like a dram-drinker, whose ordinary life is passed in dull sobriety, her unsophisticated intelligence gulped down his rococo allurements with peculiar zest. She became intoxicated, entranced. Believing all that he told her of herself, she completely regained the self-confidence which had been slipping away from her throughout the dark period that followed Albert's death. She swelled with a new elation, while he, conjuring up before her wonderful Oriental visions, dazzled her eyes with an imperial grandeur of which she had only dimly dreamed. Under the compelling influence, her very demeanour altered. Her short, stout figure, with its folds of black velvet, its muslin streamers, its heavy pearls at the heavy neck, assumed an almost menacing air. In her countenance, from which the charm of youth had long since vanished, and which had not yet been softened by age, the traces of grief, of disappointment, and of displeasure were still visible, but they were overlaid by looks of arrogance and sharp lines of peremptory hauteur. Only, when Mr.

Disraeli appeared, the expression changed in an instant, and the forbidding visage became charged with smiles.[1] For him she would do anything. Yielding to his encouragements, she began to emerge from her seclusion; she appeared in London in semi-state, at hospitals and concerts; she opened Parliament; she reviewed troops and distributed medals at Aldershot.[2] But such public signs of favour were trivial in comparison with her private attentions. During his hours of audience, she could hardly restrain her excitement and delight. "I can only describe my reception," he wrote to a friend on one occasion, " by telling you that I really thought she was going to embrace me. She was wreathed with smiles, and, as she tattled, glided about the room like a bird." [3] In his absence, she talked of him perpetually, and there was a note of unusual vehemence in her solicitude for his health. "John Manners," Disraeli told Lady Bradford, "who has just come from Osborne, says that the Faery only talked of one subject, and that was her Primo. According to him, it was her gracious opinion that the Government should make my health a Cabinet question. Dear John seemed quite surprised at what she said; but you are more used to these ebullitions." [1] She often sent him presents; an illustrated album arrived for him regularly from Windsor on Christmas Day. [2] But her most valued gifts were the bunches of spring flowers which, gathered by herself and her ladies in the woods at Osborne, marked in an especial manner the warmth and tenderness of her sentiments. Among these it was, he declared, the primroses that he loved the best. They were, he said, " the ambassadors of Spring," " the gems and jewels of Nature." He liked them, he assured her, " so much better for their being wild; they seem an offering from the Fauns and Dryads of Osborne." " They show," he told her, " that your Majesty's sceptre has touched the enchanted Isle." He sat at dinner with heaped-up bowls of them on every side, and told his guests that " they were all sent to me this morning by the Queen from Osborne, as she knows it is my favorite flower." [3]

As time went on, and as it became clearer and clearer that the Faery's thraldom was complete, his protestations grew steadily more highly-coloured and more unabashed. At last he ventured to import into his blandishments a strain of adoration that was almost avowedly romantic. In phrases of baroque convolution, he conveyed the

---

[1] Buckle, V, 384. [2] *Ibid.*, VI, 468. [3] *Ibid.*, VI, 629.

message of his heart. The pressure of business, he wrote, had " so absorbed and exhausted him, that towards the hour of post he has not had clearness of mind, and vigour of pen, adequate to convey his thoughts and facts to the most loved and illustrious being, who deigns to consider them." [1] She sent him some primroses, and he replied that he could " truly say they are ' more precious than rubies,' coming, as they do, and at such a moment, from a Sovereign whom he adores." [2] She sent him snowdrops, and his sentiment overflowed into poetry. " Yesterday eve," he wrote, " there appeared, in Whitehall Gardens, a delicate-looking case, with a royal superscription, which, when he opened, he thought, at first, that your Majesty had graciously bestowed upon him the stars of your Majesty's principal orders. And, indeed, he was so impressed with this graceful illusion, that, having a banquet, where there were many stars and ribbons, he could not resist the temptation, by placing some snowdrops on his heart, of showing that, he, too, was decorated by a gracious Sovereign.

" Then, in the middle of the night, it occurred to him, that it might all be an enchantment, and that, perhaps, it was a Faery gift and came from

---

[1] Buckle, VI, 248. [2] *Ibid.*, VI, 246–7.

another monarch: Queen Titania, gathering flowers, with her Court, in a soft and sea-girt isle, and
sending magic blossoms, which, they say, turn the
heads of those who receive them." [1]

A Faery gift! Did he smile as he wrote the
words? Perhaps; and yet it would be rash to con-
clude that his perfervid declarations were altogether without sincerity. Actor and spectator
both, the two characters were so intimately blended
together in that odd composition that they formed
an inseparable unity, and it was impossible to say
that one of them was less genuine than the other.
With one element, he could coldly appraise the
Faery's intellectual capacity, note with some surprise that she could be on occasion " most interesting and amusing," and then continue his use of
the trowel with an ironical solemnity; while, with
the other, he could be overwhelmed by the immemorial panoply of royalty, and, thrilling with the
sense of his own strange elevation, dream himself
into a gorgeous phantasy of crowns and powers
and chivalric love. When he told Victoria that
" during a somewhat romantic and imaginative
life, nothing has ever occurred to him so interesting as this confidential correspondence with one
so exalted and so inspiring," [2] was he not in earnest

[1] Buckle, VI, 464–7.   [2] Buckle, VI, 238.

after all? When he wrote to a lady about the Court, " I love the Queen—perhaps the only person in this world left to me that I do love," [1] was he not creating for himself an enchanted palace out of the Arabian Nights, full of melancholy and spangles, in which he actually believed? Victoria's state of mind was far more simple; untroubled by imaginative yearnings, she never lost herself in that nebulous region of the spirit where feeling and fancy grow confused. Her emotions, with all their intensity and all their exaggeration, retained the plain prosaic texture of everyday life. And it was fitting that her expression of them should be equally commonplace. She was, she told her Prime Minister, at the end of an official letter, "yours aff'ly V. R. and I." In such a phrase the deep reality of her feeling is instantly manifest. The Faery's feet were on the solid earth; it was the *rusé* cynic who was in the air.

He had taught her, however, a lesson, which she had learnt with alarming rapidity. A second Gloriana, did he call her? Very well, then, she would show that she deserved the compliment. Disquieting symptoms followed fast. In May, 1874, the Tsar, whose daughter had just been married to Victoria's second son, the Duke of

---

[1] Buckle, VI, 462.

Edinburgh, was in London, and, by an unfortunate error, it had been arranged that his departure should not take place until two days after the date on which his royal hostess had previously decided to go to Balmoral. Her Majesty refused to modify her plans. It was pointed out to her that the Tsar would certainly be offended, that the most serious consequences might follow; Lord Derby protested; Lord Salisbury, the Secretary of State for India, was much perturbed. But the Faery was unconcerned; she had settled to go to Balmoral on the 18th, and on the 18th she would go. At last Disraeli, exercising all his influence, induced her to agree to stay in London for two days more. "My head is still on my shoulders," he told Lady Bradford. "The great lady has absolutely postponed her departure! Everybody had failed, even the Prince of Wales; . . . and I have no doubt I am not in favour. I can't help it. Salisbury says I have saved an Afghan War, and Derby compliments me on my unrivalled triumph." [1] But before very long, on another issue, the triumph was the Faery's. Disraeli, who had suddenly veered towards a new Imperialism, had thrown out the suggestion that the Queen of England ought to become the Empress of India. Vic-

[1] Buckle, V, 414–5.

toria seized upon the idea with avidity, and, in
season and out of season, pressed upon her Prime
Minister the desirability of putting his proposal
into practice. He demurred; but she was not to
be baulked; and in 1876, in spite of his own un-
willingness and that of his entire Cabinet, he found
himself obliged to add to the troubles of a stormy
session by introducing a bill for the alteration of
the Royal Title.[1] His compliance, however, finally
conquered the Faery's heart. The measure was
angrily attacked in both Houses, and Victoria was
deeply touched by the untiring energy with which
Disraeli defended it. She was, she said, much
grieved by " the worry and annoyance " to which
he was subjected; she feared she was the cause of
it; and she would never forget what she owed to
" her kind, good, and considerate friend." At the
same time, her wrath fell on the Opposition. Their
conduct, she declared, was " extraordinary, incomprehensible, and mistaken," and, in an emphatic
sentence which seemed to contradict both itself and
all her former proceedings, she protested that she
" would be glad if it were more generally known
that it was *her* wish, as people *will* have it, that
it has been *forced upon her!* "[2] When the affair
was successfully over, the imperial triumph was

1 Buckle, V, 456–8; VI, 457–8.   2 *Ibid.*, V, 468–9, 473.

celebrated in a suitable manner. On the day of the Delhi Proclamation, the new Earl of Beaconsfield went to Windsor to dine with the new Empress of India. That night the Faery, usually so homely in her attire, appeared in a glittering panoply of enormous uncut jewels, which had been presented to her by the reigning Princes of her *Raj*. At the end of the meal the Prime Minister, breaking through the rules of etiquette, arose, and in a flowery oration proposed the health of the Queen-Empress. His audacity was well received, and his speech was rewarded by a smiling curtsey.[1]

These were significant episodes; but a still more serious manifestation of Victoria's temper occurred in the following year, during the crowning crisis of Beaconsfield's life. His growing imperialism, his desire to magnify the power and prestige of England, his insistence upon a " spirited foreign policy," had brought him into collision with Russia; the terrible Eastern Question loomed up; and when war broke out between Russia and Turkey, the gravity of the situation became extreme. The Prime Minister's policy was fraught with difficulty and danger. Realising perfectly the appalling implications of an Anglo-Russian war, he was

1 Hamilton, 120; *Quarterly Review,* cxxxix, 334.

yet prepared to face even that eventuality if he could obtain his ends by no other method; but he believed that Russia in reality was still less desirous of a rupture, and that, if he played his game with sufficient boldness and adroitness, she would yield, when it came to the point, all that he required without a blow. It was clear that the course he had marked out for himself was full of hazard, and demanded an extraordinary nerve; a single false step, and either himself, or England, might be plunged in disaster. But nerve he had never lacked; he began his diplomatic egg-dance with high assurance; and then he discovered that, besides the Russian Government, besides the Liberals and Mr. Gladstone, there were two additional sources of perilous embarrassment with which he would have to reckon. In the first place there was a strong party in the Cabinet, headed by Lord Derby, the Foreign Secretary, which was unwilling to take the risk of war; but his culminating anxiety was the Faery.

From the first, her attitude was uncompromising. The old hatred of Russia, which had been engendered by the Crimean War, surged up again within her; she remembered Albert's prolonged animosity; she felt the prickings of her own greatness; and she flung herself into the turmoil with

passionate heat. Her indignation with the Opposition—with anyone who ventured to sympathise
with the Russians in their quarrel with the Turks
—was unbounded. When anti-Turkish meetings
were held in London, presided over by the Duke
of Westminster and Lord Shaftesbury, and attended by Mr. Gladstone and other prominent
Radicals, she considered that " the Attorney-
General ought to be set at these men "; " it can't,"
she exclaimed, " be constitutional." [1] Never in her
life, not even in the crisis over the Ladies of the
Bedchamber, did she show herself a more furious
partisan. But her displeasure was not reserved
for the Radicals; the backsliding Conservatives
equally felt its force. She was even discontented
with Lord Beaconsfield himself. Failing entirely
to appreciate the delicate complexity of his policy,
she constantly assailed him with demands for vigorous action, interpreted each finesse as a sign of
weakness, and was ready at every juncture to let
slip the dogs of war. As the situation developed,
her anxiety grew feverish. " The Queen," she
wrote, " is feeling terribly anxious lest delay
should cause us to be too late and lose our prestige for ever! It worries her night and day." [2]
" The Faery," Beaconsfield told Lady Bradford,

---

[1] Buckle, VI, 106–7.   [2] *Ibid.*, VI, 144.

" writes every day and telegraphs every hour; this
is almost literally the case." [1]   She raged loudly
against the Russians.   " And the language," she
cried, " the insulting language—used by the Russians against us!   It makes the Queen's blood
boil!" [2]   " Oh," she wrote a little later, " if the
Queen were a man, she would like to go and give
those Russians, whose word one cannot believe,
such a beating!   We shall never be friends again
till we have it out.   This the Queen feels sure of." [3]

The unfortunate Prime Minister, urged on to
violence by Victoria on one side, had to deal, on
the other, with a Foreign Secretary who was fundamentally opposed to any policy of active interference at all.   Between the Queen and Lord
Derby he held a harassed course.   He gained, indeed, some slight satisfaction in playing off the
one against the other—in stimulating Lord Derby
with the Queen's missives, and in appeasing the
Queen by repudiating Lord Derby's opinions; on
one occasion he actually went so far as to com-
pose, at Victoria's request, a letter bitterly attacking his colleague, which Her Majesty forthwith
signed, and sent, without alteration, to the Foreign
Secretary.[4]   But such devices only gave a tem-

1 Buckle, VI, 150.   3 *Ibid.*, VI, 217.
2 *Ibid.*, VI, 154.   4 *Ibid.*, VI, 157-9.

porary relief; and it soon became evident that Victoria's martial ardour was not to be side-tracked by hostilities against Lord Derby; hostilities against Russia were what she wanted, what she would, what she must, have. For now, casting aside the last relics of moderation, she began to attack her friend with a series of extraordinary threats. Not once, not twice, but many times she held over his head the formidable menace of her imminent abdication. "If England," she wrote to Beaconsfield, " is to kiss Russia's feet, she will not be a party to the humiliation of England and would lay down her crown," and she added that the Prime Minister might, if he thought fit, repeat her words to the Cabinet.[1] " This delay," she ejaculated, " this uncertainty by which, abroad, we are losing our prestige and our position, while Russia is advancing and will be before Constantinople in no time! Then the Government will be fearfully blamed and the Queen so humiliated that she thinks she would abdicate at once. Be bold! "[2] " She feels," she reiterated, " she cannot, as she before said, remain the Sovereign of a country that is letting itself down to kiss the feet of the great barbarians, the retarders of all liberty and civilisation that exists."[3] When the Russians ad-

[1] Buckle, VI, 132.   [2] *Ibid.*, VI, 148.   [3] *Ibid.*, VI, 217.

vanced to the outskirts of Constantinople she fired
off three letters in a day demanding war; and
when she learnt that the Cabinet had only decided
to send the Fleet to Gallipoli she declared that
" her first impulse " was " to lay down the thorny
crown, which she feels little satisfaction in retaining if the position of this country is to remain as it
is now." [1] It is easy to imagine the agitating effect
of such a correspondence upon Beaconsfield. This
was no longer the Faery; it was a genie whom he
had rashly called out of her bottle, and who was
now intent upon showing her supernal power.
More than once, perplexed, dispirited, shattered
by illness, he had thoughts of withdrawing altogether from the game. One thing alone, he told
Lady Bradford, with a wry smile, prevented him.
" If I could only," he wrote, " face the scene which
would occur at headquarters if I resigned, I would
do so at once." [2]

He held on, however, to emerge victorious at
last. The Queen was pacified; Lord Derby was
replaced by Lord Salisbury; and at the Congress
of Berlin *der alte Jude* carried all before him.
He returned to England in triumph, and assured
the delighted Victoria that she would very soon be,

[1] Buckle, VI, 243-5. [2] *Ibid.*, VI, 190.

if she was not already, the " Dictatress of Europe." [1]

But soon there was an unexpected reverse. At the General Election of 1880 the country, mistrustful of the forward policy of the Conservatives, and carried away by Mr. Gladstone's oratory, returned the Liberals to power. Victoria was horrified, but within a year she was to be yet more nearly hit. The grand romance had come to its conclusion. Lord Beaconsfield, worn out with age and maladies, but moving still, an assiduous mummy, from dinner-party to dinner-party, suddenly moved no longer. When she knew that the end was inevitable, she seemed, by a pathetic instinct, to divest herself of her royalty, and to shrink, with hushed gentleness, beside him, a woman and nothing more. " I send some Osborne primroses," she wrote to him with touching simplicity, " and I meant to pay you a little visit this week, but I thought it better you should be quite quiet and not speak. And I beg you will be very good and obey the doctors." She would see him, she said, " when we come back from Osborne, which won't be long." " Everyone is so distressed at your not being well," she added; and she was, " Ever yours very aff'ly, V.R.I." When the royal letter was given him, the strange old comedian, stretched on his bed of death, poised it in his hand, appeared to consider deeply, and then whispered to those about him, " This ought to be read to me by a Privy Councillor." [1]

[1] Buckle, VI, 613–4.

CHAPTER IX

OLD AGE

I

MEANWHILE in Victoria's private life many changes and developments had taken place. With the marriages of her elder children her family circle widened; grandchildren appeared; and a multitude of new domestic interests sprang up. The death of King Leopold in 1865 had removed the predominant figure of the older generation, and the functions he had performed as the centre and adviser of a large group of relatives in Germany and in England devolved upon Victoria. These functions she discharged with unremitting industry, carrying on an enormous correspondence, and following with absorbed interest every detail in the lives of the ever-ramifying cousinhood. And she tasted to the full both the joys and the pains of family affection. She took a particular delight in her grandchildren, to whom she showed an indulgence which their parents had not always enjoyed, though, even to her grandchildren, she could be, when the occasion demanded it, severe.

The eldest of them, the little Prince Wilhelm of Prussia, was a remarkably headstrong child; he dared to be impertinent even to his grandmother; and once, when she told him to bow to a visitor at Osborne, he disobeyed her outright. This would not do: the order was sternly repeated, and the naughty boy, noticing that his kind grandmama had suddenly turned into a most terrifying lady, submitted his will to hers, and bowed very low indeed.[1]

It would have been well if all the Queen's domestic troubles could have been got over as easily. Among her more serious distresses was the conduct of the Prince of Wales. The young man was now independent and married; he had shaken the parental yoke from his shoulders; he was positively beginning to do as he liked. Victoria was much perturbed, and her worst fears seemed to be justified when in 1870 he appeared as a witness in a society divorce case. It was clear that the heir to the throne had been mixing with people of whom she did not at all approve. What was to be done? She saw that it was not only her son that was to blame—that it was the whole system of society; and so she despatched a letter to Mr. Delane, the editor of *The Times,* asking him if

[1] Hallé, 296.

QUEEN VICTORIA IN 1897.

he would " frequently *write* articles pointing out the *immense* danger and evil of the wretched frivolity and levity of the views and lives of the Higher Classes." And five years later Mr. Delane did write an article upon that very subject.[1] Yet it seemed to have very little effect.

Ah! if only the Higher Classes would learn to live as she lived in the domestic sobriety of her sanctuary at Balmoral! For more and more did she find solace and refreshment in her Highland domain; and twice yearly, in the spring and in the autumn, with a sigh of relief, she set her face northwards, in spite of the humble protests of Ministers, who murmured vainly in the royal ears that to transact the affairs of State over an interval of six hundred miles added considerably to the cares of government. Her ladies, too, felt occasionally a slight reluctance to set out, for, especially in the early days, the long pilgrimage was not without its drawbacks. For many years the Queen's conservatism forbade the continuation of the railway up Deeside, so that the last stages of the journey had to be accomplished in carriages. But, after all, carriages had their good points; they were easy, for instance, to get in and out of, which was an important consideration, for the

1 *Notes and Queries,* May 20, 1920.

royal train remained for long immune from modern conveniences, and when it drew up, on some border moorland, far from any platform, the high-bred dames were obliged to descend to earth by the perilous foot-board, the only pair of folding steps being reserved for Her Majesty's saloon. In the days of crinolines such moments were sometimes awkward; and it was occasionally necessary to summon Mr. Johnstone, the short and sturdy Manager of the Caledonian Railway, who, more than once, in a high gale and drenching rain with great difficulty " pushed up "—as he himself described it—some unlucky Lady Blanche or Lady Agatha into her compartment.[1] But Victoria cared for none of these things. She was only intent upon regaining, with the utmost swiftness, her enchanted Castle, where every spot was charged with memories, where every memory was sacred, and where life was passed in an incessant and delightful round of absolutely trivial events.

And it was not only the place that she loved; she was equally attached to " the simple mountaineers," from whom, she said, " she learnt many a lesson of resignation and faith." [2] Smith and Grant and Ross and Thompson—she was devoted

---

[1] Neele, 476-8, 487.   [2] *More Leaves, v.*

to them all; but, beyond the rest, she was devoted
to John Brown. The Prince's gillie had now become the Queen's personal attendant—a body
servant from whom she was never parted, who
accompanied her on her drives, waited on her during the day, and slept in a neighbouring chamber
at night. She liked his strength, his solidity, the
sense he gave her of physical security; she even
liked his rugged manners and his rough unac-
commodating speech. She allowed him to take
liberties with her which would have been unthinkable from anybody else. To bully the Queen, to
order her about, to reprimand her—who could
dream of venturing upon such audacities? And
yet, when she received such treatment from John
Brown, she positively seemed to enjoy it. The
eccentricity appeared to be extraordinary; but,
after all, it is no uncommon thing for an auto-
cratic dowager to allow some trusted indispensable
servant to adopt towards her an attitude of authority which is jealously forbidden to relatives or
friends: the power of a dependant still remains,
by a psychological sleight-of-hand, one's own
power, even when it is exercised over oneself.
When Victoria meekly obeyed the abrupt commands of her henchman to get off her pony or
put on her shawl, was she not displaying, and in

the highest degree, the force of her volition? People might wonder; she could not help that; this was the manner in which it pleased her to act, and there was an end of it. To have submitted her judgment to a son or a Minister might have seemed wiser or more natural; but if she had done so, she instinctively felt, she would indeed have lost her independence. And yet upon somebody she longed to depend. Her days were heavy with the long process of domination. As she drove in silence over the moors she leaned back in the carriage, oppressed and weary; but what a relief!— John Brown was behind on the rumble, and his strong arm would be there for her to lean upon when she got out.

He had, too, in her mind, a special connection with Albert. In their expeditions the Prince had always trusted him more than anyone; the gruff, kind, hairy Scotsman was, she felt, in some mysterious way, a legacy from the dead. She came to believe at last—or so it appeared—that the spirit of Albert was nearer when Brown was near. Often, when seeking inspiration over some complicated question of political or domestic import, she would gaze with deep concentration at her late husband's bust. But it was also noticed that sometimes in such moments of doubt and hesitation Her Majesty's looks would fix themselves upon John Brown.

Eventually, the "simple mountaineer" became almost a state personage. The influence which he wielded was not to be overlooked. Lord Beaconsfield was careful, from time to time, to send courteous messages to "Mr. Brown" in his letters to the Queen, and the French Government took particular pains to provide for his comfort during the visits of the English Sovereign to France. It was only natural that among the elder members of the royal family he should not have been popular, and that his failings—for failings he had, though Victoria would never notice his too acute appreciation of Scotch whisky—should have been the subject of acrimonious comment at Court. But he served his mistress faithfully, and to ignore him would be a sign of disrespect in her biographer. For the Queen, far from making a secret of her affectionate friendship, took care to publish it to the world. By her orders two gold medals were struck in his honour; on his death, in 1883, a long and eulogistic obituary notice of him appeared in the *Court Circular;* and a Brown memorial brooch—of gold, with the late gillie's head on one side and the royal monogram on the other—was designed by Her Majesty for presentation to her Highland servants and cottagers, to be worn by them on the anniversary of his death, with a mourning scarf and pins. In the second series of extracts from the Queen's Highland Journal, published in 1884, her "devoted personal attendant and faithful friend" appears upon almost every page, and is in effect the hero of the book. With an absence of reticence remarkable in royal persons, Victoria seemed to demand, in this private and delicate matter, the sympathy of the whole nation; and yet—such is the world!— there were those who actually treated the relations between their Sovereign and her servant as a theme for ribald jests.[1]

II

The busy years hastened away; the traces of Time's unimaginable touch grew manifest; and old age, approaching, laid a gentle hold upon Victoria. The grey hair whitened; the mature features mellowed; the short firm figure amplified and moved more slowly, supported by a stick. And, simultaneously, in the whole tenour of the Queen's existence an extraordinary transformation came to pass. The nation's attitude towards her, critical and even hostile as it had been for so many

[1] *More Leaves,* passim; Crawford, 326–31; private information.

years, altogether changed; while there was a corresponding alteration in the temper of Victoria's own mind.

Many causes led to this result. Among them were the repeated strokes of personal misfortune which befell the Queen during a cruelly short space of years. In 1878 the Princess Alice, who had married in 1862 the Prince Louis of Hesse-Darmstadt, died in tragic circumstances. In the following year the Prince Imperial, the only son of the Empress Eugénie, to whom Victoria, since the catastrophe of 1870, had become devotedly attached, was killed in the Zulu War. Two years later, in 1881, the Queen lost Lord Beaconsfield, and, in 1883, John Brown. In 1884 the Prince Leopold, Duke of Albany, who had been an invalid from birth, died prematurely, shortly after his marriage. Victoria's cup of sorrows was indeed overflowing; and the public, as it watched the widowed mother weeping for her children and her friends, displayed a constantly increasing sympathy.

An event which occurred in 1882 revealed and accentuated the feelings of the nation. As the Queen, at Windsor, was walking from the train to her carriage, a youth named Roderick Maclean fired a pistol at her from a distance of a few

yards. An Eton boy struck up Maclean's arm
with an umbrella before the pistol went off; no
damage was done, and the culprit was at once
arrested. This was the last of a series of seven
attempts upon the Queen—attempts which, taking
place at sporadic intervals over a period of forty
years, resembled one another in a curious manner,
All, with a single exception, were perpetrated by
adolescents, whose motives were apparently not
murderous, since, save in the case of Maclean,
none of their pistols was loaded. These unhappy
youths, who, after buying their cheap weapons,
stuffed them with gunpowder and paper, and then
went off, with the certainty of immediate detection,
to click them in the face of royalty, present a
strange problem to the psychologist. But, though
in each case their actions and their purposes
seemed to be so similar, their fates were remarkably varied. The first of them, Edward Oxford,
who fired at Victoria within a few months of her
marriage, was tried for high treason, declared to
be insane, and sent to an asylum for life. It
appears, however, that this sentence did not commend itself to Albert, for when, two years later,
John Francis committed the same offence, and
was tried upon the same charge, the Prince pronounced that there was no insanity in the matter.

"The wretched creature," he told his father, was "not out of his mind, but a thorough scamp." "I hope," he added, "his trial will be conducted with the greatest strictness." Apparently it was; at any rate, the jury shared the view of the Prince, the plea of insanity was set aside, and Francis was found guilty of high treason and condemned to death; but, as there was no proof of an intent to kill or even to wound, this sentence, after a lengthened deliberation between the Home Secretary and the Judges, was commuted for one of transportation for life. As the law stood, these assaults, futile as they were, could only be treated as high treason; the discrepancy between the actual deed and the tremendous penalties involved was obviously grotesque; and it was, besides, clear that a jury, knowing that a verdict of guilty implied a sentence of death, would tend to the alternative course, and find the prisoner not guilty but insane—a conclusion which, on the face of it, would have appeared to be the more reasonable. In 1842, therefore, an Act was passed making any attempt to hurt the Queen a misdemeanour, punishable by transportation for seven years, or imprisonment, with or without hard labour, for a term not exceeding three years—the misdemeanant, at the discretion of the Court, "to

be publicly or privately whipped, as often, and in
such manner and form, as the Court shall direct,
not exceeding thrice." [1] The four subsequent attempts were all dealt with under this new law;
William Bean, in 1842, was sentenced to eighteen
months' imprisonment; William Hamilton, in
1849, was transported for seven years; and, in
1850, the same sentence was passed upon Lieu-
tenant Robert Pate, who struck the Queen on the
head with his cane in Piccadilly. Pate, alone
among these delinquents, was of mature years; he
had held a commission in the Army, dressed himself as a dandy, and was, the Prince declared,
" manifestly deranged." [2] In 1872 Arthur O'Con-
nor, a youth of seventeen, fired an unloaded pistol
at the Queen outside Buckingham Palace; he was
immediately seized by John Brown, and sentenced
to one year's imprisonment and twenty strokes of
the birch rod. It was for his bravery upon this
occasion that Brown was presented with one of his
gold medals. In all these cases the jury had refused to allow the plea of insanity; but Roderick
Maclean's attempt in 1882 had a different issue.
On this occasion the pistol was found to have
been loaded, and the public indignation, emphasised as it was by Victoria's growing popularity,

[1] Martin, I, 88, 137–43.   [2] *Ibid.*, II, 285.

was particularly great. Either for this or for
some other reason the procedure of the last forty
years was abandoned, and Maclean was tried for
high treason. The result was what might have
been expected: the jury brought in a verdict of
" not guilty, but insane "; and the prisoner was
sent to an asylum during Her Majesty's pleasure.[1]
Their verdict, however, produced a remarkable
consequence. Victoria, who doubtless carried in
her mind some memory of Albert's disapproval of
a similar verdict in the case of Oxford, was very
much annoyed. What did the jury mean, she
asked, by saying that Maclean was not guilty? It
was perfectly clear that he was guilty—she had
seen him fire off the pistol herself. It was in
vain that Her Majesty's constitutional advisers reminded her of the principle of English law which
lays down that no man can be found guilty of a
crime unless he be proved to have had a criminal
intention. Victoria was quite unconvinced. " If
that is the law," she said, " the law must be
altered ": and altered it was. In 1883 an Act
was passed changing the form of the verdict in
cases of insanity, and the confusing anomaly remains upon the Statute Book to this day.[2]

1 *The Times,* April 20, 1882.
2 Letter from Sir Herbert Stephen to *The Times,* December 15, 1920.

But it was not only through the feelings—commiserating or indignant—of personal sympathy that the Queen and her people were being drawn more nearly together; they were beginning, at last, to come to a close and permanent agreement upon the conduct of public affairs. Mr. Gladstone's second administration (1880-85) was a succession of failures, ending in disaster and disgrace; liberalism fell into discredit with the country, and Victoria perceived with joy that her distrust of her Ministers was shared by an ever-increasing number of her subjects. During the crisis in the Sudan, the popular temper was her own. She had been among the first to urge the necessity of an expedition to Khartoum, and, when the news came of the catastrophic death of General Gordon, her voice led the chorus of denunciation which raved against the Government. In her rage, she despatched a fulminating telegram to Mr. Gladstone, not in the usual cypher, but open;[1] and her letter of condolence to Miss Gordon, in which she attacked her Ministers for breach of faith, was widely published. It was rumoured that she had sent for Lord Hartington, the Secretary of State for War, and vehemently upbraided him. "She

[1] Morley, III, 167.

rated me," he was reported to have told a friend, "as if I'd been a footman." "Why didn't she send for the butler?" asked his friend. "Oh," was the reply, "the butler generally manages to keep out of the way on such occasions."[1]

But the day came when it was impossible to keep out of the way any longer. Mr. Gladstone was defeated, and resigned. Victoria, at a final interview, received him with her usual amenity, but, besides the formalities demanded by the occasion, the only remark which she made to him of a personal nature was to the effect that she supposed Mr. Gladstone would now require some rest. He remembered with regret how, at a similar audience in 1874, she had expressed her trust in him as a supporter of the throne; but he noted the change without surprise. "Her mind and opinions," he wrote in his diary afterwards, "have since that day been seriously warped."[2]

Such was Mr. Gladstone's view; but the majority of the nation by no means agreed with him; and, in the General Election of 1886, they showed decisively that Victoria's politics were identical with theirs by casting forth the contrivers of Home Rule—that abomination of desolation—into

[1] Private information.   [2] Morley, III, 347-8.

outer darkness, and placing Lord Salisbury in power. Victoria's satisfaction was profound. A flood of new unwonted hopefulness swept over her, stimulating her vital spirits with a surprising force. Her habit of life was suddenly altered; abandoning the long seclusion which Disraeli's persuasions had only momentarily interrupted, she threw herself vigorously into a multitude of public activities. She appeared at drawing-rooms, at concerts, at reviews; she laid foundation-stones; she went to Liverpool to open an international exhibition, driving through the streets in her open carriage in heavy rain amid vast applauding crowds. Delighted by the welcome which met her everywhere, she warmed to her work. She visited Edinburgh, where the ovation of Liverpool was repeated and surpassed. In London, she opened in high state the Colonial and Indian Exhibition at South Kensington. On this occasion the ceremonial was particularly magnificent; a blare of trumpets announced the approach of Her Majesty; the "National Anthem" followed; and the Queen, seated on a gorgeous throne of hammered gold, replied with her own lips to the address that was presented to her. Then she rose, and, advancing upon the platform with regal port, acknowledged the acclamations of the great assembly by

a succession of curtseys, of elaborate and commanding grace.[1]

Next year was the fiftieth of her reign, and in
June the splendid anniversary was celebrated in
solemn pomp. Victoria, surrounded by the highest dignitaries of her realm, escorted by a glittering galaxy of kings and princes, drove through the
crowded enthusiasm of the capital to render thanks
to God in Westminster Abbey. In that triumphant hour the last remaining traces of past antipathies and past disagreements were altogether
swept away. The Queen was hailed at once as
the mother of her people and as the embodied
symbol of their imperial greatness; and she responded to the double sentiment with all the
ardour of her spirit. England and the people of
England, she knew it, she felt it, were, in some
wonderful and yet quite simple manner, *hers.*
Exultation, affection, gratitude, a profound sense
of obligation, an unbounded pride—such were her
emotions; and, colouring and intensifying the rest,
there was something else. At last, after so long,
happiness—fragmentary, perhaps, and charged
with gravity, but true and unmistakable none the
less—had returned to her. The unaccustomed
feeling filled and warmed her consciousness.

[1] Jerrold, *Widowhood,* 344; private information.

When, at Buckingham Palace again, the long ceremony over, she was asked how she was, " I am very tired, but very happy," she said.[1]

III

And so, after the toils and tempests of the day, a long evening followed—mild, serene, and lighted with a golden glory. For an unexampled atmosphere of success and adoration invested the last period of Victoria's life. Her triumph was the summary, the crown, of a greater triumph—the culminating prosperity of a nation. The solid splendour of the decade between Victoria's two jubilees can hardly be paralleled in the annals of England. The sage counsels of Lord Salisbury seemed to bring with them not only wealth and power, but security; and the country settled down, with calm assurance, to the enjoyment of an established grandeur. And—it was only natural—Victoria settled down too. For she was a part of the establishment—an essential part as it seemed—a fixture—a magnificent, immovable sideboard in the huge saloon of state. Without her the heaped-up banquet of 1890 would have lost its distinctive quality—the comfortable

[1] Lee, 487.

order of the substantial unambiguous dishes, with their background of weighty glamour, half out of sight.

Her own existence came to harmonise more and more with what was around her. Gradually, imperceptibly, Albert receded. It was not that he was forgotten—that would have been impossible—but that the void created by his absence grew less agonising, and even, at last, less obvious. At last Victoria found it possible to regret the bad weather without immediately reflecting that her " dear Albert always said we could not alter it, but must leave it as it was "; she could even enjoy a good breakfast without considering how " dear Albert " would have liked the buttered eggs.[1] And, as that figure slowly faded, its place was taken, inevitably, by Victoria's own. Her being, revolving for so many years round an external object, now changed its motion and found its centre in itself. It had to be so: her domestic position, the pressure of her public work, her indomitable sense of duty, made anything else impossible. Her egotism proclaimed its rights. Her age increased still further the surrounding deference; and her force of character, emerging at length in all its plenitude, imposed itself abso-

[1] *More Leaves*, 23, 29.

lutely upon its environment by the conscious effort
of an imperious will.

Little by little it was noticed that the outward
vestiges of Albert's posthumous domination grew
less complete. At Court the stringency of mourning was relaxed. As the Queen drove through
the Park in her open carriage with her Highlanders behind her, nursery-maids canvassed
eagerly the growing patch of violet velvet in the
bonnet with its jet appurtenances on the small
bowing head.

It was in her family that Victoria's ascendency
reached its highest point. All her offspring were
married; the number of her descendants rapidly
increased; there were many marriages in the third
generation; and no fewer than thirty-seven of her
great-grandchildren were living at the time of her
death. A picture of the period displays the royal
family collected together in one of the great rooms
at Windsor—a crowded company of more than
fifty persons, with the imperial matriarch in their
midst. Over them all she ruled with a most potent
sway. The small concerns of the youngest aroused
her passionate interest; and the oldest she treated
as if they were children still. The Prince of
Wales, in particular, stood in tremendous awe of
his mother. She had steadily refused to allow him

the slightest participation in the business of government; and he had occupied himself in other ways. Nor could it be denied that he enjoyed himself—out of her sight; but, in that redoubtable presence, his abounding manhood suffered a miserable eclipse. Once, at Osborne, when, owing to no fault of his, he was too late for a dinner party, he was observed standing behind a pillar and, wiping the sweat from his forehead, trying to nerve himself to go up to the Queen. When at last he did so, she gave him a stiff nod, whereupon he vanished immediately behind another pillar, and remained there until the party broke up. At the time of this incident the Prince of Wales was over fifty years of age.[1]

It was inevitable that the Queen's domestic activities should occasionally trench upon the domain of high diplomacy; and this was especially the case when the interests of her eldest daughter, the Crown Princess of Prussia, were at stake. The Crown Prince held liberal opinions; he was much influenced by his wife; and both were detested by Bismarck, who declared with scurrilous emphasis that the Englishwoman and her mother were a menace to the Prussian State. The feud was still further intensified when, on the death of

[1] Eckardstein, I, 184-7.

the old Emperor (1888), the Crown Prince succeeded to the throne. A family entanglement
brought on a violent crisis. One of the daughters
of the new Empress had become betrothed to
Prince Alexander of Battenberg, who had lately
been ejected from the throne of Bulgaria owing
to the hostility of the Tsar. Victoria, as well as
the Empress, highly approved of the match. Of
the two brothers of Prince Alexander, the elder
had married another of her grand-daughters, and
the younger was the husband of her daughter, the
Princess Beatrice; she was devoted to the handsome young man; and she was delighted by the
prospect of the third brother—on the whole the
handsomest, she thought, of the three—also becoming a member of her family. Unfortunately,
however, Bismarck was opposed to the scheme.
He perceived that the marriage would endanger
the friendship between Germany and Russia,
which was vital to his foreign policy, and he announced that it must not take place. A fierce
struggle between the Empress and the Chancellor
followed. Victoria, whose hatred of her daughter's enemy was unbounded, came over to Charlottenburg to join in the fray. Bismarck, over
his pipe and lager, snorted out his alarm. The
Queen of England's object, he said, was clearly

political—she wished to estrange Germany and
Russia—and very likely she would have her way.
" In family matters," he added, " she is not used
to contradiction "; she would " bring the parson
with her in her travelling bag and the bridegroom
in her trunk, and the marriage would come off on
the spot." But the man of blood and iron was not
to be thwarted so easily, and he asked for a private
interview with the Queen. The details of their
conversation are unknown; but it is certain that
in the course of it Victoria was forced to realise
the meaning of resistance to that formidable personage, and that she promised to use all her influence to prevent the marriage. The engagement
was broken off; and in the following year Prince
Alexander of Battenberg united himself to Fräulein Loisinger, an actress at the court theatre of
Darmstadt.[1]

But such painful incidents were rare. Victoria
was growing very old; with no Albert to guide
her, with no Beaconsfield to enflame her, she was
willing enough to abandon the dangerous questions of diplomacy to the wisdom of Lord Salisbury, and to concentrate her energies upon objects
which touched her more nearly and over which she
could exercise an undisputed control. Her home

[1] Grant Robertson, 458-9; Busch, III, 174-88; Lee, 490-2.

—her court—the monuments at Balmoral—the livestock at Windsor—the organisation of her engagements—the supervision of the multitudinous details of her daily routine—such matters played now an even greater part in her existence than before. Her life passed in an extraordinary exactitude. Every moment of her day was mapped out beforehand; the succession of her engagements was immutably fixed; the dates of her journeys— to Osborne, to Balmoral, to the South of France, to Windsor, to London—were hardly altered from year to year. She demanded from those who surrounded her a rigid precision in details, and she was preternaturally quick in detecting the slightest deviation from the rules which she had laid down. Such was the irresistible potency of her personality, that anything but the most implicit obedience to her wishes was felt to be impossible; but sometimes somebody was unpunctual; and unpunctuality was one of the most heinous of sins. Then her displeasure—her dreadful displeasure— became all too visible. At such moments there seemed nothing surprising in her having been the daughter of a martinet.[1]

But these storms, unnerving as they were while they lasted, were quickly over, and they grew

[1] *Quarterly Review*, cxciii, 305–6; 308–10.

more and more exceptional. With the return of
happiness a gentle benignity flowed from the aged
Queen. Her smile, once so rare a visitant to those
saddened features, flitted over them with an easy
alacrity; the blue eyes beamed; the whole face,
starting suddenly from its pendulous expression-
lessness, brightened and softened and cast over
those who watched it an unforgettable charm.
For in her last years there was a fascination in
Victoria's amiability which had been lacking even
from the vivid impulse of her youth. Over all
who approached her—or very nearly all—she
threw a peculiar spell. Her grandchildren adored
her; her ladies waited upon her with a reverential
love. The honour of serving her obliterated a
thousand inconveniences—the monotony of a court
existence, the fatigue of standing, the necessity for
a superhuman attentiveness to the minutiæ of time
and space. As one did one's wonderful duty one
could forget that one's legs were aching from the
infinitude of the passages at Windsor, or that
one's bare arms were turning blue in the Balmoral
cold.

What, above all, seemed to make such service
delightful was the detailed interest which the
Queen took in the circumstances of those around
her. Her absorbing passion for the comfortable

commonplaces, the small crises, the recurrent sen-
timentalities, of domestic life constantly demanded
wider fields for its activity; the sphere of her own
family, vast as it was, was not enough; she became the eager confidante of the household affairs
of her ladies; her sympathies reached out to the
palace domestics; even the housemaids and scul-
lions—so it appeared—were the objects of her
searching inquiries, and of her heartfelt solicitude
when their lovers were ordered to a foreign station, or their aunts suffered from an attack of
rheumatism which was more than usually acute.[1]

Nevertheless the due distinctions of rank were
immaculately preserved. The Queen's mere presence was enough to ensure that; but, in addition,
the dominion of court etiquette was paramount.
For that elaborate code, which had kept Lord
Melbourne stiff upon the sofa and ranged the
other guests in silence about the round table according to the order of precedence, was as punctiliously enforced as ever. Every evening after
dinner, the hearth-rug, sacred to royalty, loomed
before the profane in inaccessible glory, or, on
one or two terrific occasions, actually lured them
magnetically forward to the very edge of the

[1] *Quarterly Review*, cxciii, 315–6; Miss Ethel Smyth, *London Mercury*, November, 1920; private information.

abyss. The Queen, at the fitting moment, moved towards her guests; one after the other they were led up to her; and, while dualogue followed dualogue in constraint and embarrassment, the rest of the assembly stood still, without a word.[1] Only in one particular was the severity of the etiquette allowed to lapse. Throughout the greater part of the reign the rule that ministers must stand during their audiences with the Queen had been absolute. When Lord Derby, the Prime Minister, had an audience of Her Majesty after a serious illness, he mentioned it afterwards, as a proof of the royal favour, that the Queen had remarked " How sorry she was she could not ask him to be seated." Subsequently, Disraeli, after an attack of gout and in a moment of extreme expansion on the part of Victoria, had been offered a chair; but he had thought it wise humbly to decline the privilege. In her later years, however, the Queen invariably asked Mr. Gladstone and Lord Salisbury to sit down.[2]

Sometimes the solemnity of the evening was diversified by a concert, an opera, or even a play. One of the most marked indications of Victoria's enfranchisement from the thraldom of widowhood

[1] *Quarterly Review,* cxciii, 325; Miss Ethel Smyth, *London Mercury,* November, 1920.

[2] Buckle, V, 339; Morley, III, 347, 514.

had been her resumption—after an interval of
thirty years—of the custom of commanding dramatic companies from London to perform before
the Court at Windsor. On such occasions her
spirits rose high. She loved acting; she loved a
good plot; above all, she loved a farce. Engrossed
by everything that passed upon the stage she
would follow, with childlike innocence, the un-
winding of the story; or she would assume an
air of knowing superiority and exclaim in triumph,
" There! You didn't expect *that,* did you?"
when the *dénouement* came. Her sense of humour was of a vigorous though primitive kind.
She had been one of the very few persons who
had always been able to appreciate the Prince
Consort's jokes; and, when those were cracked
no more, she could still roar with laughter, in
the privacy of her household, over some small
piece of fun—some oddity of an ambassador, or
some ignorant Minister's *faux pas.* When the
jest grew subtle she was less pleased; but, if it
approached the confines of the indecorous, the danger was serious. To take a liberty called down
at once Her Majesty's most crushing disapproba-
tion; and to say something improper was to take
the greatest liberty of all. Then the royal lips
sank down at the corners, the royal eyes stared

in astonished protrusion, and in fact the royal
countenance became inauspicious in the highest
degree. The transgressor shuddered into silence,
while the awful " We are not amused " annihilated
the dinner table. Afterwards, in her private en-
tourage, the Queen would observe that the person
in question was, she very much feared, " not discreet "; it was a verdict from which there was no
appeal.[1]

In general, her æsthetic tastes had remained
unchanged since the days of Mendelssohn, Landseer, and Lablache. She still delighted in the
roulades of Italian opera; she still demanded a
high standard in the execution of a pianoforte
duet. Her views on painting were decided; Sir
Edwin, she declared, was perfect; she was much
impressed by Lord Leighton's manners; and she
profoundly distrusted Mr. Watts. From time
to time she ordered engraved portraits to be taken
of members of the royal family; on these occasions she would have the first proofs submitted to
her, and, having inspected them with minute particularity, she would point out their mistakes to
the artists, indicating at the same time how they
might be corrected. The artists invariably dis-

---

[1] *Quarterly Review*, vol. 193, pp. 315, 316-7, 324-5, 326; *Spinster
Lady*, 268-9; Lee, 504-5.

covered that Her Majesty's suggestions were of
the highest value. In literature her interests were
more restricted. She was devoted to Lord Tennyson; and, as the Prince Consort had admired
George Eliot, she perused "Middlemarch": she
was disappointed. There is reason to believe,
however, that the romances of another female
writer, whose popularity among the humbler
classes of Her Majesty's subjects was at one
time enormous, secured, no less, the approval of
Her Majesty. Otherwise she did not read very
much.[1]

Once, however, the Queen's attention was drawn
to a publication which it was impossible for her
to ignore. "The Greville Memoirs," filled with a
mass of historical information of extraordinary
importance, but filled also with descriptions, which
were by no means flattering, of George IV,
William IV, and other royal persons, was brought
out by Mr. Reeve. Victoria read the book, and
was appalled. It was, she declared, a "dreadful
and really scandalous book," and she could not
say "how *horrified* and *indignant*" she was at
Greville's "indiscretion, indelicacy, ingratitude
towards friends, betrayal of confidence and shame-

[1] *Quarterly Review*, vol. 193, pp. 322–4; Martin, *Queen Victoria*,
46–9; private information.

ful disloyalty towards his Sovereign." She wrote
to Disraeli to tell him that in her opinion it was
" *very important* that the book should be severely
censured and discredited." " The tone in which
he speaks of royalty," she added, " is unlike anything one sees in history even, and is most repre-
hensible." Her anger was directed with almost
equal vehemence against Mr. Reeve for his having published " such an abominable book," and
she charged Sir Arthur Helps to convey to him
her deep displeasure. Mr. Reeve, however, was
impenitent. When Sir Arthur told him that, in
the Queen's opinion, " the book degraded royalty,"
he replied: " Not at all; it elevates it by the contrast it offers between the present and the defunct
state of affairs." But this adroit defence failed
to make any impression upon Victoria; and Mr.
Reeve, when he retired from the public service,
did not receive the knighthood which custom entitled him to expect.[1] Perhaps if the Queen had
known how many caustic comments upon herself
Mr. Reeve had quietly suppressed in the published
Memoirs, she would have been almost grateful to
him; but, in that case, what would she have said
of Greville? Imagination boggles at the thought.
As for more modern essays upon the same topic,

1 Buckle, V, 349–51; Laughton, II, 226.

Her Majesty, it is to be feared, would have characterised them as " not discreet."

But as a rule the leisure hours of that active life were occupied with recreations of a less intangible quality than the study of literature or the appreciation of art. Victoria was a woman not only of vast property but of innumerable possessions. She had inherited an immense quantity of furniture, of ornaments, of china, of plate, of valuable objects of every kind; her purchases, throughout a long life, made a formidable addition to these stores; and there flowed in upon her, besides, from every quarter of the globe, a constant stream of gifts. Over this enormous mass she exercised an unceasing and minute supervision, and the arrangement and the contemplation of it, in all its details, filled her with an intimate satisfaction. The collecting instinct has its roots in the very depths of human nature; and, in the case of Victoria, it seemed to owe its force to two of her dominating impulses—the intense sense, which had always been hers, of her own personality, and the craving which, growing with the years, had become in her old age almost an obsession, for fixity, for solidity, for the setting up of palpable barriers against the outrages of change and time. When she considered the multitudinous objects which belonged to her, or, better still, when, choosing out some section of them as the fancy took her, she actually savoured the vivid richness of their individual qualities, she saw herself deliciously reflected from a million facets, felt herself magnified miraculously over a boundless area, and was well pleased. That was just as it should be; but then came the dismaying thought—everything slips away, crumbles, vanishes; Sèvres dinner-services get broken; even golden basins go unaccountably astray; even one's self, with all the recollections and experiences that make up one's being, fluctuates, perishes, dissolves . . . But no! It could not, should not be so! There should be no changes and no losses! Nothing should ever move—neither the past nor the present—and she herself least of all! And so the tenacious woman, hoarding her valuables, decreed their immortality with all the resolution of her soul. She would not lose one memory or one pin.

She gave orders that nothing should be thrown away—and nothing was. There, in drawer after drawer, in wardrobe after wardrobe, reposed the dresses of seventy years. But not only the dresses —the furs and the mantles and subsidiary frills and the muffs and the parasols and the bonnets—

all were ranged in chronological order, dated and complete. A great cupboard was devoted to the dolls; in the china room at Windsor a special table held the mugs of her childhood, and her children's mugs as well. Mementoes of the past surrounded her in serried accumulations. In every room the tables were powdered thick with the photographs of relatives; their portraits, revealing them at all ages, covered the walls; their figures, in solid marble, rose up from pedestals, or gleamed from brackets in the form of gold and silver statuettes. The dead, in every shape—in miniatures, in porcelain, in enormous life-size oil-paintings—were perpetually about her. John Brown stood upon her writing-table in solid gold. Her favourite horses and dogs, endowed with a new durability, crowded round her footsteps. Sharp, in silver gilt, dominated the dinner table; Boy and Boz lay together among unfading flowers, in bronze. And it was not enough that each particle of the past should be given the stability of metal or of marble: the whole collection, in its arrangement, no less than its entity, should be immutably fixed. There might be additions, but there might never be alterations. No chintz might change, no carpet, no curtain, be replaced by another; or, if long use at last made it necessary, the stuffs and the patterns must be so identically reproduced that the keenest eye might not detect the difference. No new picture could be hung upon the walls at Windsor, for those already there had been put in their places by Albert, whose decisions were eternal. So, indeed, were Victoria's. To ensure that they should be the aid of the camera was called in. Every single article in the Queen's possession was photographed from several points of view. These photographs were submitted to Her Majesty, and when, after careful inspection, she had approved of them, they were placed in a series of albums, richly bound. Then, opposite each photograph, an entry was made, indicating the number of the article, the number of the room in which it was kept, its exact position in the room and all its principal characteristics. The fate of every object which had undergone this process was henceforth irrevocably sealed. The whole multitude, once and for all, took up its steadfast station. And Victoria, with a gigantic volume or two of the endless catalogue always beside her, to look through, to ponder upon, to expatiate over, could feel, with a double contentment, that the transitoriness of this world had been arrested by the amplitude of her might.[1]

[1] *Private Life,* 13, 66, 69, 70–1, 151, 182.

Thus the collection, ever multiplying, ever en-
croaching upon new fields of consciousness, ever
rooting itself more firmly in the depths of instinct,
became one of the dominating influences of that
strange existence. It was a collection not merely
of things and of thoughts, but of states of mind
and ways of living as well. The celebration of
anniversaries grew to be an important branch of
it—of birthdays and marriage days and death
days, each of which demanded its appropriate
feeling, which, in its turn, must be itself expressed
in an appropriate outward form. And the form,
of course—the ceremony of rejoicing or lamenta-
tion—was stereotyped with the rest: it was part
of the collection. On a certain day, for instance,
flowers must be strewn on John Brown's monument at Balmoral; and the date of the yearly
departure for Scotland was fixed by that fact.
Inevitably it was around the central circumstance
of death—death, the final witness to human muta-
bility—that these commemorative cravings clustered most thickly. Might not even death itself
be humbled, if one could recall enough?—if one
asserted, with a sufficiently passionate and reiterated emphasis, the eternity of love? Accordingly,
every bed in which Victoria slept had attached to
it, at the back, on the right-hand side, above the

pillow, a photograph of the head and shoulders of Albert as he lay dead, surmounted by a wreath of immortelles.[1] At Balmoral, where memories came crowding so closely, the solid signs of memory appeared in surprising profusion. Obelisks, pyramids, tombs, statues, cairns, and seats of inscribed granite, proclaimed Victoria's dedication to the dead. There, twice a year, on the days that followed her arrival, a solemn pilgrimage of inspection and meditation was performed. There, on August 26—Albert's birthday—at the foot of the bronze statue of him in Highland dress, the Queen, her family, her Court, her servants, and her tenantry, met together and in silence drank to the memory of the dead. In England the tokens of remembrance pullulated hardly less. Not a day passed without some addition to the multifold assemblage—a gold statuette of Ross, the piper— a life-sized marble group of Victoria and Albert, in medieval costume, inscribed upon the base with the words: " Allured to brighter worlds and led the way "—a granite slab in the shrubbery at Osborne, informing the visitor of " Waldmann: the very favourite little dachshund of Queen Victoria; who brought him from Baden, April 1872; died, July 11, 1881." [2]

[1] *Private Life,* 19.

[2] *Ibid.,* 207, 212.

At Frogmore, the great mausoleum, perpetually enriched, was visited almost daily by the Queen when the Court was at Windsor.[1] But there was another, a more secret and a hardly less holy shrine. The suite of rooms which Albert had occupied in the Castle was kept for ever shut away from the eyes of any save the most privileged. Within those precincts everything remained as it had been at the Prince's death; but the mysterious preoccupation of Victoria had commanded that her husband's clothing should be laid afresh, each evening, upon the bed, and that, each evening, the water should be set ready in the basin, as if he were still alive; and this incredible rite was performed with scrupulous regularity for nearly forty years.[2]

Such was the inner worship; and still the flesh obeyed the spirit; still the daily hours of labour proclaimed Victoria's consecration to duty and to the ideal of the dead. Yet, with the years, the sense of self-sacrifice faded; the natural energies of that ardent being discharged themselves with satisfaction into the channel of public work; the love of business which, from her girlhood, had been strong within her, reasserted itself in all its vigour, and, in her old age, to have been cut off from her

[1] *Private Life*, 233.　　　　[2] Private information.

papers and her boxes would have been, not a relief, but an agony to Victoria. Thus, though toiling Ministers might sigh and suffer, the whole process of government continued, till the very end, to pass before her. Nor was that all; ancient precedent had made the validity of an enormous number of official transactions dependent upon the application of the royal sign-manual; and a great proportion of the Queen's working hours was spent in this mechanical task. Nor did she show any desire to diminish it. On the contrary, she voluntarily resumed the duty of signing commissions in the army, from which she had been set free by Act of Parliament, and from which, during the years of middle life, she had abstained. In no case would she countenance the proposal that she should use a stamp. But, at last, when the increasing pressure of business made the delays of the antiquated system intolerable, she consented that, for certain classes of documents, her oral sanction should be sufficient. Each paper was read aloud to her, and she said at the end " Approved." Often, for hours at a time, she would sit, with Albert's bust in front of her, while the word " Approved " issued at intervals from her lips. The word came forth with a majestic sonority; for her voice now—how changed from the silvery treble of her girlhood!—was a contralto, full and strong.[1]

IV

The final years were years of apotheosis. In the dazzled imagination of her subjects Victoria soared aloft towards the regions of divinity through a nimbus of purest glory. Criticism fell dumb; deficiencies which, twenty years earlier, would have been universally admitted, were now as universally ignored. That the nation's idol was a very incomplete representative of the nation was a circumstance that was hardly noticed, and yet it was conspicuously true. For the vast changes which, out of the England of 1837, had produced the England of 1897, seemed scarcely to have touched the Queen. The immense industrial development of the period, the significance of which had been so thoroughly understood by Albert, meant little indeed to Victoria. The amazing scientific movement, which Albert had appreciated no less, left Victoria perfectly cold. Her conception of the universe, and of man's place in it, and of the stupendous problems of nature and philosophy remained, throughout her life, entirely unchanged. Her religion was the religion which she had learnt

[1] Lee, 514–5; Crawford, 362–3.

from the Baroness Lehzen and the Duchess of
Kent. Here, too, it might have been supposed
that Albert's views might have influenced her.
For Albert, in matters of religion, was advanced.
Disbelieving altogether in evil spirits, he had had
his doubts about the miracle of the Gaderene
Swine.[1] Stockmar, even, had thrown out, in a
remarkable memorandum on the education of the
Prince of Wales, the suggestion that while the
child "must unquestionably be brought up in the
creed of the Church of England," it might nevertheless be in accordance with the spirit of the
times to exclude from his religious training the
inculcation of a belief in "the supernatural doctrines of Christianity."[2] This, however, would
have been going too far; and all the royal children
were brought up in complete orthodoxy. Anything else would have grieved Victoria, though her
own conceptions of the orthodox were not very
precise. But her nature, in which imagination
and subtlety held so small a place, made her instinctively recoil from the intricate ecstasies of
High Anglicanism; and she seemed to feel most at
home in the simple faith of the Presbyterian
Church of Scotland.[3] This was what might have

[1] Wilberforce, Samuel, II, 275.
[2] Martin, II, 185-7.
[3] *Quarterly Review,* vol. 193, pp. 319-20.

been expected; for Lehzen was the daughter of a Lutheran pastor, and the Lutherans and the Presbyterians have much in common. For many years Dr. Norman Macleod, an innocent Scotch minister, was her principal spiritual adviser; and, when he was taken from her, she drew much comfort from quiet chats about life and death with the cottagers at Balmoral.[1] Her piety, absolutely genuine, found what it wanted in the sober exhortations of old John Grant and the devout saws of Mrs. P. Farquharson. They possessed the qualities, which, as a child of fourteen, she had so sincerely admired in the Bishop of Chester's " Exposition of the Gospel of St. Matthew "; they were " just plain and comprehensible and full of truth and good feeling." The Queen, who gave her name to the Age of Mill and of Darwin, never got any further than that.

From the social movements of her time Victoria was equally remote. Towards the smallest no less than towards the greatest changes she remained inflexible. During her youth and middle age smoking had been forbidden in polite society, and so long as she lived she would not withdraw her anathema against it. Kings might protest; bishops and ambassadors, invited to Windsor, might be re-

[1] Crawford, 343.

duced, in the privacy of their bedrooms, to lie
full-length upon the floor and smoke up the chim-
ney—the interdict continued.[1] It might have been
supposed that a female sovereign would have lent
her countenance to one of the most vital of all the
reforms to which her epoch gave birth—the eman-
cipation of women—but, on the contrary, the mere
mention of such a proposal sent the blood rushing to her head. In 1870, her eye having fallen
upon the report of a meeting in favour of Wom-
en's Suffrage, she wrote to Mr. Martin in royal
rage—" The Queen is most anxious to enlist
everyone who can speak or write to join in check-
ing this mad, wicked folly of 'Woman's Rights,'
with all its attendant horrors, on which her poor
feeble sex is bent, forgetting every sense of
womanly feeling and propriety. Lady —— ought
to get a *good whipping*. It is a subject which
makes the Queen so furious that she cannot con-
tain herself. God created men and women different—then let them remain each in their own position. Tennyson has some beautiful lines on the
difference of men and women in ' The Princess.'
Woman would become the most hateful, heart-
less, and disgusting of human beings were she
allowed to unsex herself; and where would be the

1 Eckardstein, I, 177.

protection which man was intended to give the weaker sex? The Queen is sure that Mrs. Martin agrees with her." [1] The argument was irrefutable; Mrs. Martin agreed; and yet the canker spread.

In another direction Victoria's comprehension of the spirit of her age has been constantly asserted. It was for long the custom for courtly historians and polite politicians to compliment the Queen upon the correctness of her attitude towards the Constitution. But such praises seem hardly to be justified by the facts. In her later years Victoria more than once alluded with regret to her conduct during the Bedchamber crisis, and let it be understood that she had grown wiser since. [2] Yet in truth it is difficult to trace any fundamental change either in her theory or her practice in constitutional matters throughout her life. The same despotic and personal spirit which led her to break off the negotiations with Peel is equally visible in her animosity towards Palmerston, in her threats of abdication to Disraeli, and in her desire to prosecute the Duke of Westminster for attending a meeting upon Bulgarian atrocities. The complex and delicate principles of the Constitution cannot be said to have come within the

[1] Martin, *Queen Victoria*, 69–70.
[2] *Girlhood*, II, 142.

compass of her mental faculties; and in the actual developments which it underwent during her reign she played a passive part. From 1840 to 1861 the power of the Crown steadily increased in England; from 1861 to 1901 it steadily declined. The first process was due to the influence of the Prince Consort, the second to that of a series of great Ministers. During the first Victoria was in effect a mere accessory; during the second the threads of power, which Albert had so laboriously collected, inevitably fell from her hands into the vigorous grasp of Mr. Gladstone, Lord Beaconsfield, and Lord Salisbury. Perhaps, absorbed as she was in routine, and difficult as she found it to distinguish at all clearly between the trivial and the essential, she was only dimly aware of what was happening. Yet, at the end of her reign, the Crown was weaker than at any other time in English history. Paradoxically enough, Victoria received the highest eulogiums for assenting to a political evolution, which, had she completely realised its import, would have filled her with supreme displeasure.

Nevertheless it must not be supposed that she was a second George III. Her desire to impose her will, vehement as it was, and unlimited by any principle, was yet checked by a certain shrewdness. She might oppose her Ministers with extraordinary violence; she might remain utterly impervious to arguments and supplications; the pertinacity of her resolution might seem to be unconquerable; but, at the very last moment of all, her obstinacy would give way. Her innate respect and capacity for business, and perhaps, too, the memory of Albert's scrupulous avoidance of extreme courses, prevented her from ever entering an *impasse*. By instinct she understood when the facts were too much for her, and to them she invariably yielded. After all, what else could she do?

But if, in all these ways, the Queen and her epoch were profoundly separated, the points of contact between them also were not few. Victoria understood very well the meaning and the attractions of power and property, and in such learning the English nation, too, had grown to be more and more proficient. During the last fifteen years of the reign—for the short Liberal Administration of 1892 was a mere interlude—imperialism was the dominant creed of the country. It was Victoria's as well. In this direction, if in no other, she had allowed her mind to develop. Under Disraeli's tutelage the British Dominions over the seas had come to mean much more to her than ever before, and, in particular, she had grown enamoured of the East. The thought of India fascinated her; she set to, and learnt a little Hindustani; she engaged some Indian servants, who became her inseparable attendants, and one of whom, Munshi Abdul Karim, eventually almost succeeded to the position which had once been John Brown's.[1] At the same time, the imperialist temper of the nation invested her office with a new significance exactly harmonising with her own inmost proclivities. The English polity was in the main a common-sense structure; but there was always a corner in it where common-sense could not enter—where, somehow or other, the ordinary measurements were not applicable and the ordinary rules did not apply. So our ancestors had laid it down, giving scope, in their wisdom, to that mystical element which, as it seems, can never quite be eradicated from the affairs of men. Naturally it was in the Crown that the mysticism of the English polity was concentrated—the Crown, with its venerable antiquity, its sacred associations, its imposing spectacular array. But, for nearly two centuries, common-sense had been predominant in the great building, and the little, unexplored, inexplicable corner had attracted small attention.

[1] Lee, 485; private information.

Then, with the rise of imperialism, there was a change. For imperialism is a faith as well as a business; as it grew, the mysticism in English public life grew with it; and simultaneously a new importance began to attach to the Crown. The need for a symbol—a symbol of England's might, of England's worth, of England's extraordinary and mysterious destiny—became felt more urgently than ever before. The Crown was that symbol: and the Crown rested upon the head of Victoria. Thus it happened that while by the end of the reign the power of the sovereign had appreciably diminished, the prestige of the sovereign had enormously grown.

Yet this prestige was not merely the outcome of public changes; it was an intensely personal matter, too. Victoria was the Queen of England, the Empress of India, the quintessential pivot round which the whole magnificent machine was revolving—but how much more besides! For one thing, she was of a great age—an almost indispensable qualification for popularity in England. She had given proof of one of the most admired characteristics of the race—persistent vitality. She had reigned for sixty years, and she was not out. And then, she was a character. The outlines of her nature were firmly drawn, and, even

through the mists which envelop royalty, clearly
visible. In the popular imagination her familiar
figure filled, with satisfying ease, a distinct and
memorable place. It was, besides, the kind of
figure which naturally called forth the admiring
sympathy of the great majority of the nation.
Goodness they prized above every other human
quality; and Victoria, who had said that she
would be good at the age of twelve, had kept
her word. Duty, conscience, morality—yes! in the
light of those high beacons the Queen had always
lived. She had passed her days in work and not
in pleasure—in public responsibilities and family
cares. The standard of solid virtue which had
been set up so long ago amid the domestic happiness of Osborne had never been lowered for an
instant. For more than half a century no divorced lady had approached the precincts of the
Court. Victoria, indeed, in her enthusiasm for
wifely fidelity, had laid down a still stricter ordinance: she frowned severely upon any widow
who married again.[1] Considering that she herself
was the offspring of a widow's second marriage,
this prohibition might be regarded as an eccentricity; but, no doubt, it was an eccentricity on
the right side. The middle classes, firm in the

[1] Lee, 555.

triple brass of their respectability, rejoiced with a special joy over the most respectable of Queens. They almost claimed her, indeed, as one of themselves; but this would have been an exaggeration. For, though many of her characteristics were most often found among the middle classes, in other respects—in her manners, for instance—Victoria was decidedly aristocratic. And, in one important particular, she was neither aristocratic nor middle-class: her attitude toward herself was simply regal.

Such qualities were obvious and important; but, in the impact of a personality, it is something deeper, something fundamental and common to all its qualities, that really tells. In Victoria, it is easy to discern the nature of this underlying element: it was a peculiar sincerity. Her truthfulness, her single-mindedness, the vividness of her emotions and her unrestrained expression of them, were the varied forms which this central characteristic assumed. It was her sincerity which gave her at once her impressiveness, her charm, and her absurdity. She moved through life with the imposing certitude of one to whom concealment was impossible—either towards her surroundings or towards herself. There she was, all of her—the Queen of England, complete and obvious; the world might take her or leave her; she had nothing more to show, or to explain, or to modify; and, with her peerless carriage, she swept along her path. And not only was concealment out of the question; reticence, reserve, even dignity itself, as it sometimes seemed, might be very well dispensed with. As Lady Lyttelton said: " There is a transparency in her truth that is very striking—not a shade of exaggeration in describing feelings or facts; like very few other people I ever knew. Many may be as true, but I think it goes often along with some reserve. She talks all out; just as it is, no more and no less." [1] She talked all out; and she wrote all out, too. Her letters, in the surprising jet of their expression, remind one of a turned-on tap. What is within pours forth in an immediate, spontaneous rush. Her utterly unliterary style has at least the merit of being a vehicle exactly suited to her thoughts and feelings; and even the platitude of her phraseology carries with it a curiously personal flavour. Undoubtedly it was through her writings that she touched the heart of the public. Not only in her " Highland Journals," where the mild chronicle of her private proceedings was laid bare without a trace either of affectation or

[1] Lyttelton, 331.

of embarrassment, but also in those remarkable messages to the nation which, from time to time, she published in the newspapers, her people found her very close to them indeed. They felt instinctively Victoria's irresistible sincerity, and they responded. And in truth it was an endearing trait.

The personality and the position, too—the wonderful combination of them—that, perhaps, was what was finally fascinating in the case. The little old lady, with her white hair and her plain mourning clothes, in her wheeled chair or her donkey-carriage—one saw her so; and then—close behind—with their immediate suggestion of singularity, of mystery, and of power—the Indian servants. That was the familiar vision, and it was admirable; but, at chosen moments, it was right that the widow of Windsor should step forth apparent Queen. The last and the most glorious of such occasions was the Jubilee of 1897. Then, as the splendid procession passed along, escorting Victoria through the thronged re-echoing streets of London on her progress of thanksgiving to St. Paul's Cathedral, the greatness of her realm and the adoration of her subjects blazed out together. The tears welled to her eyes, and, while the multitude roared round her, "How kind they are to

me! How kind they are!" she repeated over and
over again.[1] That night her message flew over the
Empire: "From my heart I thank my beloved
people. May God bless them!" The long journey was nearly done. But the traveller, who had
come so far, and through such strange experiences, moved on with the old unfaltering step.
The girl, the wife, the aged woman, were the
same: vitality, conscientiousness, pride, and simplicity were hers to the latest hour.

[1] *Quarterly Review,* vol. 193, p. 310.

CHAPTER X

THE END

THE evening had been golden; but, after all, the day was to close in cloud and tempest. Imperial needs, imperial ambitions, involved the country in the South African War. There were checks, reverses, bloody disasters; for a moment the nation was shaken, and the public distresses were felt with intimate solicitude by the Queen. But her spirit was high, and neither her courage nor her confidence wavered for a moment. Throwing herself heart and soul into the struggle, she laboured with redoubled vigour, interested herself in every detail of the hostilities, and sought by every means in her power to render service to the national cause. In April 1900, when she was in her eighty-first year, she made the extraordinary decision to abandon her annual visit to the South of France, and to go instead to Ireland, which had provided a particularly large number of recruits to the armies in the field. She stayed for three weeks in Dublin, driving through the streets, in spite of the warnings of her advisers, without an armed escort;

and the visit was a complete success But, in the
course of it, she began, for the first time, to show
signs of the fatigue of age.[1]

For the long strain and the unceasing anxiety,
brought by the war, made themselves felt at last.
Endowed by nature with a robust constitution,
Victoria, though in periods of depression she had
sometimes supposed herself an invalid, had in
reality throughout her life enjoyed remarkably
good health. In her old age, she had suffered
from a rheumatic stiffness of the joints, which had
necessitated the use of a stick, and, eventually, a
wheeled chair; but no other ailments attacked her,
until, in 1898, her eyesight began to be affected by
incipient cataract. After that, she found reading more and more difficult, though she could still
sign her name, and even, with some difficulty,
write letters. In the summer of 1900, however,
more serious symptoms appeared. Her memory,
in whose strength and precision she had so long
prided herself, now sometimes deserted her; there
was a tendency towards aphasia; and, while no
specific disease declared itself, by the autumn there
were unmistakable signs of a general physical de-
cay. Yet, even in these last months, the strain
of iron held firm. The daily work continued;

[1] *Quarterly Review*, vol. 193, pp. 318, 336-7.

nay, it actually increased; for the Queen, with an astonishing pertinacity, insisted upon communicating personally with an ever-growing multitude of men and women who had suffered through the war.[1]

By the end of the year the last remains of her ebbing strength had almost deserted her; and through the early days of the opening century it was clear that her dwindling forces were only kept together by an effort of will. On January 14, she had at Osborne an hour's interview with Lord Roberts, who had returned victorious from South Africa a few days before. She inquired with acute anxiety into all the details of the war; she appeared to sustain the exertion successfully; but, when the audience was over, there was a collapse. On the following day her medical attendants recognised that her state was hopeless; and yet, for two days more, the indomitable spirit fought on; for two days more she discharged the duties of a Queen of England. But after that there was an end of working; and then, and not till then, did the last optimism of those about her break down. The brain was failing, and life was gently slipping away. Her family gathered round her; for a little more she lingered, speechless and ap-

[1] Lee, 536–7; private information.

parently insensible; and, on January 22, 1901, she died.[1]

When, two days previously, the news of the approaching end had been made public, astonished grief had swept over the country. It appeared as if some monstrous reversal of the course of nature was about to take place. The vast majority of her subjects had never known a time when Queen Victoria had not been reigning over them. She had become an indissoluble part of their whole scheme of things, and that they were about to lose her appeared a scarcely possible thought. She herself, as she lay blind and silent, seemed to those who watched her to be divested of all thinking—to have glided already, unawares, into oblivion. Yet, perhaps, in the secret chambers of consciousness, she had her thoughts, too. Perhaps her fading mind called up once more the shadows of the past to float before it, and retraced, for the last time, the vanished visions of that long history—passing back and back, through the cloud of years, to older and ever older memories—to the spring woods at Osborne, so full of primroses for Lord Beaconsfield—to Lord Palmerston's queer clothes and high demeanour, and Albert's face under the green lamp, and

[1] Lee, 537–9; *Quarterly Review*, cxciii, 309.

Albert's first stag at Balmoral, and Albert in his blue and silver uniform, and the Baron coming in through a doorway, and Lord M. dreaming at Windsor with the rooks cawing in the elm-trees, and the Archbishop of Canterbury on his knees in the dawn, and the old King's turkey-cock ejaculations, and Uncle Leopold's soft voice at Claremont, and Lehzen with the globes, and her mother's feathers sweeping down towards her, and a great old repeater-watch of her father's in its tortoise-shell case, and a yellow rug, and some friendly flounces of sprigged muslin, and the trees and the grass at Kensington.

BIBLIOGRAPHY

LIST OF REFERENCES IN THE NOTES, ARRANGED
ALPHABETICALLY.

ADAMS. *The Education of Henry Adams: an autobiography.* 1918.

ASHLEY. *The Life and Correspondence of H. J. Temple, Viscount Palmerston.* By A. E. M. Ashley. 2 vols. 1879.

BLOOMFIELD. *Reminiscences of Court and Diplomatic Life.* By Georgiana, Lady Bloomfield. 2 vols. 1883.

BROUGHTON. *Recollections of a Long Life.* By Lord Broughton. Edited by Lady Dorchester. 6 vols. 1909-11.

BUCKLE. *The Life of Benjamin Disraeli, Earl of Beaconsfield.* By W. F. Monypenny and G. E. Buckle. 6 vols. 1910-20.

BULOW. *Gabriele von Bülow,* 1791-1887. Berlin. 1893.

BUNSEN. *A Memoir of Baron Bunsen.* By his widow, Frances, Baroness Bunsen. 2 vols. 1868.

BUSCH. *Bismarck: some secret pages of hi. history.* By Dr. Moritz Busch. (English translation.) 3 vols. 1898.

CHILDERS. *The Life and Correspondence of the Rt. Hon. Hugh C. E. Childers.* 2 vols. 1901.

CLARENDON. *The Life and Letters of the Fourth Earl of Clarendon.* By Sir Herbert Maxwell. 2 vols. 1913.

Cornhill Magazine, vol. 75.

CRAWFORD. *Victoria, Queen and Ruler.* By Emily Crawford. 1903.

CREEVEY. *The Creevey Papers.* Edited by Sir Herbert Maxwell. 2 vols. 1904.

CROKER. *The Croker Papers.* Edited by L. J. Jennings. 3 vols. 1884.

DAFFORNE. *The Albert Memorial: its history and description.* By J. Dafforne. 1877.

DALLING. *The Life of H. J. Temple, Viscount Palmerston.* By Lord Dalling. 3 vols. 1871-84.

Dictionary of National Biography.

DISRAELI. *Lord George Bentinck: a political biography.* By B. Disraeli. 1852.

ECKARDSTEIN. *Lebens-Erinnerungen u. Politische Denkwür-digkeiten.* Von Freiherrn v. Eckardstein. 2 vols. Leipzig. 1919.

ERNEST. *Memoirs of Ernest II, Duke of Saxe-Coburg-Gotha.* 4 vols. 1888. (English translation.)

FITZMAURICE. *The Life of Earl Granville.* By Lord Fitzmaurice. 2 vols. 1905.

GASKELL. *The Life of Charlotte Brontë.* By Mrs. Gaskell. 2 vols. 1857.

GIRLHOOD. *The Girlhood of Queen Victoria.* Edited by Viscount Esher. 2 vols. 1912.

GOSSART. *Adolphe Quetelet et le Prince Albert de Saxe-Cobourg.* Academie Royale de Belgique, Bruxelles. 1919.

GRANVILLE. *Letters of Harriet, Countess Granville.* 2 vols. 1894.

GREVILLE. *The Greville Memoirs.* 8 vols. (Silver Library Edition.) 1896.

GREY. *Early Years of the Prince Consort.* By General Charles Grey. 1867.

HALLE. *Life and Letters of Sir Charles Hallé.* Edited by his Son. 1896.

HAMILTON. *Parliamentary Reminiscences and Reflections.* By Lord George Hamilton. 1917.

HARE. *The Story of My Life.* By Augustus J. C. Hare. 6 vols. 1896-1900.

HAYDON. *Autobiography of Benjamin Robert Haydon.* 3 vols. 1853.

HAYWARD. *Sketches of Eminent Statesmen and Writers.* By
A. Hayward. 2 vols. 1880.

HUISH. *The History of the Life and Reign of William the
Fourth.* By Robert Huish. 1837.

HUNT. *The Old Court Suburb: or Memorials of Kensington,
regal, critical, and anecdotal.* 2 vols. 1855.

JERROLD, EARLY COURT. *The Early Court of Queen Victoria.*
By Clare Jerrold. 1912.

JERROLD, MARRIED LIFE. *The Married Life of Queen Victoria.* By Clare Jerrold. 1913.

JERROLD, WIDOWHOOD. *The Widowhood of Queen Victoria.*
By Clare Jerrold. 1916.

KINGLAKE. *The Invasion of the Crimea.* By A. W. Kinglake. 9 vols. (Cabinet Edition.) 1877-88.

KNIGHT. *The Autobiography of Miss Cornelia Knight.* 2
vols. 1861.

LAUGHTON. *Memoirs of the Life and Correspondence of
Henry Reeve.* By Sir John Laughton. 2 vols. 1898.

LEAVES. *Leaves from the Journal of our Life in the Highlands, from 1848 to 1861.* By Queen Victoria. Edited
by A. Helps. 1868.

LEE. *Queen Victoria: a biography.* By Sidney Lee. 1902.

LESLIE. *Autobiographical Recollections by the late Charles
Robert Leslie, R.A.* Edited by Tom Taylor. 2 vols.
1860.

LETTERS. *The Letters of Queen Victoria.* 3 vols. 1908.

LIEVEN. *Letters of Dorothea, Princess Lieven, during her
residence in London, 1812-1834.* Edited by Lionel G.
Robinson. 1902.

The London Mercury.

Lovely Albert! A Broadside.

LYTTELTON. *Correspondence of Sarah Spencer, Lady Lyttelton, 1787-1870.* Edited by Mrs. Hugh Wyndham. 1912.

MARTIN. *The Life of His Royal Highness the Prince Consort.* By Theodore Martin. 5 vols. 1875-80.

MARTIN, QUEEN VICTORIA. *Queen Victoria as I knew her.* By Sir Theodore Martin. 1908.

MARTINEAU. *The Autobiography of Harriet Martineau.* 3 vols. 1877.

MAXWELL. *The Hon. Sir Charles Murray, K.C.B.: a memoir.* By Sir Herbert Maxwell. 1898.

MORE LEAVES. *More Leaves from the Journal of a Life in the Highlands, from* 1862 *to* 1882. By Queen Victoria. 1884.

MORLEY. *The Life of William Ewart Gladstone.* By John Morley. 3 vols. 1903.

MURRAY. *Recollections from* 1803 *to* 1837. By the Hon. Amelia Murray. 1868.

NATIONAL MEMORIAL. *The National Memorial to H.R.H. the Prince Consort.* 1873.

NEELE. *Railway Reminiscences.* By George P. Neele. 1904.

OWEN. *The Life of Robert Owen,* written by himself. 1857.

OWEN, JOURNAL. *Owen's Rational Quarterly Review and Journal.*

PANAM. *A German Prince and his Victim.* Taken from the Memoirs of Madame Pauline Panam. 1915.

PRIVATE LIFE. *The Private Life of the Queen.* By One of Her Majesty's Servants. 1897.

The Quarterly Review, vols. 193 and 213.

ROBERTSON. *Bismarck.* By C. Grant Robertson 1918.

SCOTT. *Personal and Professional Recollections.* By Sir George Gilbert Scott. 1879.

SMITH. *Life of Her Majesty Queen Victoria.* Compiled from all available sources. By G. Barnett Smith. 1887.

SPINSTER LADY. *The Notebooks of a Spinster Lady.* 1919.

STEIN. *Denkschriften über Deutsche Verfassungen.* Herausgegeben von G. H. Pertz. 6 vols. 1848.

STOCKMAR. *Denkwürdigkeiten aus den Papieren des Freiherrn Christian Friedrich v. Stockmar,* zusammengestellt von Ernst Freiherr v. Stockmar. Braunschweig. 1872.

TAIT. *The Life of Archibald Campbell Tait, Archbishop of Canterbury.* 2 vols. 1891.

The London Times.

The Times LIFE. *The Life of Queen Victoria,* reproduced from *The London Times.* 1901.

TORRENS. *Memoirs of William Lamb, second Viscount Melbourne.* By W. M. Torrens. (Minerva Library Edition.) 1890.

VITZTHUM. *St. Petersburg und London in den Jahren 1852-1864.* Carl Friedrich Graf Vitzthum von Eckstädt. Stuttgart. 1886.

WALPOLE. *The Life of Lord John Russell.* By Sir Spencer Walpole. 2 vols. 1889.

WILBERFORCE, SAMUEL. *Life of Samuel Wilberforce, Bishop of Oxford.* By his son, R. G. Wilberforce. 3 vols. 1881.

WILBERFORCE, WILLIAM. *The Life of William Wilberforce.* 5 vols. 1838.

WYNN. *Diaries of a Lady of Quality.* By Miss Frances Williams Wynn. 1864.

INDEX

431

have that institution changed; he votes therefore against the oft-made proposal to give Cabinet officers seats in Congress. He is fully alive to the embarrassing role often played by the Senate in foreign relations, but concludes that on the whole the American system works as well as the English or the French. On only two matters, indeed, does Mr. Laski suggest reforms. He would have the Senate abandon the system of "Senatorial courtesy," and he would deprive the Congress of power to make appropriations not specifically requested by the executive.

This book represents Mr. Laski at his best. It has all the clarity of statement, the felicity of phrasing, the acute intelligence and reasonableness, of such earlier books as the "History of Liberalism" and the "Parliamentary Government in England," and is undisturbed by the Marxist interpretation of some of the other books. It is not a profound study, nor even an original one, but it is throughout reflective and suggestive. For purposes of the average reader it is the best analysis of the Presidency in our literature.

HENRY STEELE COMMAGER

THE AMERICAN PRESIDENCY

AN INTERPRETATION

★

THE PATTEN FOUNDATION

Mr. Will Patten of Indianapolis (A.B., Indiana University, 1893) made in 1931 a gift for the establishment of the Patten Foundation at his Alma Mater. Under the terms of this gift, which became available upon the death of Mr. Patten (May 3, 1936), there is to be chosen each year a Visiting Professor who is to be in residence several weeks during the year. The purpose of this prescription is to provide an opportunity for members of the University, students and faculty to enjoy the privilege and advantage of personal acquaintance with the Visiting Professor. The Visiting Professor for the Patten Foundation in 1938-1939 was

PROFESSOR HAROLD J. LASKI
London School of Economics and Political Science
University of London

THE AMERICAN PRESIDENCY, AN INTERPRETATION

By

HAROLD J. LASKI

PROFESSOR OF POLITICAL SCIENCE IN
THE UNIVERSITY OF LONDON

* * * * * * * * * *

HARPER & BROTHERS PUBLISHERS

New York and London

CONTENTS

✣

PREFACE

IN THE spring of 1939 Indiana University honored me with an invitation to lecture there on the Patten Foundation; this volume is, substantially, the course I delivered. I should like to thank President H. B Wells for an experience as stimulating as it was delightful. I should add that, in their printed form, these pages owe much to the discussions I had in Bloomington with many members of the faculty, and, in particular, to my friends Dean Bernard Gavit, and Professors Ford Hall and Fowler Harper. I shall long remember their kindness, and that of Mr. S. Yellen and Mr. Harry Engel.

This book is, as its subtitle seeks to indicate, less a treatise on the presidency of the United States than an attempt, made through English eyes, to interpret the way in which it actually works. I am, I hope, sufficiently aware of the dangers to which any student is exposed who seeks to explain a foreign institution. I can only plead that there is a sense in which I have been watching the presidency at work, sometimes from near at hand, ever since I began to teach at Harvard nearly twenty-five years ago; and there are few of the arguments I have ventured to put forward that have not had the benefit of criticism from many American friends, both academic and political, and not least from the friend to whom I have been permitted to dedicate this book. Its errors are, of course, all my own. But I should indeed be ungrateful if I did not acknowledge the immense debt it owes for what merit it may possess to those friends. In particular, its obligation to Mr. Justice Frankfurter and to Dr. Alfred E. Cohn is quite beyond my power of repayment.

I owe much, too, to some of the standard works on the subject. In particular, I should like to mention how much I have been helped by the writings of Professors Lindsay Rogers, Charles Beard, and Thomas Reed Powell. I found also immense assistance in the elaborate investigation of Professor Dangerfield into the relation of the Senate to the treaty-making power. I should add that the biographies and autobiographies of leading American statesmen, above all the superb *Diary* of John Quincy Adams, as abridged by Allan Nevins from the *Memoirs*, are an indispensable source of understanding.

American scholars have done so much, especially in recent years, for the study of English institutions, that I hope this little book may stimulate British students to realize something of the interest and fascination of American history and politics. If it does this even in a small degree, it will not have been written wholly in vain.

H. J. L.

Little Bardfield,
 Essex.

THE AMERICAN PRESIDENCY

AN INTERPRETATION

★

I

INTRODUCTORY

I

INSTITUTIONS are living things, and they do not easily yield their secrets to the printed word. Predominantly, that is not because they are in themselves mysterious. It is rather because they change with changes in the environment within which they operate, and partly because they differ, from one moment to the other, in terms of the men who operate them. The premiership of Great Britain was one thing in the hands of Mr. Lloyd George in time of war; it was a different thing in the hands of Mr. Baldwin in time of peace; it is a different thing, again, in the hands of Mr. Neville Chamberlain. So, too, with the presidency of France. Though the books warn us that here is the one head of a state whose constant characteristic is that he neither reigns nor governs, in fact, the office has been very different in the hands of its various holders; notably it has hardly seemed the same thing in the hands of M. Poincaré as what it has been in the hands of M. Doumergue.

No important institution, moreover, is ever merely what the law makes it. It accumulates about itself traditions, conventions, ways of behavior, which, without ever attaining the status of formal law, are not less formidable in their influence than law itself could require. The prerogatives of the Crown in Great Britain are perhaps the supreme example of this habit; many of them retain their formal status as law and yet could hardly be revived without what would amount to a constitutional revolution. The habits of one period, this is to say, can hardly hope to determine the conduct of its successor. The dynamics of life require a continuity of adaptation which almost always means that the formal appearance is different, at any given moment, from the actual reality. To penetrate that reality, therefore, is always a difficult matter. In part, it is obscured, as most institutional phenomena are obscured, by the complexity of the material itself. The processes of government are very like an iceberg; what appears on the surface may be but a small part of the reality beneath. How difficult it is to judge that reality is well known to every historian. Even those most closely concerned in the processes may totally misjudge their meaning. Both the king of France and the tsar of Russia wholly failed to grasp the events, respectively, of 1789 and 1917; and Mr. Asquith's resignation, in December, 1916, was intended to lead to the elimination, and not to the triumph, of Mr. Lloyd George.

The observation of institutions is difficult for another reason. No student can fail, consciously or unconsciously, to bring his own scheme of values to them. He may be detached; he cannot hope to be impartial. For he brings to the task of observation not

[2]

merely the experience in which he is involved—an experience which is bound to color his power to see what is before him. He brings to it, also, his own hopes and fears, his judgment of good and bad, significant and insignificant. And this is more certain to be the case when he seeks to explain an institution which he sees from without. There, he is almost bound to be impressed by what in it is alien from the routine to which he is accustomed. He sees more emphatically the unwonted side than the side which resembles the experience with which he is familiar. More than this. In seeking to understand its operation, he is bound to rely upon the judgment of men who have themselves seen it from within. But they, in their turn, as they describe its working to him, bring to that description a body of assumptions the meaning of which he can grasp only as he is conscious that they are being made. Everyone knows that Gibbon's great history derives a considerable part of its unique character from the fact that its author was a philosophic rationalist of the eighteenth century. Everyone knows, also, how much Sir Henry Maine's judgment of popular government was colored by his years as Legal Member of the Viceroy's Council in India. Even a work like Stubbs's *Constitutional History* was profoundly influenced, as Vinogradoff has pointed out,[1] by the rising tide of Victorian liberalism; and that, be it added, even though its author regarded himself as an orthodox Conservative.

I am to speak, being an Englishman, of the supreme political office in the United States. I am aware of my

---

[1] *Villainage in England* (1892), Preface.

temerity. But to emphasize my sense that the adventure is a delicate one, I should like to give one more example of what I mean by the influence of one's environment upon the judgment. Save perhaps the *Democracy in America* of de Tocqueville, no more famous book on that theme has been written than Bryce's *American Commonwealth*; from the moment of its appearance, just over fifty years ago, it at once took its place as a work of classic quality. Its author was already an eminent historian and a jurist of exceptional distinction. He had traveled widely all over the United States. He was intimately acquainted with many of the leading figures in its political and intellectual eye. He had taken more pains to examine the United States, and with greater energy, than any previous observer. Certainly he knew more of the American political scene, when he wrote, than any European, not even excluding de Tocqueville, had previously known.

Yet Bryce was also a Gladstonian Liberal, immersed in the special philosophy represented by that experience. When he came, therefore, to look at the American industrial scene, he viewed its substance, both as to the mind of the labor movement, on the one hand, and as to the relation of labor to the governmental process, on the other, very much with the mental outlook of a Victorian Liberal, who mainly noted the better economic condition of the workingman in America, his ampler margins of opportunity, compared to those enjoyed by the workingman in England. He did not examine American trade unions at first hand. He took his view of the problems of law and order created by industrial unrest either from the political figures whom he met at Washington, or from political journals, like the *Nation* then edited by his friend Godkin, which accepted a social philosophy akin to his own. The result was that he hardly knew how profound was the American labor problem in his day; and nearly every judgment he made about its influence on governmental policy has subsequently been called into question by later historical investigation. He was wholly wide of the mark in his judgment of the Haymarket riot;[2] he knew nothing of the inner and dubious details which went to the making of Cleveland's decision to aid the railroads;[3] even the revised edition of 1910 takes no account of the existence of the American Federation of Labor.[4] His revised edition was made two years before the great upheaval of 1912 and the famous Pujo Committee of 1913.[5] Yet he has no knowledge of the Populist movement except as an incident in the Democratic party's acceptance of a free silver policy in 1896. He is not aware of the degree to which Populism looks backward in its implications to the first political struggles of the republic, or forward to that Roosevelt epoch in which so many of the outlines of contemporary controversies began to emerge. Of the great strikes led by the Knights of

[2] *American Commonwealth* (ed. of 1911), II, 646. Cf. Henry David, *The History of the Haymarket Affair* (1936), and Samuel Yellen, *American Labor Struggles* (1936), Chap. II.

[3] *Ibid.*, II, 599. Cf. Yellen, *op. cit.*, Chap. IV.

[4] Trade unions do not even appear in the index to his book.

[5] On the Pujo Committee see L. D. (Mr. Justice) Brandeis, *Other People's Money* (1915).

Labor on the railroads, he can write that "when recently a gigantic organization of workingmen, purporting to unite the whole of American labor, attempted to enforce its sentences against particular firms or corporations by a boycott in which all laborers were urged to join, there was displeasure, but no panic, no call for violent remedies. The prevailing faith in liberty and in the good sense of the mass was unshaken; and the result soon justified this tranquil faith."[6]

There is hardly a phrase in these sentences that would stand examination today;[7] and they are not less revealing for their underlying assumptions than they are for their factual inaccuracies. Bryce accepted the simple faith in liberty of contract as between individual employer and individual worker that was characteristic of his time; and he had no conception that its implications were largely obsolete even when he wrote the first edition of his book. He brought with him to America, in a word, a social philosophy, a way of life, that set the criteria not only of what he was to look for, but also of what he found. He mingled in America almost wholly with the same type of men he was accustomed to meet in England—college presidents, statesmen, editors, bankers, and eminent industrialists; men, that is to say, who shared, overwhelmingly, his own point of view. It is not, therefore, surprising that his judgment of what he ought to look for in America was confirmed by them; or

[6] *Op. cit.*, II, 646.
[7] Cf. *op. cit.* Yellen.

[6]

that, very largely, his judgment of what he found was their judgment. Bryce was a disinterested and detached observer, if ever there was one. Yet his account of what he saw is, in this particular context, a striking example of how the subconscious personal equation is vital in the conclusions at which even a disinterested and detached observer will arrive.

I use the illustration of Bryce's book because it shows how careful one must be in seeking to estimate, especially as an Englishman, an institution so intricate and, I add, psychologically unfamiliar, as the American presidency. Part of its functions are like those of the British Crown; part of them can be made to appear like those of the British prime minister; and the temptation is great to think of them in these terms. Yet it is fundamental to remember that, in each part, the resemblances are far less striking than the differences, and that the functioning of the institution as a whole results in the unique consequences which cannot be predicted when those parts are separately surveyed. It is not, I think, merely a platitude to say that the essence of the presidency is the fact that it is an *American* institution, that it functions in an American environment, that it has been shaped by the forces of American history, that it must be judged by American criteria of its response to American needs. To us in England, for example, it appears wholly wasteful that, after the immense experience the tenure of such an office confers, only one American president should have been able to utilize it in political life after his term had expired. (The brief senatorial service of Andrew

[7]

Johnson hardly counts.) Yet the whole ethos of the American political system would be different if that were not the case; and to argue, for example, that Americans ought to have a House of Lords in which ex-presidents can function usefully is to miss the vital fact that the very nature of American politics prevents either house of Congress from functioning in any way like the House of Lords.

Englishmen, again, are tempted to remark on the fact that many of the presidents of the United States have been very ordinary men, not to be distinguished from several millions of their fellows; Lord Bryce has a chapter in his book entitled "Why Great Men Do Not Become Presidents." But the judgment, I suggest, is a facile one. On any showing, eleven American presidents have been extraordinary men, whatever may be our view of the handling of their office. That is a proportion not less high than the proportion of remarkable men who have become prime minister in the same period; and, among those who could not be judged extraordinary, two at least, Tyler and Polk, seem on the evidence that has now accumulated to have been at least as fit for the office they held as were, say, Sir Henry Campbell-Bannerman or Mr. Bonar Law for the office of prime minister. A foreigner may distrust the methods by which the president is chosen; certainly there is a good deal of truth in Bagehot's famous aphorism, apropos of Lincoln, that "success in a lottery is no argument for lotteries." But, of course, the assumption of his remark is that the choice of Lincoln in 1860 was an accident. That is not the case. Few choices have ever been more carefully or-

ganized in a presidential convention. It is true that
Lincoln was nationally known only a short time before his nomination. But it is worth remembering that
Mr. Baldwin was hardly known at all when he became
prime minister, and that, so far, each Labour leader
in England, with only one exception, has been chosen
as a result of a series of fortuitous circumstances none
of which was foreseen. And it is far from rare in our
party history to find that the prime minister is less
the obvious man than the most available man. We train
our leaders differently, and we keep them longer. But
we must not transfer the criteria of our own system
to that of the United States without a care greater
than we usually exercise.

A good deal, in fact, of the literature upon American institutions applies to the standards derived from
European experience. That is true, it is worth while to
add, even of much that has been written by Americans themselves. The classic work of Woodrow Wilson, for example, would hardly have come to some of
its conclusions—that on the procedure of the Senate,
for instance—if its author had not been steeped in
Burke and Bagehot and had not seen a good deal of
American government through their eyes. We compare the long political career of an English prime
minister with the brevity of that of an American president; but the true comparison is surely between the
periods in which each held the highest office in the
state, and, if we make that comparison, more American presidents have held office for eight years than
have British prime ministers since the younger Pitt.

We speak of the long apprenticeship to politics that an English prime minister serves before he reaches 10 Downing Street; we forget, I think, not only that American conditions altogether rule out (I do not think wisely) that kind of apprenticeship, but also that, in the postwar years in England, the apprenticeship we have come to regard as habitual has been notably abridged in time.

Older commentators, again, and, especially Bagehot, complained of the poor quality of political writing in the American newspapers as compared with that in the English press; and they attributed this to the influence of the fixed presidential term in the United States as compared with the dramatic elasticity of the English system. Later history has made it possible to doubt this conclusion. For the increasing rigidity of the English party structure, on the one hand, and the decline of importance, especially in the postwar years, of the editorial page, on the other, have combined with the reduction of the press to a department of big business to give it, except in moments of gravest emergency, far less importance in its influence on political decisions than was true in Bagehot's day. In America, however, while the influence of the editorial page has continued to decline, there has been the rise of the independent political commentator whose articles probably have a more far-reaching influence than the work of any English editors, and whose status in American public life is comparable with that of Delane in the most important days of the London *Times*. The reasons for these developments are complicated; but one of them, at least, is the fact that party structure in the United States remains far less rigid than in Great Britain and the influence of the independent voter, influenced in his turn by the political commentator, is far greater. There are many journals in the United States the columns of which are mainly studied for articles of this kind. They shape the climate of American opinion very much as does the work of the great English cartoonist, David Low. They build a stereotype of ideas which slowly, but incisively, makes its impact upon those who shape decisions in Washington.

Any discussion, therefore, of so essentially American an institution as the presidency must seek to analyze its working in American terms. Whatever the intention of the founders, the history of the United States has molded it in ways they could not have foreseen; and its ways of behavior, the criteria by which it is to be judged, must be set by the conditions in which it has to work. There is no foreign institution with which, in any basic sense, it can be compared, because, basically, there is no comparable foreign institution. The president of the United States is both more and less than a king; he is, also, both more and less than a prime minister. The more carefully his office is studied, the more does its unique character appear. We are, indeed, entitled to criticize the results of its operation; and, particularly, we can compare those results with the consequences which follow from the operation of other systems. But we must constantly bear in mind that the transplantation of methods from other countries to American soil would, in all human probability, produce results quite different from any which their advocates have been inclined to anticipate; after all, the British parliamentary system has been different in each country of its adoption, just as American federation has undergone a decisive sea-change with its transference to other climes. Not the least danger in the study of politics is the attempt to construct large generalizations which flow from the comparison of two unlikes, on the ground that the institutions involved have a similar part to play in the respective governmental systems. The more fully we avoid generalizations of this character, the more likely we are to understand the nature of the material with which we have to deal.

2

No one who studies the proceedings of the constitutional convention can fail to see one emphasis in its construction of the presidency which has remained a living part of the traditions in which it is imbedded. Fear of executive despotism is, for reasons intelligible enough in the light of American origins, evoked in the public approach to the office. Though Lincoln and Woodrow Wilson both exercised, in the pressure of wartime conditions, an almost dictatorial power, it is, I think, true to say that each wielded it with uneasiness; and the exercise of that power was in each case followed by a strong reaction toward congressional control of presidential action. It is not, I suggest, accident that for twenty years after Lincoln there was no strong president until Cleveland; and that the twelve years after Woodrow Wilson saw the effective leadership of American policy outside the White House. For the first few months of his period of office, President Franklin Roosevelt dominated both houses of Congress; but it is notable that, after the summer of 1933, the development of congressional challenge to his authority mounted constantly in volume.

The reasons for this are, I suspect, threefold in character. Partly, they lie in the constitutional position of the office itself. The president is at no point the master of the legislature. He can indicate a path of action to Congress. He can argue, bully, persuade, cajole; but he is always outside Congress, and subject to a will he cannot dominate. He is, while in office, the national leader of his party; of set purpose, he is not, and cannot be, its congressional leader. Even if his party has a majority in both houses, he has to win the good will of his party in Congress; he cannot exact it. A president, indeed, who sought to do so would soon discover the limits of his power. Mr. F. D. Roosevelt was resoundingly beaten on his Court plan shortly after his remarkable triumph of 1936. Successive presidents, since 1920, have recommended in vain the adherence of the United States to the Permanent International Court. The lobby of the American Legion has proved more successful with both houses, ever since the end of the War of 1914, than any pressure, even including the exercise of the veto power, that the president could bring to bear.

He can initiate policy; he cannot control it. The emergency of war apart, that has been the constant characteristic of his position ever since 1789. That was the intent of the founders; and, broadly, it has continued to win the approval, as an intent, of public opinion. If its origin was, as I have said, a natural fear of executive despotism, its continuance must be sought in other directions. Partly, I think, it lies in the nature of American conditions from 1789 until almost the other day. The wide opportunities, the boundless resources, the habits of a frontier civilization, all these made against the idea of a positive state. Americans did not feel they needed strong government. They felt, out of an experience which seemed continually to reverify itself, that they could rely upon their own exertions for material advancement. *Ne pas trop gouverner* was the lesson extracted by their business men from their marvelous success in developing the continent. A strong executive meant the risk of interference from Washington. Interference meant a disturbance of the confidence upon which business men depend. Government regulation and business prosperity were deemed—are largely still deemed—mighty opposites. Whenever a strong president—Jackson, Tyler, Theodore Roosevelt, Wilson, Franklin Roosevelt—has been in office, business men have always been alarmed by the tendency of affairs.

"We are," wrote Henry Clay, when Jackson was in office, "in the midst of a revolution, hitherto bloodless, but rapidly leading towards a total change of the pure republican character of the government and to the concentration of all power in the hands of one man. The powers of Congress are paralyzed except when exerted in conformity with his will." Jackson was a strong president; yet no student but is aware how baseless was the view Clay here expressed. Yet it is an attitude which has been taken by men not less able than Clay in each instance when a president of strong will has shown himself in the White House. And so far, in each instance, the constant reiteration of a baseless warning has resulted in the choice of a successor to a strong president who has half-abdicated from the control of policy.

The third reason for this suspicion of the strong executive lies, I believe, in the reasons that have led to his choice. In each case, so far, his election has been the outcome of a popular revolt, more or less conscious, against the business man's dominating influence upon the exercise of political power. Jefferson represented a revolt of the West against the narrow property interests of Eastern Federalism. Jackson embodied the nascent agrarian suspicion of Eastern banking power. Cleveland and Theodore Roosevelt were both, as it were, protest presidents—the one against corruption, and Northern domination of the South; the other against the growth of corporate power. Woodrow Wilson embodied the hostility of the little man to the trusts, his fear of being dominated by the octopus of Wall Street. Franklin Roosevelt was elected, as he himself said, by the "forgotten man," the trade unionist, the worker on relief, the little shopkeeper, the tenant-farmer, the millions, in short, who had abruptly discovered the hollowness of the permanent prosperity the Coolidge-Mellon epoch had seemed to foreshadow.

It is notable that the tendency to strong presidents coincides with epochs of difficulty in the United States; it is notable, also, that strong presidents have come with greater frequency in more recent times than in early American history. The reason is the obvious one that, with the exhaustion of frontier conditions, the problems of America have become increasingly the same in essence as those of a typical capitalist democracy in western Europe. No doubt, the economic opportunities are still larger, the social stratification much less intense, the ability to experiment far wider, than in Europe. But there has finally emerged a vast working-class which needs the protection of the state if it is to have security and the minimum conditions of civilized living. There is a vast concentration of wealth in relatively few hands; and there is an increasing centralization of economic power. Every problem in the European scene reproduces itself in the United States; and none of the problems is capable of solution without executive leadership of the political forces involved.

This presents two issues of major magnitude in the context of the presidency. As things are, leadership can come from the president alone; for reasons that I shall discuss later, there is no other source of direction which can secure the attention of the whole nation. But the forces which operate against continuity of presidential leadership are immense. There are the forces inherent in the Constitution—an absolute division of powers, a system of checks and balances as between executive and legislative which gives to each an interest in the diminution of authority instead of in its consolidation, a tendency to destroy something of the president's prestige as his first term draws to an end, and to weaken most of it in the latter part of his second. There are the forces, secondly, inherent in the nature of business enterprise—their fear of governmental regulation in general, the timidity and inertia of property before economic innovation, the depressing effect upon business enterprise of the level of taxation usually implicit in any economic innovation that comes from government. There are the forces of the cultural heritage, which always make the relation between political forms and social needs disproportionate; a disproportion which is intensified by the fact that, since a strong president is usually the outcome either of emergency or of profound discontent, he must usually be spectacularly successful if he is to maintain increased authority without abridgment. For increased authority will always meet with resistance from those whose interest it is to stand by the ancient ways; and, on the evidence, they will exhaust all their power and ingenuity to prevent the prospect of any spectacular success.

It cannot be too often remembered that the founders of the Constitution were working in a predominantly agricultural society in which the consequences of the Industrial Revolution could not be even dimly realized. They feared the masses. They were adamant about the "rights" of property. Liberty to them predominantly meant protection of vested interests from the invasions of the multitude. No one can read the proceedings of the Philadelphia convention without seeing how infinite were the precautions they took against the creation of a presidential office which should lend the color of its personality to the scheme of government. At every point, the limits of its possible operations were narrowly set; and we can see in the *Diary* of Maclay how jealously its activities were watched. History has made it possible for some of these limitations to be transcended. Certainly, the use of the presidency in Franklin Roosevelt's hands would have been unthinkable—Lincoln, perhaps, apart—to any president before Theodore Roosevelt, and even to most of his successors. But the original conception of the office has, both legally and psychologically, profoundly influenced the limits of the direction it may attempt. Every failure in such an attempt causes the pendulum of opinion to swing back to a more negative conception of the office; and, since the positive conception is at once new and exceptional, in the mind of the most powerful class in America there is an almost a priori case against its operation. Men cling tenaciously to their wonted routines. The American people are not yet accustomed to think of the presidency as the essential keystone of the political arch. We have to remember that, as recently as the era of Woodrow Wilson, the office seemed a source of supplement and correction to business control rather than an agency which was to set the pace and direction of the nation's political life.

The grave question of the future is whether it will be able to do so. There are many factors which make this dubious. A president limited by the will of Congress is always like a sailor on an uncharted sea; he cannot proceed with certainty upon his course. There is the problem of winning a renomination, and the price he may have to pay for it. There is the problem of whether a term that, so far, has not exceeded eight years gives time enough, within the character of the system, to implement any full scheme of ideas; a Republican president might easily work havoc with the New Deal, and even a Democratic successor might jeopardize its outstanding features. There is the problem of securing not merely the legislative but also the administrative co-operation he requires. There is the problem, always omnipresent to an innovating president, of the Supreme Court; the accidents of the appointing power have made a good deal of history in the judicial sphere. Even if we grant, as I should at once grant, that a great president today has more chance of having his way than at any previous time in the history of the office, it is still an open question whether the conditions under which the Constitution itself, and the traditions it has imposed, still operate give him the elbowroom he requires for a fully constructive job.

It is not as though, in the American system, the initiative is supplied from elsewhere. For reasons that I shall discuss in another chapter, the Congress is not a body capable of constructive leadership; the functions it performs most effectively are those of criticism and investigation rather than responsibility for the direction of affairs. It is, indeed, true of any legislative assembly that its coherence for action depends upon its being so organized that it acts under a continuous sense of responsibility. This the Congress does not do, and, as I shall argue, from its own inherent nature can hardly do. And since the cabinet is no more than the president's advisory council, to be used in the degree, but no more than the degree, that he thinks fit, it cannot be looked to for initiative of this kind. The only person responsibly charged with thinking and planning in terms of the whole Union is the president; and it is a striking, even startling, feature of the American scheme of government that he has no way of seeing that his conception of his duty will, as a normal feature of the political process, be weighed from the angle that he considers imperative.

He has, of course, ways at his disposal of enforcing consideration. A message from the president, especially upon an important matter, is always news that will be nationally debated. The president can also, through the press and radio, insure that Congress is driven to take some action upon his proposals. And his patronage gives him a power of bringing pressure to bear upon individuals of both houses that is bound to count for a good deal. What he cannot assure to himself is that the policy he sets will be his policy. He must always take account of the fact that the Congress is a co-ordinate authority, jealous of its rights, likely, except in the gravest emergency, to resent any attempt upon his part to enforce his views upon its acceptance.

It is likely, indeed, to emphasize some divergence from those views in order to make it plain that he is not its master. This will be the case even when the party he leads is in power in both houses; his position will, naturally, be immensely more difficult when the opposition party controls one or both of the houses. Then, the whole interest of the opposition is to paralyze the presidential office in order to have the best possible chance of victory at the next election. How devastating that situation can be was decisively shown in the last two years of President Wilson's second administration.

It is, of course, an answer to this view to urge that its assumptions involve the idea of an executive responsible to the legislature in the British sense; and it is plain that this has been at no point a characteristic of the American scheme. But my argument is based upon a different foundation. It assumes only that the political evolution of the last forty years has shown that the modern state requires a strong executive, whose plans, of course suitably criticized and controlled, form the staple food of legislative digestion. I am arguing that the presidential conception of political needs must overwhelmingly square with the legislative conception if there is to be effective responsibility in government. The inference I draw from American experience is that this responsibility is minimized by the system. That was relatively unimportant before the Civil War; it has become increasingly important since that time. And though it is true that, on the whole, presidential leadership has been far more thoroughgoing since the Civil War than before it, that has been due, not to a public nor to a congressional recognition that it must be the case, but to external necessities that have imposed it. And, generally, both Congress and a good deal of public opinion, especially business opinion, have sought, at the earliest opportunity, to escape from the consequences of these essential necessities. The facts make against the continuous recognition of what is involved in leadership in the positive state. The risks a strong president must encounter if he wishes to exert his strength are both profound and manifold. He is not only running counter to the purpose of the Constitution. He is also arraying against himself all the forces in American politics to whom his strength is bound to be obnoxious. And included in those forces is Congress itself. For the greater his strength appears, the more he appears to dwarf Congress by its exercise. The more, accordingly, he tempts it to seek a trial of strength with him in order that it may vindicate its own claims to its co-ordinate share in power. The gravity of this position is obvious.

For the question it raises goes to the root of the whole scheme of American government. Just as it is an open question whether the division of powers between the federal government and the states is any longer compatible with efficient administration, even more, with full response to social needs,[8] so it is an open question whether the system of checks and bal-

---

[8] Cf. my article in the *New Republic* of May 3, 1939, "The Obsolescence of Federalism."

ances is not incompatible, as it is now operated, with a proper relation between executive and legislature. Even if we grant that the strong practical instinct of Americans has done much to lessen the creaking of the machine, the price that has to be paid for that diminution is a very heavy one. It is, no doubt, a price that a strong and courageous president will always be willing to pay; and it is no doubt true, also, that the stronger and more courageous he is the more likely he will be to enlist an effective public opinion on his side. But it is perhaps equally true that his strength and courage will seem to his critics to be more like blindness and obstinacy; and the measure of their exercise may serve to exacerbate opposition rather than to defeat it. Nor is there assurance that, when the time demands great leadership, it will be necessarily forthcoming. A good deal of the tragedy of the American depression might have been avoided if it were certain that the hour would produce the man. In fact, there is no such certainty. There is rather the danger that, in any save the gravest crisis, any continuous attempt to transcend the implications of the checks and balances will result in the charge of dictatorship. There is no charge to which, rightly enough, American public opinion is more sensitive, and there is none, therefore, that an American president is more anxious to avoid. But his very anxiety to avoid it means that he is continually searching for paths of compromise in realms where he doubts its wisdom.

The system, in fact, allows only a very great man to be himself. Even as strong a personality as Theodore

Roosevelt was broken by the system. Few presidents have avowed more frankly the price prudence exacts for the right to walk boldly along the highroad; and the record of Theodore Roosevelt is largely one of immense verbal emphasis and actual timidity. Indeed, despite his thunder and lightning, in his own favorite realm of "trust-busting," the record of President Taft, whom he accounted a weak president, is somewhat more impressive. It is unlikely that presidential courage will again encounter so bitter a fate as Andrew Johnson's. But Johnson's experience, with the vast repercussions it has had on American history, is important evidence of what the system of checks and balances can effect. It cannot only paralyze the presidential office. It may have the far more evil effect of completely destroying any idea of responsibility in government. And this dissipation of responsibility will matter far more in the coming years than it has done at any previous stage of American history, simply because the need of a positive policy will be greater. The problems that the United States will confront are, both in scale and complexity, far more delicate than those of any previous time.

It may be said that this is to exaggerate the position. The president, after all, may not be right; and the predominance of the cabinet over the House of Commons shows, it may be argued, the excessive penalties attached to executive control over the legislature. I am not here urging that a president is infallible; the evidence is too grimly the other way. My argument is, first, that a democracy needs clear direction, and that it cannot get this unless the central motive force in a political system rests in the executive's hands. He may be right or wrong; what is important is that the plans put into operation should essentially be plans for which he is willing to accept full responsibility. And, secondly, it is not possible in the modern state to separate legislation from administration. In the making of policy, an assembly as miscellaneous as a legislature is bound to be cannot organize itself for creative action unless those who direct organization are also those who will apply it in action. In the United States, this is not the case. There is always a separation, which, at times, may amount to an antithesis, between them. The system, in fact, gives to the legislature functions which, nearly three-quarters of a century ago, John Stuart Mill pointed out it is least fitted to perform. As it is constructed, the interest of the legislature is to avoid the accusation of being a rubber stamp for presidential policy. To emphasize that avoidance, it always tends to develop a policy of its own. It is always inclined to build as much as possible upon the independence of its initiative in matters of legislation. This is bound to mean the erosion of responsibility. For the president can always claim that the policy by which he is bound is not his policy; while the legislature, in its turn, insists that the failure of a measure lies in the weakness of its application. Public opinion has rarely the materials upon which to form a valid judgment; and the matter involved, as in the realm of currency, for example, may be one upon which it is very difficult, from its nature, for any judgment to be formed at all.[9]

3

No one can examine the character of the American presidency without being impressed by its many-sidedness. The range of the president's functions is enormous. He is ceremonial head of the state. He is a vital source of legislative suggestion. He is the final source of all executive decision. He is the authoritative exponent of the nation's foreign policy. To combine all these with the continuous need to be at once the representative man of the nation and the leader of his political party is clearly a call upon the energies of a single man unsurpassed by the exigencies of any other political office in the world. In England, the main burden of ceremonial is taken from the shoulders of the prime minister by members of the royal family; and his political obligations are shared with a cabinet in which two or three other men are likely to carry a considerable part of his responsibility. The prime minister, moreover, knows that, in all normal circumstances, he will not have to face a recalcitrant House of Commons.

The ceremonial side of the presidency is, no doubt, fatiguing and delicate rather than important; but it is a great call upon the physical powers of any man. The president may on Monday be accepting a portrait of George V for the National Gallery at Washington.

[9] Cf. the debates in Congress on the proposed renewal of the president's power to devalue the dollar. *New York Times*, June 28-July 1, 1939.

He may have to greet the Daughters of the American Revolution on Tuesday, and the National Education Association on Wednesday. Washington's birthday calls for one kind of speech, and Jefferson's birthday, from a Democrat, for another. There may be a message to the Boy Scouts, a royal visitor from another country, the dinner to the judiciary (no easy matter when the president is at variance with the majority of the Supreme Court), the necessary entertainment of the diplomatic corps. He has to see enough of the Congress to make it feel that, at the least, it is not socially neglected. Attention must be paid to ceremonial recognition of the defense forces. A great government experiment, like Boulder Dam or Grand Coulee, must be visited. There must be tours at least wide enough in scope to give the impression that the president realizes that the United States is not merely Washington; and each of these must be chosen with an eye to its political repercussions. Any such tour, moreover, exacts an orgy of long speeches, the omission of any of which may offend an important district or a congressman whose support is significant. All of this, in its range and intensity, is enough to occupy the full attention of a single man. And all of this is conducted in a blare of pitiless publicity which makes the lightest word or act of the president, even of his wife,[10] a possible theme of national discussion.

But ceremony is, of course, merely the decorative penumbra of the office. It is the range of functions, and the pressure under which decisions have to be taken,

[10] Cf. William Allen White, *A Puritan in Babylon* (1938), pp. 353-7.

which, given their responsible character, constitute the immense burden of the office. And this burden will be the greater, the more positively the office is conceived. The president may get some aid (though less than one might expect) from his cabinet. He may get some more from those trusted advisers in non-official positions upon whom, it is probable, the modern president is coming more and more to rely. No doubt, too, the presence in Congress of a group of trusted politicians, of whose impact upon both houses he can be sure, counts for a good deal; it relieves the sense of an ever constant need for unrelaxing vigilance at the Capitol. But when all possible deductions have been made, there is no problem of which it cannot be said that it may be material upon which the president, and no one but the president, must make up his mind. Upon most of them he cannot hope to be an expert. Upon most of them, also, the people will look for some pronouncement from him; and upon most of those pronouncements he must expect the most expert criticism that opposition can produce. For it is by that criticism that the opposition hopes to replace him. Nothing that he can do is immune from public scrutiny; everything that he attempts may be the subject of the most rigorous investigation. He knows that, from the day he takes office, all that can be said against his policies legitimately, and, not seldom, illegitimately, is certain to be said.

What are the qualities called for by so vast and intense a range of functions? Above all, I think, the power to handle men, the ability almost intuitively to recognize the efficient human instrument for his purpose. That power has been more rare than is usually imagined. Lincoln, for instance, though he had an amazing insight into character, was never able to discover those instruments; no small part of the history of his administration is the record of his painful effort to transcend the results of that situation. Franklin Roosevelt has possessed it, as he showed when he chose, in remarkable circumstances, Mr. Ickes to be his secretary of the interior. Woodrow Wilson lacked it very largely; and no doubt a good deal of his final tragedy was due to that lack. So, also, did Calvin Coolidge; and he thereby prepared the road which led straight to the great depression.

There is the need for a president to come to office not only with a sense of the general direction in which he wishes to move, but with a sense, also, of the direction in which the times require him to move; these are very different things. Mr. Coolidge knew that he wished to pursue a policy of masterly inactivity; he assumed that the less he hampered the activities of business men the more prosperous would be the position of the country. The result of that attitude was an encouragement of speculative finance which he did not know enough to check at the right time, and which had assumed such proportions by the time Mr. Hoover took office that it is at least doubtful whether the latter would have been in a position to check it even if he had wished to do so.

And a president, further, must be able to think and decide rapidly; time is of the essence of perhaps half of his decisions. He needs not only the pertinacity to abide by them when they are made, but the instinct which tells him both when to give way and when he may wisely return to a policy about which he has been compelled at one stage to give way. Few things better illustrate this sense of time than President Wilson's approach to the problem of American intervention in the War of 1914. He created an atmosphere in which the mass of the people was persuaded to accept his view that intervention was inescapable; and he took, accordingly, a practically united people into the war. Had he acted much before he did, that psychological success would have been dubious enough at least to risk the chance of his re-election in 1916. The same quality is apparent in Franklin Roosevelt's handling of the neutrality issue. Again and again his search for the acceptance of his own formulae of international policy has been baffled by the dislike of the American people for European entanglements. Again and again, also, the president has utilized the changing circumstances to drive home the necessity of his view. If it be said that his problem has been rendered easier by the brutality of German and Italian policy since 1933, it has been rendered constantly more difficult by American doubt, which he may himself conceivably have shared, whether the governments of France and England read into his formulae the same ends as he sought to secure.

The presidential ability to co-ordinate is fundamental; and this largely depends upon the ability to distinguish between the significant and the insignificant.

The president who cannot delegate, and trust when he has delegated, is lost. For the most part, he can only concern himself with outlines; the details of the picture must be filled in by subordinates. Here, certainly, an art is required which must operate upon a scale quite different from any with which a prime minister is concerned. For the dignity of cabinet colleagues, and the relative certainty with which he can control the House of Commons, means that he is free, once policy in the large is settled, to leave its implementation alone. But a president may lose a bill in Congress if a subordinate proceeds untactfully. His strategy of action is necessarily far more delicate than any English prime minister requires. Every delegation of power is therefore a risk to be taken, and this makes his judgment of men a matter of supreme importance. He must know that the men he uses will see things through his eyes. He must feel confident not only that they will not bother him unduly, but even more that they will refer back to him at the point where his pressure only can produce the required result. He must delegate, too, knowing that at best he is bound to make mistakes both in men and in things. This is above all the case in matters of foreign policy. There, he is dependent upon the eyes and ears of men who, however skilfully he chooses them, will be less under his control and influence in Paris or London than in Washington. And the men to whom he delegates complicate his problem because they must delegate in their turn. Anyone who considers the relation of Lincoln to Stanton will see that the issue is an intricate one. To go too far is to risk the fulfilment of his aims; not to go far enough is to overwhelm himself in a multiplicity of detail which may no less jeopardize those aims.

Any president, almost in the nature of things, is in a position of aloofness. The eminence of his position is so great, the calls upon him so numerous, that it is not easy for him to avoid a sense of profound separation from his fellows. He cannot cultivate the kind of intimacy with his critics that is born of the almost instinctive good-fellowship of the House of Commons. He is rarely dealing, either in his cabinet or in his party-relations, with men to whose intimate friendship he has become accustomed by long experience. It is difficult for him to build a body of friends outside his official family upon whom he can rely for advice and action; the experience of Mr. Wilson with Colonel House, and of Franklin Roosevelt with Mr. Moley, shows that this is the case. In the result, a president who is to do his job adequately requires certain psychological qualities which cannot be too sufficiently emphasized. He must not be an unduly sensitive person. By his position, he is the central target for criticism, and he must be able to shake off its effect without repining. The danger of an inability to immunize himself against attack is shown clearly by Mr. Wilson's career in the White House. A president, no doubt, needs self-confidence; but he must not have that arrogant self-confidence which assumes, first, that his policies are infallibly right, and, therefrom, that criticism of them is original sin. It is pretty evident, from the documents, that Mr. Wilson lacked this ability to withstand attack. When he was pricked he bled; and he magnified the authors of the pinpricks into assassins. The result was that he predominantly surrounded himself, as in his cabinet, with second-rate men whom he could always overbear by superior intelligence, or, outside it, with men like Colonel House who were prepared simply to indulge in agreement for the pleasurable sensation of living at the center of power. At every critical moment after 1917, therefore, Mr. Wilson never had the personal instruments upon whom he could depend. He had either enemies whom he could not trust, or friends who had been sterilized into ineffective silence. A president in that position is bound to risk, and probably meet, disaster.

I do not mean that a president must not possess self-confidence; he could not do his work without a considerable measure of it. He has to pass judgment upon a mass of problems, not least in international affairs, upon which his actual knowledge must be small. Unless he was able to feel reliance upon that judgment, clearly he would fall into the hands of any associate strong-minded enough to establish an ascendency over him. Broadly, indeed, it is true to say that a lack of self-confidence has not been the besetting sin of presidents; Buchanan apart, it is difficult to think of one in whom irresolution was the outstanding characteristic. In general, it is almost true to say that entrance upon the office itself breeds self-confidence; that is interestingly true in the case of men so different as Polk and Coolidge. The problem for the president is to have sufficient of it to be able to plow ahead in his own way, and yet never so much that he is insensitive to the significance of counsel and criticism. He will get both in abundance, and the delicacy of his task, as Lincoln so supremely knew, lies above all in being able to make himself sufficiently remote from both as to be certain that it is his own mind that is making the decision.

I have spoken of the aloofness which surrounds the presidential office. No one can watch the president at work without the sense of its profundity, and the realization, therefore, that in an ultimate way, the president is bound to be a lonely man. I do not mean lonely in the sense that Lincoln was lonely; Lincoln's loneliness derived from an inner and utter melancholy that gave him friends but never intimates. His ultimate self was always withdrawn from his fellows; the greater the responsibility he bore, the greater was his loneliness. It is clear, for instance, that his famous storytelling was, above all, a protective coloration against its consequences upon his relations. I mean a loneliness that comes partly from the knowledge that no one can share the steep eminence upon which he is poised, and that, therefore, no one can really share the burden of responsibility he has to carry.

This fact, I think, makes two things important. No president must be too far ahead of his time if he is to be a successful president. He must see what he sees with the eyes of the multitude upon whose shoulders he stands. To get anywhere he must win understanding; to win it, the policy he pursues must never be so remote from the views about him that he cannot get that understanding. At bottom, his real power is in the popular support he can rally for the direction he proposes to follow; and it is generally unlikely that he will be able to rally support of any considerable volume for the novel plan or the unlooked-for principle. A good illustration of this was, I think, the Court plan of President Roosevelt in 1937. There, it is interesting to note, while he sought an objective intelligible to, and sympathized with, by that great majority which renewed his power in 1936, he sought its achievement by ways with which the tradition had not familiarized the masses; in ways, indeed, to which the tradition had made the masses hostile. He was too ingenious, both in concept and in mechanism, for a multitude which sees the broad highways only. He had insufficiently prepared it for so circuitous a divagation from those highways. It is the one instance, so far, in Mr. Roosevelt's presidency in which his hold of the opinion upon which presidential power depends was unsure in method and defective in execution. The result was his resounding defeat. I suspect that when the secret history of the Court proposals comes to be written we shall find that no small part of that defeat was the outcome of lesser men's urgency prevailing over his own normal realization that the way to win the confidence of the people is to take them fully into your confidence. On the Court fight, he was not in a realm made familiar to him by technical experts; and he made the mistake of relying upon advisers who did not understand that no statesman can ever successfully attack fundamental institutions by sidestepping them.

The president must never be ahead of his time; he achieves the maximum unity by moving to objectives that are expected as well as desired. And, in so moving, it is important that he should always retain the common touch without ever being controlled by it. A president who lacks this gift, the two Adamses, for example, is bound to suffer defeat. Without this gift, the presidential power to rally opinion in his support is paralyzed. Andrew Jackson always gave his forces the impression that his thoughts were theirs; he symbolized them in a way that made them an army of adherents. Lincoln marvelously made the ordinary man feel that the tragic sufferings of the war were his sufferings too. Mr. Roosevelt's use of the radio has made him a living and intimate part of millions of homes in which, otherwise, his policies would have been remote abstractions. He has symbolized to them, in an epoch of economic crisis, that zeal for the "forgotten man" which millions have wished to see embodied in the contours of policy. It is this absence of the common touch that was, I think, largely responsible for the defeat of Mr. Hoover. He was full of good will; he worked relentlessly at his task. But he never gave his constituents the impression of entering into their problems upon the plane on which they encountered them. He saw them from angles so different that, so to say, they did not seem the same problems. And since the remedies he recommended were those which, in the previous two years, the electorate had been engaged in largely repudiating, the general impression was

conveyed (though quite wrongly conveyed) that Mr.
Hoover simply did not realize there was a crisis at all.

What I am seeking to argue was well put by
Bagehot in a classic discussion of Sir Robert Peel. A
democratic statesman, he said, must be "an uncommon
man of common opinions." That, I think, is as good a
description as any of the successful president. The
nature of the office requires a man who is marching
with his times and is not remote from them. The
things he must emphasize in his policy, however in-
geniously he elaborates them, must be the big themes
of common discussion. Vast innovations for which
the public is unprepared are almost bound to fail, because they are almost certain to shock. There can be
experiment in the tactics of policy; there can hardly,
without great danger, be experiment in fundamental
ideas. Those observers who say that Mr. Roosevelt
missed a great opportunity in 1933 when he did not
nationalize the banking system seem to me wholly to
misconceive the nature of the presidential office.
While it is possible that, at that grave moment, the
president might have carried through such a scheme,
it was so widely outside the range of common expectation that it would have destroyed his authority for the
rest of his term of office. Nothing in previous discussion had prepared the public for such a measure. Nothing in the electoral conception of Mr. Roosevelt had
prepared the public to associate him with such a strategy. He might have won the battle; he would have
lost the campaign. For in democratic politics, the
justification for drastic expedients is long familiarity

with the idea; their possible coming must be part of the current coin of political controversy. Otherwise, the routine of the common man is dangerously disturbed; and once that occurs, he easily becomes the victim of those manufactured panics which are the staple opportunities of men like Hitler or Huey Long.

He must have "common opinions." But it is equally imperative that he be an "uncommon man." The public must see themselves in him, but they must, at the same time, be confident that he is something bigger than themselves. They must see someone who compels respect. They must see someone who can say in the grand way what they half-articulately feel. They must have the sense that they are a part of significant events. Dull government can only endure when government is unimportant; a long period of extraordinary prosperity will, as in the Coolidge regime, persuade men that dullness is the same as soundness. But where any significant part of the population is hard pressed, it looks to the president for relief; and it is then urgent that he give the appearance of active intervention on their behalf. A dull president will not last long in a period of crisis. His temptation, just because he is dull, is to throw the burden of responsibility upon the leaders in Congress. He thus ceases to be the symbol of action, and the nation feels deprived of that leadership to which it feels itself entitled. It was a sound instinct which persuaded Theodore Roosevelt, when he was in the White House, always to provide a public pronouncement for Monday morning. It was a still more sound instinct which led Woodrow Wilson to revive the custom, which had lapsed since Jefferson's time, of addressing Congress in person. And it has, I think, been something like a stroke of genius on the part of Franklin Roosevelt to transform the press conference at the White House from the stiff interchange that took place under his predecessors to the full and frank discussions of which we have now so intimate and revealing a record.[11] To make the public see how some, at least, of the wheels go round is to admit them to a sense of the range and magnitude of the office. That is one of the ways in which a masterful president can do most to educate his electorate to the understanding of his policies. It is, of course, part of the technique of propaganda, as well as of information, and, as such, has its very real dangers.[12] The president may say the wrong thing,[13] or he may be misrepresented; and there is the danger of premature disclosure. But, all in all, the White House press conference is probably a necessary method of driving home to an electorate of nearly fifty millions the presidential attitude of mind. It cannot compete with a good radio address as a source of direct impact; but the latter is a weapon likely to diminish in value if it makes the president oppressively familiar. There is an important sense in which his remoteness is not less important than his friendliness as an instrument in making effective his policy.

There is no formula for the "uncommon man"; his

[11] See *The Public Papers and Addresses of Franklin D. Roosevelt*, Vols. I-V, for a full sample of them.

[12] Lindsay Rogers, *The American Senate* (1926), pp. 215 f.

[13] For an amusing example see Rogers, *op. cit.*, p. 218.

qualities vary with the person who fills the office. It is one thing with Washington, and a very different thing with Jefferson or Madison. It is one thing with Andrew Jackson, and again, a very different thing with Franklin Roosevelt. In general, it is worth noting that, even with ordinary men, the momentum of the office has the power to call out the best that is in them. James Polk had few exceptional qualities either of mind or of character; yet it is difficult to read his *Diary* without the sense that he grew consistently in stature throughout his incumbency in the White House. There was nothing intellectually extraordinary in Grover Cleveland; yet his rugged obstinacy gave his periods of office a certain distinction which has had its influence upon the subsequent tradition of the presidency. Colorless presidents, indeed, have been more exceptional than the critics have been wont to admit; Franklin Pierce, Fillmore, James Buchanan, Benjamin Harrison, and Warren Harding stand out in this regard. The fact is that the opportunities the office affords are so great that an ordinary man is usually dignified by it, while an exceptional man is stimulated as by no other post in a democratic state. Partly, I think, this arises from its very elevation. The depth of interest it evokes among the American people is a challenge to the best in a man. Bagehot, with his usual prescience, has noted the extraordinary growth in Lincoln's stature during his presidency. That is, of course, outstanding, though perhaps less remarkable in so great a figure than in the case of lesser men from whom, on the previous evidence, so much less was to be expected.

The cases of Tyler and Polk are more outstanding; for without the office neither would have seemed, historically, the exceptional man he became. The influence of the office on the personality of its holder is, in fact, a fascinating study in the dynamics of political power.

4

The founders of the Constitution were especially proud of the method they adopted for choosing the president; none of their expectations has been more decisively disappointed. The presidential candidates are now chosen at national conventions of the respective parties; and the decision is made by the whole electorate, voting in such fashion that, as shown in several elections, a plurality of votes does not necessarily carry with it the certainty of election. It is, indeed, a desirable thing that the method should be made to correspond to the facts. A constitutional amendment which simply stated that the candidate with the most votes should be deemed to have been elected would be a wise safeguard against possible difficulties in the future.

An American presidential convention is like nothing else in the civilized world; and the critics of the system—which, in its modern form, is just a hundred years old—have exhausted the language of vituperation in attack upon its character. The power of money; the persuasive power of hidden and corrupt influence; the undue authority of the "doubtful" state; the overt and hidden prejudices against particular types of candidates, as, for instance, members of the Roman Catholic Church; the "deals" which accompany the capture of a delegation for one candidate as against another; the mythology of the "favorite son"; the casual influence, notable in the case of Lincoln's selection, of the choice of the convention city; the undue impact, as in the Democratic convention of 1896, of a single speech by a potential nominee; the operation of the technique of the "dark horse" candidate; the exploitation of the "stalking-horse" behind whom some well-organized group has its carefully prepared selection whose name is put forward at the right moment; and, finally, the raucous, complex, and hectic atmosphere of the convention itself; its well-improvised enthusiasms; its fantastic horse-play; its immunity to thought; its wild rumors; its incredible conspiracies; all these characteristics, none of which can ever suffer exaggeration, seem to the outsider, and especially to the European outsider, about the worst possible way in which to choose a man to occupy the highest executive post in a democratic commonwealth.

The convention itself is, of course, predominantly an organ for registering decisions that have been made behind the scenes. Occasionally, an utterance upon its floor may exercise a real influence upon its outcome. Senator Conkling did Grant irreparable damage in 1880; and the contrast between his speech and that of Garfield, who nominated Sherman, had a good deal to do with the emergence of Garfield as the Republican candidate. So, also, the famous speech of Bryan in 1896 turned the balance of opinion in his favor. But

in general the actual nomination is decided in part by
the pre-convention campaign and in part by bargains
actually concluded in and around the convention itself. The pre-convention campaign is of great importance. It was decisive, for instance, in the selection of
Franklin Roosevelt in 1932; the spadework done by
Mr. Farley in the two preceding years was the condition precedent to his nomination. Bargaining at the
convention is, of course, a special art. Its importance
emerges either when there are a number of outstanding candidates between whom choice is difficult—as
with the Republicans in 1880 and 1920, and with the
Democrats in 1924—or when a powerful group has
made up its mind to try to force a "dark horse" upon
the convention. Accident, in fact, plays a much
smaller part in the choice of the candidate than is imagined. Many people, for example, expected either
Governor Lowden or General Wood to be the Republican candidate in 1920; and immense sums had
been expended in promoting their interests. But the
skilful proponents of Senator Harding's name had long
foreseen that the acuteness of their rivalry would make
neither possible, and they had long foreseen the probability of Harding's success. "At the proper time after
the Republican national convention meets," said Mr.
Daugherty, Senator Harding's manager, "some fifteen
men, bleary-eyed with loss of sleep, and perspiring
profusely with the excessive heat, will sit down in seclusion round a big table. I will be with them, and will
present the [name] of Senator Harding to them and

[43]

before we get through, they will put him over."[14] That is precisely what occurred.

Out of all this complexity, there has emerged the doctrine of "availability." The party needs a candidate who, positively, will make the widest appeal and, negatively, will offend the least proportion of the electorate. On the whole, he ought to come from a doubtful state; a Democrat from New York is more "available" than one from the solid South because he is likely to win votes which might otherwise be uninterested. It seems still to be true that it is difficult to elect a Roman Catholic; half the solid South refused to vote for Governor Smith in 1928. He must not be anti-religious; that would offend the great vested interest of the churches. He must be sound on the tariff; he must be against wild currency adventures; he must not be too overtly internationalist in outlook. Administrative experience, like the governorship of a state, is important. It is helpful if he is a self-made man; the "log cabin to White House" tradition is still, despite the two Roosevelts, an influential one. He ought not to possess any nostrum which can be represented as extreme. In the aftermath of a war period, it is important that he should have played his part in the army; from Jackson and Taylor onwards, the military hero has had an immense appeal to the electorate. It is undesirable that he should have too close an association with the big interests, especially Wall Street; Wilson, in 1912, owed his

[14] *New York Times*, June 13, 1920. For a full account of Mr. Daugherty's technique, see H. M. Daugherty and Thomas Dixon, *The Inside Story of the Harding Tragedy* (1932), pp. 32-55.

nomination to Mr. Bryan's famous pronouncement that he would not support anyone under obligation to "Morgan, Ryan, Belmont, or any other member of the privilege-seeking favor-hunting class." He must have a sufficiently flexible mind to accept the implications of the trading necessary to build his majority. He must not be the kind of man whom it is obviously easy to ridicule in a campaign, either because he is "viewy," or for any other reason.

All of which means, as a general rule, that the outcome of a presidential convention is likely to be a compromise of some kind. But it is important to realize that it is not a compromise in which, without cause, the outstanding candidate is certain to be defeated. Henry Clay never became president because the political judgment of his party warned it against nominating him in the years when its chances for success were brightest. Blaine never became president because even many of his admirers profoundly felt that his association, to say no more, with dubious political methods left too much to be explained away. Governor Fuller of Massachusetts could not be nominated because, as Senator Borah said, Sacco and Vanzetti would thereby have become issues in the campaign.[15] Senator Lodge was for forty years an outstanding figure in the Senate. But he could not have secured the Republican nomination simply because his own party realized that, whatever his qualities, those years in politics were a continuous demonstration of his unfitness for high

[15] As governor of his state in 1927, Mr. Fuller did not intervene to prevent their execution.

executive office. Mr. Hoover was undoubtedly the leading Republican in 1936; and, on the precedent of Cleveland's nomination in 1892, was the natural recipient of the candidature. But he was unavailable because the party leaders felt, quite rightly, that he was too closely associated with Republican failure in the depression to be an acceptable candidate.

It is notable, in short, that whenever an obvious contender for the nomination does not receive it, there is usually a quite adequate explanation for his failure. It is notable, further, that when a "dark horse" nominee emerges, he has been held in reserve for just such an opportunity by powerful influences which are waiting for their moment. It is possible for someone, like Franklin Pierce, who is unknown to the general public, to emerge from the ordeal. But it is to be noticed that, if he does, his emergence is always due to special circumstances, and that there is to be detected behind him a substantial cohort who know precisely what they are doing. A "dark horse," that is to say, is a compromise candidate in much the same way as Mr. Bonar Law was a compromise between Sir Austen Chamberlain and Mr. Walter Long in 1911, or Sir Henry Campbell-Bannerman as Liberal leader after 1895. Much the same situation obtains in the complicated intrigues of French politics. It is difficult for the outsider to follow the tortuous internal events which make now M. Herriot, now M. Chautemps, and now M. Daladier the leader of the Socialist Radicals. Immediacy on the basis of "availability" there also explains the result that is reached. It is as natural for

Henry Clay or James G. Blaine to have missed the presidency as it is for Lord Curzon or Sir Austen Chamberlain to have missed the premiership in their country.

The real difference, of course, lies in the prior experience of those who are chosen as nominees. Other things being equal, a prime minister in Great Britain or France will have served a long apprenticeship in the legislative assembly before obtaining the supreme office. He will be a figure in the House. He will be known to the party. He will probably have had considerable administrative experience in a lesser office. He will be pretty intimately known to those whom he is to lead. In the United States, none of this is necessarily true. Since the Civil War, a distinguished career in Congress has rarely been a passport to the nomination. Attainment of cabinet office has had no direct relevance to a candidature in any except two cases; and, of these, Mr. Hoover's name was made rather by his war record than by his experience in the Department of Commerce. A state governorship has counted for much. But it is pretty true to say that most of the chosen candidates have been names in the nation rather than in Washington. They have not known with any intimacy those with whom they would, as president, be expected to work.

The position is in curious contrast with the pre-Civil War period. The first four presidents of the United States almost nominated themselves; and, among their successors, there was hardly a candidate for the nomination who was not a person of considerable political consequence. One feature, indeed, is constant. No presidential candidate in the whole record has been a business man. The vocation, clearly, is a full-time one; and the qualities which make for business success make, also, against the possibility of nomination. It is true that, in his engineering period, Mr. Hoover was mainly a company organizer. But after his return to America all his energies were devoted to politics. Business men have played a not inconsiderable part in the conventions as king-makers; but it is a curious fact that in a civilization perhaps more dominated by business men than by any other, they have had to surrender the hope of being king. The lawyer, the soldier, the rentier and politician, the man who lives by his earnings as politician; these are the types from whom the candidates have been chosen. The business man may hope for cabinet office. He is likely to be important in negativing ambitions the realization of which would not be regarded with favor by the big interests. But, on the record, he must be the power behind the throne; he cannot hope to occupy it.

The reason, I think, is simple. The small man cannot hope to afford the risks of a political career. The great one, a Rockefeller, a Vanderbilt, even an Owen D. Young, would not be an "available" candidate simply because he would arouse the suspicion that the party which nominated him was in bondage to the money-power. The influence of the business outlook upon the parties must, therefore, be indirect. It is real enough, as the election of McKinley makes clear. But it must always seek to veil itself in a decent obscurity if it is not to prove a source of violent opposition from the interests of labor and the small farmer. Franklin Roosevelt gained great strength from both these sources by the fact that the Liberty League, an organization dominated by the great business interests, was opposed to his re-election.

The big problem that is raised by the American method of nominating presidential candidates is whether it puts a premium, as Lord Bryce argued, against the opportunity of first-rate men to receive consideration. I do not think his case is proved by making a list of first-rate men, Clay and Calhoun and Webster, for example, who missed nomination. The answer to that argument is, first, that many first-rate men have become president by reason of the system; and second, that the reasons which stopped others would have been powerful reasons against their elevation in any representative democracy. It is, I think, at least doubtful whether the elevation of a Roman Catholic to the premiership would be regarded favorably in Great Britain. A great business man, both in England and France, will operate mainly behind the political scene rather than in front of it; of our three business men who have become prime ministers one was, in fact, a rentier, and the others had long retired from active participation therein. Few people could easily explain the nuances that account for the failure of one man to reach the top, and the success of another. And in estimating the meaning of "availability" we must remember, always, that there is a real sense in which the more strong the candidate, supposing that he represents a special point of view, the more strong, also, are likely to be his enemies. Not infrequently, an easy nomination—so long as the renomination of an existing president is not involved—merely means, as it meant with Horace Greeley in 1872, with Judge Parker in 1904, with Governor Landon in 1936, that rival candidates do not consider there is much prospect for their party's success, and they are not anxious to be associated with a dismal failure at the polls, with a view of a later nomination.

Granted, this is to say, the greatness of the prize, and the necessity of popular election, it is difficult to see what other method than the nominating convention is available; more, it is true to say that, on balance, it has worked well rather than badly. The criticisms that are brought against it are rather, in their real substance, criticisms of the place of the presidency in the American constitutional scheme than of the method whereby the president is chosen. It is regrettable that an inexperienced man may come to reside in the White House; the answer is that few of those who have reached it have been inexperienced men. If it be said that men like Harding and Coolidge were unfit for the great post they secured, the answer is that the first had considerable experience both in the Ohio legislature and in the Senate, while the second had been a successful Massachusetts politician, twice occupying the governorship, for twenty years. If we take the presidents of the twentieth century, there is not one who had not been prepared for presidential office by a long experience of politics; and, with the possible exception of the Democratic candidate in 1904, that is true, also, of their defeated rivals. What is lacking in their training is mostly the art of handling Congress; and the rules of that art are only partly dependent upon the character of the president for the time.

It must be remembered that, in making the choice, there are two fundamental considerations in the background of which the meaning of "availability" must be set. The first is that the party choosing a candidate wants, if it can, to win; and second, it knows that if it does win, and its nominee becomes president, there is great likelihood of its having to adopt him a second time, since not to do so is to condemn an administration for which it has to bear responsibility. While, therefore, it is quite true that a party convention provides an opportunity for the art of such a dubious wire-puller as Mr. Daugherty, it is also true that the managers of a great party are anxious to avoid, if they can, the consequences of success in that type of manipulation. One has only to read the account of an experience of conventions like that of Senator Hoar of Massachusetts to see that a scrupulous and honorable man will approach the task of selection with all the seriousness that its consequences require.[16]

All in all, I doubt whether the methods of the system are very different from those of other countries. They are, perhaps, more open and crude than in Great Britain. There is no generosity in the fight for power. There is a passionate determination on the part

[16] G. F. Hoar, *Autobiography* (1903), I, 378-421.

of organized interests to get the "safe" man who can be relied upon to live up to the commitments exacted from him. There is the fierce conflict of rival ambitions. There is the organization of every sort of cabal to win a victory for its man. Press and radio and platform are vigorously manipulated to this end. Immense promises are made, pretty ugly deals are effected. Yet I suggest that anyone who knows the life of a political party from within Great Britain will not feel inclined to cast a stone at the American system. It fits, well enough, the medium in which it has to work. It achieves the results that the needs of the people require.

For there is at least one test of the system that is, I think, decisive. There have been five considerable crises in American history. There was the need to start the new republic adequately in 1789; it gave the American people its natural leader in George Washington. The crisis of 1800 brought Jefferson to the presidency; that of 1861 brought Abraham Lincoln. The War of 1914 found Woodrow Wilson in office; the great depression resulted in the election of Franklin Roosevelt. So far, it is clear, the hour has brought forth the man. It is of course true, as Bagehot said, that "success in a lottery is no argument for lotteries." I agree that no nation can afford a succession of what Theodore Roosevelt termed "Buchanan Presidents"— men whose handling of the issues is uncertain and feeble. But the answer is that the nation has never had that succession; an epoch of Hardings and Coolidges produces, by the scale of the problems to which it gives rise, its own regeneration. The weak president, as I have argued, comes from the fact that a strong predecessor has set the feet of the nation on level ground. He is chosen because, after a diet of strong occasions, a nation, like an individual, turns naturally to the chance of a quiet time. "Normalcy" is always certain to be popular after crises. The issue is whether, when a crisis comes, the system can discover the man to handle it. On the evidence, this has so far been very remarkably the case. To urge that it is chance is, I think, a superficial view. It is the outcome of the national recognition that energy and direction are required, and the man chosen is the party response to that recognition. The phenomenon is as natural as the replacement of Mr. Asquith by Mr. Lloyd George in 1917, as instinctive, one may say, as the widespread demand, in the England of 1939, for the strengthening of the personnel of the "National" government. The American scheme involves delay; Mr. Roosevelt did not come to office until the nation had suffered three years of depression. But the essential fact is that he came to office. Nor is there reason to suppose that this is accidental. The more deeply we penetrate the working of the system the more clearly does it emerge that the result is inherent in its nature.

5

Quite different considerations apply to the position of a president after election. The tasks that confront him even before he assumes the burden of office are manifold. He has to choose, not merely his cabinet colleagues, but a vast horde of minor officials in an atmosphere that is not seldom akin to pandemonium. He has to work out at any rate some of the general principles of the policy he proposes to follow. He has to arrive at a *modus vivendi* with the leaders of his party in Congress. There are the delicate problems of the transition between the old regime and the new; two months now elapse between election and assumption of office. Every action of his, every thought almost, is surrounded by a fierce light of publicity which makes the calm appropriate to thought almost impossible. The historians have described the almost fantastic atmosphere which preceded the inauguration of Garfield, and ended in his assassination at the hands of a disappointed office seeker. More delicate even was the type of problem confronted by Franklin Roosevelt before his entrance into the White House on March 4, 1933. For President Hoover was still in office, even though discredited by defeat. The country was in a state of crisis; and Mr. Hoover was engaged in difficult negotiations about the international economic situation. On both aspects of policy, his views and those of Mr. Roosevelt were as far apart as the poles. He could hardly act without consulting his successful opponent; yet he was not prepared to act upon the only assumptions Mr. Roosevelt was prepared to accept. The complicated minuet they jointly performed in those months, with Mr. Hoover seeking collaboration on his own terms and Mr. Roosevelt delicately insisting that the responsibility was necessarily the president's, indicates the range of the issues the president-elect has to decide.

And he does not approach those issues as, in any full sense, a free man. The president is the subject of compulsions which begin to operate from the day he has been nominated as a candidate. He has to pay a price in men; he has to pay a price in measures. He has to reward the more outstanding, at least, of those who have been responsible for his election; how great that price may be will be evident to anyone who looks at the membership of President Harding's cabinet. To assure his election, he will have made or have acquiesced in the making of innumerable, and not seldom dubious, commitments. He will have had to placate or persuade vested interests, like Wall Street, or the farming community, or organized labor, or the Catholic vote. Some deference he must pay to the outline of the party platform; though here a convenient and rhetorical vagueness will usually leave him a diversity of possible interpretation. He has to think in terms of the profound sectionalism by which he is confronted. He has to bend his mind to decision upon a multiplicity of issues about which he has hardly before had to concern himself. It is not, I think, exaggeration to say that the day of a successful election is the day on which the president ceases to be a free man.

For there is not only the price, in men and measures, of election. There is the price for laying the foundations of a possible re-election; and that will begin almost as soon as he assumes the reins of office.

Few presidents have been willing to forgo the chance of a second term; and no president can so act as to deprive his party at least of the chance of a second term for its nominee. He has to pay the price exacted for the power to maintain the control of his party, above all in Congress; and there he is bound to remember that he faces a power which is, at best, co-ordinate with himself and may, unless skilfully handled, insist on seeking to become his superior rival. No doubt he can always appeal against it—as both Woodrow Wilson and Franklin Roosevelt have remarkably done—to the force of public opinion outside. But he can never be the master of his party in the sense that a British prime minister with a majority in the House of Commons is. He cannot appeal from an antagonistic Congress to an electorate whose support he believes himself to possess. He must persuade and cajole; he can rarely afford to threaten. Whatever be the growth in the magnitude of the executive power in the United States, in the nature of things it cannot even remotely be described, at least with accuracy, as approaching dictatorial proportions.

For the punitive powers by which a president can hew his way to his goal are cribbed and confined by the system at every turn. He can do something with the patronage; though the limits of its influence are, in the realm of major policy, more narrow than the critics of the executive are prone to admit. He cannot threaten a dissolution. He cannot even, as Franklin Roosevelt learned in the congressional elections of 1938, successfully appeal to his supporters to purge the critics of his own party. His real reliance is simply upon the public opinion he can muster in his behalf. Two-thirds of the senators are largely beyond his power of control; they were there before he came to office, and they can normally expect to remain there long after he has gone. And even though the turnover of members of the House of Representatives is much greater than in the Senate, its proportions depend much more upon local than upon national considerations, at least within the party itself. The experience of Franklin Roosevelt is, again, decisive in this regard. The defeat of his plan for the reform of the Supreme Court was, after all, accomplished by his opponents within six months of the most triumphant victory in the history of the presidency.

Nor does presidential power have the right to confidence even when its majority in Congress is assured. Behind and above its authority, there looms the Supreme Court which may, at any moment, strike an act of Congress into impotence. And it cannot be said that this depends merely upon the composition of the Court, that a liberal president is safe if he has a liberal majority there, and vice versa. In the *Schechter* case,[17] all the liberal members of the Court were united with their conservative colleagues to find the National Industrial Recovery Act—one of the most important, if one of the most dubious, experiments of Franklin Roosevelt's first term—unconstitutional. No president can seriously hope for a

[17] *Schechter* v. *U. S.* (1935), 295 U. S. 495.

constitutional amendment in this realm that is likely to be of assistance to him within the time-limit during which he must work. He may be fortunate in obtaining vacancies on the Court which he can fill with men of his own outlook; but he is bound to remember the experience of Theodore Roosevelt with Mr. Justice Holmes and know that not even the most careful scrutiny will give him a positive assurance that he will be upheld.[18] Here the truth is that the constitutional limits within which both the president and a Court that is scrupulous in its technique of interpretation must work are probably more narrow than the needs of the United States. On any showing, the powers left to the states cover matters which hamper the prospect of rapid and decisive federal action, should any number of them be recalcitrant; and the difficulties of the commerce clause, in the age of giant industry, will be obvious on the most superficial examination.[19]

No doubt in an emergency, the Supreme Court will act with a certain generosity or acumen; its attitude to the Adamson law in 1916[20] and to the gold clause in 1934[21] is proof that it is far from indifferent to the political consequences of its decisions. Members of the Supreme Court dwell upon Olympian heights; but they display all the human characteristics we associate

---

[18] *Correspondence between Theodore Roosevelt and H. C. Lodge* (1928), I, 517-519.

[19] Cf. E. S. Corwin, *The Twilight of the Supreme Court* (1936).

[20] *Wilson* v. *New* (1917), 243 U. S. 332.

[21] Cf. the interesting discussion of P. J. Eder. "The Gold Clause Cases in the Light of History," 23, Georgetown *Law Review*, pp. 359-388, 722-760.

with dwellers upon Olympus. Some of them, at least, are keen politicians by training, keen enough to yearn for the presidency even after they have become justices of the Supreme Court; it is not, indeed, an exaggeration to say that, at any given time, one or two of the justices are potential candidates for the presidency. It is not unimportant, in this context, that Chief Justice Taft did not think it incompatible with his high office to act as a personal adviser to Mr. Coolidge throughout his presidential terms;[22] and though we do not yet fully know the part played by Chief Justice Hughes and by some, at least, of his associates in the defeat of Mr. Roosevelt's Court plan in 1937, there can be little doubt that it was considerable. Any president who chooses to embark upon an ample legislative program, especially if it touches, as an ample program can hardly fail to touch, the delicate problems of the limits of the federal power, must keep one eye firmly fixed upon its possible repercussions upon the Supreme Court.

Not only is this the case upon any narrow partisan ground. Two, at least, of the great conflicts between the executive and the judiciary in American history rest upon a far wider foundation than that of narrow party advantage. That is certainly the case in the conflict between Marshall and Jefferson; it is also true of the conflict between Marshall and Jackson. In each instance, what was at stake was a philosophy of the Constitution. In each instance, also, it is easy to

[22] W. Allen White, *A Puritan in Babylon* (1938), pp. 245, 252, 284-288, 348-350, 374-376.

understand the wide differences which separated the protagonists. They were not at variance over a small measure. They were at variance over the pivotal question of the place of the judiciary in the American constitutional scheme. For Marshall, rightly or wrongly—I myself think wrongly—the duty of the Court was not merely to strengthen the national power; even more it was to strengthen it as a weapon of property against the possible assault of the masses. The whole ethos of his conception of the Court's function lay in his belief that the power of democracy must be limited by the right of property to security; and he saw in the instrument of judicial review the highroad to this end. Neither Jefferson nor Jackson sympathized with this outlook, and the issue was bound to be joined between them. It is bound, I add, to be joined—emergency apart—between the Court and any president who seeks a rapid redefinition of the place of property in the state. For to redefine that place means legislation which is, in its nature, not only bound to traverse basic precedents in the history of the Court; it runs very quickly toward a re-assessment of the division of powers contemplated by the Constitution. And since it is likely that, save in the most exceptional periods, the majority of the judges of the Court will be successful lawyers whose outlook has been shaped by long years of service to the business interests, they are not apt to view with favor legislation which seeks the control of these in a way likely to be regarded by business itself as detrimental to the national well-being.

A president, therefore, especially an actively liberal
president, is bound to have regard to the possible attitude of the Court to his innovations; and he is bound
to remember that only emergency will persuade the
Court to abdicate from its historic function—the real
achievement of Marshall—of guardian of the rights
of property. But the compulsions upon him do not
end there. He must pay continuous attention to the
attitude of business itself. To disturb its confidence
is, always, to jeopardize his chance of a smooth passage
during his years of office. It is not merely that invest-
ment may lag, with its rapid repercussion upon unemployment and the standard of life. It is not merely,
either, that American business is as powerful a "lobby"
in Washington as there is anywhere in the world. It
is also that the interstitial connections between business and politics in the United States give to its
actions a quite special and immediate authority of
which he dare not be neglectful. It is to big business
that his party must look for essential campaign contributions. There are states whose senators depend
upon some great corporation for their place in Washington. Its influence in the national committee of
his party will always be profound. It will tend to
have behind its views the main weight of the legal
profession—a serious matter in a legislative system
where the lawyer plays so large a part. The president
who arouses the suspicion that he is not a "sound"
man from the angle of business philosophy is bound
to run into heavy weather. And "soundness" from
the business angle means a minimum of interference

[61]

with the established practices of commercial and industrial enterprise. The way of an innovating president, who is anxious for massive social legislation, is not likely to be strewn with roses.

This generalization is proved not only by the experience of Franklin Roosevelt. It is remarkably exemplified by the career of Mark Hanna; he was nothing so much as the business agent of capitalism in the Senate and at the White House in the later years of his career.[23] It is shown by the problems Theodore Roosevelt confronted when he sought to deal with conservation and the trusts. It is shown, again, by the fact that though the revelations of the Pujo Committee in 1913 depicted a situation of which the outcome was clearly prophesied at the time by Mr. Justice Brandeis,[24] nothing was done about it until the depression of 1929 put a new driving force behind the urgency of reform; and even now, it is a problem to know how far the substance of the legislation passed as a result of the Black Committee is likely to be permanent in its influence. An innovating president may appeal against the business criteria of "soundness" to public opinion. In an emergency period he is likely to obtain wide support for his attitude. But he is in the difficulty that the continuance of this support depends, to a considerable degree, upon his power to obtain the conditions of economic revival; and this power, in its turn, depends upon his ability to secure that co-operation from business men

[23] Cf. Herbert Croly, *Mark Hanna* (1912), for an illuminating picture of his views and activities.

[24] See his now-classic exposé, *Other People's Money* (1915).

which, by definition almost, his reform program repels. It is significant, for example, that Franklin Roosevelt's rearmament program evoked widespread assent from business men because it is a classic form of expenditure upon public works to which they are habituated by tradition. But expenditure on the experiments of the Works Progress Administration, of which the social value has been literally inestimable, has been bitterly denounced from its inception, rarely upon any factual basis, and mainly because its assumptions run counter to those of the classic form.

What I am concerned to show is that the "inarticulate major premises" of the presidential office limit by definition the area within which the president is free to move. The position itself imposes boundaries of action upon him. He is limited as to the men he may use as the instruments of his policy. He is limited by the interplay of the institutions with which he must cooperate. He is limited by the division of powers which the Constitution imposes, and the interpretation which is likely to be placed on the implications of that division by the courts. He is limited by the fact that he must conciliate his party and cannot coerce it; to be too far ahead of its conceptions is necessarily to court defeat. He is limited by the need to carry with him the members of a business community whose strategic position gives to it an economic and psychological authority unexampled, I think, in any other country in the world. To transcend these limitations either the president must be, like Lincoln, a supremely great man, or he must inherit an emergency, like war, as with Woodrow Wilson, or economic chaos, like Franklin Roosevelt, which so act upon public opinion as to suspend the normal assumptions of the American system.

And there is one other limitation to which attention must be directed. In a sense, the category of time is more important to the president of the United States than to any other political leader in the world. His term of office is for four years. But at the end of two, he is faced with a congressional election, in which the results of his policy are judged. He has, therefore, if he wants to make an impact upon the electoral mind, to do so with extraordinary rapidity. To be successful, indeed, he ought really to come into office with a pretty clear notion of the lines upon which he is to act. He has only six months between nomination and election; only eight months between nomination and accession to office. In five of these, the campaign, with its fatiguing journeys and endless speeches, is necessarily the first consideration; in the remaining three, he is the predestined victim of every important person and interest requiring consideration. After the mid-term congressional election, he has to make arrangements for his re-election, if he can. The whole impetus, accordingly, of the second half of his first term is set in the perspective of that necessity. Granted that he is likely to secure it—a refusal of the party to renominate is taken as a confession of failure—he has still to be careful lest he offend the powerful by his policy. And if he secures renomination, he is faced by the knowledge of two facts: there is, first, the mid-congressional election, with all its hazards, of his second term, and there is the virtual certainty that, two years later, he will have done with office forever. John Quincy Adams is the only president who, so far, has played a significant part in politics after leaving the White House. The knowledge, accordingly, that the scepter must pass from him, at the furthest, at the close of his second term operates decisively to weaken his influence in the last two years of his reign. Few presidents have had any substantial results to show during that period.

This raises the very interesting question of the proper length of the presidential term. The present limitation to two terms is, of course, simply a convention born of Washington's decision to retire at that stage. Had he wished for a third nomination, he could have had it, and Gouverneur Morris is only one of many who urged him strongly to continue. So far, no president has secured a third term, though it is possible that Jefferson and Jackson might have had it if they had wished. Grant eagerly desired a third term, but the strength of tradition and the dubious persons with whom he had surrounded himself while in office prevented his nomination. Theodore Roosevelt practically, though not technically, ran for a third term, but he did not secure the official nomination of his party. Certainly the pressure of public opinion against a third term is very strong. There is not only the power of tradition, in a country where tradition exercises very great authority. There is an important truth in the argument of Professor Cushman that "the American people would grow very restive under a long, executive term of office . . . the change for which they so loudly clamor every four years is a safety valve for their prejudices and sentiments."[25]

It is clear, I think, that a single four-year term does not give elbowroom, especially when the danger of a loss of control of Congress at the mid-term election is remembered, to a president who has a big program in view. The persuasion of a democracy to big changes is at best a slow process, and a relatively small part of the president's time can be given to that purpose. This was seen by de Tocqueville a century ago. "It is impossible to consider," he wrote,[26] "the ordinary course of affairs in the United States without perceiving that the desire to be re-elected is the chief aim of the president; that his whole administration, and even his most indifferent measures, tend to this object; and that, as the crisis approaches, his personal interest takes the place of his interest in the public good." Nor is he in better case if he has decided not to run for a second term. Polk made that decision, and a revealing passage in his *Diary* shows the result of that self-denying ordinance. "With a large nominal majority in both houses," he wrote[27] about mid-way in his term, "I am practically in a minority. The several cliques and sections of the Democratic Party are manifestly more engaged in managing for their respective

[25] S. P. Orth and R. E. Cushman, *American National Government* (1931), p. 246.
[26] *Democracy in America* (ed. 1900), pp. 1, 136.
[27] *Diary of James K. Polk* (ed. Nevins, 1929), p. 186.

favorites in the next presidential election than they are in supporting the government in prosecuting the [Mexican] war, or in carrying out any of its great measures. The only corrective is in the hands of the people."

Four years is, clearly, too short a period of office in the light of the circumstances confronted by the president; and it has the great disadvantage that, without re-eligibility, it gives him the advantage of an experience of which it would then deprive the American people. But if there is to be, as there now is, re-eligibility, the difficulty de Tocqueville noted is an important consideration; the president, as John Randolph said in the convention,[28] "should not be left under a temptation to court a re-appointment." It is this which led Chief Justice Taft to suggest a change in the present system. "I am strongly inclined to the view," he wrote,[29] "that it would have been a wiser provision, as it was at one time voted in the convention, to make the term of the president six or seven years, and render him ineligible thereafter. Such a change would give to the executive greater courage and independence in the discharge of his duties. The absorbing and diverting interest in the re-election of the incumbent, taken by those federal civil servants who regard their own tenure as dependent upon his, would disappear and the efficiency of administration in the last eighteen months of a term would be maintained."

[28] Farrand, *Records of the Federal Convention*, I, pp. 104 f.
[29] *Our Chief Magistrate and His Powers* (1916), p. 4.

It is, I think, difficult to read the documents without the conviction that Mr. Taft was right. If there is to be no re-eligibility, a term of four years is too short; if there is to be re-elegibility, the argument against a third term is not a very convincing one. The fear of monarchy which pervaded the mind of some, at least, of the founders is no longer valid; the fear of Caesarism uttered by contemporary critics omits the vital fact that the whole framework of the American scheme of government is utterly incompatible with Caesarism. A Caesar, if some crisis led to his emergence in the United States, would have to do far more than is implied in mere re-election upon the basis of the present presidential powers. The true and only issue involved in the problem of a third term is whether, on a balance of considerations, the American people want any given incumbent who offers himself; and that, after all, is a question which the American people alone are competent to decide.

There are, of course, important considerations to be weighed. The burden of the office is very heavy, especially in critical times; few men could easily carry it for more than eight years. It needs an incumbent who is at the height of his powers. A president must be thirty-five; but he is, as a rule, in early middle age on election. An eight-year period of office brings him near to the middle sixties; after that, the strain begins to tell if it is borne continuously. On the other hand, there are exceptional men who bear the years with relative indifference, Mr. Gladstone, for instance, and Bismarck. Peel was seventy when he was killed;

and there was no evidence of any decline in his powers. From this angle, the whole problem is clearly individual to the man, and all generalizations are out of place.

It is, indeed, true that democracy is based on the thesis that no man is indispensable; therein lies one of its most vital differences from a dictatorial regime, which usually finds insoluble the problem of the succession to the dictator. But here, the electorate has its own remedy; it has the power to choose or not to choose the given incumbent for a further term as it will. If, patently, he seems superior to any alternative, it must seem to the outsider a grievous waste of human resources to put a president on the shelf mainly because, for private reasons, George Washington decided to serve for two terms only. The power to plan, the experience gained, the stability of personnel established, the sense acquired by the nation of continuity in direction—all these are valuable assets, if they cohere about the right person. To discard them for a mechanical formula is to miss altogether the central essence of what government requires. Part of the virtue of popular choice lies in its ability to keep the right man when it has found him. Certainly a good deal of the merit of the British system has lain in the full utilization of that capacity. To argue otherwise is, I think, to argue in favor of a single-term system. The case for that method is, no doubt, a strong one. But the case against it is the decisive one that it is not the method upon which the presidential office has been built.

II

THE PRESIDENT AND HIS CABINET

I

ALMOST from the outset of Washington's administration, the executive heads of departments began to assume the character of a cabinet; and the fact that it is so referred to by name in Marshall's decision in *Marbury* v. *Madison*[1] is proof enough that it had already become an integral part of the institutional framework of the United States. But it is important to realize at once that the American cabinet hardly corresponds to the classic idea of a cabinet to which representative government in Europe has accustomed us.

Its members, of course, cannot, under the Constitution, be members of either house of Congress; and tradition, which perhaps goes back to Jefferson's fear of Hamilton's powers of persuasion, prevents them from taking part in debate there. Cabinet officers in the United States are essentially presidential advisers. They may give information to Congress. They may appear before committees in defense of the measures they have recommended. They may make public speeches in support of the general policy of the ad-

[1] (1803) 1 Cranch 137.

ministration. They may even initiate a line of policy which, granted presidential approval, is recognized as their own special contribution to affairs; so the agricultural policy of Mr. Wallace and the reciprocal low-tariff agreements of Mr. Hull are associated, in Franklin Roosevelt's administration, with a line of thought to which each of these ministers attaches special significance. But, in general, the American cabinet minister lives and moves and has his being in the context of presidential thought. However able and distinguished, he is bound to be eclipsed by the major significance of his chief.

It is, indeed, rare for a majority of any given cabinet to have outstanding importance in the political life of America. The composition of a cabinet is unpredictable. Many of its members, after their term of office, retire into the obscurity from which their elevation brought them. It is comparatively rare for a figure of outstanding distinction in Congress, at least since the Civil War, to choose cabinet office in preference to the continuance of his congressional career; and this is true even though men like Clay and Webster, Calhoun and Blaine, Bryan and Root served in this capacity. The office has rarely served, since Jackson's time, as a highroad to the presidency. Membership is rather a phase in a life-career; it is not itself an integral part of a career. No one thought of Mr. Newton D. Baker as a possible secretary of war before 1916; and, though he was a possible candidate for the Democratic nomination in 1932, he held no national office before or after that four years' interlude in his law practice. Miss Perkins was well known in New York before she became secretary of labor in 1933; but she had never possessed an important political position before that time. In the British and the French systems, cabinet office is the goal toward which a member of the legislative assembly seeks continually to move; accession to it is the crown of a political career. With Americans, this is not the case; and it may even be said that there is no special reason why the fact that a man has attained cabinet rank should assure him any pivotal part in the political world.

That is shown in many ways. Not only does the resignation of a cabinet member make little or no difference to the strength of the president's position; it is almost assumed that some members of the cabinet will resign during his term. Nor is it likely that, because a man is in the cabinet, he will, thereby, exercise influence with Congress; on the record, it is rare for this to be the case unless he has previously been a member of either house, and popular there. To bring a man from the back benches of the House to the cabinet in England is at once to clothe any announcement he may make with definite importance; but a speech, say, of the chairman of the Senate Committee on Foreign Affairs will always rival in significance any utterance that may be made even by the secretary of state. A prime minister in England or in France hazards his head when he dispenses with a powerful colleague; Lord John Russell did not long survive his dismissal of Palmerston in 1851. And an

English politician who refuses cabinet office may thereby risk bringing his effective political career to a close—as Sir Robert (now Viscount) Horne did when he refused to become minister of labor in Mr. Baldwin's government of 1925. But a president does not have to consider the danger of dispensing with a powerful colleague just because, from his angle, he has no powerful colleagues in the cabinet who may jeopardize his position. A politician does not take risks by refusing cabinet office, if he already has national prestige on other grounds; Senator Glass could have been secretary of the treasury in 1933. But everyone understood the grounds upon which he preferred to stay in the Senate.

The cabinet is a body of advisers to the president; it is not a council of colleagues with whom he has to work and upon whose approval he depends. There is, indeed, as a rule, a weekly cabinet meeting at which discussion takes place upon those issues the president wishes to raise. But there is no collective responsibility. Issues of the gravest importance need not be, indeed are not, submitted to the cabinet at all; Franklin Roosevelt went forward with his Court plan without most of the cabinet's having any knowledge of it. Even a united cabinet cannot prevail against the will of the president. There is hardly a department in which the direction of, and initiative in, policy is not his if he wants to assume them. He is a court of appeal from them all, and his verdict is decisive against them. They make, collectively, no impact upon Congress or the nation, as he does; their relation is one of departmental interstitiality. No doubt some of them are in a position to influence his decisions; they are never in a position to control them. A member of the cabinet differs from the president at his peril. Even so renowned a party leader as Mr. Bryan never recovered from the consequences of his resignation. After 1915, he never exerted the influence that was previously his. A cabinet officer, normally, must assume that he will live his term in the presidential shadow. What substance is his depends upon the will of the president.

It is, of course, true that the relation varies. A weak president, like Buchanan or Harding, gives far more leeway to his colleagues, sometimes with disastrous results. A strong president may place special reliance upon a particular colleague; Lincoln did upon Stanton and Theodore Roosevelt upon Elihu Root. But Mr. Wilson, in all matters of major importance, treated his secretaries of state like office boys; and it is clear that the vital initiative in all major matters has lain with the White House under Franklin Roosevelt. How impossible it is for a cabinet officer, however eminent, to control a president who has made up his mind was shown by the relations between Lincoln and Seward. The latter was far more widely known than the president when he took office, was, indeed, far more experienced; and it is clear that he hoped to act as a kind of tutelary deity to a man whose inferiority he did not hesitate to assume. He was rapidly undeceived; and, from first to last, every major action of the State Department bears the mark of Lincoln's own hand.

Polk, too, rode his cabinet on a tight rein; and his *Diary* makes it clear that he had never any doubt who was master. Under Coolidge, on the other hand, at least three of the cabinet shaped the lines of their policy with but little interference from the president; though the incisiveness of his control, when he thought the credit of his government was at stake, is shown clearly enough by his dismissal of his attorney-general.[2]

Not only is the initiative in policy a matter for presidential discretion. In areas of supreme importance a president may rely upon councilors who have, technically, no official status at all. As early as the thirties of last century, Andrew Jackson had his "kitchen cabinet," which was far more influential with him than his official family. None of Mr. Wilson's colleagues ever carried with him the weight of authority of Colonel House. Mark Hanna had much the position of House at the height of his power; and it is probable that not more than two of Franklin Roosevelt's colleagues have ever had the weight of half a dozen advisers outside. Alongside this, the American system makes it almost inevitable that the leaders of his party in both houses of Congress, and especially the Senate, should have an authority with the president to which no cabinet officer can pretend. It is upon them that he must depend for the passage of his measures. In face of their recalcitrance he is lost, where he can always overcome the obstinacy of a cabinet member. Vis-à-vis Congress, indeed, the

[2] William Allen White, *A Puritan in Babylon* (1938), pp. 271-272.

president may be said to be dealing with something akin to a shadow-cabinet which argues with him on terms far more approaching equality than the official cabinet can hope to do.

This is intelligible enough, from one angle. The leaders of Congress ought to exercise great influence for the simple reason that they are charged with an independent responsibility. To the foreigner, the influence of the unofficial advisers is more startling. They are not, necessarily, politicians of standing, nor expert in the subject matter with which they deal. Colonel House, on the evidence, seems to have been a simple, rather vain man, with a great affection for Mr. Wilson, and an immense liking for the kind of diplomacy in which he could exercise influence without responsibility. For a brief period, a Professor Warren, whose specialism was agriculture, persuaded President Franklin Roosevelt to embark upon a disastrous currency experiment of immense magnitude. Professor Moley was, indeed, the undersecretary of the State Department; but, if his own account be accurate, for the first fifteen months of Franklin Roosevelt's first administration he exercised more authority over the president than all his cabinet together;[3] though it must be added that his own account makes it clear that the phases of policy in which he played his part were determined by the president. The problem created by these unofficial advisers is clearly the twofold one that they have no responsibility for the advice they give, and their hour of authority depends

[3] See his account of his appointment, *After Seven Years* (1939).

upon their ability to persuade the president to listen to them. In Colonel House's case, that ability mainly took the form of advising the president to act in the way he intuitively guessed the president wished to act. The famous break of 1919, which he always declared he did not understand, obviously arose from the fact that, at the Peace Conference, he passed beyond that function and began to act as though he were an independent agent. Such positions, in fact, are comparable to those of a favorite at Court; and it is, I think, wholly undesirable that they should reach as far as Colonel House made his effort go. For, out of them, as his papers show, there arise understandings, and even commitments, which are not of the kind to be made by unofficial agents, especially when these are unknown to those who are called officially to assist the president in the making of policy.

2

This position of the cabinet arises from the conditions under which it has to be made. An English prime minister, when he assumes office, is largely given the men upon whom he must rely. Disraeli must have Cairns; Gladstone must have Hartington; Campbell-Bannerman must have Asquith. The party expects certain men to be in the cabinet; the country, also, expects them to be there. No doubt the prime minister, once he has passed beyond certain obvious peaks, has a real discretion; Mr. Baldwin's choice of Mr. Churchill as chancellor of the exchequer in 1925 was a surprise; so, also, was Mr. Chamberlain's choice of Lord Chatfield as minister for the co-ordination of defense in 1939. But Mr. Churchill, after all, had been for nearly twenty years a distinguished figure in British politics; and Lord Chatfield was an eminent naval officer chosen for a post in which his special *expertise* had peculiar relevance at the time when he was called.

The attorney-general apart, it is rare for any American cabinet officer to have any special claims to the post he fills. There are, of course, exceptions; the appointment of Mr. Henry Wallace to the Department of Agriculture in 1933 was—apart from the fact that his previous party connections were Republican—natural in the light of his position as one of the outstanding editors of an agricultural paper in America. But the considerations a president must have in mind as he forms his cabinet are quite different from those a British or a French prime minister must have in mind. The latter, first of all, is building a team whose basic purpose is the maintenance of unity as a team. Most of them have been well known to Parliament for a considerable period. Most of them, also, have acted in opposition as a shadow-cabinet and know one another's ways. Many of them, normally, will have held office before and will be accustomed to the habits of public administration. All of them can rely upon a skilled collaboration from the civil service; and many of them will know with some intimacy the high officials with whom they are going to collaborate.

Little of this position confronts the president. He

is not, in the first place, making a team. Some of his colleagues may hardly be known to him when he chooses them; some of them, at least, will not be known at all to one another. He must have one or two men who are likely to be influential with Congress; the choice of a Calhoun or a Webster or a Clay becomes at once explicable on this ground. One, at least, must be a person directly expert in the handling of the party machine; Mr. Walter Brown, under President Hoover, Mr. Farley, under Franklin Roosevelt, obviously fills the role. There must be representatives of the territorial sections of the country; a cabinet constructed wholly of Easterners would be offensive to the West and the South. There ought, desirably, to be representatives of the predominant religions of the United States; a prominent Methodist and an outstanding Catholic layman will always make presidential relations more easy. It is said that Theodore Roosevelt made Mr. Oscar Straus the secretary of commerce in the belief that this would incline the support of the large Jewish vote in America toward the Republicans. It has been usual for the secretary of labor to be chosen from the ranks of important trade unionists; and it is notable that this custom caused President Franklin Roosevelt some little difficulty when he ignored it to appoint Miss Frances Perkins in that office. Her choice is interesting, since it may well compel a future president to include a woman in the cabinet as a measure designed to please the women in America, not least in view of their powerful organization in such bodies as the League of Women Voters.

But this is not all. A president has also to pay for his nomination and election. Mr. Wilson, obviously enough, selected Mr. Bryan as his secretary of state as a reward for the latter's decision to support him as against Mr. Champ Clark in the Democratic convention of 1912. Cleveland chose Gresham as his secretary of state, though he was a Republican, and a former member of President Arthur's cabinet, in order to gratify the low-tariff Republicans who had become "Mugwumps." President Harding rewarded his campaign manager, Mr. Harry Daugherty, with the office of attorney-general—an appointment as disastrous as any in the history of modern administrations. Mr. Mellon's contribution to the Republican campaign fund in 1920 was largely responsible for his choice as secretary of the treasury. McKinley and Theodore Roosevelt both gave gold-Democrats places in their cabinets to mark their gratitude to men who supported them as a protest against the danger of "Bryanism" among their opponents. At the end of his administration Mr. Wilson appointed Mr. Bainbridge Colby, a Republican, as successor to Mr. Lansing in the State Department in a vain effort to persuade some of the Republicans to help him force the Versailles Treaty upon the Senate.

It is a tradition, broken only once in modern times,[4] that the presidential appointments to the cabinet should

---

[4] In 1925 when the Senate refused twice to ratify Mr. Coolidge's choice of Mr. Charles B. Warren as his attorney-general.

be confirmed by the Senate; it is rightly felt that the president had better choose the men with whom he has to live. And, political expediency apart, the personal view of the president always plays a considerable part in the selection of his colleagues. The choice of Mr. Hull and Mr. Swanson by President Franklin Roosevelt was obviously dictated by political considerations; on the other hand, that of Mr. Woodin, for the Treasury, of Mr. Ickes for the Interior, of Miss Perkins for Labor, were obviously definitely personal appointments. So, at a later stage, was the appointment of Mr. Morgenthau to succeed Mr. Woodin on the latter's death. So, also, was that of Mr. Hopkins to succeed Mr. Roper in the Department of Commerce. Mr. Hopkins' appointment, indeed, was in a sense an outstanding example of the tradition which gives the president free play. Mr. Hopkins, until 1932, was a social worker of some distinction, but of no very definite political leanings. He came under the notice of Mr. Roosevelt and was chosen to head the Works Progress Administration. In that position, he grew rapidly into perhaps the closest adviser of the president, certainly his most intimate friend; and his elevation to the cabinet was nothing so much as a signal mark of personal friendship made in order to answer passionate criticism of Mr. Hopkins which emanated hardly less from the president's own party than it did from his opponents. Hardly less interesting was the choice of the attorney-general in 1939. It had long been expected that Mr. Cummings' resignation would be followed by the appointment of the solicitor-general, Mr. Robert Jackson, whose work, both as lawyer and as politician, had been of exceptional distinction. But Mr. Roosevelt nominated Mr. Frank Murphy, a former governor of Michigan, who had just been defeated in his contest for re-election, despite the special support of the president. It is not, I think, unfair to suppose that Mr. Jackson was passed over as a result of the president's desire to mark in an exceptional way the confidence and regard he had for Mr. Murphy.

On the whole it is true, I believe, to say that a Democratic cabinet contains more surprises than a Republican cabinet, especially in recent years. This is largely because the divisions within the parties have grown wider. Anyone who studies the relations, for example, between the progressive Republicans and their more conservative colleagues for the last twenty-five years will have some difficulty in believing that the same party label can cover men of such divergent views. Presidents, not unnaturally, have sought to take advantage of these differences. Cleveland's appointment of Gresham, and Franklin Roosevelt's appointment of Mr. Ickes may, I think, not unfairly be represented as attempts to assure themselves support which would transcend the normal differences between parties. For the allegiance of the voter is a pretty shifting thing. An unexpected appointment, whether in terms of party, or section, or even religious creed, may make a considerable difference to the hold a president has upon his volatility.

What is striking in the result that emerges is how

little can be known of the administrative capacity of cabinet members, whether as individuals, or as a team, until they have got under way. They have rarely, as a team, had continuity of contact with great affairs. They have not learned to be a unity in the sense that the members of an English cabinet are a unity before they begin their work. Some of them, even, do not know either their chief or one another, except in the most casual way, until they find themselves in office. They come and go upon grounds which not seldom are very different from those to which a European is accustomed. At the end of 1938, for example, the attorney-general resigned in order, by a return to legal practice, to recoup his personal fortunes. And only a minority has any serious hold upon the outside public. Not more than one or two can speak in the name of the administration in the sense in which an English cabinet minister can. For the most part, also, the substance of their speeches tends to be narrowly departmental in character. Mr. Ickes or Mr. Hull may take a roving commission in discourse; Mr. Farley may, as chairman of the National Democratic Committee, generalize upon the wider aspects of policy. But the American public would be surprised if Miss Perkins, as secretary of labor, suddenly spoke her full mind upon international affairs, or if Mr. Morgenthau, as secretary of the treasury, were to express his views upon the conflict between the A. F. of L. and the C. I. O. In the main, generalizations are a presidential prerogative; and it is not customary for the cabinet officer to think at all profoundly over a wide field.

This does not mean that the president does not consult his cabinet; the documents make it plain that he does so with some continuity. But they suggest that the technique of cabinet functioning is not a pooling of the minds in the British or French sense. It is not merely that the president is always free to make his own decisions; it is not merely, either, that he always tends to develop a special relation with one or two intimates in a cabinet, as Theodore Roosevelt did with Elihu Root. It is that cabinet discussion is the collection of opinions by the president with a view to clarifying his own mind, rather than a search for a collective decision. A cabinet officer may resent a presidential determination about which he has not been consulted, as Mr. Root is said[5] to have resented Theodore Roosevelt's decision to prosecute, under the Sherman Act, the Northern Securities case; but he is not entitled to resent it and his resentment has no effective remedy. For if he resigns, as Mr. Wilson's secretary of war resigned, because he disagrees with presidential policy, he normally retires into obscurity without in any serious way affecting the position or policy the president may choose to follow.

How complete is the absence of collective responsibility was strikingly shown in the oil scandals under President Harding. Three members of the cabinet were concerned; all of them were compelled to resign; two of them were criminally indicted, and one

[5] H. F. Pringle, *Theodore Roosevelt* (1931), p. 255.

of them served a prison sentence. The matter in which they were involved raised issues of high policy; and it was passionately discussed in Congress and the press. Yet it seems, throughout, to have been treated as an interdepartmental matter upon which any decision, when public opinion became involved, was a presidential prerogative. Mr. Hoover, who was later the president of the United States, and Mr. Hughes, who was later to become its chief justice, were both members of the cabinet throughout its operative period. Neither seems ever to have concerned himself with the issue, or to have regarded it as one with which he was concerned; nor did the public treat it as one in which their honor was in any way involved. Yet it is inconceivable that a similar situation in England, in which, say, the three defence ministers were parties to a corrupt bargain that became a theme of intense public discussion, would not have its impact upon the status of the cabinet as a whole. And this aloofness is not novel, for it is, in its way, a reproduction of a similar scandal in the cabinet of President Grant.

The decisions of the cabinet are thus in the nature of advice to the president rather than a corporate act. Anyone who reads the letters of Theodore Roosevelt, or the documents we now possess about the Wilson administration, will see how largely this is the case. The cabinet officer may well expect to be consulted about his own department, though he has no assurance that his advice will be taken; he does not know that he will be generally consulted, and he has no title to general consultation. He may find himself no better informed upon a momentous decision before it has been taken than a member of the ordinary public; and he may find that an important senator or congressman is regarded as far more relevant than he is to the process which leads to its making. Not many of Mr. Wilson's cabinet can have been aware of the intimate substance of Colonel House's vital negotiations with Sir E. Grey in 1915-16, still less that the president's mind was made up, as early as 1916, to intervene, if need be, to prevent the defeat of the allies. It may well be that awareness would have resulted in their agreement; certainly their published memoirs suggest that this would have been the case. But, as a cabinet, they were not taking part in the making of policies; they were accepting decisions already arrived at in the presidential mind. And they had no alternative but to accept them.

In this situation, it is intelligible enough that, as a career, membership in the cabinet does not compare with that of a senator. The latter has a sphere of influence in which, so long as he secures re-election, he is his own master, and he has a platform second only to that of the president from which to address the nation. It may be doubted whether any cabinet officer, in the period since Hamilton was the secretary of the treasury, has had the influence or the attention of Senator Aldrich or of Senator Borah. One has only to compare the trembling uncertainty of John Hay about his tenure of the Department of State after the assassination of McKinley, with Senator Norris' rugged defiance of Harding and Coolidge to realize the difference in position. Few presidents are likely to consult their cabinet colleagues with any continuity about, for example, judicial appointments; but it is well known that Senator Borah's influence was decisive in placing Mr. Justice Cardozo on the Supreme Court, and it is believed that Senator Norris played an important part in the nomination of Mr. Justice Frankfurter—in this case against the pressure of President Roosevelt's first attorney-general. And, of course, where senatorial courtesy is concerned, the Senate will act as a unit against the president to enforce that consideration of a colleague which it considers his due.

Cabinet office, this is to say, is an interlude in a career; it is not itself a career. There is no technique of direct preparation for it; there is no certainty that it will continue because it has begun; there is no assurance that the successful performance of its functions will lead to a renewal of office in a subsequent administration. It is, no doubt, an exaggeration to say that the cabinet officer is simply the president's man in charge of a particular department; but it is not an exaggeration to say that he must be prepared, without repining or resigning, to be the president's man on any particular point about which the president is adamant. He does not increase his political influence, when he differs from his chief, by resigning in order to appeal beyond him to public opinion; for his position is such that there is no public opinion to which he may appeal. He does not even make himself available as a presidential candidate by successful administration. Where a cabinet officer, like Clay or Taft or Mr. Hoover, has attained this position, his cabinet reputation has been but a small factor in his nomination. If, indeed, a cabinet officer has presidential ambitions, he is more likely than not to arouse the suspicions of the president unless, as with Taft and Theodore Roosevelt, the president has determined to push his candidature. "No candidate for the presidency," wrote James K. Polk,[6] "ought ever to remain in the cabinet. He is an unsafe adviser." That is a view that any president is likely to take if the aspirant's convictions differ from his own. For, save in exceptional cases, he is bound to feel that the advice he is offered is governed less by the evidence than by the cabinet officer's judgment of its effect upon his chances of the nomination. That view is not easily compatible with an honest and disinterested relationship.[7]

The truth is that the relation between the president and his cabinet, however harmonious, does not seriously diminish the burden which rests upon the former; and, above all, it does not relieve him in the vital realm of foreign affairs. Partly, this is the case simply because in the last resort the cabinet is not a responsible body; it is the president, and the president alone, who is responsible for its actions. But partly, also, it is not, like its European analogues, a policy-making body; every major item of affairs ultimately is settled by the president's view of what is desirable.

[6] *Diary of James K. Polk* (ed. Nevins, 1929), p. 308.
[7] Cf. Polk's view, *ibid.*, p. 64 (Buchanan) and p. 72 (Calhoun).

Partly, further, the result of this concentration of power in the president's hands is to make him, almost necessarily, a court of appeal from departmental decisions wherever the person appealing is powerful enough to have direct influence in the White House. An important member of either house of Congress, a powerful commercial interest, a great trade union, can always feel pretty confident that he will have the opportunity, if he is dissatisfied with a departmental decision, of stating his case directly to the president. In a sense, indeed, an appeal of this kind is almost a matter of common form. An American citizen of standing would hardly feel that his case had been properly dealt with unless its ultimate disposition had been a matter of presidential thought.

That is because collective cabinet responsibility does not exist; the matter disposed of is always one the form of which it is assumed the president may shape differently from his adviser. And he may well so shape it. It may be an appointment to the Supreme Court; it may be the stabilization of international currencies; it may be the attitude of the administration to some pivotal point in labor policy. It is not, I think, too much to say that a large proportion of business that in England would be disposed of departmentally, that, even if submitted directly to the prime minister, would be remitted by him for ultimate disposal by a cabinet colleague, is, in the United States, business not merely that the president will decide, but also that he will be expected to decide. The relief, therefore, that he can expect from his colleagues is far smaller than it is in England. And if it were not smaller, the whole system would be very different from what it is. The expectation of direct thought from the president by the citizen-body of the United States is greater than the analogous expectation of any similar citizen-body elsewhere. In England, we blame an anonymous entity "the Government" if things go wrong, or a mistake is made; in the United States it is the president who is blamed. A decision of the Supreme Court is regarded as adverse to *his* policy; a defeat in Congress is a blow to *his* prestige; the mid-term congressional elections affect *his* policy, for good or ill. No one thinks of them in terms of their effect upon his cabinet. For the purpose of action, it is he alone who is fundamentally involved.

The temptation is to say that the result is to place upon the shoulders of the president a burden greater than any man can be asked to bear. In a sense, no doubt, this is unquestionably the case. The range of issues he may be called upon to handle is by all odds greater than any man can hope, or be expected, to handle wisely, and there is rarely the kind of consideration available to him that he needs for a wise judgment. He lacks the kind of *expertise* the civil servants of an English department will, for the most part, place at the disposal of their minister. He lacks, from most of his cabinet, the kind of counsel that comes from men who are equally sharing with him in the adventure of government. The colleagueship of the leaders of his party in Congress, even supposing his party to be in a majority, is not, as the record

shows plainly, of that intimate character which relieves the sense of perpetual strain under which any
president must live. And most presidential correspondence reveals that sense of strain. It emerges not only
in the letters and diaries of men who, like Lincoln,
were engaged in dealing with a crisis of the first magnitude. It emerges, also, with presidents whose path, like
that of Taft, was relatively smooth. Whatever the
intimacies a president may build, he is ultimately a
lonely figure. The burden of office is, in a special
sense, his and his only; there is no one who can share
it with him, or take it from him. He is not a dictator,
whose will is certain to be imposed upon his followers.
He is not even sure, like a prime minister, that in the
absence of major blunders he can maintain his hold
upon his party. His position makes him a target to be
attacked by every person or interest at all critical of
his purposes. He is there, in all cases, to be blamed;
and there is no one, in any real sense, who can help
him to bear the burden of the blame.

Part of this, no doubt, is due to the nature of politicians; part of it has been shaped by the history of the
office; and part of it is due, I think, to the psychological habits of the American people. The politician, almost by definition, is a person eager for
power. He is a man who is anxious that his will should
prevail against other and competing wills. The presidency gives to men of this temper an opportunity of
which, unless they are weak in will, they are almost
bound to take full advantage. Even an easy-going
president, like Taft, who did not himself want the

office,[8] is almost driven by its immanent logic to attempt a leadership the maintenance of which means that, when differences occur, he must make his own decisions. And that attitude is reinforced by the nature of the presidency. He is the only person, on the executive side, who holds an independent position; his cabinet officers, however eminent, are there because he has willed that they shall be there. However eminent, they hold office at his pleasure; they must go whenever he decides that he no longer wants their co-operation. They lack, that is to say, that sense of being necessary to the strength of the president which an important English cabinet officer has. Mr. Lloyd George in the Asquith government, Mr. Chamberlain in that of Mr. Baldwin, Sir William Harcourt in that of Lord Rosebery, Mr. Arthur Henderson in the first and second governments of Mr. Ramsay MacDonald, had each an independent position in the eyes of the nation; with the American cabinet officer such independence is so rare as to be almost a negligible factor in its operation. He cannot hope to break the president; it is even rare for him to be able to injure his prestige. No one is in a position to enforce an alternative view against him save Congress. For the years, in short, in which he holds office the denials he must face, the criticisms he must encounter, are always external to the executive power; they are never inherent in it.

And so momentous is the internal prestige of the office that internal denials and criticisms never come to him in such a way as to assure that the full weight of

[8] Pringle, *op. cit.*, p. 498.

their inner logic will be attached to them. The men who are playing for presidential influence on their side, within the framework of the executive power, are never certain that they will carry it just because they are members of the cabinet. That is clear, for instance, in foreign policy. No one can read Polk's own account of the Mexican War without the realization that, though he may have listened to the advice of his cabinet, the real motive-power to action was, throughout, a policy upon which he himself had made up his mind. That was true, also, of Lincoln; it was true of Woodrow Wilson; and it seems pretty clear that, when the documents are available, it will be true also of Franklin Roosevelt. Indeed, there is a sense in which the more positive and independent the affirmations of the president, the more, so to say, the springs of his policy are in himself, rather than shared with others, the profounder will be the impact he makes upon the national life. A president who is believed not to make up his own mind rapidly loses the power to maintain that hold. The need to dramatize his position by insistence upon his undoubted supremacy is inherent in the office as history has shaped it. A masterful man in the White House will, under all circumstances, be more to the liking of the multitude than one who is thought to be swayed by his colleagues. Even when, as with Theodore Roosevelt, great verbal audacity is accompanied by a relative caution in action, the mere fact that the president insists upon being the center of the stage continuously strengthens his position. It is, it should be added, an attitude that is expected of him.

For the president is news, in a way that cannot be said of any member of his cabinet. Every action of his will be reported; his lightest word, almost, is discussed and repeated, and the last ounce of possible meaning extracted from it. That is not the case with the cabinet. Its members must take steps to bring themselves before the public; and, even if they are successful in doing so, they must be content to live under the presidential shadow. It is even, I think, true to say that whereas the criticism that a president may evoke is to some extent restrained by the very fact that he is the president—the resemblance here to a member of the British royal family is notable—no such restraint is deemed incumbent upon the critics of a cabinet officer. And whereas the president's opinions are all of them, at least temporarily, significant, the cabinet officer must, for the most part, confine himself to his departmental functions if he wants to be heard. If Mr. Roosevelt chose to speak on American art, it is certain that a public discussion of his opinions would follow; but if the secretary of the treasury spoke on such a theme, most people would wonder why he strayed so far from the path of common sense. The president, in a word, symbolizes the whole nation in a way and to a degree that admits of no competitor while he is in office. Alongside his, the voice of a cabinet officer is, at best, a whisper, which may or may not be heard.

Indeed, what is striking in the American scene is

the number of voices, the president apart, which compete for attention with those of the cabinet officers. An outstanding banker, like the late J. P. Morgan, for example, will usually command not less attention than the secretary of the treasury in matters of finance; an eminent labor leader, like Mr. John L. Lewis, will at least rival in interest the opinions of the secretary of labor. The president of Harvard University has a national position which compares not unfavorably with that of any but the two or three outstanding cabinet officers. A great industrialist, like Mr. Ford, can make his pronouncements "news" in a sense that few cabinet members can rival, unless they are known to be speaking in the name of the president on some great public theme. None of them is likely to surpass in public significance a senator of any considerable standing; and a congressman who is either Speaker of the House, or the chairman of an important committee, has at least equal standing. My point is that his membership in the cabinet, as such, is never a guarantee either that he will make policy in any important way, or that he will assume a position of national significance by reason of it. The context in which he is set is that of presidential exigency; in that context he lives and moves and has his being.

That is true of the cabinet as a group of individuals; it is true, also, of the cabinet as a collective entity. During the war, President Wilson held no cabinet meetings; policy was made by him in the light of personal consultation with different members of it. Even after his return from Versailles, this continued to be the case. He was ill from September, 1919, until April, 1920, during which period no cabinet meeting was held. When a railroad strike seemed to call for such a meeting, Mr. Lansing, who, as secretary of state, was the senior member of the cabinet, called his colleagues together for consultation. He did so only after careful discussion, and because neither he nor they were allowed access to the president, and because no member of the cabinet was willing to take important action on his own initiative. Mr. Wilson's response to that action was summarily to dismiss Mr. Lansing. That was, on any showing, an extraordinary action, for there is not an atom of reason to suppose that Mr. Lansing was trying to do other than his best under very difficult circumstances. And even if we attribute Mr. Wilson's harshness in part to his natural arrogance and in part to the obvious petulance of a sick man, the fact that his action passed with but little criticism is sufficient proof of the degree to which presidential control defines the sphere of initiative within which the cabinet officer may hope to move. He originates at his peril.

3

This situation may be related to the effort, which goes back for three-quarters of a century, to secure the right to speak, though not, of course, to vote,[9] upon the floor of Congress. As long ago as February, 1864, Mr. Pendleton, a congressman from Ohio, sought to secure that "heads of executive departments

[9] Voting would, of course, be unconstitutional.

may occupy seats on the floor of the House of Representatives"; and his proposal was strongly supported by James A. Garfield, then also a congressman from Ohio, in a remarkable speech. The committee to which the resolution was referred then introduced a bill containing two proposals: (1) cabinet officers were to have the right, in their own discretion, to attend debates when matters concerning their departments were under discussion; and (2) their attendance was to be made compulsory on certain days for the purpose of answering questions.[10] An ardent discussion took place upon the bill, but it was not voted on. Fifteen years later, Pendleton, then a member of the Senate, raised the question a second time. The committee to which his resolution was referred produced a long and valuable report;[11] but, as in 1864, no vote was taken upon the proposed measure. In 1886, Mr. J. D. Long, later a secretary of the navy, introduced a measure which permitted members of the cabinet to attend and speak, at their own pleasure, in the House of Representatives; but, on this occasion, the bill was not reported out of committee. The proposal then slumbered for twenty-five years. It was revived by President Taft who supported the idea of cabinet representation in Congress with considerable vigor; but his proposal came to nothing. It was renewed in 1921 and 1924; in neither case did it arouse any serious public interest or discussion.

The case for the Pendleton proposal has been well

[10] House Rep. 43. 38th Congress, 1st Session (1864).
[11] Sen. Rep. 837. 46th Congress, 3rd Session (1881).

stated by President Taft. "Without any change in the Constitution," he wrote, "Congress might well provide that heads of departments, members of the president's cabinet, should be given access to the floor of each house to introduce measures, to advocate their passage, to answer questions, and to enter into the debate as if they were members, without, of course, the right to vote. . . . This would impose on the president greater difficulty in selecting his cabinet, and would lead him to prefer men of legislative experience who have shown their power to take care of themselves in legislative debate. It would stimulate the head of each department by the fear of public and direct inquiry into a more thorough familiarity with the actual operations of his department and into a closer supervision of its business. On the other hand, it would give the president what he ought to have, some direct initiative in legislation, and an opportunity, through the presence of his competent representatives in Congress, to keep each house advised of the facts in the actual operation of the government. The time lost in Congress over useless discussion of issues that might be disposed of by a single statement from the head of a department, no one can appreciate unless he has filled such a place."[12]

The case is obviously a powerful one; and it has had the support of men so experienced as Mr. Justice Story, Senator Ingalls, and James G. Blaine. The case is the stronger with the immense growth, in recent years, of the congressional appetite for information

[12] *Our Chief Magistrate and His Powers* (1916), p. 32.

from and investigation of the departments, much of which, if it is to be really effective, demands their friendly collaboration. There can be little doubt that it would greatly enhance the significance of congressional debate; and, thereby, it would give to it a character of responsibility and a popular significance which, compared to those of the House of Commons, are in considerable degree lacking. There is, too, much to be said for breaking down the antagonism between Congress and the departments; at present it is not untrue to say that many of the amendments each house makes to bills derive less from a knowledge of their value than from a desire to emphasize its power. I have myself heard Mr. Theodore Roosevelt insist that this method was not only likely to produce a wiser selection of cabinet officers; it was also, in his judgment, the best way to deal with the inherent difficulties of tariff legislation and of the "pork-barrel" bills which still remain a blot of no mean dimensions on the record of the legislature.

The argument, however, has not yet penetrated deeply into the popular consciousness. It is notable that in neither of his remarkable books on the American system did Woodrow Wilson think it worth while discussing, though he paid great attention to the relation between the executive and the legislature; while Lord Bryce, who knew Senator Pendleton personally, relegates it to a footnote in his *American Commonwealth*.[13] The reason, I think, is clear. The change is not a superficial one. Its ramifications are,

[13] *American Commonwealth* (ed. of 1911), I, 86.

in fact, so wide that they might easily change the whole balance of power in the American system. They might change it, not merely as between the executive and the legislature, but within the elements of the executive itself. The failure to give the plan the consideration it deserves is not, I think, due to inertia, but rather, as Professor Cushman rightly suggests,[14] to "the vaguely uneasy feeling that the plan would unwisely upset the traditional and established relationship between the executive and legislative departments with consequences that cannot be accurately foreseen and appraised."

Close analysis makes this at once apparent. If the cabinet is to sit in Congress, the president must choose its members from those who are likely to be influential with it. This at once narrows his choice. It makes him think of the men who already have some standing in its eyes, and some direct knowledge of its complicated procedure. But this means putting a premium on the experienced members of either house as cabinet material. It means, further, that the more successful they are upon the floor of Congress, the more independent they are likely to be vis-à-vis the president. They will develop a status of their own as they become known as the men who are able to make Congress take their views about the bills they promote. They are likely, in fact, to become rivals of the president himself for influence with Congress. The problem, in this situation, of maintaining cabinet unity would necessarily become a difficult matter. Congress

[14] *American National Government* (1931), p. 316.

might easily tend to weaken the administration by playing off the cabinet, or some part of it, against the president and some other part. The loyalty of the cabinet officer would be divided. Is he, for example, to support the president on a scheme like the Court plan, and thereby to weaken his standing with Congress; or is he discreetly to make known his dislike for the plan in the hope that he may thereby win approval for some bill in which he is interested?

The president's problem of changing his cabinet would, moreover, be immensely intensified. Is he to keep an officer about whose full loyalty he is dubious, but whose influence on Congress is clearly great? Can he prevent such an officer's so nearly rivaling his own authority as to make his own position exceptionally difficult? Would not the position of a president like Lincoln, whose hold on his own colleagues was small when he assumed power, become virtually untenable if Congress were in a position to play them off against him? Is there not, indeed, the danger of a powerful cabal of cabinet officers' becoming the effective mediator between the president and Congress with a vital shift, as a consequence, in the present delicate balance of power? Would it not, further, be likely that a tendency would rapidly develop for any cabinet officer who became outstandingly influential with Congress to become the rival of the president himself, and, where the latter was weak, in actual fact his master?

More than even this is, I think, involved. There would develop the tendency for the president to

choose his cabinet from Congress in order to maximize his influence with it, and thus to transfer the
leadership of his party there to a room, so to say, of
which he only had the key. There would be a tendency for cabinet officers to use their relation with
Congress as a platform from which to reach the presidency, with all the difficulties of colleagueship of this
position, and more, that Polk emphasized. It is difficult, moreover, not to feel that, in these circumstances,
the advice of the cabinet member upon questions of
patronage would be given under conditions altogether
different from and inferior to those upon which they
now depend. The danger of trading posts for measures is already profound enough in the American system; it is difficult not to feel that it would be greatly
intensified if a cabinet officer were independent of
the president in his power to influence Congress. The
coherence that is now given to administrative action
by the supremacy of the president might easily be
jeopardized by this aspect alone.

The Pendleton scheme suggested that cabinet members should have access to debates upon the floor of
the House. But in fact, the main business of Congress
is performed in secret committees to which the public has no access. No cabinet officer could adequately
look after his measures unless he penetrated the committee rooms also. But were he to do so, the control
over him of the president would be still further diminished; and the relation between him and Congress
would rival in closeness that with the executive of
which the president is the head. This seems scarcely

desirable in a system where there is no collective cabinet responsibility, and where the unity of the executive structure is supplied by presidential control. In these circumstances, no cabinet member can be transformed into an automaton who merely reflects the presidential will. For first, in such a transformation as this innovation portends, he would have been chosen just precisely because he is not an automaton; and second, to the degree that he seeks to act like one, he defeats the whole object of the innovation.

There are two further difficulties in the scheme, moreover, to which adequate attention has hardly been given in discussion of it. It raises most delicate and complicated questions of the relation between the cabinet officer, as a quasi-member of Congress, and the senator or congressman who is in charge of the bill in which he is interested. By whom is the concession to be made to a proposed amendment? How will chairmanships be arranged so as to secure a proper harmony in congressional proceedings between the cabinet officer and the chairman of his committee? On a bill, for example, like that of President Roosevelt's Court plan, the position of the attorney-general would be well-nigh intolerable unless he were at one with the chairman of the Judiciary Committee. The fact is that, on the present system, where the chairmen of the important committees of both houses form a kind of quasi-executive within the two branches of the legislature, the position of cabinet officers would be impossible at every point where they disagreed with that quasi-executive. Either they would be tempted into a position of continuous inferiority for the sake of agreement, in which difficult questions of loyalty to the president would be involved; or they would differ openly with the official chairmen of the legislative committees, in which case, they would greatly add, by that difference, to the burden the president had to carry.

Nor is this all. The Pendleton scheme seems to assume that each cabinet officer is to sit in Congress merely in relation to his own department. But the categories of government are far from being as simple as this view would make them appear. The range of modern legislation makes the secretary of the treasury as ubiquitously relevant as the chancellor of the exchequer in relation to most government proposals. The interrelations of modern problems of defense make half the issues which arise matters of co-ordination to which the secretary of the treasury, the secretary of war, and the secretary of the navy are all relevant. On foreign affairs, every vital matter is at least a joint operation between the president and the secretary of state; the latter could hardly offer an opinion in Congress save as he affirmed that outlook for which he had prior approval from the president; and in matters of supreme importance it is the president only whose attitude it is vital for Congress to know. There, as the Wilson administration makes clear, he supersedes the secretary of state far more emphatically than, in an analogous situation, the prime minister of England supersedes (he rather supplements) the foreign secretary. Similar difficulties

arise as between the Departments of Commerce and
Labor; and the Department of Justice, especially in
the context of prosecutions such as those under the
Sherman Act, has a vital relation to many other departments. It is, in fact, difficult to see how any cabinet officer except the postmaster-general could be
confined within any rigidly defined domain. In the
result, most cabinet officers would—whatever the system started as—be bound to develop roving commissions of general relevance not very different from the
part that a cabinet minister plays in the British House
of Commons.

It must, moreover, be remembered that in the
American system the initiative in legislation does not
lie, as with Great Britain, for effective purposes in the
government only. No doubt a special pre-eminence attaches to bills which have, so to say, the imprimatur of
the president. But the source of a good deal of important legislative action lies in the hands of individual
senators and congressmen; in this respect it is only
necessary to remember how much has been done,
often despite the administration, by men like the late
Senator La Follette and by Senator Norris. It would
be far from easy to adjust the delicate relations which
would arise from this dual relationship, not least if
the president were in a minority in Congress. And if
members of the cabinet were admitted only to the
floor of both houses, they would, for the most part,
miss the chance of participation in the pivotal consideration of bills; while, if they were permitted their

full share in the committee processes, the duality of leadership would create almost insoluble problems.

The Pendleton scheme, in short, does not meet the real problems created by the presidential system. The facts of American life have concentrated literally enormous power in the hands of the president; and it is no doubt true that the exercise of this power produces, above all in a second term, grave congressional doubts of the wisdom of its extent. At some time in the tenure of a president with a majority, the accusation of autocracy is almost bound to arise. But the real outcome of the Pendleton scheme, or any variant upon it, would be, I think, to transfer the essential features of presidential leadership to the cabinet. Its operations in Congress would be bound, sooner or later, to become the axis upon which the authority of the administration turned. I believe, indeed, that properly to perform its function in Congress the cabinet would be bound to try and discover the terms upon which it could become a unity; a unity, be it noted, not only against the Congress, but against the president also. The latter would be compelled to spend a good deal of his energy in maintaining his authority against colleagues who would have developed an interest and prestige at least parallel to his own, and, conceivably, different from it. None of them could fail to be aware that outstanding success in the handling of Congress was the highroad to the kind of reputation out of which a presidential nomination could be secured. Some of them, at least, would be bound to play for that nomination; and the problem, in those circumstances, of maintaining presidential supremacy would be at every point delicate and complicated.

The real result, in a word, of the adoption of such a scheme as Senator Pendleton proposed would be very rapidly to transform the president into a person more akin to the president of the French Republic than to that of the United States. He could not avoid the certainty that his colleagues who became pivotal in Congress would soon become indispensable to him. He could hardly avoid the concentration of public attention upon their activities in Congress rather than upon his relations with it. He would have to watch those activities with a jealous eye lest they impinge upon the sphere of influence that is at present his own. The man among them who became the congressional leader of the cabinet would soon become a figure akin in character and influence to the prime minister; the president would be dependent upon him for every legislative move in the fulfilment of his program. Indeed, I think it not unlikely that the president would become rather the adviser than the master of the man to whom Congress looked for the formulation and defense of the presidential program; he would be moved to second place. He would find it difficult to resist the pressure of a cabinet officer who was influential with Congress; he might well jeopardize his own position if he asked for his resignation. A hostile Congress might even play off the cabinet, or some section of it, against him.

On any showing, this is to say, the Pendleton

scheme would wholly alter the balance of forces history has evolved in the American system of government. I do not say that it would necessarily alter them for the worse; any such estimate depends upon a comparison between the presidential and parliamentary systems that is here out of place. All I am concerned to argue is that latent in the scheme is a revolution in the historical conception of the presidency. As it now operates, the nation looks to the president for executive leadership, and, in the long run, circumstances make it difficult for that leadership to be found elsewhere. Such a scheme as Pendleton's inherently threatens that authority. While it separates him from his cabinet, on the one hand, it builds a bridge between the cabinet and Congress, on the other; and the president cannot walk across that bridge. It gives the cabinet an interest against him, not only with the legislature, but also with the party. A generation which has seen the vice-president of the United States use his influence in Congress to intrigue against the president should have no difficulty in seeing what his position might become if to his influence were joined that of any considerable part of the cabinet. At present, at any rate, when the president and Congress are at odds, the former's power of direct appeal to the nation makes the issue between them a clear one upon which public opinion can make up its mind. A cabinet that moved toward independence of him would make such a clarity of choice a difficult matter. It would, almost necessarily, divert a good deal of attention away from the case the president has to make. It would offer the possibility of great rewards to those about him who were prepared to risk the penalties of disloyalty to him. Anyone who reflects upon the position that might have arisen if Stanton had been able to utilize Congress as a platform against Andrew Johnson can see the potentialities that are latent in this change.

It may be, as I have said, that it should be attempted; for it may well be that the burden which the present situation imposes upon the president is greater than any statesman, above all in a democratic community, should be asked to bear. But the change should not be attempted without a full knowledge that it will profoundly alter the historic contours of the presidential system. It may not, in the first instance, transform it on the lines of the parliamentary system; it is bound, I have argued, in the long run to move it toward those lines. It cannot do so, on all experience, without two results. It must first depreciate the position of the man who cannot directly influence the congressional process; those, to use my earlier metaphor, are bound to be nearer to it who cross the bridge than those who stay on the other side. And if men are sought who can influence Congress, men are bound to be sought by whom Congress is prepared to be influenced. That does not only mean the device of a different kind of cabinet officer from those of the past. It means also, in the long run, men who realize that the way to influence a legislative assembly is to be responsive to its will; and that is the first step toward responsibility to its wishes. Fundamentally, this is to alter the whole balance of the American Constitution. It is to make it desirable to build a cabinet which can sway Congress. That makes the main lever of executive authority resident in the cabinet rather than in the president. While this may be a better scheme than the present one, its possible merits cannot conceal the fact that it is a constitutional revolution of the first magnitude. It is to dig into the foundations of the state; and that, as Edmund Burke insisted, is always a dangerous adventure.

III

THE PRESIDENT AND CONGRESS

I

UNDER all normal circumstances, it is difficult not to feel that the president of the United States must envy the legislative position of a British prime minister. The latter is the head of an assured parliamentary majority; unless he has made a grave blunder, it is nowadays the electorate, and not Parliament, which destroys his measures. He and his cabinet have the effective initiative in all legislation, above all in finance; and they do not find it necessary, save on the rarest occasions, to yield to sectional pressure. The prime minister has no interest he need consult in the making of appointments; there is unlikely to be serious question even about those of which there are grave doubts among his followers. He takes the fundamental part in the definition of all issues. While he remains prime minister, he is the unquestioned master of his party machine. He is, moreover, the master of the House of Commons through his power over its dissolution; he decides when the moment is propitious for an election. He is unlikely to retire from the leadership of his party except at his own discretion; and the fact that he will lead it to the polls means, normally, the nearer the approach of a general election, the more complete will be his power over his party. No doubt, over a period, the condition of his hold is that he shall be successful; but, granted that he can lead it to victory once in a decade, he has little reason to fear the emergence of a rival.[1]

At almost every point in the pattern British practice has traced, there is a wide divergence from the presidential situation. The president is never the master of Congress, except in relatively brief intervals of emergency. He does not know that it will accept his principles of action; as Polk insisted,[2] and as Franklin Roosevelt has learned, even a great majority in both houses is no guarantee of his control. He may not even have a nominal majority, and, in that event, he can be sure that the main purpose of Congress will be to discredit his administration. He cannot exercise over either house the threat of dissolution; whether he will or no, its elections are determined by a time-table over which he has no say. He may influence the choice of congressional leaders but he cannot determine them; all the prestige of Franklin Roosevelt only enabled Senator Barkley to succeed Senator Robinson by a single vote. There is no continuous power to secure disciplined voting; and Mr. Coolidge found that a small number of recalcitrant legislators may be fatal to his plans. Neither he nor his cabinet directly participate in the work of Congress; they are dependent upon legislators whose own view of the wise course

[1] Cf. my *Parliamentary Government in England* (1938), pp. 239-241.
[2] *Op. cit.*, p. 186.

to follow is not less important than theirs. He can, no doubt, exercise some discipline over rebels in his own party; but the attempted "purge" of 1938 makes it clear that this authority reaches but a little way. He may initiate legislation; and he can be sure that a respectful attention will be given to his proposals. But he will always find that there are, in either house, perhaps half a dozen men with independent authority to promote legislation independently of him. He can be sure, too, that whatever his convenience, either house, or both houses, will spend a considerable part of their energies investigating his administration; and unlike the British prime minister, he will be largely unable to determine to his own advantage the composition of the investigating committees. While he is nominally the head of his party, and, while in office, the chief factor in the operation of its machine, the knowledge that in eight years at most he will have ceased to be president profoundly limits his power to determine the uses to which it shall be put.

To grasp the difference between the two systems, it is essential to bear certain points in mind. The House of Commons is only formally a legislative assembly; in this context its real business is to act as the cabinet's organ of registration. It may secure minor amendments; it may even, on rare occasions, secure the withdrawal of a proposal. But, fundamentally, legislation is shaped in Whitehall, and not in Westminster. With Congress, this is not the case. Legislation is the main business of both houses. They do not act under the instructions of the president; they may co-operate with him if they feel so inclined. But they are at every point, save in periods of grave crisis, equal partners with him, and in the event of difference they, rather than he, are likely to have their way. He has, of course, the right of veto; but that is rather a reserve weapon of last instance than one of habitual use. It is, indeed, true to say that the influential members of Congress have, in their legislative capacity, more power than any private members of any other legislative assembly in the world.

This is the case for a number of reasons. It is inherent, in the first place, in the division of powers; the founders of the Constitution did not intend the president to have authority to do more than indicate a general direction; particularity was assumed to be the proper business of a legislature. It is the case, secondly, because Congress is the legislature of a continent rather than of a country in the European sense of the word. A member of Congress is expected, by reason of the vast size of the United States, to think in terms of sectional not less than national interests. He has to think about the effect of the measures to be considered upon the character of the particular area for which he sits; and what he believes (sometimes wrongly) to be its will, may not infrequently cut across the will of the administration. A member of the House of Representatives must be constantly aware that every two years he will be judged by his constituents; and this makes him far more responsive to his judgment of what will please them than he is likely to be to what will satisfy the president. For him, normally, the local issue and its repercussions are likely to seem far more acute than the national, not least if the outcome of the next primary is at all seriously in dispute. A congressman, moreover, whose fate may depend upon the judgment of a local boss (in his turn, perhaps, the creature of an important public utility corporation) is likely to feel that the advice of the boss is far more relevant to his future than that of the president. The members of Congress from the silver-producing states would not lightly go back to their constituencies and explain that, in the national interest, they saw no alternative but to accept the views of Wall Street upon the gold standard; and a president who sought to enforce stringent legislation against lynching would find that he encountered a definitely particularistic view from Southern congressmen and senators. There is a real sense in which all but a handful of especially eminent senators, whose return to the Senate has become almost a tradition, may be regarded as members of "special areas," for whose interests they must press, and to whose peculiarities they must yield, whatever be the outlook of the president and the party.

It is important, thirdly, that the Congress has an interest separate from that of the president. No doubt the common tie of party binds them together; but it is vital to realize that it never binds them into a unity. From the first presidency of Washington onward, Congress has made its will to independence apparent; and only war, or an emergency like that of March, 1933, has secured the transcendence of that will. Partly, it is a matter of pride; the Congress must show that it takes its orders from none but itself. Partly, it is the realization that the life of the administration does not depend on its having its own way. Partly, no doubt, the individual congressman feels that he is more genuinely a person by enforcing his right to assert himself. For there is always a real fear in Congress of being overshadowed by the president. To enforce alterations is to draw attention to itself, to secure understanding that he is not the unqualified master of the nation. There can be no doubt that, in its own eyes, Congress establishes its prestige when it either refuses to let the president have his own way, or compels him to compromise with it. Unlike the House of Commons with the prime minister, it can do so without penalty. So far as possible, therefore, it likes to make every measure submitted to it a little different from the form in which it is received. That enhances its stature in its own eyes, and, on occasion, it enhances its stature in the eyes of the electorate. There is always a pleasure in informing the head of the nation that there are limits to his power.

The system, I think, makes both for incoherency and irresponsibility, not least in the realm of finance. It makes for the first because, whatever the effort the president may make, the legislation of any given Congress is not unified; it does not derive from a single mind. Some measures are directly presidential in principle; though it will be rare for them to have the exact form the president may wish to give them. Others may come from the will of an important senator who can count on the backing of his colleagues; others, again, may derive from a sectional group, irrespective of party, who demand them as the price of supporting other measures. Particularly in finance, where the American system forbids any real unity of control either in ways and means or in appropriation, the outlook of a powerful chairman may make a great difference to the measures Congress will pass; and to this the budgetary system introduced nearly twenty years ago has made little difference. It is perhaps an exaggeration to say that the opinion of the chairman of the Senate Committee on Interstate Commerce will, on a big railroad question, count as much as the opinion of the president; but it is not, I think, an exaggeration to say that, where they differ, the Senate will compel the president to make sufficient of a compromise with its chairman to show that the senator has not been defeated by the presidential will. There is certainly no appropriations act which does not spend literally millions of dollars upon objectives the president does not approve and is compelled to accept as the price for securing other objectives about which he feels keenly.

The system makes also for irresponsibility. Because the influences which go to make legislation are so diverse, there can be no clear allocation of blame. Each house of Congress can proceed upon its own lines; only too often, they evolve a compromise which does not satisfy either, and is not the legislation which the president intended. There are, too, measures of considerable importance, like that, for instance, relating to the soldiers' bonus, which Congress will pass in defiance of the presidential veto simply because it dare not risk the unpopularity a powerful lobby like the American Legion may seek to organize against it. It will yield to sudden gusts of ignorant temper. The Reorganization Bill of 1938, for example, (which it passed in substantially similar form in 1939) was defeated largely as the result of indefensible propaganda which represented it, quite inaccurately, as a vast enlargement of presidential power. If it be true that the British member of Parliament obeys too rigidly the crack of his party whip, it is still more true that the member of Congress is prone to an anarchism about the substance of measures for which there is no defense. The "pork barrel" legislation of the last century is the measure of this anarchism. Without regard to the problems the president confronts, it has been built upon an interchange of sectional interests for which, quite unjustifiably, the taxpayer has been called upon to pay. Much the same is true of pensions; much the same is true of the tariff; much the same is true of agricultural measures like the McNary-Haughen bill. The separation of powers erodes responsibility by dividing it; and the result is not only an immense increase of the costs of government.

It is also a temptation to a weak president to evade the responsibility of leadership. This was true, very notably, of men like Buchanan and Harding and Coolidge. They do not tackle the problems they ought to tackle; they accept measures they think mistaken both in principle and in detail because they are afraid to have trouble with Congress. The system not only

results in a prenatal control of legislation upon subjects either difficult or unpopular. It offers an opportunity to powerful lobbies to multiply the area in
which prenatal control operates with a weak president by playing on his fears. No one can read the history of the attempts to deal with the slavery question
without seeing that this is the case. No one, either,
can read the painful effort of Edward Moseley to secure essential legislation for railroad safety[3] without
seeing how a lobby as powerful as that of the railroads can persuade both president and Congress to
neglect an obvious duty. Even a strong president, like
Franklin Roosevelt, is driven to postpone issues which
he believes to be urgent by the fact that one or other
of the lobbies at Washington may dissipate party coherency through the local influences it can bring to
bear. With a weak president, this leads to the making
of concessions which he knows to be indefensible.
And even if the pressure of public opinion, as with
the trusts, compels Congress, under presidential impulse, to action, the positive execution of the measure
concerned will halt. That has certainly been the case
with the Sherman Act. Even a president as positive as
Theodore Roosevelt engaged largely in shadow-box-
ing with the great corporations for fear of the influence they might bring to bear at the other end of
Pennsylvania Avenue.

The system, further, puts a premium on sectionalism. It is difficult, anyhow, to draw any clear line be-

[3] See the history of his achievement admirably related in James
Morgan's biography of him.

tween the major American parties; and the degree to which they hold the field is shown by the fact that, with but five exceptions since 1860, the Republican and Democratic parties have polled, between them, over 90 per cent of the votes in presidential elections. It is, however, true to say that with the possible exception of some of the major measures since 1933, there is no measure that has been put upon the statute-book by one party which could not have been put there by another. The parties gain their majorities by the appeal they make to sectional interests;[4] and individual members take leave to think in sectional rather than in party terms. There is, in fact, more in common between a Democrat like Senator Wheeler of Montana and a Republican like the late Senator Borah of Idaho, than there is between Senator Glass, the Democratic senator from Virginia, and Mr. Wheeler, or between Senator Hastings of Delaware, a conservative Republican, and a Senator Borah. The votes of each are determined by considerations which transcend party lines in a way hardly understood in Great Britain; and the presidential problem of securing coherency is greatly aggravated as a consequence. In legislation regulating hours and wages in commodities of interstate commerce, for instance, a Democratic senator or congressman from Massachusetts is bound to think less of the party line than of the effect on his constituency of so voting as to offer the prospect of being criticized in Massachusetts because he has sacri-

[4] See this well worked out by Professor A. N. Holcomb in E. B. Logan, *The American Political Scene* (1938), pp. 1-52, 289-304.

ficed its industrial interests to the lower standard of life which prevails in the South. A progressive-minded Southerner like Mr. Maury Maverick of Texas is pretty certain to pay by defeat for insisting that southern industry ought not, in matters of industrial legislation, to be parasitic upon its low standard of life. *Mutatis mutandis*, this is true of a large part of the field of social and economic action.

All this is to say that it tempts the Congress to avoid unity of outlook except under immense pressure from the White House. It follows the presidential lead instinctively only when it would be fatal for it not to follow that lead. Fatality depends on three things. There may be external war, as in 1898 and 1917; there may be grave internal emergency, as in 1933; or there may be a public opinion so widespread in favor of the presidential policy that the Congress finds it unwise to follow its own bent. But the result is the clear one—the mechanism of which I shall discuss later—that the means a president must use to secure the unity he requires are all quite different from anything the founders could have imagined. They built a weak executive, they divided the sources of legislative power, because at the time they did their work the mental climate of the time called for that attitude. It is even possible to argue that it was an intelligible outlook down to some such period as the Civil War. Since then, and in increasing degree, it has been a hindrance, and not a help, to the proper performance of the president's duties. And this conclusion is not vitiated by the fact that some presidents—Mr.

Coolidge, for example—had rarely any idea in the situation they confronted of what those duties were.

The situation is difficult enough when the president's party is in a majority in both houses. Then, at least, the party interest in re-election enables him to use the pressures at his disposal to maintain some measure of effective power. But if he loses that majority, as was evident in the administration of Hayes and in the last years of Wilson's presidency, he is in a hopeless position. In those circumstances the Congress naturally feels that it has nothing to gain by co-operating with him; and its term is passed in a mutual evasion of responsibility which has rarely any point save playing for advantage at the next presidential election. Measures may well be passed, even with a presidential majority, to which the president himself has the strongest possible objection; and, if his veto is inoperative, he is compelled—the supreme folly in administration—to execute policies of which he disapproves. A good example of this habit was the decision of Congress in 1939 to discontinue the cultural experiments made under the Works Progress Administration. All observers of them who had any serious acquaintance with their achievement were aware that they represented an epoch in the history of the relation between government and the arts. They were sacrificed because the opposition to the president had determined to make "economy" an issue of the campaign of 1940; and, though the sum involved was small, his nominal supporters took the view that the enemy could not be allowed to put—what they would in any case put—the need for economy before the electorate as an issue. The cultural experiment was therefore abandoned, despite the pressure of the president. But he was still left with the important administrative issue of how to find effective means of relief for those who would be rendered unemployed by reason of their abandonment.

2

This leads to one conclusion which is of great importance to the proper understanding of the relation between Congress and the president. Its own instinctive and inherent tendency is, under all circumstances, to be anti-presidential. It may respect him; it may even fear him; it may give him a general if spasmodic support. But it is always looking for occasions to differ from him, and it never feels so really comfortable as when it has found such an occasion for difference. In doing so, it has the sense that it is affirming its own essence. It is more truly itself because it is exalting its own prestige. Some members, no doubt, act in this way because to fight the president is the highroad to notoriety. Others, the late Senator Borah, for example, are constitutionally uncomfortable if they support any president while he is in office. In the Senate, especially, a good deal of truth lies in the remark of President Coolidge that most senators think they ought to be president, and that, in any case, they know more than he does. In the Senate, again, something is due to the fact that the chairman of an important committee is likely to have been there for many years. He has become a specialist in his allotted field. He has seen presidents and cabinet officers come and go; it is only human, perhaps, for him to think, first, that his own view of what should be done is better than their view, and, second, that to enhance his own prestige it is important for him to change any presidential measure sufficiently to leave his own mark upon it. Mark Hanna and Roscoe Conkling are perhaps extreme instances of men who sought to move their colleagues to take the view, in the one case privately, in the other by public dispute, that the credit of their institution depended upon keeping the president in its leading strings.

The history of Congress, and especially of the Senate, might well from one angle be summarized as a continuous effort to make the president its creature; of the Senate, in particular, because its relation to the appointing power and to foreign relations, in addition to the fact that the career of the average senator will normally outlast that of several presidents, give it a special advantage in seeking to enforce its view. No one can read such documents as the diaries of John Quincy Adams, of Polk, of Gideon Welles, or the autobiographies of senators like Blaine and Hoar of Massachusetts without seeing that this is the case. The administration of President Grant was, no doubt, a particularly flagrant example of a Congress without any real sense of obligation; but it is notable that even from a senator with cabinet experience it evoked no blame. "The executive department of a republic like ours," wrote John Sherman, "should be subordinate to the legislative department. The president should obey and enforce the laws, leaving to the people the duty of correcting any errors committed by their representatives in Congress."[5] "The most eminent senators," wrote Hoar, then a congressman, of this period, "would have received as a personal affront a private message from the White House expressing a desire that they should adopt any course in the discharge of their legislative duties that they did not approve. If they visited the White House, it was to give, not to receive, advice. Any little company or coterie who had undertaken to arrange public policies with the president and to report to their associates what the president thought would have rapidly come to grief. . . . Each of these stars kept his own orbit and shone in his sphere, within which he tolerated no intrusion from the president or from anybody else."[6]

No doubt the aftermath of the Civil War was an exceptional period; but for at least the fifteen years succeeding it, the thesis of the Senate was that presidents should run in leading strings that it would control. Even the cabinet of Hayes was not confirmed until a storm of popular disapproval had arisen.[7] The actions of the Senate in those years are inexplicable except upon the assumption that it was determined to make the president no more than its creature. Even when its claims had to be diminished under the force

[5] *Recollections of Forty Years in the House, Senate and Cabinet* (1895), p. 447.
[6] *Autobiography* (1903), II, 46.
[7] *Diary of R. B. Hayes* (ed. Williams, 1922), entries for March, 1877.

of public opinion, they remained as a threat to become operative at the first opportunity. It assumed the right to supervise in itemized detail the conduct of every executive agency it had brought into being. It believed that it was its duty to investigate each executive action, and, as in the classic case of Cleveland's nomination of Burnett to the office of district attorney in Alabama, to see all confidential papers in connection with the administrative process.[8] The impression produced on a careful observer of this period is worth noting. Congress, wrote Woodrow Wilson,[9] "does not domineer over the president himself, but it makes the secretaries its humble servants. Not that it would hesitate, upon occasion, to deal directly with the chief magistrate himself; but it has few calls to do so, because our latter-day presidents live by proxy; they are executives in theory, but the secretaries are executives in fact." Until at any rate the late eighties of the last century it is not unfair to accept Wilson's description of the president as, in the eyes of Congress, "merely the executor of the sovereign legislative will."[10] Only a few years later Lord Bryce was recording the view that "the president's wishes conveyed in a message have not necessarily any more effect on Congress than an article in a prominent party newspaper . . . and, in fact, the suggestions which he makes, year after year, are usually neglected, even when his party has a

[8] Cleveland, *Presidential Problems* (1904), pp. 46 f.
[9] *Congressional Government* (1885), p. 45.
[10] Cf. his illuminating article, "The Presidency in 1879" in the *International Review*, VI, 46.

majority in both houses, or when the subject lies outside party lines."[11]

From Grant to the election of McKinley the center
of effective power was in Congress, and save for an
occasional revolt most of the presidents seemed, at
least publicly, content that it should be so. The picture
of what, in an eminent Republican's eyes, they ought
to seek to be, was drawn for Benjamin Harrison by
John Sherman. "The president," he wrote,[12] "should
have no policy distinct from that of his party, and
this is better represented in Congress than in the executive." Hayes and Cleveland may have had their
moments of challenge, but even the fact that they
were supported in them by public opinion did not lead
them to attempt any continuity of leadership. It was
not until McKinley arrived at the White House that
the balance began to swing in the presidential direction. Partly, no doubt, this was due to the fact that
the Spanish-American War forced upon him, as war
forced upon the Whig Lincoln, a direction he could
hardly avoid; partly, too, his long period in the House
of Representatives gave him a skill in congressional
maneuver that his predecessors from Grant onward
had lacked. Senator Hoar, indeed, after a generation's
experience, expressed the view that no president, save
possibly Jackson, had exercised the influence over the
Senate that McKinley did.[13] Perhaps this was because
the entrance of America into international politics as

[11] *American Commonwealth* (1908), I, 230.
[12] *Op. cit.*, p. 1032.
[13] *Op. cit.*, II, 47.

a world power gave him, consciously to himself, a new status; there is significance in his remark that "I can no longer be called the president of a party; I am now the president of the whole people."[14]

The leadership that McKinley exercised in an unostentatious way was exercised by Theodore Roosevelt with a determined aggressiveness that had been unknown since Jackson. He had, as he has himself told us, a theory of the presidential power which placed its exponent in the forefront of the political stage. "The executive power," he wrote,[15] "was limited only by specific instructions and prohibitions appearing in the Constitution, or imposed by Congress under its constitutional powers. My view was that every executive officer, and above all every executive officer in a high position, was a steward of all the people bound actively and affirmatively to do all he could for the people. . . . I did not usurp power, but I did greatly broaden the use of executive power." That was not an unfair description of his practice. It ought to be added that much of its success was due to his collaboration with Speaker Cannon,[16] that in the last years of his presidency there was a visible and significant decline in the force of his leadership, and that his successor, William Howard Taft, whom he virtually nominated, went back to a view of the presidential office more akin to that of Cleveland than to that of Roosevelt.[17] Woodrow Wilson, in his turn, re-

[14] Olcott, *Life of William McKinley* (1916), II, 296.
[15] *Autobiography* (1913), p. 389.
[16] L. W. Bushey, *Uncle Joe Cannon* (1927), p. 219.
[17] *Our Chief Magistrate* (1916), pp. 139-142.

newed and extended the Roosevelt conception. It was not merely that he was the first president since Washington personally to place his program before Congress. Even before he took office he had revolted against the notion that he was the instrument of congressional purposes. "The president is at liberty," he wrote in 1906,[18] "both in law and in conscience to be as big a man as he can. His capacity will set the limit." He is entitled to seek the leadership of the nation because, if he succeeds, it is because "the president has the nation behind him and Congress has not. . . . The Constitution explicitly authorizes the President to recommend to Congress 'such measures as he shall deem necessary and expedient,' and it is not necessary to the integrity of even the literary theory of the Constitution to insist that recommendations shall be merely perfunctory. . . . The Constitution bids him speak, and times of stress must more and more thrust upon him the attitude of originator of policies."[19]

Those last words are significant, and they must be read, I think, in terms of the development he gave them just after his election and before he took office. "The president," he wrote,[20] "is expected by the nation to be the leader of his party, as well as the chief executive officer of the government, and the country will take no excuses from him. He must play the part, and play it successfully, or lose the country's confidence. He must be prime minister, as much con-

[18] *Constitutional Government in the United States* (1907), p. 69.
[19] *Ibid.*, pp. 70-73.
[20] Letter to A. Mitchell Palmer in H. J. Ford, *Woodrow Wilson* (1916), where it is printed as an appendix.

cerned with the guidance of legislation as with the just and orderly execution of law, and he is the spokesman of the nation in everything, even the most momentous and delicate dealings of the government in foreign affairs." The theory of Woodrow Wilson corresponded closely to his practice. In the first two years of his administration, Congress was driven to pass an important series of domestic measures of which he was himself the chief architect. With the coming of war, he assumed the headship of the nation to a degree, and with powers, beyond any that Lincoln received. It is significant that he refused to accept a cabinet of national concentration, and that he stopped the movement which sought to repeat the Lincolnian precedent by associating with him a committee of both houses of Congress to assist him in the conduct of the war. Until the eve of the armistice, he was the unquestioned master of the nation. "Senators of sovereign states and leaders of parties," writes one commentator,[21] "grovelled in their marble corridors, so terrified were they of public opinion."

But Wilson pushed public opinion too far. With the coming of peace, the idea of the almost personal sovereignty he had exercised aroused discontent everywhere; and his opponents won a majority in the Congress of 1918. Thenceforward, he was impotent; and until 1932 the pendulum swung back to a stage where the effective leadership was in Congress and not in the president. In part, at least, this was due to the presidents themselves. Both Harding and Coolidge

[21] G. R. Brown, *The Leadership of Congress* (1922), p. 187.

were mediocrities. The first had pledged himself, before election, to a "revival of party government as distinguished from personal government," by which he meant that he would follow Congress and not lead it; and, indeed, his nomination was mainly due to the realization of the chiefs of the Republican party that he was the type of man who would accept guidance. The treatment of his first budget in Congress, of which he expressed the hope that Congress would make no substantial changes, is typical of the treatment he received. The Committee on Appropriations examined the estimates of his Bureau of the Budget so minutely that the printed testimony of their examination occupies over twenty thousand pages of print; and they reduced them by over three hundred million dollars.[22] Mr. Coolidge was hardly in better case. There were, in fact, few subjects upon which he had any ideas, and his general approach to politics was built upon the assumption that there was, in any circumstances, too much legislation. He did not, therefore, try to give any lead. "I have never felt," he wrote,[23] "that it was my duty to attempt to coerce senators or representatives, or to take reprisals. The people sent them to Washington. I felt I had discharged my duty when I had done the best I could with them. In this way I avoided almost entirely a personal opposition, which I think was of more value to the country than to attempt to prevail through arousing personal fear." The period, in fact, from

[22] *Congressional Record* (67th Congress, 2nd Sess.), p. 11, 665.
[23] *Autobiography* (1929), p. 232.

1921 to 1929 was the era of conscious abdication from power on the part of the president. Neither really appealed to the country for support against Congress, because neither had any policy for which to appeal. Each was content to give his party a free run of power; and each assumed that the idea of the free run for the party meant the almost unfettered dominance of Congress. Congress, of course, was content to accept this view.

The problem of the Hoover administration was a different one. Harding and Coolidge were mediocre hack politicians whose main recommendation to their colleagues was their very mediocrity. Mr. Hoover, with little political experience, came to office as an expert administrator, more or less in specific contrast to his predecessors. He encountered an emergency hardly less great than the war itself; yet he seemed entirely unable to assume the leadership of Congress in that emergency. What is the reason? Partly, no doubt, it derives from his acceptance of a rigorous concept of the separation of powers. "The weakening of the legislative arm," he wrote in 1934,[24] "[leads] to encroachment by the executive upon the legislative and judicial functions, and inevitably that encroachment is upon individual liberty. If we examine the fate of wrecked republics over the world we shall find first a weakening of the legislative arm." Something of this affirmation is, of course, a direct criticism of the policy pursued by his successor, Franklin D. Roosevelt. But it is also explicit in his actual relations

[24] *The Challenge to Liberty* (1934), pp. 125-126.

with Congress. Tariffs and farm relief, he said shortly after taking office, are matters for Congress to determine; his duty was merely to draw attention to them.[25] Though he cordially disapproved of the Hawley-Smoot tariff, he refused to use his influence against it, on the ground that he could not know enough of its details to recommend specific alterations of them. He was deeply unpopular in Washington; and this seems to have bred a self-distrust in him which made him shrink from the emphasis of leadership.[26] Perhaps, also, the depth of his attachment to a laissez faire philosophy inhibited him from recommending that positive action which would have meant government interference with matters he conceived as the concern of business men only. While he was in office, at any rate, it was in Congress and not in him that the direction of affairs was centralized. It is not, I think, unfair to suggest that it was the public consciousness of the fact that he did not lead in the face of the great depression which was largely responsible for his defeat in the election of 1932.

Though the last six years are still living events, it happens that, in the context of this discussion, we are better informed about them than about any of the three previous administrations. The publication by President Roosevelt of his papers[27] makes available not only his public addresses, but also his private conferences with the press, and his annotations upon the

[25] Cf. the criticism in the *New Republic*, Vol. 58, p. 184.
[26] *New Republic*, June 4, 1930.
[27] *The Public Papers and Addresses of Franklin D. Roosevelt* (1938), 5 vols.

whole. It is hardly too much to say that these give us an insight into the working of the presidency such as we have not had since the diaries of John Quincy Adams and of Polk. From our angle, what they represent is a revival and extension of the theory of the presidency of which Theodore Roosevelt and Woodrow Wilson were the exponents. The drive to action comes from the White House. Franklin Roosevelt's conception of his office is intensely positive. Whether in foreign policy or in domestic affairs, the material Congress is made to consider is material for which he demands consideration. I shall discuss later the methods by which he has enforced consideration. Here it is sufficient to say that he has throughout chosen to lead, and has compelled Congress to follow.

But what is significant in the experience of Franklin Roosevelt is not merely the extent and the intensity of the lead he has given; what is significant also is the growth and dissent from the fact of this leadership in Congress. In the first "hundred days," the emergency was so great that he secured from Congress everything for which he asked. It responded without limit to the challenge he uttered. "In the event," he told it,[28] "that the Congress shall fail to take these courses, and in the event that the national emergency is still critical, I shall not evade the clear course of duty that will then confront me. I shall ask the Congress for the one remaining instrument to meet the crisis—broad executive power to wage a war against the emergency as great as the power that would be given to me if we

[28] *Public Papers* (1938), II, 15.

were in fact invaded by a foreign foe." The remark of the Republican leader in the House of Representatives in the debate on the emergency banking bill best expresses the attitude of Congress to this challenge. "The house," he said,[29] "is burning down, and the President of the United States says this is the way to put out the fire." It may be doubted whether, even during the World War, there had been so complete an acceptance of presidential leadership as in those hundred days.

In the president's first term, it is broadly true to say that the fulness of his direction was maintained. There was a good deal of confusion; there was muttering against his program; in one or two cases, there was even the threat of open revolt. But they came to nothing. "The victory of the president," wrote the most eminent of living American historians,[30] "was complete all along the line. . . . After the democratic processes of debate and confusion were given free rein, leadership emerged in the end. When results were surveyed at the end of the discussion and uproar, it could truly be said that seldom, if ever, in the long history of Congress had so many striking and vital measures been spread upon law books in a single session." The public seemed to confirm that view in the triumphant return of Mr. Roosevelt to power in the election of 1936.

But a change developed rapidly in the second term.

[29] Cf. E. P. Herring, *American Political Science Review*, Vol. 28, p. 70.
[30] Professor C. A. Beard in *Current History*, October, 1935, p. 64.

He was defeated over the Court plan. His first effort at administrative reorganization suffered a similar fate. In measures relating to relief and agriculture he was compelled to accept drastic changes. In the realm of foreign policy, at a vital juncture in international affairs, he was unable to secure acceptance of the proposals he made for changes in neutrality legislation which would have enlarged his discretionary powers. The Republicans gained heavily in the mid-term elections of 1938, and it was clear that the divisions in the ranks of the Democratic party jeopardized the president's control of it. Mr. Roosevelt could, indeed, at the adjournment of 1939, well have repeated Polk's complaint of ninety years before.[31] He had a nominal majority in both houses, but that majority was far more interested in maneuvers for the 1940 campaign than in the consideration of presidential policies. Complaints of presidential autocracy were loud even among members of the Democratic party; and the latter were prepared to enforce against the president the implications of senatorial courtesy over a judicial appointment even in a case where it was admitted that the proposed nominee was in every way appropriate for the position. It had become clear, in short, that with the disappearance of the more immediate gravities of the depression Congress generally, and the Senate in particular, was resentful of presidential leadership and eager to reduce it so far as they judged public opinion would permit. Mr. Roosevelt was not so disastrously placed as Mr. Wilson was in 1918; and

[31] *Op. cit.*, p. 186.

the brilliance of his maneuvers, combined with the depth of his personal hold on the electorate, combined to prevent Congress from going too far in its resentment. But there was nothing like the magical atmosphere of the first two years of his presidency. The desire of Congress to recover its authority was unmistakable. An attack upon presidential leadership was clearly becoming a primary issue of the political scene.

3

In the absence of special circumstances, this is to say, the hostility of Congress to the president is a part of its inner essence. Before we discuss its meaning, however, it is important to discuss the methods at the disposal of the president for influencing Congress. How does he get his way? What are the methods at his disposal for securing unity of outlook between the executive and the legislature?

One answer is to say at once that there is no general rule. Every president has his opportunities of influence; the way he uses them depends partly on his own personality and partly on the situation that he confronts. A president in an emergency is, obviously, likely to be far more influential than a president who, like Coolidge, is held to be ruling in a period of profound prosperity. A president whose party is in the majority in Congress has opportunities far greater than one who is in a minority in the House or the Senate or both. A president like McKinley, who knows Congress intimately, is obviously more likely to be successful in his handling of Congress than one who, like Mr. Hoover, is largely unaccustomed to its peculiar mental climate, and, in any case, unskilled in dealing with men. A president like John Quincy Adams, who is by nature aloof from public contact, is less likely to be successful than one who, like Theodore Roosevelt, has a genuine and instinctive liking for people. There is no general rule which enables one to predict with confidence that the relation between Congress and the president will be harmonious. Rather is it natural, on the record, to say that even if the normal conditions of harmony are present, at some stage strain is pretty certain to occur.

The first great element which makes for unity is the fact that the president and his party have a common interest in remaining in power. However great their differences, neither can do without the other. It is rarely enough for a man to be president; the drive that has placed him there makes him want to be a successful president; and this, in its turn, makes him seek to find the best terms of accommodation he can with his party. Usually, too, he wants renomination at the end of his first term; and this is always a strong ground for persuasion toward common ends. The party, too, needs the president. It lives by his record. To break with him in any thoroughgoing way is to risk the support of public opinion at the next election. Psychologically, the persistence of acute strain between the president and his party is always a major advantage to their opponents; it leads to defections from the ranks, and these, in doubtful areas, may be pivotal to the result. Senator Norris' loss to the Republican party in 1932, for example, undoubtedly brought many wavering voters to Mr. Roosevelt's side. And unity between them is important, too, in a material sense. A party lives by the spoils it has to distribute. The successful use of these is the condition of its effective organization. Unless some degree of harmony reigns between executive and legislature, there is always the danger that the advantages of office may be dissipated by their maldistribution.

It is important to realize that, the case of Andrew Johnson apart, no president has so far been completely deserted by his party. There have been grim periods of strain, as notably during the presidency of Tyler; but, in the end, some sort of outer harmony has been arranged. Deep, also, as the quarrel may be, it is rarely so deep, perhaps curiously, as between one party and another. I say curiously, because the line of cleavage between the parties is always more apparent than real; there is far more agreement between a progressive Republican like Senator La Follette and President Franklin Roosevelt than, say, between the former and Senator Hastings of Delaware. But it would take something like a constitutional revolution for Senator La Follette to emerge as a Democratic candidate for the presidency. Few Democrats were so critical of the Republican presidents of the last thirty years as the Republican Senator Borah; but he never "bolted" the party, and each presidential election found him offering at least a pinch of incense on the Republican altar.

A certain degree of harmony usually prevails in the first months of a presidential term. The incumbent is new to office; he has to feel his way; there is a general understanding, both in Congress and in public opinion, that he shall not be attacked until he is accustomed to his routine. This is not, indeed, always the case. Harding's death had hardly elevated Calvin Coolidge to the White House before the Senate rejected his nominee for the post of attorney-general, an event unprecedented in fifty years. In the first year of his administration they passed the soldiers' bonus over his veto. They refused to accept his view of Japanese immigration policy. They rejected his proposal of adherence to the World Court, and they mangled, despite a threatened veto, his super-tax proposals so that the body became a corpse. But this is comparatively rare. A president who has something real to say and do—the condition is important—can usually count on a "honeymoon period" in which what he asks for will, in large measure, have assurance of being granted. It is usually toward the close of his first congressional session that the buttons are taken off the foils.

The patronage, moreover, is an immense and necessary element in the making of this unity. Senators and congressmen want posts for their followers; and they know how much of their own future depends upon their ability to get them. To quarrel with the president may mean the withholding of the post from a man whose re-election begins to loom; it may even mean that a party rival in his own state or district becomes influential, with the possible result of his loss of the nomination at the next primary. It is the disposal of the patronage that keeps the party machinery oiled; and the loss of influence through opposition to the president may be a serious matter. President Cleveland used this weapon to force through the repeal of the Silver Purchase Act. President Wilson obtained the support of Senator Tillman for his most distinguished nomination to the Supreme Court by a similar method. Democrats who had waited for twelve long and hungry years for the patronage were easily stimulated, in the presence of crisis, to avoid discussion by an apt reminder from the president that the distribution would be delayed until the necessary measures were on the statute-book.[32] How vital an element in the retention of power the patronage may be is shown by the famous controversy between Garfield and Roscoe Conkling. Even a cabinet minister, as Polk has made plain,[33] may have "sleepless nights" because "the impression was becoming general . . . . that the patronage of the government here was being wielded against him." The immense extension of government service under President Franklin Roosevelt has not only been a direct cause of his great hold on Congress; its growth, also, has been a cause of Republican bitterness. It is natural to expect presidential influence to decline when the jobs have been distributed. But the Roosevelt policies have resulted in the creation of new agencies with large patronage almost

[32] Earle Looker, *The American Way* (1933), p. 67.
[33] *Op. cit.*, p. 40.

continuously through the administration of two terms. In these circumstances, exploitation of the differences between the president and his supporters in Congress has been a far more difficult matter than it usually is.

The president has also the veto power, in its various forms, as a method of influence. No one now accepts the view of Washington that a bill should be vetoed only upon the ground of its probable unconstitutionality. "If anything has been established by actual practice," wrote President Taft, "it is that the president, in signing a bill, or returning it unsigned, must consider the expediency and wisdom of the bill, as one engaged in legislation and responsible for it. The Constitution used the word 'approve,' and it would be a narrow interpretation to contract this into a mere decision as to legal validity."[34] This is the generally accepted view; even Benjamin Harrison, as much the mere agent of Congress as any president, vetoed seventeen measures. The president, he wrote,[35] "does not deal with bills submitted for his approval upon the principle that he should approve only such as he would have voted for if he had been a member of Congress. Much deference is due to the Congress, and vetoes have customarily been used only when the fault in the legislation was serious in itself or as a precedent." On the whole, it cannot be said that the power is a great one, or that it has been widely used; and Congress can always overrule the

[34] *The Presidency* (1916), pp. 13-14.
[35] *This Country of Ours* (1901), p. 133. On the general subject the best treatment is still E. C. Mason, *The Veto Power* (1890).

[142]

president by a two-thirds majority of the members who constitute a quorum in either house.[36] Eight presidents (seven of them in office before the Civil War) did not exercise their veto power at all. Of the earlier presidents, Washington exercised it twice, Madison on six occasions, and Monroe once. Jackson vetoed twelve measures and Tyler nine. In the post-Civil War period, Grant vetoed forty-three bills, Roosevelt forty, and Woodrow Wilson twenty-six. Cleveland vetoed no less than 358 measures; but the vast majority of them were private pension bills of an indefensible character. The passage of a bill over the president's veto is infrequent. No such passage occurred in the first fifty years of the republic. When it has been so passed, as with the Immigration Act of 1917 (which, in substantially the same form, had been vetoed successively by Cleveland, Taft, and Wilson), or the soldiers' bonus acts, passed over the vetoes of Coolidge, Hoover, and Franklin Roosevelt, the reason usually lies in the pressure of an organized opinion outside so strong that the Congress is not willing to take the risk of leaving the presidential veto as final.

The great defect in the veto power is the fact that it is total and not partial. The president must reject or accept a bill as a whole; he cannot, like the governors of several states, veto particular items and approve the rest. It is upon this fact that Congress has erected the gigantic structure of the "pork barrel" in general appropriation bills, and the device of

[36] *Missouri Pac. Ry. Co.* v. *Kansas* 248 U. S. 276 (1919).

the "rider" as an attachment thereto. Few presidents will have the courage to veto this type of legislation, objectionable though it be, simply because the failure to secure necessary financial legislation hampers so greatly the process of administration; though both Taft and Wilson were brave enough to do so.[37] President Grant vainly requested Congress to pass an amendment giving him authority to veto parts of bills. No doubt the new Budget Act of 1921 has effected some improvement in the financial powers of Congress. But it is still true to say in this regard that few financial measures go to the president for signature without items in them representing a gift to some special interest for which no defense is possible and which even the most lax president must be desirous of expunging if he could. The veto power, in short, though real, reaches but a little way. It will rarely be exercised in that financial realm where it is most needed; and, outside that realm, it mostly marks either constitutional doubts on the part of the president's advisers, or a difference between him and Congress so acute that its exercise rather marks the degree of strain than enables him to overcome it.

The real source, the patronage apart, of presidential power lies, ultimately, in the appeal to public opinion. This power has a twofold source. On the one hand, it derives from the fact of the president's position; being the one element in the government

---

[37] In Wilson's case the rider, abolishing daylight saving, was passed as a separate bill over his veto. The matter is now dealt with separately by each state.

which derives from the nation as a whole, it is natural
for it, especially in times of crisis, to look to him for
leadership. On the other, the public is naturally interested in the process of government; and a president of dominant personality can utilize that interest
to his advantage. Each of these sources deserves some
detailed exploration.

The position of the president in the national life
is hardly to be understood by anyone who has not
seen it both continuously and at first hand. For the
nation, while he is in office, he is in a real sense its
embodiment. It has made him president; that act of
creation gives him for it a reality and a respect quite
different in character from any that a hereditary monarch possesses. Members of the nation may hate and
fear him; Franklin Roosevelt is, in some ways, the
most hated and feared president since Andrew Johnson. They may even despise him, as Calvin Coolidge
was frankly despised by a considerable number of
those who had any intimate contact with him. But,
fear or hate, or even contempt, there is inherent in
his office a sense of respect which brooks no denial.
It is a part of the make-up of the American citizen.
He can no more escape it than the Englishman can
escape the sense that royalty is somehow different
from ordinary clay. And because every American
has that sense, he looks up to the president, listens to
him, watches with attention his every action. The
president, by historic tradition, is placed on an eminence which not even so distinguished a figure as the
chief justice of the United States can rival. The

citizen may gossip about, and, as the various "whispering" campaigns have made clear, even against, the president. There may grow up, as in the case of President Coolidge, a whole saga of anecdotes about his habits. But the degree to which the president maintains interest, while he is president, even in the citizen most indifferent to politics, is an astonishing thing to the outsider.

The result is that he looks to the president for views. He expects leadership from him. He assumes that the president has opinions about every subject from the place of the Boy Scout movement in the national life to the problems of soil erosion. He expects consideration for those opinions. He expects his congressman or his senator to have opinions about those opinions. And because the president is not only the ceremonial head of the nation but also its executive head, he follows with some closeness what happens to presidential opinions upon matters of significant public import. Every president has an incomparable audience waiting for the pronouncement he may choose to make; to whomever else the Americans may not listen—and they are, in any case, a nation of listeners—they will listen to *him*. In any crisis, in the discussion of any big problem, they expect him to speak; in a very real sense, when he has spoken, they feel that the nation has spoken. To give a lead upon the issues of his time is not merely a constitutional function to be exercised in a formal way; it is, it increasingly becomes, an essential part of the presidential office. The more the president gives the lead, the greater the stature he assumes. He makes things intelligible, discussable almost, by speaking out. The people expect to be interested by their president; that is one of the reasons why they have elected him. They want to see him in action, to hear him speak. The foreigner may hear amusement, even contempt, about members of Congress; he will rarely hear anything but respect for the presidential office as such.

This attitude provides a basis which makes an appeal from the president to public opinion a matter of enormous significance. The audience is there to be interested; it is its president who speaks to it. No one else has the power that he has to mobilize public opinion; no one else can reach it so profoundly; no one else's judgment is, so decisively, "front page" news. The president, therefore, when he is at variance with Congress, starts with the advantage that there is a wide public opinion on his side. He is pretty sure to command a good deal of respect for his point of view; he is certain to command an interest with which no one else can compare. And a skilful president can, of course, maximize the opportunities at his disposal. His messages and speeches can prepare the ground. His press conferences are nothing so much as propaganda by which, through information and suggestion, he secures receptivity for his attitude. Phrases of his will become the current coin of conversation; Franklin Roosevelt's "horse and buggy" utterance has passed into the tradition of the nation. The effective use of the radio—which gives him almost the whole nation as an audience—offers him the certainty that his case will be heard and known as he wishes it heard and known. He has a means at his disposal for creating confidence in his point of view which far surpasses that at the disposal of any rival factor in the nation. He will be heard even if, as in the election of 1936, the overwhelming bulk of the press is opposed to him.

All this means that a president with the gift for leadership can, in Professor Cushman's phrase,[38] "usually find it possible to create a public sentiment . . . . which party leaders in and out of Congress dare not ignore." He must, of course, be determined and persistent. He must take care to see that the public mind is really concentrated upon his measure. He must have arguments on its behalf that are simple and direct and intelligible. He must avoid springing novelties upon the public which touch traditions which the record has—like that of the Supreme Court —made sacred. He must try to appear as the reasonable man battling against wilful obstinacy or vested interests. He must have, like Theodore Roosevelt, the power of accurate timing in his appeals, or, like Franklin Roosevelt, something akin to genius for making the complex appear simple and obvious. Even a dull president, like Rutherford Hayes, can arouse the nation if the fighting ground against him is badly chosen by Congress.[39] A president with a dominating temper can always be certain that if he has chosen

[38] *American National Government* (1931), p. 303.
[39] Cf. Burgess, *The Administration of President Hayes* (1916), pp. 65 f.

his issue well and phrased it skilfully he will win widespread popular support for his point of view. Granted, indeed, that the president really believes in his cause, and has persistency, he can so educate the nation in his support that a difficult case will make its way to victory.

There are many instances to prove this. The fight of Theodore Roosevelt for conservation is one example of it. The ability with which Woodrow Wilson took a united nation with him into the War of 1914 is another; for brilliance of timing, indeed, it would be difficult to surpass that achievement when it is remembered that, only five months before, the slogan "he kept us out of war" was one main cause of Wilson's re-election. Even Franklin Roosevelt's unsuccessful campaign against the Supreme Court prepared public opinion to believe that it was a reactionary body the composition of which was unsatisfactory; and this prepared the way for the virtually unanimous acceptance by the Senate of nominations which, but a short time before, would undoubtedly have been stoutly challenged. So, too, skilful use by the president of the congressional power of investigation may prepare the way, through the revelations it effects, for the acceptance of legislation which Congress itself is dubious about, and against which all the pressure of powerful "lobbies" is being exerted at the Capitol. The ruthless but salutary investigation of Wall Street at the hands of Judge Pecora undoubtedly made possible the drastic regulation of the New

York Stock Exchange.[40] It prepared the public mind for the notion that a cleansing was necessary by turning, under presidential inspiration, the pitiless light of publicity upon the habits of men who had previously seemed beyond the reach of public criticism. The pathetic appearance, under examination, of men like Andrew Mellon, "the greatest secretary of the treasury since Hamilton," broke the worship of idols whom it was necessary to break if the presidential policies were to be driven through Congress.

Obviously enough, great though the power is, there are limits to it. A president who offends certain deep traditions in the American mental climate will find that a recalcitrant Congress, if it is stubborn enough, can resist the pressures he can mobilize. A demand for innovation will, normally, force its way to acceptance in a crisis. But if habituation to the crisis develops, persistency in innovation may then break on the rock of older habituations the cultural lag of which has been stayed, rather than broken, by the crisis. This, I suspect, has been in part the explanation of the adverse fortune of Franklin Roosevelt with Congress since 1936. With the passage of the supreme emergency on the crest of whose wave he rode, certain normal American ideas, the divine right of the business man to be free from government interference, the idea of a balanced budget, the belief (now wholly untrue) that any energetic American can find a job if he really tries, that that government is best which spends least, that the budget ought to be

[40] Ferdinand Pecora, *Wall Street Under Oath* (1939).

[150]

balanced annually (an interesting fiscal superstition), have all resumed something of their wonted authority. The breakdown of business control gave the trade unions an immense opportunity, behind which the president put considerable pressure; and the National Labor Relations Act was the result. But American conditions have not, historically, been favorable soil for a strong trade union movement, and the reaction against its gains has, despite the president, made considerable headway in Congress. The president, in a word, can compel attention for the things he desires; but his chance of victory for those things is not one of which he can be certain. Almost always, his success depends upon the presence of a mental climate it is beyond his power to control.

His authority, moreover, is limited for another reason. Not only Congress grows anxious under a president who too frequently cracks the whip. Beyond it, there is always a powerful current of opinion adverse to a strong president as such. There is fear that the legislative branch of the government may be excessively dominated by the executive; that is un-American. It is pretty clear that some of the judges, of unquestionably liberal outlook, who shared in finding the National Industrial Recovery Act unconstitutional, were moved by fears that it conferred dangerously excessive powers of delegated legislation upon the president.[41] And there is a widespread fear, especially prevalent among farmers and business men of "too much government"; the tradition of laissez faire

[41] *Schechter v. U. S.*, 295 U. S. 495.

has still deep roots in the American consciousness. The period in which the realm of federal intervention was both narrow and expected to be narrow, is still near enough for such intervention to encounter the cross-current of suspicion that it is eroding that individual responsibility the anxiety for which is a legacy inherent in a civilization still hardly a generation distant from the traditions of the frontier.

The president, moreover, must pick his issues carefully. They must be wide enough to be genuinely interesting. They must be of the type that, emotionally, can be made pretty rapidly to seem important. They must, if possible, transcend the inherent sectionalism of Congress. And the appeal to the public must not be made too frequently. Just as an excessive use of the radio would dull its influence by making it over-familiar, so the president must not appear as a man who simply cannot "get on" with Congress. His case must be of the kind upon which the electorate is likely to feel strongly—strongly enough, at least, for them to feel that they must express themselves about it either in letters to the press or by personal communication with their senator or congressman. It must, too, be the kind of issue that is familiar enough in its general outline to have a historic basis upon which presidential sentiment can be built up. When Franklin Roosevelt pressed for the Securities and Exchange Act, he had behind him the memories, far from dim, of Theodore Roosevelt's thunder against "malefactors of great wealth," and Woodrow Wilson's "new freedom" for the little man. When he protested against the Nazi rape of Czecho-Slovakia, he could rely, not only upon the still vivid memories of the war years, but upon the deep emotions of a large number of Czech-Americans to whom the rebirth of their native land in 1918 had been one of the two or three supreme public events in their lives.

The success of the president, I have said, often depends upon factors outside his control. The immense complications of the neutrality tangle of 1938-39 are interesting evidence of this. The president is searching for a free hand. He confronts in Congress an opposition, largely reflected in the country at large, which is compounded of a variety of factors. Some of it is the traditional demand for American isolation; Washington's warning against "permanent alliances" is still one of which every president must take account. Some of it is due to the revelations of congressional inquiries, of which that of Senator Nye into the armaments industry is perhaps outstanding, that have made many Americans—not least those of liberal temper—fearful of what the free hand may, in practice, conceal. Some of it, no doubt, is due to a suspicion that there is not so much to choose between Herr Hitler and Mr. Chamberlain; the profound psychological impact of Munich upon American opinion is unquestionable, especially upon that liberal opinion so important to Mr. Roosevelt. A good deal of it is sheer maneuvering for position in the next presidential election; the more the president can be discredited by defeat the less will he be a vital factor when that issue is determined.

Yet none of these factors is a tithe so important as what may happen in Europe itself. The issue of American neutrality will be largely determined by the limits of the aggression attempted by the Fascist powers.

4

To what conclusions does this argument lead? First, I think, it should be noted that a distinction must be drawn between the "crisis" situation and the "normal" situation. In the first, the president's position is so overwhelming that it is, broadly, imperative for Congress to follow where he chooses to lead. Then, the nation requires action, and it looks to the president to define the kind of action that is required. It assumes the necessity, in crisis, for the conference upon him of wide powers; it is impatient of doubt about, or hostility to, their conference. It may, indeed, almost be said that it is too impatient; no one can analyze, for instance, the workings of the Espionage Act of 1917 without seeing that Congress then practically abdicated before the president.[42] Much the same is true of the "hundred days" of Franklin Roosevelt. It would have been literally impossible, in the face of public opinion, for Congress to have resisted the pressure to give the president what he chose to demand; there are, indeed, careful observers who believe that if, at that moment, he had demanded even so drastic a measure as the nationalization of the banks, Congress would have had to accept it. In a

[42] Cf. Walter Nelles, *Espionage Act Cases* (1920), and Z. C. Chaffee, *Freedom of Speech* (1920).

crisis, to put it shortly, public opinion compels the abrogation of the separation of powers. There is really only one will in effective operation, and that is the will of the president. He is as powerful, while the emergency has a psychological hold on the country, as the British prime minister at a moment of national emergency.

But in a "normal" situation the position is very different. The American system, in its ultimate foundations, is built upon a belief in weak government. It must never be forgotten that the Constitution is the child of the eighteenth century; that the influence of Locke and Montesquieu is written deeply into its clauses. Those who made it were, out of actual and inferred experience, above all afraid of arbitrary power. They constructed a system of checks and balances as a bulwark against its emergence. They did so because they believed, with Madison, that "the accumulation of powers in a single hand is the very definition of tyranny." They did so because the effective citizen whom they were above all considering was the bourgeois man of adequate property who needed protection, on the one hand against an ambitious executive, and on the other against a legislature unduly under the influence of the propertyless mob. Naturally enough, in their day, the good state seemed to be the negative state. They were not unduly enamored of democracy, even if few of them would have said openly with Alexander Hamilton that the people was "a great beast." They believed profoundly in fundamental law; and their interpretation of its substance, whether they were Federalists like John Marshall or Democrats like Thomas Jefferson, was that it guaranteed their conception of the rights of property against legislative invasion. The state they constructed was the negative state that a nation of small property owners required; the state, be it noted, that under similar pressures, if in different form, was being simultaneously created in England and in France. The nineteenth century seemed, in large degree, to vindicate their notions; for, slavery apart, the immense physical resources at the disposal of the nation saved it from the deep social tensions of Europe for nearly a hundred years after 1787. It was not until such a period as the Haymarket Riots that an observer could claim general acceptance for the view that there was no qualitative difference between the problems of America and those of Europe. The remarkable insights of men like Orestes Brownson[43] fell upon ears largely deaf. He was speaking of class conflict when little else could be perceived but that contest over slavery which, by its intensity, seemed to transcend all other forms of social difference.

The idea of weak government fitted into the pattern of the first century of American development. It was aided by the facts, first, that the major parties were dominated by business men whom that idea suited; and second, that until the turn of the century trade unions were not a serious force to be reckoned with

---

[43] There is now a good biography of this remarkable man by Arthur Schlesinger Jr., *Orestes Brownson* (1939); see also an excellent analysis by Helen Mims in *Science and Society*, Spring, 1939.

in American politics. Legislative experiments in a positive direction were hampered at every turn by the courts filled predominantly by judges whose ideas of constitutional validity were shaped by devotion to the ideal of the negative state. Until almost the time of Woodrow Wilson, it is not unfair to describe the Senate as a rich man's club; and the attitude of Theodore Roosevelt to what now appear to be the very moderate ideas of the elder La Follette makes it obvious that the difficulties against which positive ideas in social legislation had to struggle were very great.[44] The power, moreover, of the business forces over the parties was immense; the history both of the Bryan campaign and of the Progressive movement is evidence of that. Even if the farmers were, on occasion, tempted "to raise less corn and more hell," they were uninterested in problems—the hours of labor, for example— which went beyond their narrow horizon. The disposition of forces in American politics, in short, all made toward the idea of a government which did not disturb those conditions of confidence which business men approved.

It was to the maintenance of those conditions that Congress largely directed its attention. On examination, it will be found that practically every major occasion in which there has been conflict between Congress and the president was, from Jackson onward, an occasion when the policy of the president seemed likely to disturb them. With Jackson, it was the bank; with Andrew Johnson, it was the fulfilment of the

[44] Cf. Pringle, *op. cit.*, pp. 547-548.

triumph of the industrial North against the agrarian South; with Theodore Roosevelt and Woodrow Wilson, it was a struggle against monopolies, with Franklin Roosevelt, it has been an effort to subdue the operations of business enterprise to a larger social purpose. In each case, also, the structure of the American Constitution, by dividing initiative in policy, through the legacy of a belief that weak government is desirable, has confused that initiative. The result has mainly been a compromise satisfactory to neither side. Few presidents, except in emergency, have secured what they sought; few Congresses have been able to prevent all they have desired to prevent from being enacted. No plan of action has been legislated coherently, or administered coherently. No allocation of direct responsibility for failure on either head has been seriously possible.

For once the need for a positive state began to be admitted—as it was reluctantly admitted in the presidency of Theodore Roosevelt—one outstanding principle was clear. It was the principle, long ago adumbrated by John Stuart Mill, that the formulation of legislative proposals is not a task for which a legislature is fitted. A legislature can criticize; it can ventilate grievance; its power to investigate through committees is invaluable; and, not least, as it fulfils these tasks it provides a process of public education which is pivotal to democratic government. But a legislature like Congress is at once too big and too incoherent of itself to devise an organic and unified approach to the problems of the time. It is not effectively organized to take a continuous initiative. Its members are not compelled to think by their position in terms of the problems of the whole nation. Each house of Congress has a separate prestige; their common prestige is, by their nature, inherently anti-presidential in character. To be something, Congress is forced to take a stand against the president; it cannot be anything if it merely follows his lead. And the weakness of the system is magnified by the fact that though it can seek its own elevation only by discrediting him, it cannot destroy him. He is there, whether it will or no, for his term; and his power to appeal against its decisions is but interstitial in character. The result of the system, normally, is therefore to dissipate strength rather than to integrate it. The president is usually less than he might be, because the stature of Congress is diminished the more fully he has his way; and Congress is never all that it might become, because it is so organized as to prevent the acceptance of clear sailing directions.

It is, of course, true that the ties of party provide a barrier against the consequences of this dissipation of strength. The president and his supporters have always a common interest in getting something done because their record measures the chance of later success at the polls. Yet that common interest is tempered by a number of hindrances. It is hindered by the fact that the committee system makes a number of little presidents, as it were, in the congressional sphere; there is a dual quasi-executive within the legislature, even though it does not enjoy executive power.

It is hindered again by the fact that, as the president's term draws to its close, the temptation to withdraw from him what allegiance the party system enforces is maximized. If the president, like Hayes, is not seeking re-election at the end of his first term, his power is likely to be small. "The very fact," writes Professor Commager,[45] "that Hayes was not a candidate for re-election accentuated the question of the succession, and bedevilled his administration with some of the most bitter political conflicts in our history—intraparty conflicts into which Hayes himself was drawn." And it is notable that the second term of those presidents who have been re-elected has in each case been less creative than the first. The problem of the succession means far more to congressional politics than the fruits of the legislative process.

No president is in a position to prevent this disintegration in normal times; even Washington could not do so, for it was in his second term that the forces were aligned which ultimately became the Federalist and Republican parties. An American party is not a unity in the English sense; it is a loose confederation of interests each of which is playing for power. It is therefore engaged, not merely in a fight against the opposing party, but also in a fight against factions within itself. No president can be sure that he will not have to pay the price for that factionalism. "I learned tonight," wrote Polk, on the twenty-first of

[45] See his illuminating article, "One, Two, or Three Terms," *New York Times Magazine*, July 23, 1939.

April, 1846,[46] "that the Senate, by the votes of Mr. Calhoun and his wing of the Democratic party, united with the whole Whig party, had rejected the nomination of Dr. Amos Nourse as collector. . . . This is, in addition to other evidence, a pretty clear indication that Mr. Calhoun intends to oppose my administration. He has embarrassed the administration on the Oregon question. He is playing a game to make himself president. . . ." On June 24, 1846, he is complaining of further rejections through the influence of certain senators. "The sooner," he comments,[47] "such party men go into the ranks of the Whig party, the better." "Democratic and Whig senators," he writes on February 28, 1848,[48] ". . . . act solely with the view to the elevation of themselves or their favorites to the presidential office. . . . Senators act as if there was no country and no public interests to take care of." Many later presidents must have re-echoed these sentiments.

In "normal" times, indeed, the relation between the president and Congress has a curious analogy with that between the French governments of the Third Republic and the Chamber of Deputies. No doubt, there is far greater executive stability in the American system; the Constitution provides for that. But there is in both an incoherence and irresponsibility in the relations between executive and legislature which it is impossible not to remark; in both, also, factionalism tends

[46] *Op. cit.,* p. 72.
[47] *Op. cit.,* p. 117.
[48] *Op. cit.,* p. 313.

[161]

greatly to destroy the prospect that any government may hope continuously to drive through an ample program of social change. In both, also, embarkation upon that program results in a withdrawal of business confidence; and a reforming government is presented with the alternatives of recovery or reform. In both, too, the individual legislator is prone to take every opportunity to mark his independence of the executive; and his support, only too often, has to be purchased by administrative favors. Both show, especially in the last generation, the striking phenomenon of "normal" governments being succeeded, every so often, by "crisis" governments, in which legislative irresponsibility compels the conference of wide powers upon the executive as a remedy for the irresponsibility. In both, also, a return to "normality" produces a return to the earlier characteristics. Neither shows any propensity to embark upon those fundamental reforms which the incoherence and instability suggest as imperative.

It may, of course, be said that the present system in the United States has served it well enough for a century and a half; that each crisis has demonstrated on the part of Congress a willingness to confer sufficient powers upon the president to cope with it. The answer to this view is, I think, twofold. It is, in the first place, clear that the basis of an institutional system framed for a negative state cannot easily be adequately adapted to the needs of a positive state. The legislative program in the latter type of organization needs an integration and a coherent continuity that it cannot attain under the American system; more, it requires standards of administrative performance and experience which cannot be improvised every four or eight years. And in the second place, no democracy in the modern world can afford a scheme of government the basis of which is the inherent right of the legislature to paralyze the executive power. Presidential programs often suffer from grave inadequacies; presidential leadership is often smaller than the problems it confronts. However inadequate, and however small, they are the only programs and leadership which are projected upon a national plane; more, they alone are so operated in the open as to focus upon themselves the whole force of public opinion. The weakness of the relationship established between the president and Congress is that it gives the latter a constant interest in the diminution of his power. It is not merely that, so to say, he is on the way out as he is on the way in. It is also that the sanctions he possesses are not continuous enough in their operation to make his leadership continuously effective except under conditions the avoidance of which is the purpose of every scheme of government. Whatever the weaknesses of the British system, it makes responsibility for action clear and direct and intelligible. An executive which cannot command the confidence of the legislature may appeal beyond it to the electorate. So long as it controls the legislature, its authority is coherent and integrated. These are immense advantages. The authority may be abused; but at least the responsibility for the abuse is always clearly indicated. The energy of the executive is not continually dissipated in patching up the majorities it requires for some degree of the program it has urged. The allegiance of its supporters is not constantly shifting on its axis. There is not a continuous interest in the legislature to develop a policy of its own at the cost of executive credit.

No doubt a good deal in the American pattern is easily explicable in historical terms. But that still leaves open the vital question whether past history is an excuse for present inadequacy. The modern state requires disciplined leadership; the American system leaves no assurance of its continuous availability. It is, indeed, built upon foundations that are inherently suspicious of leadership as such. From the foundation of the republic, as we can see from the pages of Maclay's *Diary*, the president has run in the leading strings of congressional control. This control has not presented a clear alternative to his leadership. Rather, for the most part, its result has been a confusion of the public mind. He may move in one direction; that is almost an invitation to Congress to move in several other directions. The clash of opinion about the wisdom of the alternative he emphasizes does not lead back to the people from whom his authority emanates. Rather does it result in an interregnum of power while the forces in opposition are maneuvering for an advantage they can only seize at stated intervals without chronological coincidence with national necessity.

These are momentous difficulties which reach down into the foundations of the Constitution. They are not touched, I venture to think, by any of the minor expedients of reform that have so far been proposed. The central problem of representative government in a democracy is, I repeat, to make the source of responsibility for action unmistakable, and to reach at once that citizen-body whose verdict upon its exercise is alone decisive. That problem, I suggest, is not solved in the American system. Its very nature is to dissipate responsibility by substituting the politics of maneuver for the politics of policy. No doubt, as Adam Smith said, there is a great deal of ruin in a nation; and emergency will always force a unity upon forces which the system is constructed to divide. But a government does not prove its adequacy because it can transcend its own principles in an emergency; its adequacy is born of its ability to prevent the outbreak of emergency. That is the test by which the relationship between the president and Congress must be judged. At the least, there are grounds for grave doubt whether it can meet this test successfully.

IV

FOREIGN RELATIONS

I

IF NO democratic people has yet satisfactorily solved the problem of its control of foreign relations, it can at least be said that nowhere has a more careful effort been made toward that end than in the United States. The president may have immense powers in negotiation; but in the ultimate disposition of its result he is the subject of the Senate before whose power of veto and amendment he must bow. Where the House of Commons is, in this realm, the virtual creature of any government that is not the author of overt disaster, the Senate of the United States is in a position at least to scrutinize every step of the executive, and, in large degree, to control its outcome. It cannot be said, I think, that a satisfactory balance between the president and the Senate has so far been attained; indeed it is in a real sense difficult to state their relations in any precise way. For, in the first place, ever since the administration of Washington a controversy has been proceeding between them as to the exact degree of power each is entitled to exercise; and, in the second, the relation changes as the international situation contributes a different emphasis to

American history. Different presidents, moreover, have viewed their foreign problems quite differently, and this, also, has changed the emphasis. But whatever the international situation, and whoever has occupied the presidential office, it can, I think, be truly said that no legislative assembly in the world rivals the Senate of the United States in its influence in the international sphere.

The provisions of the Constitution give but a partial index to the nature of the relationship. The president, it lays down, "shall have power, by and with the consent of the Senate, to make treaties, provided two-thirds of the senators present concur."[1] Negotiation is the prerogative of the president; but the treaty is binding upon the citizens of the United States only with the consent of the Senate. There is a sense, also, in which the relation of the House of Representatives to a treaty is important; for no money can be raised to complete its implementation without the consent of that house. The declaration of war, moreover, is a joint act of both houses. The Senate, further, is directly concerned in foreign relations since it must confirm the appointment of all ambassadors and other diplomatic representatives. This is the formal framework of the structure as the founders of the Constitution defined it. I need not say that it supplies but a partial clue to the grasp of the whole network of relations that have been built upon it.

It may fairly be said that two substantial principles emerge upon which the whole presidential relation to

[1] Art. II, Sec. 2, clause 2.

foreign affairs has been built. The first cannot be better stated than in the classic words of Thomas Jefferson: "The transaction of business with foreign nations is executive altogether." This, as a general rule, has come to be the accepted practice of the United States. Apart from that process of approval and consent of which the Constitution speaks, whether in relation to instruments or persons, it is the president who decides what degree of consultation shall precede the formal submission of the result of his negotiations. From this wide freedom there follows, I think logically, the second principle that Congress, and above all the Senate, shall not be prejudiced constitutionally in the exercise of its powers in its own sphere, by what the president has done in his. No doubt, in fact, there is continuous reciprocity of influence. But that is not held to deter either authority from independent action in its allotted field.

This allocation of functions has, in fact, come to mean that the president has a decisive hand in the shaping of foreign affairs, even though the Congress, and especially, of course, the Senate, retains a negative voice. He is considerably dependent upon the secretary of state, whose department has grown from the four clerks, a French interpreter, and two messengers under Jefferson to some six hundred officials in Washington and some three thousand employed all over the world. But exactly as the prime minister of Great Britain has a specially close relation to, even supremacy over, the foreign secretary, so it has been the case, in general, for the president of the United States to

take the main hand in shaping at least the large outlines of foreign policy. Some presidents, indeed, like
Jefferson, Polk, Theodore Roosevelt, and Woodrow
Wilson, have been, to all intents and purposes, their
own secretaries of state; others, like Harding and
Coolidge, have left a large discretion to the State Department. Woodrow Wilson seems to have allowed
Mr. Bryan some elbowroom in the field of the latter's
special hobby of arbitration, while retaining a general
oversight of his work; and I suspect that this would
not be an unfair description of the relations between
Mr. Hull and President Franklin Roosevelt. Great
men, no doubt, whose collaboration it has not been
easy to subjugate, have presided over the State Department; five of them subsequently became presidents,
two chief justices, while three others, Clay, Webster and Calhoun, are among the outstanding figures
in American history. Nevertheless, one cannot read
the essential documents without the clear inference
that the overmastering impulses in foreign affairs derive from the presidential mind. An occasional president may be content to play a secondary role; but I
do not think this can be said of more than four presidents, and, with all but Grant, foreign affairs played
a comparatively minor part in his administration.
Whatever the degree of consultation with his colleagues, in the cabinet or in Congress, the president remains the chief architect in this field.

This can be seen if we consider briefly the range of
his initiative. It is for him to choose, and to dismiss,
his chief collaborators; the secretary of state who does

not agree with him must go. The ambassador with whom he is not satisfied may, like Mr. Page, remain in office; but it is a sufficient commentary upon his influence that, after Mr. Wilson's death, a great mass of Page's letters to him were discovered unopened. The president has unlimited discretion in the recognition of new governments. How powerful that influence has been in the recent history of Mexico it is unnecessary to emphasize. But it has had, also, an immense influence in the history of Europe; Franklin Roosevelt's recognition of the Soviet government, for example, may well prove to have been a real turning point in its history, as may his refusal so far[2] to recognize the Japanese conquest of Manchuria or the German absorption of Czecho-Slovakia. He has a wide and undefined authority to send special agents abroad; the part played by Colonel House in the European War of 1914-18 is only the supreme example of policies shaped and understandings secured by this means. He has an undefined power, further, to enter into compacts that are less than treaties without the participation of the Senate; the consequence of this power may be only slightly less than actual entrance into a treaty. He has the exclusive and unchallengeable right to negotiate treaties up to the point of their acceptance by the Senate; though here it should be added that history, especially the history of the Treaty of Versailles, makes the lesson clear that in treaty-making full consultation with at least the vital figures in the Senate Committee on Foreign Affairs is pivotal to the suc-

[2] August, 1939.

cessful conclusion of any treaty which arouses serious debate. He has a wide initiative in the official formulation of the national foreign policy; and though, no doubt, this is in some degree a hazardous political adventure, there is no field in which the president has so full an opportunity of giving a lead. No European, certainly, of my own generation is likely to forget how Woodrow Wilson, between 1917 and 1919, voiced in his public utterances the aspirations of the common people all over the world. The president, moreover, is the commander-in-chief of the armed forces of the United States. In that aspect, he may legitimately take action, as the history of Mexico bears ample witness, which leaves Congress no alternative but to follow the lead he has chosen to give.

I am summarizing too briefly a vast range of function. It must be understood that in each of its aspects, especially in a critical time, the whole world is watching with attention the direction a president may follow. There is no doubt, for example, that British policy in the Far East at the present moment is largely conditioned by the president's attitude to Japanese aggression in China. There is little doubt, either, that the Fascist powers had, for a long time, been largely deterred from risking a European war by fear that Mr. Roosevelt might persuade America to place at least its boundless material resources at the service of the democracies. The leadership provided by the president in foreign affairs is, without any doubt, the pivotal influence in framing foreign policy. Whatever part the Constitution may assign to the legislative

[171]

agency, the spirit of the presidential purpose, especially in a situation of gravity, is the overwhelming factor in forming the direction and the decision.

It is, of course, inevitable that it should be so. Whatever may have been the intention of the founders, the framing of foreign policy and its negotiation cannot be carried on by a numerous assembly. The interviews, the documentation, the understandings of personal intercourse all forbid it. Some degree of secrecy is inescapable in matters of international intercourse; anyone, for instance, can see that negotiations like those for an Anglo-Soviet pact could not be carried on to the accompaniment of full public discussion at each of its stages; a proposal of marriage must be made in private, even if the engagement is later discussed in public. That the balance of diplomatic power should, therefore, be in the president's hands, arises almost from the nature of things.

It is, of course, a limited power. The Senate has very fully maintained its right to confirm treaties, to reject them, or to amend them before offering its concurrence. The House of Representatives has always insisted upon its right to refuse appropriations which become necessary under ratified and confirmed treaties; though I believe it has never exercised that right. The Congress has insisted, as with the Russian Treaty of 1911, upon its power to abrogate treaties. Acts of Congress may also limit the presidential initiative; in 1939, for example, the area within which the president might maneuver was clearly limited by the implications of the Neutrality Act of 1937. In an extreme instance the fact that a declaration of war must be made by both houses of Congress is a safeguard against a supreme presidential indiscretion. Seward, for instance, was in favor of declaring war against France and Spain to cement the union; had he persuaded Lincoln to accept his view, the result might have been grave indeed. Against misjudgment of that kind, the congressional power is a check, even if its limits are obvious.

Taken as a whole, the record of American presidents in the making of foreign policy is a remarkable one. There have been, no doubt, the heavy sins of "dollar diplomacy"; this is not, however, a realm in which a European can afford to cast the first stone. There has been a good deal of brag and bluster, as with Polk over the Oregon boundary, with Cleveland over Venezuela, with the quite indefensible actions of Theodore Roosevelt in the diplomatic prelude to the building of the Panama Canal. If, indeed, there is a general case to be made against presidential leadership in foreign affairs, it is less upon the grounds of policy than upon the grounds of the defective organization he has built for informing himself about the affairs of foreign nations. In the post-Civil War period, American diplomatic representation in at least the major states has been the reward for standing in the party, often financial standing only, rather than for *expertise* in foreign affairs. A rich newspaper proprietor, the owner of a large department store, the husband of a great heiress to a fortune made in patent foods, have, to take stray examples, been accounted adequate holders of posts which, in most other countries, go only to men who have proved their fitness by long political or diplomatic experience. An embassy, perhaps, is less important in the days of the transatlantic telephone than it was when Jefferson and Monroe and Charles Francis Adams made the place of the United States so formidable in diplomatic discussion by their skill and force. This may explain the increasing tendency of the president to rely for the information he requires upon the special envoy, often appointed outside the categories which require senatorial confirmation, on the ground that he enjoys in a peculiar degree the private confidence of the president. But, for reasons I have already suggested, I think the development an unfortunate one. Its tendency is necessarily toward the choice of men whose contacts are not only interstitial, but who are almost bound, like Colonel House, to be "yes-men" for the president in order to retain their influence with him. They tend, therefore, as the *House Papers* make evident, to see mainly what the president wants them to see; and they lack that independence and responsibility which are the hallmarks of the expert diplomatist.

The record of the presidents, I have said, is on the whole remarkably good in foreign policy, and it is worth while speculating why this should have been the case. With the earlier presidents, it is easy to understand. From Washington to Monroe, every president, by the experience through which he had passed, had received a severe schooling in the technique of diplomatic intercourse. That was true, also, of John Quincy

Adams, whose claim to the authorship of the Monroe
Doctrine is no small one. From Jackson to the Civil
War, the main pressure of foreign policy is concerned with affairs within the American hemisphere—
Mexico, the Oregon boundary, and so on; in each of
these, either the power of the United States as against
any possible opponent was overwhelming, or, as with
the Oregon boundary question, it was dealing with an
antagonist who was always eager for an honorable
compromise. The Civil War, indeed, presented questions to the president of great delicacy and magnitude;
and there is no more remarkable proof of the inherent
and inescapable greatness of Lincoln than in the study
of his alterations of Seward's dispatches.[3] After Lincoln, there was no president until Cleveland with any
close grip on foreign affairs; Grant's handling of the
Santo Domingo problem is merely one of many proofs
of his unfitness for the presidential office. But from
Cleveland onward, it is, I think, true to say that only
Harding and Coolidge showed an ignorance of and unfitness for the control of foreign affairs; though in each
case those defects were merely particular instances of
a general incapacity. Theodore Roosevelt may have
had, to excess, the Palmerstonian truculence, and in
a less degree this is true of Cleveland also. But both
Woodrow Wilson and Franklin Roosevelt showed, in
this realm, a capacity to speak in world-terms which
has already given them a special place in history; while

[3] Mr. Justice Holmes, who as a young officer in the Civil War
knew Lincoln personally, was fond of telling how he first realized the
greatness of Lincoln by the study of these dispatches.

the limited opportunities Mr. Hoover had showed him, in this aspect, as a man capable of wide perspectives. American foreign policy is, by reason of the processes in which it is involved, a thing far more complex to make effectively than is the case in Europe. The grasp, therefore, which presidents have held upon it is all the more striking.

The reasons, I suggest, are complicated. In the first place, it is so because the president is not, as Lord Bryce thought, likely to be merely an "available" man. The capacities which make him president are likely, therefore, to be displayed in foreign affairs as in other realms. The remoteness, further, of America from Europe and the Far East gives him in relation to their problems a sense of poise which is less easily attainable by the statesmen of other powers. And it is important that in the United States, differently from in Europe, foreign affairs are party problems in a high degree. The president, therefore, who seeks success in this realm has to rely far more on public opinion than is the case elsewhere; and to rely upon it, he has to educate it. Anyone who watched the process by which Woodrow Wilson brought a united nation into the war of 1914-18, or who has scrutinized narrowly the effort of Franklin Roosevelt to persuade the American people into the acceptance of his views, will realize how large a part the factor of public opinion plays. It does so for another reason. America is an amalgam of the most diverse national strains. Each of them has not only its special views on foreign policy; more important, each of them is likely to have a spokesman in

Congress whose views will count. And what is true of national strains is true also, if in a lesser degree, of religious faiths. American policy to tsarist Russia was profoundly influenced by anti-Jewish pogroms there; Franklin Roosevelt, in his attitude to the Spanish Civil War of 1936-39 was deeply influenced, perhaps over-influenced, by the knowledge of an immense Roman Catholic population in the United States; Protestant missionary zeal has had a considerable effect on policy in Turkey and China. The delicacy involved in handling these interests has, almost of itself, been a training in diplomatic technique; and to this must be added the fact that a wise president learns from his dealings with Congress many of the qualities which are important in international intercourse.

Yet in the postwar years, I think the source of presidential authority has lain in two different directions. There can be little doubt, despite his defeat over the Peace of Versailles, that the emergence during the war of Woodrow Wilson as a world-figure equaled only by Lenin has given the American people an interest in foreign politics which provides the president with an audience for his ideas upon them greater than at any previous time. No one who saw the almost painful intensity with which every move of the Czech crisis in September, 1938, was followed throughout the United States can doubt that this is the case. And because there is this interest, the notion of the president as the leader of the nation has come to have a special relevance in foreign affairs. He is expected to play a big part there. The citizen looks to his pronouncements with exceptional anxiety. He has the sense, as never before, that America is a world-power, and that his president must play his part in a manner proportionate to the influence of the United States in world affairs. This attitude is new in its intensity; but its beginnings can be traced back to the presidency of Theodore Roosevelt. In the aftermath of the Spanish-American War, men began to realize that the part America was to play was different from anything that they had previously expected. They felt that a new epoch had arrived in their destiny. They had colonies; they were exporting capital; they had begun to have, as in China, spheres of special influence. There grew up in America even before the war the consciousness of a world-destiny; and this consciousness has been profoundly reflected in the attitude of the presidents.

I do not think this conclusion is vitiated by the fact that every president, in his endeavor, if he will, to play this world-part, is confronted by a profound isolationism which affects considerable areas of the country. We are told that the Middle West and the Far West are uninterested in European affairs; and we are bidden to remember that no president, as he frames a world-policy, can neglect the immense influence of, for example, German, Italian, and Irish settlers. I do not think he can neglect them; there is a real truth and significance in Henry Adams' picture of Senator Lodge scouring round Washington to do favors for Irish and Greek constituents.[4] But I think that their influence can easily be exaggerated. In the first place,

4 *The Education of Henry Adams* (1918), p. 419.

the experience of Woodrow Wilson suggests very clearly that great leadership in a president can always transcend the power of these elements in a great emergency. In the second place, the interest of the West in Far Eastern issues is profound; and these become daily more related, and are understood to be related, to European problems. The United States, moreover, is now, for good or ill, an exporting country in which the influence of international finance is fundamental; and this plays a part in pushing any president toward a leadership likely, I think, to grow more, and not less, significant. Nor must one forget that every national group which pushes him to isolationism is usually counterbalanced by another national group which is pushing him against it. In the result, I think he is bound to choose a position which gives his people as a whole the sense, not only that the United States has something important to say on world-problems, but that it has power enough behind what it says to compel the world to listen.

The president, in fact, shapes and voices the foreign policy of the United States to a degree that no other competing power can rival. The treaty-making power apart—I shall discuss this later—he is, subject to the influence of public opinion, incomparably the master of the field. His speeches have an influence that is supreme. His ambassadors act under his instructions. It is with him that foreign ministers must engage in the give-and-take of diplomatic intercourse. And we must never forget that he is the commander-in-chief of the armed forces of the United States. What this means the experience of the Central and South American republics has made constantly manifest. What it means, also, was shown by the decision of Franklin Roosevelt, in the spring of 1939, to concentrate the major American fleet in the Pacific; that has had a palpable influence at least upon the Japanese attitude to American interests in the Far East and possibly beyond that sphere. His ability to make "understandings" short of treaties counts for a good deal, as witness Theodore Roosevelt's relations with Japan and Panama and Santo Domingo. There is an immense authority latent in his power of recognition. I do not for a moment say that he has unlimited power; pretty clearly, he must keep in step with the predominant public opinion he encounters. But I do not think that anyone can survey the record of those presidents who have deliberately sought influence in foreign affairs, and deny that he has immense power to shape the public opinion he will encounter. That was true of Polk; it was true of Cleveland; it was true of Theodore Roosevelt and of Woodrow Wilson. I think it has been true, also, of Franklin Roosevelt.

For I do not think it would be easy to deny that, in the momentous years since 1933, the president's attitude to the dictator-powers has carried immense weight with his people. He has trained them to an expectancy that he will act; and they have been led to look to him for action. It has, no doubt, been true that he has not been able, as the debate over neutrality legislation has made clear, to persuade them as far as he himself would probably have wished. But what I think the historian will observe in the record is the fact that each of his initiatives in these years has widened the gulf between the support he can elicit and that gained by those in opposition to him. He may lose, as it were, particular battles; he retains, and is understood to retain, the power of the offensive in the campaign. Partly, that is the outcome of his persistence. He is at the task every day; the attention of his opponents is continually diverted by other interests. Partly, also, and very importantly, the play of the drama is on his side. He can see, as his opponents cannot see, several moves ahead in the maneuver for position. He has the papers; he engages in the conversations; he can strike at the moment when emotions grow hot. It is immensely important, as a psychological factor in the exercise of his potential power, that at each pivotal moment in the drama people ask: "What is the United States going to do?" And that is, in effect, to ask what the president is going to do. So long as this remains the case, he is bound, almost, to give some sort of lead. The authority at his disposal is immense and elastic. He is in the position in which his own people would, in these circumstances, feel that a refusal to play a part was not merely his personal abdication but that of the United States also. So that, in effect, its prestige is embodied in him. He can loose, and he can be sure that he can loose, the immense forces behind that prestige. He may, indeed, later on pay the price for loosing them, as Woodrow Wilson did over the rejection of the Peace of Versailles. And I do not for a moment deny that he courts defeat by the risks he has to take. My point is the different one that he is compelled by his position to take the risks, and that, if in his judgment it is wise to take them, it is improbable that anyone can say him nay. "The transaction of business with foreign powers," to repeat Jefferson's phrase, "is executive altogether." Because that is the case, all the fundamental relations in the building of foreign policy are in his hands. It is a field in which, in a vital sense, his discretions are acts upon which it is difficult to go back. In no other part of American political life has the separation of powers counted for so little as in the definition of this part.

2

This is a conclusion too rarely emphasized in the books. Attention, especially since the famous struggle over the Peace of Versailles, has been concentrated on the treaty-making power of the Senate; and the heaviest artillery that academic research could concentrate has been trained on the exercise of that power.[5] Critics have pointed out the scale upon which the

[5] The best general discussion is in Professor Lindsay Rogers' brilliant treatise, *The American Senate* (1926), pp. 84-87. For fuller and very important discussion see also G. H. Haynes, *The Senate of the United States* (1938), II, 569-720; R. J. Dangerfield, *In Defense of the Senate* (1933); W. Stull Holt, *Treaties Defeated by the Senate* (1933); D. F. Fleming, *The Treaty Veto of the American Senate* (1930). The early history in which the main procedural processes were established is admirably related by Ralston Hayden in *The Senate and Treaties 1789-1817* (1920). Senator Lodge's views are set out in an important essay in *A Fighting Frigate and Other Essays* (1902). The Department of State published in 1931 an invaluable *List of Treaties submitted to the Senate 1789-1931 which have not gone into force*. There is also an important discussion in E. S. Corwin, *The President's Control of Foreign Relations* (1917).

Senate has interfered with the foreign policy of the executive, not only by outright rejection of treaties, but by its exercise of the right to amend them after long and complicated negotiations, not least in the case of multilateral instruments. There has been vociferous complaint of long, and often vexatious, delay. It is argued that much of the senatorial action is the outcome, not of defects in the treaties themselves, but of causes wholly extraneous to them. Sometimes, Senate action has been traced to bitter and, it is argued, unjustifiable partisanship; the relation of Senator Lodge to President Wilson over the Versailles Treaty has been most often cited, in recent years, as the worst example of such partisanship. Sometimes it is traced to the determination of the Senate to enhance its prestige in foreign affairs, at the expense of the executive, and whatever may be the consequences of its action. Sometimes the relation is blamed on the fact that the necessity of a two-thirds majority of those voting is necessary for "approval and consent"; and it is argued that the result of this requirement is, in fact, to make a minority of the Senate the masters of the fate of a proposed treaty. It is urged that, not seldom, the senators are themselves far less well informed about the subject matter they decide than those whom they embarrass by their action; and they yield, it is said, to all kinds of pressure from interests—personal, national, economic—in reaching a decision.

The whole process is urged as unsatisfactory. It means that the president of the United States cannot submit a treaty to the Senate with the certainty either that, even if it is reasonable, it will be ratified at all, or that it will emerge, if approved, with amendments that are likely to be approved by the other contracting party involved. "The American Constitution," wrote Lord Grey, after his fruitless visit to the United States as ambassador in 1919,[6] "not only makes possible, but, under certain conditions, renders inevitable, a conflict between the executive and the legislature." "I have told you many times," wrote John Hay, in 1898,[7] "that I did not believe another important treaty would ever pass the Senate." It is even argued that the present status of the treaty-making power is a handicap to the influence of the United States in foreign affairs, by reason of the uncertainties it creates, and that the operation of the present mechanism has deprived her of great opportunities that would otherwise have been available.

The critics of the present system have, undoubtedly, a powerful case on their side. But, before we see what truth it contains, it is important to see that case in its proper perspective. The most careful estimate of the statistical aspect of the problem was made by the Department of State in 1935. Of 969 treaties submitted between 1789 and 1934, 682 have been accepted by the Senate; 173 have been amended; 15 have been rejected by it.[8] But, as Professor Dangerfield has shown,[9] of those so amended, the amendments in nearly 59 per cent were insignificant, and in 23 per

[6] London *Times*, January 31, 1920.
[7] W. R. Thayer, *Life of John Hay* (1912), II, 170.
[8] Haynes, *op. cit.*, II, 603.
[9] Dangerfield, *op. cit.*, p. 170.

cent were only moderate in character; vital amendments relate to 18 per cent of the treaties submitted for Senate approval. It is worth noting that, of the treaties submitted, fewer were rejected than the number (53) which, after unconditional approval by the Senate, were never proclaimed by the president.[10] Over 80 per cent of the treaties submitted were ratified within three months, and over 92 per cent were ratified within seven months. Only forty treaties remained without action by the Senate for a period of over a year.[11]

Certain other considerations are important. Many of the proposed extradition treaties, for example, have been amended by the Senate in the light of its persistent refusal to allow extradition to a foreign country for political offenses; in the light of the history of the national composition of the United States, that is a wholly defensible outlook. The famous delay of twenty-one years in the approval of the well-known Isle of Pines Treaty was due to the strong opposition to it of thousands of American citizens who had, under dubious circumstances, been induced to buy land there in the belief that the island would remain under the American flag.[12] Some delay is attributable to the fact that no member of the Senate was particularly interested in securing approval. There are important cases where the president was of one political complexion and the Senate of another. There are

[10] Dangerfield, *op. cit.,* p. 91.
[11] Dangerfield, *op. cit.,* p. 94.
[12] Dangerfield, *op. cit.,* Chap. V.

important cases, the arbitration treaties, for example, where the subject matter was complex and the existence of widely divergent views about the wisdom of approval easily intelligible. There are cases where the maladroit handling by the secretary of state—John Hay is a notable example of this maladroitness—was pivotal in the Senate's attitude. There are cases, further, in which the importance of the subject matter wholly justified either the most scrupulous examination, and therefore delay, and, because of genuine differences about the wisdom of the treaty in the form presented, rejection, or approval only after what Professor Dangerfield calls "vital" reservations. Nor can it be denied that, in many cases, consideration by the Senate has forced the president to further negotiations with the other contracting parties which have resulted in what, from an American angle, is a much more advantageous treaty. And it is at least possible to sympathize with Senator Lodge's insistence that to accept the general arbitration treaties which Mr. Hay had negotiated would have taken from the Senate a power of approval which, rightly or wrongly, was conferred upon it by the Constitution.[13]

It is not, I think, a very powerful argument against the Senate's present power to say that it leaves foreign states in some uncertainty about the outcome of negotiations. It is the business of a foreign state to know the implications of the American Constitution; that is, so to say, a condition precedent to any negotia-

[13] Cf. Haynes, *op. cit.*, p. 616, and the important quotation from the report of the Committee on Foreign Relations in 1911.

tion with the United States. The statistical evidence, moreover, shows that the overwhelming bulk of treaties emerged either wholly unscathed from the ordeal of senatorial examination, or only partially scathed. And it is notable that, Russia apart, "the Senate delays less on those treaties signed with countries with which our diplomatic intercourse is most frequent."[14] For France, Germany, Italy, Great Britain, and Japan, the average is just under eight weeks—not, I think, an excessive period for the detailed examination of the outcome of what is usually prolonged diplomatic interchange.

I am not for a moment denying the force of certain criticisms I propose to consider later. Here I am concerned to note only that those who have attacked the Senate have rarely built their argument on all the facts involved. And account must be taken of the position occupied by the Senate in the constitutional structure of the United States. Rightly or wrongly, the founders associated the Senate with the process of treaty ratification. Whether, as Pierce Butler said,[15] it was their intention that the president should consult the Senate throughout the process of negotiation, it is no longer possible to say. History, in the first instance, and the size of the modern Senate in the second, have made that directness of relation impracticable; it is certainly true that the modern president clings strongly to his prerogative of being the sole effective agent in negotiation. He may consult informally with

[14] Dangerfield, *op. cit.*, p. 102.
[15] Cf. Dangerfield, *op. cit.*, p. 33.

a selected group of senators, especially with the members of the Foreign Relations Committee. He may appoint one or more senators as members of a negotiating commission. He has the means of associating Congress at an early stage with any policy of treaty-making upon which he proposes to embark; as when he asks for an appropriation to meet the expenses of a possible commission and thus obtains implicit approval for the line of action involved. But it is broadly true to say that, in the vast majority of instances, the actual process of negotiation is so wholly executive in character that the Senate is unaware of the results, except in a general way, until the treaty is actually in its hands for consideration.

On any showing, the right of the Senate to examine fully and independently any treaty that comes before it is beyond question. It takes that function seriously; and none of its critics, I presume, would wish this to be otherwise. The real problem lies in the cumbersome nature of the machinery involved, on the one hand; and on the other, in the fact that the very idea of the separation of powers leads each party to the treaty-making process to seek to exalt its own role. This, I think, emerges most fully in the struggle between President Wilson and the Senate over the approval of the Peace of Versailles. It was arrogant folly on the president's part to make the kind of party appeal he did for a Congress that would enable him to make his own kind of peace. It was at least unwise of him to refuse to associate any members of the Senate with the American delegation to the Peace Conference. It was still more unwise to boast that he had made the kind of treaty which made acceptance of American association with the League of Nations inevitable of Senate acceptance. In short, the whole tragic history of the Versailles Treaty was, in the context of the record of the treaty-making power, nothing so much as a wanton defiance of the Senate by the president which, in the light of the fact that he had lost his majority there, was certain to be met with equal defiance.[16] That Senator Lodge, the leader of the opposition to Mr. Wilson in the Senate, was moved by the meanest personal considerations in the excesses to which he allowed himself to go is, of course, made plain by the amazing letter to Mr. Henry White he allowed himself to write even before the Peace Conference began to sit.[17] But, unjustifiable as was the partisanship he displayed, it is, I suggest, undeniable that there was bitter partisanship, also, on the president's side.

The truth is that the treaty-making power displays the whole American scheme of government at its worst. It multiplies all the difficulties that are inherent in the separation of powers. It provides a channel for institutional expression to every form of personal and political antagonism that has developed during the president's term of office. It heightens the natural tendency of every legislature to expand its power at the expense of the executive. None of the expedients that have been suggested for mitigating its acerbities

[16] Cf. Holt, *op. cit.*, pp. 249-308.
[17] Allan Nevins, *Henry White* (1930), pp. 353-354.

has proved satisfactory. Eleven presidents, for instance, have sought to safeguard themselves from rebuff by asking senatorial advice upon the desirability of entering upon a proposed negotiation.[18] That has had general helpfulness; but it still leaves open the fact that a proposal to negotiate upon a subject is very different from a judgment upon the result of a negotiation. Other presidents have tried to assist themselves either by the means of appointing the proposed agents of negotiation, or by influencing the Senate through appointing its own members as part of the negotiating commission. There is no doubt that this has helped, both to secure approval, and to abridge the delay in securing approval. But it has not solved the central problem. It has avoided the kind of difficulty created by the appointment of executive agents in treaty-making without senatorial consent;[19] but it has not touched the real issue of the substance of the treaty made and the Senate's duty in relation to it.

That central problem has been put in classic terms by Mr. Justice Davis. "In this country," he said,[20] "a treaty is something more than a contract, for the Federal Constitution declares it to be the law of the land. If so, before it can become a law, the Senate in whom rests the power to ratify it, must agree to it. But the Senate are not required to adopt or reject it as

[18] Haynes, *op. cit.*, p. 590.
[19] For a good discussion of these difficulties see Professor H. M. Wriston's admirable book, *Executive Agents in American Foreign Relations* (1929), esp. pp. 237-258, and 292-308.
[20] *Haver v. Yaker* (1869) 9 Wall. 32.

a whole, but may modify it or amend it." There are
certain clear advantages in the position. It prevents
the legislature from occupying that tragically subordinate position which the House of Commons has come
to occupy in foreign affairs. It is a safeguard against
the kind of secret diplomacy which characterized
Lord Salisbury's bargain with Germany over the Por-
tuguese colonies in Africa, or those of Sir Edward
Grey with tsarist Russia over Iran; it is, I think, all to
the good that one president cannot bind his successor
by the methods of secret diplomacy. It insures a full
public discussion of any proposed treaty independently of those who have negotiated it. The very fact,
moreover, of the need for the Senate's approval compels the president, in every important instance, to elicit
a public opinion upon the desirability of his policy;
from this angle, it may be said that the debates in
the Senate over the Peace of Versailles probably had
an enormous effect in awakening the people of the
United States to their responsibilities as a world-
power. Lord Harrowby's famous protest that "His
Majesty's Government can never acquiesce in the
precedent . . . the American government has attempted to establish, of agreeing to ratify such parts
of a convention as they may select, and of rejecting
other stipulations of it, formally agreed upon by a
minister invested with full powers for that purpose,"[21]
seems to me to fail because it refuses to realize that
it is the precise object of the American Constitution

---

[21] Hayden, *op. cit.*, pp. 150-152; and see his quotation of Monroe's
instructions to the American minister in Sweden in 1816, pp. 208-215.

to prevent a minister from being invested with "full powers" in the sense in which a system like the British understands that term. This has been well put by Senator Lodge. "A British secretary of state for foreign affairs," he wrote,[22] ". . . ought to realize that the Senate can only present its views to a foreign government by formulating them in the shape of amendments which a foreign government may accept, or reject, or meet with counter-propositions, but of which it has no more right to complain than it has to the offer of any germane proposition at any other stage of the negotiation."

In his *Life* of Woodrow Wilson, Mr. Ray Stannard Baker put the case against the present system with exceptional force. "It has been made impossible for America," he wrote,[23] "to speak with a bold and united voice. Nearly every important treaty the country has been called upon to make has become a bone of contention between the executive and the Senate. It is certain that in the years to come, if we are to go forward in the new paths and stand for a clear-cut world policy, we must devise some method of speaking to the world promptly, and with an undivided voice. Our present system leads to utter weakness, muddle and delay; it forces both sides to play politics, and instead of meeting the issue squarely, to indulge in a vast controversy over the prerogatives of two co-ordinate branches of the government. The deadlock between the executive and the Senate every

[22] *A Fighting Frigate* (1902), p. 224.
[23] *Woodrow Wilson and the World Settlement* (1922), I, 316.

time we face a really critical foreign problem is intolerable. It not only disgraces us before the nations, but in some future world-crisis may ruin us."

These are strong words; and it is worth while, I think, to examine them with some particularity. Mr. Baker, of course, was writing as the official exponent of Woodrow Wilson's policy, and some allowance must be made for his natural indignation at its rejection by the Senate. Broadly, it cannot seriously be said that, on most major matters, the policy of the United States has lacked a sufficient power to make itself felt in the politics of world-power. It has applied the Monroe Doctrine with irresistible force in the American hemisphere. Its policy of the "open door" has been a dominating consideration in the politics of all other powers in the Far East. Its impact on Europe, as the War of 1914 and its aftermath made clear, has been continuously profound; no small part, particularly, of British foreign policy has been motivated by the determination of successive prime ministers to keep in step with American purposes, and any failure to do so, as the Manchurian affair of 1931-32 made clear, has led to bitter criticism from the opposition. Nor do I think that anyone who examines the record since Grover Cleveland can doubt that, in general, the United States has been able to make its purposes known both "promptly" and with no more undivided power than any country built upon a system of representative government. There is lacking, it is true, the swiftness and unity of the dictatorial powers; but that is precisely because states built upon the principles of representative government must take account of the reactions of public opinion before their executives act. And Mr. Baker, I assume, would not have it otherwise.

The real pith of his attack lies in his assertion that treaty-making as such invites a controversy between the executive and the legislature. There is substance in this contention, though it must be noted that the invitation is not confined to the treaty-making power only but extends over the whole area of American government. Mr. Baker's argument is really a plea that the Senate should accept a position of inferiority in relation to the president. Upon this view there are two things to be said. First, that the Constitution deliberately provides for equality, and it would, therefore, require a constitutional amendment to attain that end, an amendment unlikely to be secured except after a formidable struggle; and second, that it is asking too much of any legislature to abdicate voluntarily from the exercise of powers upon which a considerable part of its prestige depends. It is worth remembering, moreover, that the Senate has not seldom been as right as the president in its interpretation of what public opinion demanded. Certainly its view of Grant's proposal to take over Santo Domingo, its refusal to accept, in 1868, the purchase of the Danish West Indies, and even its rejection of the Peace of Versailles, may be said to have been in public accord with the sentiment of the time.

Mr. Baker cannot argue that a treaty ought to be confirmed merely because the president has approved

it; presidents have themselves often decided to withdraw treaties that have been proclaimed. It is, too,
worth noting that the power of making executive
agreements not of treaty status—of which the reciprocal agreements of 1882 and 1896 with Mexico are examples[24]—gives any president a wide discretion of
which full advantage has been taken. In a generation,
for example, twenty agreements settling claims of
American citizens for injuries to their property were
made executively, without reference to the approval
of the Senate.[25] The Boxer Protocol of 1901 was so
arranged; as was the well-known exchange of notes
between Mr. Root, as secretary of state, and Baron
Takahira, in 1908; so, despite the discussions it provoked, was the Lansing-Ishii agreement of 1917. None
of these was submitted to the Senate.

Frequently, also, despite Senate hostility, the president has acted as though an agreement had been
made, in matters of grave moment, which was likely
to become a treaty. Theodore Roosevelt has given a
remarkable account in his *Autobiography* of one instance of this attitude on the part of the president.
Speaking of the proposed treaty of 1905 for "the
adjustment of all the Dominican debts, foreign and
domestic," he describes how "I went ahead and administered the proposed treaty anyhow, considering
it as a simple agreement on the part of the executive
which would be converted into a treaty whenever the

[24] Cf. Quincy Wright, *The Control of American Foreign Relations*
(1922), p. 242. As Professor Wright points out, this power has been
amply confirmed by decisions of the Supreme Court.
[25] Haynes, *op. cit.*, p. 643.

Senate acted. After a couple of years, the Senate did act, having previously made some utterly unimportant changes which I ratified and persuaded Santo Domingo to ratify. . . . The Constitution did not explicitly give me power to bring about the necessary agreement with Santo Domingo. But the Constitution did not forbid what I did. I put the agreement into effect, and I continued its execution for two years before the Senate acted, and I would have continued it until the end of my term, if necessary, without any action of Congress."[26] President Tyler acted in a somewhat similar way over the proposed annexation of Texas; and in this case the Senate actually rejected his proposed treaty.[27] "It is evident," as Senator Rayner said in the debate over Mr. Roosevelt's action in Santo Domingo,[28] "that the president under his unquestioned authority to make executive agreements, might go to great lengths, and make arrangements with a foreign power far more serious in character than are often stipulated by formal treaty." He can, in fact, whether by executive agreement or as commander-in-chief, virtually commit the United States to war; and his power to influence congressional action in this regard may easily reduce it to the shadow of its intended substance.

On the evidence, in short, it is ludicrous to represent the president as an embarrassed phantom in the realm of foreign affairs. Roughly, he may be said to be just as strong as the public opinion he is able to

[26] *Autobiography* (1919), pp. 551-552.
[27] *Messages of the Presidents*, IV, 317-318.
[28] Jan. 23, 1906. *Cong. Record*, XL, 1423-1424.

elicit for his policies. The complaints of the critics are, I suggest, largely misplaced, except upon the assumption that the treaty-making power is to be differently exercised than any other part of the Senate's prerogatives. It is important, further, in any assessment of the exercise of this power to remember not only that foreign affairs are more complicated in the twentieth century than they were in the nineteenth, but that the need for popular control in foreign affairs was intended to be one of the features which distinguished the American from other constitutions. It has to be remembered that most of the really important treaties which have been either modified or defeated raised issues of great significance upon which real differences of opinion were, to say the least, permissible. On the arbitration treaties, for example, the Senate's attitude has been shared by important interests in Great Britain; it is notable that the Labor government of Great Britain, in adhering to the optional clause, only did so with far-reaching reservations which deprived the adherence of a good deal of its value; and this was true, also, of British adherence to the Kellogg-Briand pact.

The real target of criticism has been the two-thirds rule. "The irreparable mistake of our Constitution," wrote John Hay,[29] "puts it into the power of one-third + 1 of the Senate to meet with a categorical veto any treaty negotiated by the president, even though it may have the approval of nine-tenths of the people of the nation." There is great weight in this

[29] Letter of August 18, 1899. Thayer, *op. cit.*, II, 219.

view. It helps enormously any group of senators, even an individual, hostile to some treaty upon grounds quite irrelevant to its substance, to organize opposition to it with some hope that it may be successful. This senator is opposed to the treaty because he dislikes the state with which it is being made; that senator hopes, by his opposition, to please a strong religious or national element in his constituency; another may feel that opposition involves the duty of preventing any success being accredited to the president of the other party; another, again, may be on bad terms with the president of his own party and use this means of expressing the fact. Yet even this criticism may be pushed too far. The subject matter of most treaties does not easily lead to popularity for the senator opposing it; except upon the largest issues it is doubtful whether such opposition arouses any widespread interest at all. I doubt, for instance, whether there is any evidence that a senator's attitude on the convention of 1883 (which was rejected for lack of a two-thirds majority) with Mexico for the retrying of claims created any strong feeling about him among the people of the United States. And it has been shown that of all the treaties submitted to the Senate, none failed of approval because of the two-thirds vote before 1860, and only twelve between that date and 1935.[30] Of the twelve it is difficult, says Professor Fleming, to regard more than two of serious importance, even though he thinks that the passage of the

[30] Haynes, *op. cit.*, II, 659.

others "would have notably improved our relations with a foreign state."[31]

The case against the two-thirds rule is, however, a substantial one on another ground. It is important because of what may be termed its prenatal effects. The knowledge that a little bloc of recalcitrant senators may hold up or modify a wise proposal has adverse effect both upon the prospect of embarking upon it and upon the process of negotiation itself. This has been well put by Mr. De Witt Clinton Poole, himself an American diplomat of long experience. "The record," he writes,[32] "does not show from what wise measures the president or his secretary has been estopped by perhaps unfounded fear of what a few senators may do, nor is it demonstrable into what brusque and harmful actions the spectre on Capitol Hill has frightened them. In the light of my own reading and my own experience in Washington, I am confident that both misfortunes have frequently befallen." No one, I think, can read the correspondence and diaries of presidents and secretaries of state without the sense that this is largely true. Anyone who reads, to take the supreme instance only, the detailed story of President Wilson's negotiations at Versailles can hardly avoid the conclusion that at each stage of his activities the shadow of Senator Lodge dogged his footsteps like an evil fate, and was not without responsibility for many of Wilson's blunders both before and after the treaty was made.

[31] *The Treaty Veto of the American Senate*, p. 304.
[32] Haynes, *op. cit.*, p. 661.

The case, therefore, for a revision of the two-thirds rule is, I think, a clear one. Before we consider possible alternatives, however, there is one general remark that it is worth while to make. No critic of the present form of the treaty-making power suggests its confinement to the hand of the executive alone. In the light both of American and of foreign experience I think this is wise. A self-willed president of dominant personality, Tyler, for instance, or Polk, or Theodore Roosevelt, or Woodrow Wilson, might easily have taken the United States into dubious foreign adventures for which public opinion was unprepared, for which, also, there would have been little justification, had it not been for the knowledge that the Senate would ultimately review the results of their activities. "The spectre on Capitol Hill" may have frightened them into many "brusque and harmful actions"; it is, I think, equally unquestionable that it has frightened them out of many they might otherwise have attempted. A president eager for imperialist adventure, or concerned to exercise influence in Europe in a particular direction, might easily, in the absence of Senate control, be a source of grave danger to the American people. And this view is, I suggest, reinforced by experience of systems like that of Great Britain where the control of foreign affairs is, in fact, "executive altogether." For the only real control of the House of Commons is of a *post-mortem* nature. It is presented by the cabinet with a *fait accompli*, rejection of which involves the defeat of the government and a subsequent general election.

There is no instance in modern times where the government has had an assured majority, upon which its supporters have been willing to take that risk. The result is that the executive in Great Britain has a primacy in foreign affairs so assured that, save where a leakage gives public opinion—as in the Hoare-Laval incident—an unexpected knowledge of events, it has little reason to trouble itself about the impact of foreign affairs upon the House of Commons. The only real limit to its powers is the decision exercised by the voters at a subsequent general election; and that decision, as in the case of the doctrine of nonintervention in Spain, or the sacrifice of Czecho-Slovakia at Munich in 1938, may come too late to affect the results of the government's policy.

What, therefore, is in dispute in the United States is not the desirability of legislative control which, in some form, is conceded by all the critics; it is the narrower question of the method by which that legislative control should be secured. Some suggest that a simple majority of the Senate should suffice for the confirmation of a treaty; others suggest that the House of Representatives should be joined with the treaty-making power and that, as with a declaration of war, a majority in both houses should suffice for confirmation. This, it is interesting to note, was the method proposed by James Wilson in the constitutional convention, though only Pennsylvania voted for its adoption there; and it has recently been approved by an eminent Democratic candidate for the presidency, who has also had ambassadorial experience, Mr. John W. Davis.[33] It has been suggested that, for the purpose of confirmation, both houses might meet as a single assembly; and Mr. S. W. McCall, at one time a well-known congressman, has urged that the treaty-making power should be transferred wholly to the House of Representatives on the ground that its frequency of re-election brings it nearer than the Senate can ever hope to be to whatever public opinion is upon issues of foreign policy.[34] Professor Dangerfield, at the close of his illuminating and elaborate examination of the treaty-making powers, will have none of these proposals. He suggests the creation of a special Foreign Relations Cabinet to consist of "the secretary of state, the under-secretary of state, a senior drafting officer, the chairman and the ranking minority members of the Senate Committee on Foreign Relations and the House Committee on Foreign Affairs." " Such a cabinet," he writes,[35] "would combine the experts of the Department, and the political leaders of both houses who deal with foreign affairs."

Of these proposals, the most logical is obviously the transference of the treaty-making power to a majority of both houses of Congress. This homologates the peace-making control of foreign policy with that involved in the making of war; and it has the further advantage, which is important, of associating with

[33] Haynes, *op. cit.*, p. 661. Mr. W. J. Bryan and Colonel House were also in favor of this method.

[34] *Atlantic Monthly* (Sept. 1920), p. 395. I have been unable to find any other supporter of Mr. McCall's proposal.

[35] Dangerfield, *op. cit.*, p. 321. Professor Dangerfield points out that this proposal was first made by Professor Quincy Wright in his *Control of Foreign Relations*, p. 371.

treaty-making that branch of the legislature which has to implement any appropriations necessary for treaty fulfilment. I do not think it is a serious objection that the House is now a large body; the Senate itself has never been small enough to act as a presidential council. It is, of course, a difficulty that the House may be of a different political complexion from that of the Senate, and that this may, in important instances, lead to a deadlock; but since the same situation already exists as between the Senate and the president, I do not think this can be regarded as an insuperable objection. It may be, as Mr. Hayden has noted,[36] that the method "abandons all attempt at secrecy, and would subject the treaty to amendment or reservation by both branches of Congress, with adjustments by compromise in conference committee." But this, in any case, is an experience with which the president is familiar, and it raises no obstacle that is not inherent in the ordinary legislative process of the United States. It is a better proposal, I think, than that of simply abolishing the two-thirds rule in the Senate for several reasons. Both houses are concerned in foreign affairs; it is therefore appropriate that both should have an equal relevance to them. And where a bicameral system based on popular election exists, it is illogical to exclude one chamber from direct concern with a fundamental branch of policy. The proximity, moreover, of the House of Representatives to election would render it valuably accessible to public

[36] Hayden, *op. cit.*, II, 661.

opinion in those issues upon which—they are rare—a strong public opinion can be formed.

I do not think there is much to be said for Professor Dangerfield's scheme. It divides executive authority and responsibility where it is least desirable to divide it—at the place where initiative must be taken and the process of negotiation begun. It jeopardizes secrecy and dispatch, especially in those periods where Congress is not in session. It raises grave difficulties for the president in every instance where the Congress, or one house of it, happens not to be of his political complexion. It would make his own relations to his secretary of state no easy matter; and it might easily divide the latter's allegiance between the president and the two chairmen, as well as the ranking minority members, of the respective congressional committees. It is, no doubt, true that where the Congress members of such a cabinet supported the treaty, they would be able to recommend it in Congress with more *expertise* than at present; but it is, on the other hand, also obvious that, where they opposed it, the passage of the treaty would thereby be rendered more difficult. The evidence Professor Dangerfield has himself so illuminatingly collected suggests that, though the strong support of the chairman of the Foreign Relations Committee of the Senate may be helpful in securing the rapid consideration of a treaty, it is very far from being decisive where confirmation is concerned. Most of the advantages urged by Professor Dangerfield for his proposal are already open to the president in other ways; and one who, like McKinley, has shown that he is skilful in handling the Senate, can obviously take full advantage of them. The dangers of the proposal seem to me to outweigh its advantages. It multiplies the present prospect of legislative encroachment upon the president's power, especially in the twilight zone of executive agreements and in that complicated area involved in his functions as commander-in-chief. It hampers his initiative, especially where he is dealing with a Congress dominated by the opposition party. It offers, also, it is worth adding, manifold opportunities for the kind of action Senator Lodge thought fit to make in the prelude to the Peace Conference of Versailles.

A foreigner may consider the alternatives; it is, happily, an American task to decide between them. I am satisfied to point out that, in my own judgment, the case against the Senate has been enormously overestimated. I do not for a moment deny that an inherent jealousy of the executive, purely partisan objections, and even personal spite, have entered into the senatorial exercise of its power. Weighing all these, I still think that, somewhere in the legislature of the United States, a power of this kind should, in the face of all its difficulties, be lodged. Despite its extent, the authority of the president in foreign affairs remains immense; he is, on any showing, the motive-power of the whole system. It has one great result which is not attained in anything like a proportionate degree in other systems, and, most notably, not attained in the British system: it enforces upon the president the obligation to give reasons for what he is doing. He is compelled to educate public opinion; he cannot drive it. There is the assurance—of immense importance in representative government—that the case against what he is doing will not only be fully stated, but that, at each stage of his activities, he will be forced to take account of that case. Not seldom, in the conflicts that have arisen, the Senate has been perverse and mistaken; but, not seldom also, the president has been perverse and mistaken too. The system leaves room, as room should be left, for wide presidential initiative; but, very wisely I think, it makes the success of that initiative largely dependent upon the power of the president to maintain his hold upon public opinion. In a democracy, I think it is right that this should be the case. An Englishman, to take a concrete case, may well regret, in the light of its aftermath, the Senate's rejection of the Peace of Versailles. But anyone who compares the process of its ratification in the Senate, on the one hand, and in the House of Commons, on the other, can hardly help concluding that, if there is to be democracy in foreign affairs, the principle which underlies the American system is by far superior to the principle which underlies the British. I cannot, further, avoid the opinion that the large superiority in the reporting of foreign news in the American press, as compared with the British, is not unconnected with the fact that the basic principle of control is in the one case democratic, while in the other it is aristocratic. It is not insignificant, in the postwar years, that much discussion has been devoted in Great Britain to the problem of democratizing the control of foreign policy. I would not, for a moment, say that the problem has been solved in the United States. But it is, I think, beyond doubt that the American safeguards against executive unwisdom —I use a neutral word—are an improvement of profound importance upon anything that Europe has so far evolved.

3

I turn to a very different, if connected, aspect of the president's relation with the Senate. That body shares with him the nominating power. He has the sole right to submit names for its approbation; but the Senate is wholly free to confirm or to reject the choice he makes. The idea of the founders was, no doubt, to prevent the president from building up an unbreakable executive power. It was assumed that the merit of the proposed appointee would be the one issue with which the Senate would concern itself. "It could hardly happen," wrote Alexander Hamilton,[37] "that the majority of the Senate would feel any other complacency towards the object of an appointment than such as the appearances of merit might inspire, and the proofs of the want of it destroy."

Rarely has the failure of a prophecy by a great man been more complete. From the beginning of Washington's administration, the Senate's share in the power of appointment has been, in its essence, exercised in

[37] *The Federalist*, No. 66.

part for party purposes, and in part on personal grounds. The senatorial veto on appointments begins with the foundation of the republic, and by the time, at any rate, of Andrew Jackson the system so gracefully called "senatorial courtesy" was well established. It has been happily defined by Professor Lindsay Rogers. "Senatorial courtesy," he writes,[38] "is a kind of 'liberum veto,' and means no more than this: that while the Senate will not suggest particular nominations, it expects that the president, in naming certain local office-holders (e.g., postmasters and collectors of the customs), will choose persons satisfactory to the senator or senators of the president's political party from the state in which the offices are located, or from which the appointees come. 'The strength of the pack is the wolf, and the strength of the wolf is the pack'; consequently, if senators are ignored, or if their objections are flouted, the Senate in most cases will not approve the nominations. It is difficult to speak with decision about a scheme of appointment the range of which is constantly changing. But it is not, I think, an exaggeration to say that, nowadays, the Senate has a contingent veto power over something like 18,000 appointments."

Some of them it will usually accept without question. It is customary to agree to the president's choice of his cabinet; though this has not always been the case. Madison was compelled to withdraw the name of Gallatin for the post of secretary of state merely because Senator Smith had a brother for whom he

[38] Lindsay Rogers, *The American Senate* (1926), p. 25.

coveted the place;[39] and I have already referred to the rejection of Mr. Coolidge's nomination—on quite intelligible grounds—of Charles B. Warren as his attorney-general. But, as a rule, the Senate realizes that where cabinet posts are in question it is desirable for the president to have his own way; after all, he knows best the team with which he can live. Much the same is true of ambassadors, though even here objection has been taken to appointments in an indefensible way; the rejection of Gallatin as ambassador to Russia, of Van Buren, who resigned the secretaryship of state to go to London, of Norman Hapgood, who had been nominated to Denmark by President Wilson, are all cases of this kind. Yet, again, proportionately speaking the Senate has not been too ungenerous, perhaps on occasion even excessively gracious, to presidential nominations to diplomatic posts.

It is in the other realms of appointment that the exercise of this power is seen at its worst. It has both a negative and a positive side. On the negative side, the worst type of rejection is that in which a senator bases his opposition merely on the ground that the proposed appointee is "personally obnoxious" to him. Senator Gallinger, of New Hampshire, after a struggle lasting over two years, prevented the nomination of a distinguished lawyer, Mr. George Rublee, to the Federal Trade Commission solely on this basis.[40] Senator Hoar has given us an account of a nomination

[39] Henry Adams, *The Life of Albert Gallatin* (1879), p. 391.
[40] Cf. *New Republic*, May 20, 1916.

by President Grant made under circumstances so dubious that it may well have been the cause of Grant's failure to secure a third term.[41] The famous struggle over the collectorship of the Port of New York between Garfield and Roscoe Conkling is well known. And we have been told by Polk of the amazing nonchalance with which senatorial recommendations are too often made to the president, which he has rarely any alternative but to accept. The power is exercised ruthlessly right up to nominations for the Supreme Court. Between 1789 and 1938 the Senate has been responsible for the withdrawal of 21 nominations out of 109 submitted to it—practically 20 per cent.[42]

It is impossible, of course, to doubt that there have been occasions when the power of veto has been wisely used. Bad presidential nominations are not, alas, rare; and Senate debates like those on the appointment of Mr. Hughes as chief justice of the United States—he was confirmed by 52 votes to 26— or that as a result of which the nomination of Judge Parker to the Court was rejected, serve a useful purpose in reminding the president of the importance of remembering the qualities for which he ought to look in an appointee to the bench. But, frankly, it is the exception rather than the rule for the Senate, even in the case of the Supreme Court, to make an impersonal assessment of qualifications. The important things are the purchase of support by the presi-

[41] Hoar, *op. cit.*, I, 212.
[42] Warren, *The Supreme Court in United States History* (1922), Vol. III, Appendix.

dent from among his own party, and the effort of the
senator to see that his relation to the distribution of
patronage is effective in consolidating his own position in the political life of the state. The misery
through which a president must pass in effecting that
distribution must be seen to be believed. He may,
like Theodore Roosevelt, take high ground about the
standards he proposes to maintain;[43] experience of the
actual operation of the power will rapidly bring him
down to lower levels.

I do not myself think that the problem the issue
presents is at all an easy one. There can be no sort
of doubt but that the Senate, especially in relation to
the practice of "courtesy" has gravely abused its
power. But there can be little doubt that, left unim-
peded by the prospect of a senatorial veto, the president's abuse of his patronage would be equally grave.
As the system stands at present, it is, I think, fair
to say that public opinion will compel some real degree of judicial-mindedness in the case of appointments to the Supreme Court and certain commissions
like that on interstate commerce and the tariff; this is
not necessarily the case, but there is at least a probability that it will be so because there is likely to be a
special public interested in, and watchful of, the
quality and fitness of the men who are chosen to fill
them. Once, however, we leave those posts on which
the eyes of the nation are fixed, the whole patronage
system is bedeviled by mean and sordid interests com-

[43] J. B. Bishop, *Theodore Roosevelt* (1920), I, 157, and cf. pp. 235,
248, 442.

peting for the party and personal advantages that can be secured by its exercise.

The obvious thing for an Englishman to say is that before the reforms of 1870 the patronage system in Great Britain was also mean and sordid; that, with the coming of the merit system, a wholly different character has been given to political appointments, and that the United States can end this problem by the simple method of replacing the spoils system by the merit system. I do not think the problem is as simple as this suggests. Political parties are real and obstinate things which have to be kept alive. In Great Britain we have largely—not wholly—removed the virus of patronage from the world of the civil service. But we have replaced it, so far as rewarding political service is concerned, by an immense extension of the system of political "honors," in which even appointment to the office of justice of the peace has become, in the overwhelming number of cases, a reward for party service. To some extent this is true, also, of appointments to the High Court;[44] and it obtains in relation to a small, but important, number of colonial governorships. And hardly a royal commission is nominated but some of the appointments to which are explicable only by the desire of the prime minister or his cabinet colleague to reward a political friend. With the growth, too, of public corporations like the British Broadcasting Corporation and the London Passenger Transport Board, there has been, in recent years, a significant increase in the paid patronage at the government's dis-

[44] Cf. my *Studies in Law and Politics* (1932), Chap. 7.

posal; and it is well known that directorships on the board of the Suez Canal Company—as well paid a sinecure as there is in the disposal of the British government—have always been used to reward the higher forms of political service.

Nominations to a title, of course, are not open to the president by the fiat of the Constitution; and a political party without this source of reward would find itself in a difficult position. There can be no doubt that much of the work which, in Great Britain, is held worthy of a peerage or a knighthood, is, in the United States, rewarded with an ambassadorship or the lucrative collectorship of a great customs port. To abolish this system would be to dig deep into the foundations of party politics. The disturbance to the national and to local political machines would be immense, and it is by no means easy to predict the consequences that would follow. It is not enough, I think, merely to say that the patronage system must end. Is it to end on the senatorial side, or the presidential, or both? For let us clearly recognize that it is an evil for which both sides are equally responsible. Since Jackson's time, at any rate, no president has had any compunction in using his power of patronage to get the support he wanted in Congress, and at least since then there have been few senators who have failed to use the influence the power of confirmation brings with it to assure their position in their constituencies. To make the whole system of appointment one based, like the British system, wholly on merit, might easily have two dangerous consequences. On the one hand, it might easily jeopardize the president's power to force through necessary or useful measures by depriving him of one of the most important sanctions of that power he now possesses. On the other, it might throw members of Congress, and especially members of the Senate, into a far greater dependence upon rich men and important interests, like the railroads and the public utilities, than is now the case. Neither, I think, would be a desirable result.

Of one thing, certainly, I am sure. It would be a great mistake to abolish the power of the Senate over appointments, leaving the president the free hand he would then possess. For it is a power so obviously capable of abuse, above all in the hands of a weak man, that it would be certain to be indefensibly administered. You have only to remember the use to which Grant and Harding, even with the present safeguards, were prepared to put that power to see that this is the case. I do not suppose for a moment that it would enable any president to build up an unbeatable machine of officeholders. But it would offer temptations of grave proportions to corrupt interests to secure the staffing of the courts and the great commissions with men willing to exchange favors in return for appointments to place. Anyone who thinks, for example, of a Securities and Exchange Commission staffed by the creatures of Wall Street; or of a National Labor Relations Board whose members shared the ideals of the National Association of Manufacturers; or of an Interstate Commerce Commission incapable of detachment upon the thorny problems of railroad rates and railroad consolidations; can at once see the dangerous vistas that are conjured up. The Senate has made its mistakes, and its sins, in the context of the appointing power, are manifold. But it has always contained a number of men, of whom the late Senator La Follette was outstanding in the last generation, and Senator Norris in our own, who have been the unpurchasable and relentless guardians of the public interest in appointments; who have played, in short, the part that Hamilton assumed the Senate as a whole would play. It is a pity that there have not been more of such men. But, so long as such men are there, they act as watchdogs of the public in a way for which, granted the president's power, nothing could compensate if it were abolished.

I believe, therefore, that so long as the president's unfettered power to nominate over the present wide range of personnel remains, so long also, with all its faults, the Senate's power of approval must remain. I confess that I should like to see the range of the power limited to proportions more akin to British practice. I think the United States, in the long run, has everything to gain and little to lose by removing as much as possible of its administrative personnel from the grip of the spoils system. But it must, on any realistic consideration, be admitted that this raises two grave problems. On the one hand, there is the issue of what compensating means the president is to have to retain his hold on Congress. On the other, there is the very difficult problem of how far precisely the limitation on his power to appoint is to go.

The first problem goes down to the root of the American scheme of government. It is not enough to say that the president will still be able to appeal to public opinion, and that where he is right he will be victorious. This is to omit both the time factor and the power of propaganda in the modern world. Granted the separation of powers, I do not see that there can be any doubt that the less the president has to offer for the votes he receives, the less will be his authority in the legislature, the weaker, accordingly, will be the pressure of leadership he can exert. Let us remember that, at best, his leadership of the party is a fleeting phenomenon; that he is dealing with innumerable local machines that are, at best, only partially responsive to his control; that he has no such sanction at his disposal as the threat of dissolution; that party discipline in the United States is, by reason of the separation of powers, much less rigid than it is in the European countries; and it becomes clear that every serious deprivation of powers he may suffer is almost an invitation to Congress to move to usurpation in a sphere that should properly be his. My friend Professor Brogan, in his remarkable book,[45] has urged at once the abolition of the senatorial power over appointment and the extension of the president's authority. I agree that this would be achieved if the spoils system remained, and if the disposal of the system were to be solely a presidential prerogative. But if the spoils system, as a principle, is to go—and the case against it is really unanswerable—then the presi-

[45] *Government of the People* (1933), p. 382.

dent's position would be far weaker than it is today. For reasons I have already indicated, I do not believe the United States, at this period of its history, can afford weak presidents. The dilemma thus presented is one that goes to the heart of the whole scheme of American institutions; and I shall try to assess its significance at the end of this book.

The second problem is, of course, a much narrower one; but its importance can easily be overlooked. The British system of appointment has, in the last seventy years, succeeded in creating an administrative personnel of high quality and great influence. It has freed both the cabinet and members of Parliament from all the nauseating habits of a patronage system. But it has brought in its train serious problems of its own. It has, it is true, given the British people a civil service unsurpassed in independence and courage. But it has also, in recent years particularly, raised the question whether the price that has been paid is not an absence of the spirit of invention, a want of imagination in seeing the need to open out new lines of state policy, which are of increasing importance. "It is one business to do what must be done," wrote Sir Henry Taylor,[46] "another to devise what ought to be done. It is in the spirit of the British government, as hitherto existing, to transact only the former business." I think that is still largely true. Where large-scale innovation has been attempted the impulse to it has usually been communicated from outside, and there have been too many occasions when its introduction has been, ably

[46] *The Statesman* (ed. of 1924), p. 113.

and pertinaciously—because civil servants at the top of their departments are able and pertinacious men —resisted from within. The tradition of a civil service like that of Great Britain is to maximize the avoidance of blunders rather than to take the risks, with the dangers of mistake, for which the future seems to call. In general, a British civil servant gets to a really influential position in his department after some twenty years' service. By that time he has been habituated to a routine of thought which deprecates large-scale departure from the traditions to which he is accustomed. It requires a minister of very notable capacity to make headway against such an habituation. I suspect that the British civil service is very nearly the perfect instrument for the negative state. I think it has yet to be proved that it is, in its present form, adequate for the positive state, particularly for a positive state which requires immense administrative experimentalism if it is to adapt itself to a rapidly changing, perhaps to a revolutionary world.[47]

Something of this problem would inevitably confront an American president if his power over patronage were as largely abolished as that power has been abolished in Great Britain. Allowances would have to be made for its existence. A performing president would have to be sure not only that he could count upon the necessary support from the bureaucracy, but also of the necessary inventiveness and risk-taking. Is a stable civil service of the British kind compatible with these qualities? My answer is that we do not yet

[47] Cf. my *Parliamentary Government in England* (1938), Chap. 6.

know; and I think it worth while to record my own impression, based, I may venture to add, upon considerable investigation, that there has been more of these two vital qualities in Washington under Franklin Roosevelt than there has been in Whitehall for something like a generation. I do not deny that Whitehall produces these men—Sir Robert Morant, for example;[48] but when they emerge, they stand out like Mount Rainier amidst the surrounding range. I am satisfied to make it as clear as I can that any effort to deal with the ramifications of the civil service problem in the United States must at least bear these considerations in mind. On the one hand, to end the spoils system is to risk the pervasiveness of the president's influence over the Congress; on the other, to provide him with a permanent civil service on the British model may well deprive him of the human instrumentalities he requires for large-scale change. The problem is of the proportions that call for the qualities of a Bentham. No one who speculates upon its implications can avoid seeing how they reach far into the foundations of the American commonwealth. It is in the degree that this is realized that it has the prospect of being met with prescience and imagination.

4

The Senate has a clear power over appointments; it has a less well-defined relation to removals from

[48] Cf. B. Allen, *Sir Robert Morant* (1934), and the last chapter of Sir George Newman's *A Century of Public Health* (1939).

office. That the consent of the Senate to removals would be necessary, Hamilton did not doubt;[49] but Madison took a very different view. "If you say that a bad man in office," he wrote,[50] "shall not be displaced but by and with the advice and consent of the Senate, the president is no longer answerable for the conduct of the officer; all will depend upon the Senate. You hereby destroy a real responsibility without obtaining even the shadows." From the outset of the republic grave fears have been expressed if the president were to have an uncontrolled power of removal; though there was little in the record of the early presidents to justify such a fear and, in a considerable degree, as Professor Thach has pointed out, it is implicit in the general nature of executive power.[51]

The first great clash came under President Jackson; and from that time onward, especially under President Johnson, the fires of controversy have waxed and waned. Cases like the removal of Duane, the secretary of the treasury, by Jackson, and the suspension of Stanton, the secretary of war, by Johnson, show the profundity of the authority claimed by the president; while senatorial pressure to remove high officials, Gouverneur Morris, for instance, as minister to France, and Denby, as secretary of the navy under Coolidge, are instances of the struggle for effective control of this prerogative on the other side. A further problem arises as to the creation of offices. May Congress, in its wisdom, attach such conditions to

[49] The Federalist, No. 77.
[50] Speech in the House of Representatives, May 19, 1789.
[51] The Creation of the Presidency (1922), p. 159.

the creation of posts as to render a dismissal dependent upon its consent? In *Myers* v. *U. S.*[52] the Supreme Court, by a majority, held that the denial of an unrestricted power of removal to the president is unconstitutional; though, on that occasion, both Mr. Justice Brandeis and Mr. Justice Holmes held that Congress was entitled to place what limitations on removal it pleased. But in *Humphrey's Executor* v. *U. S.*[53] the Court seems to have narrowed the area covered by the earlier decision and to have argued that where the post involved is not purely "executive," and concerns a removal from an "independent agency" like the Interstate Commerce Commission or the Federal Reserve Board, the Congress has the right to lay down conditions within which the president may act in removal, and that a removal outside these conditions would be illegal. There is a clear area of difficulty between the two cases; and it cannot yet be said, I think, that the legal position has been settled.

My own view is that, so far as removals are concerned, there are two divisions of the problem to which different considerations apply. On the one hand, there are the ordinary executive agencies of the government. There, as I think, the president's right to be unfettered in his discretion is unquestionable. His duty is the "faithful execution of the laws"; he is entitled to the instruments he deems suitable to that execution. He may make mistakes; he may act in a partisan way; he may, as the Senate has so often feared,

[52] (1926), 272 U. S. 52.
[53] (1935), 295 U. S. 602.

seek to use his authority to build up a personal machine. But it is difficult to see what any president will, in this realm, really gain by an unwise exercise of his discretion. Wherever he dismisses an official, he has to make a new appointment; and there is reason and to spare for supposing that the Senate will interpose its veto, as it did upon Roger Taney after the dismissal of Duane, whenever it thinks the presidential exercise has been unwarranted. So long as the official involved is carrying out a function for the proper exercise of which the president is ultimately responsible, I cannot see that interference with that responsibility is desirable. In any political system, there is a point at which trust must be placed somewhere. It is of the essence of the American scheme that, for the executive process, trust should be placed in the president. It seems to me to follow from this that legislative interference with discretion in that trust is, if it reaches the point of prohibition, wholly undesirable.

I do not mean, thereby, that Congress should be estopped from the expression of its opinion. Action like that taken in the Denby case seems to me wholly undesirable.[54] That is an expression of opinion upon which the president is free to act or to refrain from acting, as he pleases, though at his peril. In a way, a resolution such as was passed in the Denby case is like a vote of "no confidence" in a particular minister in the House of Commons. It does not, indeed, force the ministry out, as it would do in Great Britain. But

[54] For a good account of the Denby case see Haynes, *op. cit.*, II, 816 f.

it serves the wholly admirable purpose of informing the president, and beyond him the people of the United States, that grave matters are afoot, of which the legislature takes a serious view. I do not think such resolutions should be passed save in cases of exceptional momentousness. But the Denby case was such a one. Here, after all, was a cabinet minister at the least culpably negligent in an affair which led to the criminal prosecution of two of his colleagues, and the conviction of one of them. To argue, as Senator Borah did, that Congress has no right under the Constitution to pass such a resolution because the dismissal of a cabinet officer is not within its power (save through the formal and unlikely process of impeachment) is to take far too narrow a view of the legislative function. Criticism of the administration is inherent in that function, is, indeed, one of the most valuable services it can perform. To hinder its performance upon formal grounds is as harmful to the president himself as it may be to the interests it is his duty to serve.

But the judges apart (and they are separately provided for under the Constitution)[55] it seems to me clear, also, that there is a type of governmental post in which, by its very nature, there ought to be safeguards against an unlimited presidential discretion to remove. There are posts, of which the Interstate Commerce Commission is the outstanding example, the holders of which are intended to have a quasi-judicial position, or which involve the passing upon problems

[55] Art. III, Sec. 1.

[223]

that are not intended to be dealt with along the ordinary lines of the party battle. Here, I suggest, it is impossible to doubt that Congress both could and should prescribe the terms upon which removals from office may be made; and of such a post as that of the comptroller-general of the United States, it seems to me obvious that accountability to Congress rather than to the president is desirable.[56] Sometimes the congressional desire to secure independence from the passing policy of the government of the day has been attempted by a deliberate demand for a bipartisan structure of the agency concerned. Where a president has sought to get round the statutory provision, as Mr. Coolidge did with Mr. D. J. Lewis, by asking for an "undated letter of resignation as the price for sending the reappointment to the Senate,"[57] his action seems to me wholly unjustifiable. A great deal of modern administration is of a quasi-judicial nature the quality of which depends upon public faith in the maximum possible impartiality of the administrators. That Congress should be entitled, in such cases, legislatively to safeguard as much of that impartiality as it can is, I think, beyond dispute. President Franklin Roosevelt, for example, wrote to Mr. Humphrey, of the Tariff Commission, requesting his resignation on the ground that "the aims and purposes of the Commission can be carried out most effectively with per-

[56] On posts of this character see the admirable remarks of Professor Lindsay Rogers, *op. cit.*, pp. 45 f. His book contains also (pp. 257-270) a valuable list of statutes restricting the power of the president to appoint or remove.

[57] Rogers, *op. cit.*, p. 47.

sonnel of my own selection"; while, at the same time, he seems to have been wholly satisfied with the quality of Mr. Humphrey's work. The statute creating the commission lays it down[58] that removals shall be for "inefficiency, neglect of duty, or malfeasance in office." Since Mr. Humphrey was charged with none of these, it is difficult to see on what legitimate grounds he could have been asked to resign.

The case of Mr. Humphrey is clearly distinguishable from that of Dr. A. E. Morgan, at the time of his removal the chairman of the Board of the Tennessee Valley Authority.[59] Here, there was definite evidence upon which the president was entitled to find that the attitude of Dr. Morgan to his colleagues made impossible the proper fulfilment of the authority's function. The president held, personally, "hearings," in which all the evidence necessary for a judgment was before him. His decision was, no doubt, an act of "discretion"; but it was one which an average reasonable man was likely, in the circumstances, to find appropriate to the facts involved. This type of case, though it gave rise to a passionate debate in Congress, was clearly of a different order from that of Humphrey. In the latter's case, there were no charges against the official. The president seems merely to have felt that he would be more satisfied with an administrative body composed of his own nominees. But since the very nature of the statute

[58] 39 U. S. Stat. 795. S. 700.
[59] For a full account of this case see the account of the president's meetings with Dr. Morgan, together with the opinion of the solicitor-general, in his message to Congress of March 23, 1938.

under which the commission operated was intended to prevent the president from having a discretion of this kind, I cannot see any possible answer to the judgment of the Supreme Court—unanimously affirmed—that he did not possess it.

For, in cases of the Humphrey type, the object of legislation is to offer the citizen a guarantee that the official is independent of the political executive in the view he forms upon its policies. It is as legitimate to safeguard that guarantee as it is to secure the tenure of a judge from executive interference. I agree that, where a vacancy occurs, the president is entitled, once he pays due regard to whatever statutory qualifications may be exacted, to put forward men of his own way of thought rather than of that opposed to him. Such officials, like, indeed, members of the Supreme Court themselves, are in that twilight area where the facts have to be seen from an angle that, so far as is humanly possible, transcends the individual limitations of judgment. Just as a justice of the Supreme Court ought not to find a statute unconstitutional just because he thinks it unwise, so a member of one of these quasi-independent agencies ought not to stand against a presidential policy because he dislikes it. The question, for him, is whether the presidential line of policy is likely to frustrate the purpose of the agency upon which he serves, and no more; he ought, even, to lean toward that line if it has serious pretensions to "reasonableness." For administration becomes an impossible task if, within the confines of the executive power, agencies exist the end of which is, if possible, to strike into impotence the policy the administration is seeking to pursue. That task is essentially a legislative one; and, within the safeguards I have suggested, the larger the leeway that is given to the president the better. I do not doubt that this freedom may be abused or badly handled. But the correction of such errors is a task which devolves upon Congress. The answer to a bad administrative policy is, its legality apart, not a matter during the president's term of office for officials of his government; the answer is in the legislature which is elected for precisely that end. And if the legislature is incapable of performing that task of correction, it is a function which devolves upon the people. Any other policy than this destroys, I am confident, the foundations of effective government.

V

CONCLUDING OBSERVATIONS

I

THE president of the United States is elected by a
method which now bears no relation to the purpose it is intended to fulfil. A majority in the electoral
college may defeat a majority in the nation. It did so
in 1876 and in 1888; it nearly did so in 1884 and in
1916. From any angle the electoral college is an
anachronism, and the choice by states is undesirable.
It has a real effect on the choice of candidates. Because,
in all normal circumstances, the attitude of a particular
state is known, the tendency is encouraged in parties
not merely to select the candidate from a doubtful
state, but also to make "deals" before the election with
the machines of particular states, with a view to securing the nomination and the victory of a particular
candidate. The Democratic party is confident that it
will win the South; and it has tended, therefore, since
the Civil War, to take its presidential candidate from
the Eastern seaboard and particularly from New York.
The Northeast is predominantly Republican; but the
Republicans can win an election only by carrying all
the states of the Middle West, and those on the border
between the North and South. They have, therefore,

[228]

sought for candidates in the middle western states in order to achieve this alliance. "Statesmanship in this nation," wrote F. J. Turner,[1] "consists not only in representing the special interests of the leader's own section, but in finding a formula that will bring the different regions together in a common policy."

It is easy to show how much of American politics has been bedeviled, in the context of the presidency, by the search for this formula. Jefferson and Jackson owed their victories to their success in finding it, as Clay and Calhoun owed their defeats to a failure in the same pursuit. The failure of Negro suffrage in the South has been the graveyard of Republican representation there; and both in the emphasis of issues, and in the choice of candidates, it is the inherent implication of sectionalism to which fundamental attention must be paid. I think, therefore, that once it is agreed that the transcendence of sectionalism is desirable, it follows at once that the president should be elected by a direct national vote. That would have the wholly desirable effect of emphasizing his national position. It would prevent the kind of fiasco which marked the Republican convention of 1912;[2] and it would diminish, as it is urgent to diminish, the excessive regard that is paid to the claims of the machines of both parties in doubtful states. The real truth is that, at present, the state as a unit of electoral refer-

[1] *The Significance of Sections in American History* (1932), p. 50.
[2] Cf. Pringle, *op. cit.*, pp. 561 f.

ence is wholly parasitic upon the party structure. To exalt its importance, as the present method of election does, is to give an entirely undue prominence to the type of man to whom "politics" is a profession in the worst sense of the word. It would do a good deal to eliminate candidates whose claims ought never to be considered seriously; and it would do something, at any rate, to save the remainder from commitments, both as to places and measures, they ought never to be asked to make.

Two further simple reforms are worth suggesting. I cannot see any case for the present limitation upon the president's veto power in finance. He must now accept or reject congressional measures as a whole. That means, despite the reforms of the budget, that he is still at the mercy of the "pork barrel" system with all its evil implications. I should like to see Congress adopt the kind of self-denying ordinance that has worked so admirably in the House of Commons; I would deny any member the right—the power of investigation apart—to ask for an appropriation that is not sought under the direct authority of the president. This would not merely result in more rational finance; it would also prevent the Appropriations Bill from being the plaything of perhaps a hundred members of Congress, whether in the House of Representatives or in the Senate, whose sole interest in finance is the local achievement in construction they can report back to their constituencies. This is a power already conferred upon the governors of many states, and, wherever it has been tried, there is no doubt that its effect has been beneficial.[3]

My second reform is also in the nature of a self-denying ordinance. Except upon purely selfish grounds, I can see no reason for the existence of "senatorial courtesy." It is rarely invoked except for narrow reasons; and, where it is invoked, its utilization is equally rarely defensible. Its effect is simply to narrow the area of presidential choice for ends intended not for the maintenance of a standard of appointment, but for the personal power of a particular senator. For reasons I have already urged, I think that the continuance of senatorial approval for the major nominations of the president is desirable; this approval would still remain. But it is wholly unfitting that a judgeship or a collectorship of a port should be dependent, as it now is, upon the effect it may have upon the balance of internecine interests within a section of the party in power. No one can seriously argue that "senatorial courtesy" is exercised to the end that bad nominations should be rejected; the well-known cases of Roscoe Conkling and Gallinger are evidence of that. No one, either, ought to ask a president so to use his nominating power as to assist men of the type of Ben Butler to build up a machine. It may be true that the power of individual senators would be adversely affected by this change. But it would not touch the collective power of the Senate. It would leave it free, in every case in modern times

---

[3] Cf. F. A. Cleveland and A. C. Buck, *The Budget and Responsible Government* (1920), and L. Lipson, *The American Governor* (1939).

in which its approval might reasonably be regarded as a matter of doubt, to resolve its doubts by debate. On the record, it is impossible not to feel that the dignity of American public life would be definitely increased if the Senate could be persuaded to accept this view.

"The fundamental addition which is necessary to enable the president to defy the pressure of local interests incarnate in senators and representatives," writes Professor Brogan,[4] "is the right to appeal to the nation by referendum. . . . The president should have an absolute veto over constitutional amendments proposed by Congress, until the country has decided between them, and the right to propose his own amendments, and his own direct legislation to the country, whether or no Congress approves. If it is possible to make national politics out of sectional politics, it can only be done through the presidency." I agree with the end Professor Brogan has in view; I cannot help feeling that his means are ill chosen. It is not merely that most of the issues upon which there is a division between executive and legislature do not seem to me susceptible of effective discussion by popular vote, and that this has been demonstrated by the history of the referendum in the various states;[5] it is also that the experience of the United States suggests strongly that the referendum is an instrument any frequent use of which would place excessive power in the hands of the most undesirable influences

---

[4] *Government of the People* (1933), p. 382.
[5] Cf. my *Grammar of Politics* (ed. of 1938), pp. 321 f.

in politics. I am confident, moreover, that many of the issues so referred, that of the Tennessee Valley Authority, for example—one of the half-dozen most beneficent experiments in American history—would be defeated by exactly that sectionalism that Professor Brogan is anxious to transcend. I doubt, further, whether this right could be given to the president without its conference upon the people also; and so to extend that right would almost certainly in many undesirable instances—the control of public utilities is an obvious example—be to play directly into the hands of the money power. The press and the radio would be at the disposal of every evil influence which had anything to lose. Who is there who cannot see the kind of power such an occasion would give to men like Mr. William Randolph Hearst or Father Coughlin? And who is there who cannot see, also, that the more indirect their influence over the voters of the United States, the healthier and cleaner its politics are likely to be? The referendum is too blunt and crude an instrument of authority to be of real use to any president who is seeking an effective refreshment of power; and there is no reason to suppose that an appeal to its power on the national plane could ever be effectively canalized. A president might thus be easily deprived of an authority he could exert in one field because, by a narrow majority, and through purely extraneous causes, he has suffered an accidental defeat in another.

I am sure that Professor Brogan is right in his insistence that the transcendence of sectionalism is the most urgent need in American politics; and I think he is probably right in arguing that the president is the instrument through which that transcendence may be most properly effected. The stronger the president, on the whole, the more likely it is not only that the attention of Congress will be directed to matters of general importance; but the more likely it is, also, that the mind of the nation will force Congress consistently to take that attitude. But to appreciate that problem we must, I think, probe deeper. We must consider what it is that has made the Congress so deeply a sectional body. It is not, I suspect, enough to say that it is so because American parties are inherently sectional. That only pushes the inquiry back to the further stage of what forces have made them inherently sectional. The answer to this complicated problem goes deep into the roots of American life.

For anyone who looks at the spectacle it presents will, I think, be struck at once by certain obvious things. It is, in the first place, clear not only that there is no "liberal" party in the United States, at least in the European meaning of that term, but also that so far no revolt from either of the major parties has had any real staying power. There have been many of those revolts; the Populist movement, the Progressive revolt under Roosevelt, the third-party movement under the elder La Follette, are only the most notable. But none of them has had importance on a plane of continuity. Sooner or later, their major figures either have returned, like Theodore Roosevelt, to the older parties from which they came, or have become politically impotent. It is notable, also, that except for brief periods, and in particular states, American labor has played no such part on the political stage as it has in European countries. It is striking that, so far, socialism has taken no hold at all of the American voter's mind; the economic crisis has deepened continuously since 1933, but the peak of socialist strength in the United States was reached in 1920, and even then it was, in proportion to the strength of the major parties, pitiably small.

These major parties represent, to a European, a curious spectacle. Though there have been moments when their differences upon particular issues were substantial, since the Civil War the dividing line between them has never been real. Grover Cleveland, for instance, might well have been a Republican president; and I cannot see any essential item in the program of President Hayes which an average Democratic president would not have been willing to commend. The truth is, I think, that these major parties have been essentially the agents of the property interests of the United States, that, in a general way, they have served them in much the same fashion, and that where they have diverged from service to them, it has been because of a profound popular agitation failure to respond to which would have meant electoral disaster. But up to, at any rate, the New Deal of 1933, the character of the response has always been within a very limited frame of reference which did not seriously disturb the conservative character of either of the parties. Within the limits permitted them by the

Supreme Court, they have been the legislative agents of business men and, to a less degree, the farming interests of the United States. The assumption upon which they have rested—the assumption, indeed, upon which the New Deal itself rests—is the social adequacy of American capitalism. They reflect its suspicion of government action. They represent the permanent desire of the man of property to be free from interference. Where they have been driven to interfere, it was usually either in a realm of minor importance or because crisis demanded a positive policy to which, at least immediately, they were compelled to give attention.

Anyone who considers the history of American parties until 1933 will, foreign policy apart, find a notable resemblance between their character and that of British parties before the advent of the British Labour party in 1906. They held a general social philosophy in common; they diverged from it only to make concessions to particular pressure groups whose demands would not brook denial. But they did not go beyond a fairly narrow frame of reference pricked out for them by the dominant property interests as sound. In a sense, indeed, they did not deserve the respect which the prewar parties in Great Britain were able to secure. Behind the congressional façade, both of them were unduly dominated by the great corporations and their representatives; it is still true of American politics as Woodrow Wilson quotes Dale of Birmingham as saying some sixty years ago that there is in the United States "a class, including thousands and tens of thousands of the best men in the country, who think it possible to enjoy the fruits of good government without working for them."[6] Whether the issue was the tariff or the trusts, railroads or electric power, taxation or the place of labor in the community, the parties were, subject to occasional revolts, in the hands of that "invisible government" of which Elihu Root spoke; a government of which the "bosses" were, as Lincoln Steffens so remarkably showed, more the symptom than the cause. The British aristocracy had, with all its limitations, a real sense of public service. The business aristocracy of America preferred to occupy itself with the making of wealth, leaving to the political parties the definition of the terms upon which it could be made, and themselves helping to frame those terms.

In this atmosphere, it is important ceaselessly to remember two things. First, the United States is essentially a continent; the making of unity out of its various sections was bound, therefore, under any circumstances, to be a difficult adventure. Second, because it was, until the nineties of the last century, a civilization in which expansion was always internal and not external, the creation of safeguards against discontent was a relatively easy matter. Opportunity, at least in comparison with Europe, was boundless; there was abundance of land, there was no residuary feudalism, almost any taxes produced a surplus in the treasury. Few members of the working class expected to remain there; most of them enjoyed conditions far

[6] *Congressional Government* (1885), p. 331.

higher than anything the European peasant or industrial worker has ever known. The triumphs of the business man were, on any showing, immense; in three generations he had built a civilization out of a wilderness. Up to the Civil War, there might have been doubts and hesitations about the future of American civilization; there were none after the issue of secession had been decided. From the presidency of Grant onward, the United States seemed, to most, to have made a permanent bargain with fate. The less positive the action of government, the greater seemed to be the tempo of its development. Parties, therefore, adjusted themselves to an atmosphere in which weak government seemed the very condition of prosperity; and, since the weaker the government the greater was the leeway given to the power of the propertied interests, the more jealously the latter scrutinized any movement toward regulation.

The real governors of the United States, that is, wanted a weak system of rule. They were content with an atmosphere in which, as Woodrow Wilson said, "authority is perplexingly subdivided and distributed, and responsibility has to be hunted down in out-of-the-way corners."[7] Every attempt at its concentration seemed unsound to the beneficiaries of the system. It was "un-American"; it was an attack upon freedom; it was contrary to the purpose of the founders. And, in a fundamental sense, each of these charges was true. For the concentration of authority in American history has only been possible at mo-

7 *Op. cit.,* p. 331.

ments of crisis. It has been accepted dubiously, and after the crisis has passed it has been discarded as rapidly as possible. The American people, trained in the tradition of negative government, have always been suspicious of it. That suspicion has been shared by Congress since the more strong the personality of the man in the White House, the more diminished has the authority of Congress itself become. From the foundation of the American system, the inference has been drawn that the stronger the president, the graver was the threat to public freedom. The men of 1787 could hardly help remembering, as they looked at the England they knew, that a legislature which could be dominated by the executive was the enemy of public freedom. They desired, therefore, "to erect a Congress which would not be subservient and an executive which would not be despotic."[8] They did so by a separation of powers which put a premium upon the possibility of governmental paralysis. "It was to have been expected that they should regard an absolute separation of these two great branches of the system (the executive and the legislature) as the only effectual means for the accomplishment of that great end."[9]

For something over a century they had every reason to believe that they were right. The system, on occasion, creaked and trembled; but, upon balance, within that period it resulted in a triumphant progress it is impossible not to admire. It was only after a century,

[8] Wilson, *op. cit.*, p. 30.
[9] *Ibid.*

[239]

when the epoch of abnormal expansion had begun to draw to its close, that analysis could suggest how real was the resemblance between the ends they had secured and the ends they had sought to avoid. For, having distributed authority, they found that, to cope with discontent, they had to bring it together again in order to prevent its paralysis. And the method by which the co-operation was secured bore a curious resemblance to the methods by which George III had made Parliament subservient to him. The use of the patronage by the president to obtain the majority he required was not very different from the use by George III of places and pensions to secure a majority in the House of Commons. The relation of the great interests to Congress has not been so unlike the domination of the eighteenth-century Parliaments to the interests of the great landowners. The truth of Lord Bute's well-known maxim that "the forms of a free and the ends of an arbitrary government are things not altogether incompatible,"[10] has been proved again and again in American history. And its truth has been emphasized by the way in which, from John Marshall onward, the Supreme Court has acted as a third chamber of the American legislature concerned to keep a possible co-operation between president and Congress within due bounds.

The spectacle of the separation of powers is, this is to say, the spectacle of the confusion of powers. A president may seek to give a lead; there is no one else in a position in which a clear lead can be given. But

[10] Cited by Woodrow Wilson, *op. cit.*, p. 308.

he cannot hope successfully to give a clear lead unless he is on one of two roads. He is likely to get what he requires if he takes what may be termed the retail view of his function. Whenever he does so, there is unlikely to be a great issue in dispute. He is then not challenging Congress for primacy in direction, and he may hope for success. He is likely, again, to get what he requires if on the path events compel him to tread the signals are set at danger. Then, at least, the prospect of a threat to the foundations of society leads to a co-operation in which he sets the direction. But, in all normal circumstances, the more positive a president sets out to be, the more unlikely is he to be able to insist upon his primacy. The whole drive of the system is against him. He is not only thwarting the separation of powers. He is also transforming the character of a party system which is, at its very basis, antagonistic to the idea of positivism. The American scheme of government is, in its inherent principles, not only a system for fair weather. It is also a system which, as it has translated itself into party terms, does not easily accept the categories of the positive state.

And this is the more important because America has now entered the epoch where the requirements of the positive state can no longer be denied. That can be seen from many angles. It is obvious, in the first place, because the dramatic period of internal expansion is over; the problems confronted by American capitalism are similar in character and intensity to those of Europe. It is obvious, in the second, because technological and scientific development have made largely obsolete the division of powers between the center and the circumference contemplated in 1787; in the epoch of giant capitalism only the federal government can hope to confront the great industrial empires on terms of equal authority.[11] It is obvious, in the third place, because the major parties have ceased to present the electorate with rational alternatives about any of the main problems to be solved.[12] That is the more emphatically the case because neither can admit within its ranks an organized labor movement seeking the translation of its needs into statutes on any wholesale scale. It is in fact evident that the labor problem in the United States is already—without its effective entrance into politics—forcing something like a realignment of parties there. Conservative Democrats and conservative Republicans find—as their attitude to revision of the Wagner Act made evident[13]—far more in common upon the basis of hostility to the claims of labor than they do in antagonism upon other issues. And what is true of their attitude to the labor problem is true, also, of their outlook upon most of the problems which the social policy of the "New Deal" has been called upon to solve.

The result can be put quite simply by saying that, emergency always apart, no president who has a positive policy to propound continuously will find, within

[11] Cf. my "Obsolescence of Federalism" in the *New Republic*, May 3, 1939.
[12] See this well put in Brogan, *op. cit.*, p. 383.
[13] On the Wagner Act cf. the admirable work of R. R. Brooks, *Unions of Their Own Choosing* (1939).

the major parties of today, any assured body of support for it. Something of what he may want he will get in the "honeymoon period" of his office; something, also, he may be able to extract by means of the patronage. But the more relentlessly he pursues major objectives that are positive in character, the more certain he is to find himself thwarted by the inherent nature of the party of which he is the nominal and temporary leader. If he gains a temporary respite with a view to renomination for a second term, he is likely to find increasing opposition as that second term draws to its close. As he disappears from the scene, he is likely to find himself replaced by a leader with whom the party can more comfortably deal on its own terms; it is not accident that a strong president has usually been followed by a succession of weak presidents, for they suit much better the environment to which both the American scheme of government and the American party system are historically conditioned.

2

America needs strong government; it needs strong leadership to attain strong government; only the president, granted its characteristics, can provide it with the leadership it requires. But against these needs must be set all the traditional impetus of the system. The Constitution makes against it partly by its separation of powers and partly by the way in which it has distributed functions between the states and the federation. It has now become of pivotal interest to the forces of privilege in the United States to maintain for their benefit both that separation and that distribution; and it must be remembered that, constitutional amendment apart, the degree to which that distribution can be effectively transcended lives precariously by the accidental composition of the Supreme Court.

The Constitution makes against it; so also, as I have argued, does the party system on its present foundation, since, except for emergencies, it enthrones the conservative forces in permanent power. These forces live by their ability to maintain weak government, for strong government, in the sense of a government with a continuously positive direction, is necessarily hostile to their interests. That can, I suggest, be seen from the intensity of their antagonism to the New Deal; they have greeted a body of legislation in general as mild as that of the Liberal government of 1906 in England as though it were inaugurating an epoch of red revolution. Since weak government is the source from which these forces draw their power in the state, their impact upon parties is always a discouragement to leadership in a positive form. And this discouragement can take many shapes. It may appear as sectionalism. It may appear through the frustration of the executive by an encouragement of opposition to its policies in the legislature. It may appear as the exploitation of the traditional American fear of strong government; there are few accusations to which the American public lends a more ready ear than to that of dictatorship, and that even when the very foundations of the system paralyze, almost a priori, any prospect of its constitutional advent.

I do not, therefore, believe that the strong leadership America requires will be available to it until the conflict between parties is on a rational basis; and I believe that this will require a radical realignment of parties. For where the choice between policies that has to be made is real, effective party discipline will follow the fact of the reality of the choice; and a president who is anxious to lead his party will then find that he has a party anxious to follow his lead. The problem, in fact, at least as I see it, is the adjustment of American parties to the disposition of social forces in the United States. At present, there is no such adjustment. Leadership on a big scale comes only because an emergency has to be surmounted. There is no provision for its continuity. On the contrary, the whole genius of the system is against its continuity. For once it becomes continuous, all the interests are weakened which suffer from its strength. A great president is bound to weaken them by the fact that he is great. I do not think it is true to say that he dwarfs his followers in Congress by the fact that he gives a lead. I do say that, by giving it, he makes Congress a unity behind him, for purposes he defines, instead of an incoherent mass of unco-ordinated elements which find their unity in the degree that they can alter those purposes. In the present scheme, the more Congress is able to defeat the president, the bigger it appears in the life of the nation. It is thus given a vested interest in his defeat. It is tempted to it by its inevitable and natural inclination to exalt its own stature. The Senator Robinson who carries out the will of the president will never appear so big a man in the eyes of the nation as the Senator Borah who successfully thwarts him. It is, in the present position, only human for most of those who go to Congress to have the ambition to be a Senator Borah rather than a Senator Robinson.

But a legislature is not of itself capable of positive leadership unless it is organized for this function. The British system organizes the House of Commons for this end by making it accept or reject, at the peril of a general election, the policies submitted to it by the cabinet. It does not lead the cabinet. It is not a policy-making body. It is an organ of registration, an instrument of criticism, a sounding board through which the voice of the nation can make itself heard. No provision is made for this relation in the American scheme. The president may urge his policies; he has no adequate sanctions to enforce them. And, once they are urged, he has no real certainty about what may become of them. There is no effective responsibility anywhere for their fate. An influential member of the legislature is, if he is of the majority party, as likely to have his way as the president; there are even spheres in which he is more likely to have his way. Congressional organization builds an executive within the legislature that is not truly charged with the executive function. Partly, it has the function of destroying the policy of the real executive; partly, it has the function of providing an alternative to it, which is rarely a part of any coherent pattern of policy. And the composition of this executive within the legislature is continually changing. It is one set of men on one set of problems; it is another set of men upon another. Whatever set of men it may be, one of their concerns must always be to establish and to emphasize their independence of the true executive power. But to establish that independence they must prevent his leadership from possessing that continuity of which I have spoken. They must, therefore, be a rampart against strong leadership. They must be a force to deny, not a force to co-operate in affirming. The purpose of the Congress, in the present scheme, must always be to make the presidency as weak as it possibly can.

This is not, I think, a situation that can be remedied by mechanical devices. I have already sought to show that it would not be cured by the introduction of a presidential right to a referendum. Nor do I believe, as has been suggested, that it can be cured by giving to the president a right to dissolve the Congress when they are at odds and seek, thereby, a refreshment of authority from the electorate. The implications of the right of dissolution are incompatible with the congressional system. They strike at the root of the separation of powers. The defeat of the president, at an election caused by its exercise, would obviously come very near to paralyzing his effectiveness during the remainder of his term; it is, indeed, doubtful whether, after such a defeat, he could usefully remain in office. And this is to say, I think, that the counterpart of a presidential right of dissolution is presidential responsibility to the new legislature he would so bring into being. If he were conceded that power, it would not be possible to avoid a rapid development of the parliamentary system, in something like the British form, in the United States. The presidential system, in its historic contours, could hardly survive the conference upon him of so tremendous a power without the exaction of a comparable responsibility.

I believe, therefore, that the changes required in the United States are likely to be produced less by direct constitutional innovation than by the repercussion upon the political framework of the immense social and economic changes that are going on before our eyes. This is not to say that I do not believe those constitutional innovations to be desirable. On the contrary, the case made, over seventy years ago, by Bagehot against the ultimate principles of the presidential system seems to me to have been strengthened, rather than weakened, by time.[14] But I doubt whether anything short of actual revolution would cause direct changes of the kind necessary to be made. The power of tradition is too great; the interests that could be mobilized against them are too strong. One has only to consider the relative failure of most efforts at direct innovation in the separate states, whenever the basis of the Constitution has there been called into question, to see how incomparably more difficult it would be to deal directly with the heart of the federal scheme. Revolution apart, it is to the pressure of usage and habit, as these are shaped by innovation within the economic fabric of the United States, that one must look for the main sources of change.

[14] Cf. my essay in *The Dangers of Obedience* (1930), pp. 31 f.

These innovations are on an immense scale; and they are likely to increase rather than to decrease in volume. It is not only that there is now a permanent proletariat in the United States with all the problems such a proletariat involves—permanent unemployment for a great army of citizens, services to mitigate its effects, and so on. Federal aid to states and cities is bound to grow, and as it grows the authority of the central government at Washington is bound to grow greater. A new level of social provision for citizens of low income in health and housing and education is inevitable; with them will come new levels and techniques of taxation intended, upon the European model, deliberately to effect such a redistribution of income as will mitigate the worst results of social inequality. All this is bound, I believe, to make the ambit of federal regulation in the future wider than it has been in the past. The state will be forced into an attitude far more emphatically positive than anything for which, so far, the "New Deal" has been responsible. There will be exacted, if American democracy endures, a much higher price for the maintenance of privilege than any it has so far been asked to pay.

It is worth while to insist, for a moment, upon the fact that there is nothing new or startling in this development. The critics of the "New Deal" speak of it as though it were a change of revolutionary intensity. The answer, to an outsider at least, is the simple answer that its roots are deep in American history. The "New Deal" of Franklin Roosevelt is the logical development of the "New Freedom" of

Woodrow Wilson. But this, in its turn, was the outgrowth of that Progressive movement of which the ambitions, perhaps, rather than the ideas, of Theodore Roosevelt made him the picturesque symbol. Yet no one can examine the Progressive movement at all carefully without seeing how much of it is rooted in Populism. This, in its turn, is a complex phenomenon the component elements in which go back not merely to agrarian discontent, but to a multiplicity of minor movements of protest the lineage of which is traceable to those things in the first days of the republic which made Shays a rebel and Jefferson president of the United States. All of them, I venture to think, were rooted in the effort of the ordinary man to get more from the common stock of welfare than he conceived himself to be getting, in the strong belief that he was morally entitled to more. All of them were more or less placated, sometimes by a recovery which transmuted demands for reform into silence, sometimes by immense grants of land, as under the Homestead Act, sometimes by those huge grants of pensions which have followed every military adventure in which America has been engaged. It seems to me, therefore, that unless there is old-fashioned recovery, on the nineteenth-century model, in the United States—and all the evidence suggests that this is no longer possible—the alternative of reform becomes inescapable. Reform means the positive state; and the debates of American politics in the next generation will turn on the pace and the quantum of the reform the propertied class is willing to concede or driven to accept.

From the angle of the presidency this has, I think, two implications. National politics in the next generation of American history will be far more important than in the past, because all the major problems of American economic life in the phase of giant capitalism project themselves, necessarily, on to a national plane. Whether the issue is the unemployed or housing, public utilities like railroads and electric power, the position of the farmer, the place of trade unions in society, the level and methods of taxation, they are insoluble problems if they are met in a sectional way. Their range and intensity will compel the political parties more and more to confront them nationally. The interests, above all that of labor, which will be forced by them into political consciousness, will, in their turn, compel a realignment of parties into conservative and progressive. Each of them will require, if it is to be effective in dealing, not merely with an electorate as vast as that of the United States, but also with one over which the power of organization is relatively small, a coherence and a discipline far greater than in the past. But to secure these, political parties will be compelled to centralize their leadership far more than they have before been willing to do. Centralization of leadership means, inevitably, a greater concentration of power in the president's hands simply because there is no other plane upon which it can be secured. He is likely, this is to say, to bear to his party a relationship far more like that of the British prime minister to his party than at any previous time. For his followers will find that, on the larger aspects of policy, the penalty of deserting the program he embodies is certain to be electoral defeat. In the America that is coming the penalty of electoral defeat will be far more important than it is today. That, above all, is why I think that the place of the president in the constitutional scheme is likely to be greater, his national authority even more immense, than at the present time.

3

This, obviously, raises a number of interesting questions, both of general and of technical importance. I take the former first, because it is easier to dispose of them. If, as I conceive, the presidency, in the future, is to be of more and not less importance than it has hitherto been, the question of the advice upon which the president can rely becomes clearly an urgent matter. The wider the range of his functions, the more profound the leadership he is called upon to give, the more, obviously enough, he must delegate; he cannot expect, in any considerable measure, to deal with any but the largest issues, or to do more than give general directions, to be fulfilled by others, in relation to all matters with the control of which he is charged. This, I think, raises the problem of supplying him with proper assistance, both on the political and on the administrative side.

On the political side, I think it means firstly a more important type of cabinet officer than he has generally had in the past. That is, in any case, desirable in itself; and it would be no more than a return to historic precedent, since the quality of the cabinets up to Jackson's day was far higher than it has been at any time since that period. The president of our own times has been too often satisfied with men upon whom he can rely less for counsel than for a purely personal allegiance, or with men whom it is desired to reward for services that are personal to himself, rather than political in character. He needs far more men of real standing, either because their influence in the party, as with Elihu Root under Theodore Roosevelt, removes from him a considerable part of the tremendous burden he has to bear, or because their past experience gives reason to believe that they will be the type of administrator who, knowing his mind, can be left a large discretion with safety. I think myself that this means a cabinet of men who are themselves of approximately presidential quality. It may be generally true that "a ministry of all the talents" is a difficult team to drive; it is certainly true that a ministry of little talent is one that it is broadly impossible to drive at all. The evidence is clear that, the weaker the cabinet, the more the president has continually to occupy himself with a mass of petty detail that ought to be quite below his notice. He does not delegate, because he is afraid of the results of delegation. He becomes his own head of department in a number of disparate offices to the functioning of which he is simply not able to give the requisite attention. Burdened in this way with oppressive detail, either he has no leisure to think in a large way upon the big questions, or, like Woodrow Wilson, he breaks down under the strain.

[253]

A president who is to function adequately needs a cabinet that is itself a training ground for the future occupancy of his position. On European experience, nothing compensates for the lack of this. It means leisure for the president. It means not only men who, in their respective spheres, can be largely left alone; it means also men who can be expected to ease his position with the legislature. This, in its turn, means knowing the legislature, and I think this involves the kind of experience of public life that high office, whether as a member of either house of Congress, or as the governor of a state, can alone confer. For, save with the very exceptional man, success in private life is not an adequate introduction to public office. The motivation of action is too different, the relation to other persons is too different also. It is not specialists in a departmental line whom the president requires as colleagues, but men who can take the kind of view he is compelled to take of the kind of problem with which he has to deal. The successful private lawyer—Mr. Ickes is a notable exception—can rarely think in this way; still less can the successful business man who is usually of little value in politics because that blending of wills in the give and take of compromise which is a large part of its essence is rarely a quality that distinguishes him. It is, above all, the quality the politician learns from handling matters of public responsibility. He comes to realize that words, there, are checks upon public account which there must be cash to meet, if credit is to be maintained. He learns, too, that decisions in politics differ from most decisions in

[254]

private life, because they have to be defended with arguments that are certain to be attacked by the other side with all the resources at their disposal. That is why I think the cabinet of politically trained men will be indispensable to any president who is not himself so extraordinary that he could almost dispense with a cabinet altogether; and, Lincoln perhaps apart, there has been no such president in the history of the United States.

The kind of cabinet of which I am thinking is one upon which the president would be eager to rely for the definition of his general approach to his problems. I doubt whether any save the weaker presidents have had that reliance in modern times. The result has been either that they have striven to do too much, like Woodrow Wilson, or that, like Calvin Coolidge, just because they had weak counselors, they have been afraid to do anything at all. Mr. Coolidge's relation, indeed, to his secretary of the treasury, Mr. Andrew Mellon, is a supreme example of what the relation between a president and one of his cabinet officers ought not to be. Mr. Coolidge adored rich men because they were rich; and Mr. Mellon was one of the richest men in the United States. His conceptions of fiscal problems were antediluvian; and he had not the remotest idea of how to handle a legislature, a matter, indeed, of which he had no experience save indirectly through his relations with the Republican machine of Pennsylvania. But Mr. Coolidge assumed that a rich man must naturally make a successful secretary of the treasury; and the financial aspect of his policy as president was disastrous because he could not believe that, in the controversies between Mr. Mellon and Congress, the former could be wrong. A cabinet officer who had spent some years not, like Mr. Mellon, in obscuring his activities from the public, but, like Hamilton or Gallatin, in making his own views a matter of public conviction, would have been far more useful to the president. It is this type of man for whom he must seek; and, in a democracy, he is rarely to be found unless, at a comparatively early age, he has that direct experience of the art of public persuasion which is central to the achievement of the democratic purpose.

The reason, in a way, is not dissimilar from that which has made eminent naval and military men so unsuccessful in Great Britain—Lord Kitchener is the outstanding example—as ministers of the Crown. For the higher the office they reach in their respective professions, the more cut off they are from debate with other men on equal terms. No one can effectively argue with another man on his knees; and the soldier and sailor in high command have become so accustomed to the unquestioning acceptance of their views that they too seldom are accessible to that criticism which makes them state, and defend from attack, the groundwork of their basic assumptions. In the context of their cabinets, most presidents have been too much in this position. The men to whom they have been compelled to listen are too seldom independent men. In any case, the elevation of the presidency is so high that it does not make criticism from colleagues an easy matter; and, beyond this, there have been too many cabinet officers whose status had no significance in itself and except as office conferred it upon the particular occupant. That was, I may add, the inherent weakness of Colonel House's position in relation to President Wilson; his value ceased as soon as he chose to take an independent line. He was an intimate collaborator as long as he was content to be an echo; he was permanently estranged as soon as he tried to take a line of his own. A president, in the modern scene, who is likely to be successful must have about him men who are capable of taking a line of their own.

It is not, I think, an answer to this to say that the American Constitution makes provision for this necessity by the device of the separation of powers. For there is all the difference in the world between response to criticism which may be made without loss of prestige, and response which, if it is made, can at once be acclaimed as a partial surrender. The president's need is for men about him whose opinion on the general problems of his administration it is worth his while to hear, and this is a matter of finding men who are accustomed to expecting that attitude to their opinion and habituated to its formulation. Such men, as I have said, can be found in that broad category we call the public life of a nation. I do not think they can easily be found elsewhere, and because that is where they are most likely to be found, I suggest that, disregard being given to identity of general aims, their proper place is in the cabinet. A good cabinet ought to be a place where the large outlines of policy can be hammered out in common, where the essential strategy is decided upon, where the president knows that he will hear, both in affirmation and in doubt, even in negation, most of what can be said about the direction he proposes to follow. The evidence, I think, makes it clear that few American cabinets have been of this quality; they have not been a team of first-rate minds pooling their ideas in common. And until they become, by deliberate construction, as near such a team as it is possible for a president to make, he will not have at his disposal the basic human resources he needs to grapple with his formidable task.

This is a general problem: the choice of the statesmen who are to be the intimate collaborators of the president. But there is also a more technical problem in the choice of those personal subordinates who are to form his secretariat. It is an issue that is being increasingly discussed; it is one of which it would be difficult to overestimate the human importance. It is not precisely the problem of the cabinet secretariat in Great Britain, so happily devised by Mr. Lloyd George,[15] but of something that reaches beyond it. An efficient secretariat is the president's eyes and ears; it is also one of the most time-saving instruments at his disposal, and perhaps of all devices the president has most need of one that will save his time. A good secretariat has to take care that he is aware of all the currents and cross-currents of opinion amid which he has so delicately to thread his way. It has to see that the information he requires is instantly available when he

---

[15] On this cf. Jennings, *Cabinet Government* (1936), pp. 186 f. and my *Parliamentary Government in England* (1939), pp. 251 f.

requires it. It has to provide for him the contacts he ought to make and, not less important, safeguard him from those which are time-consuming without being significant. It must be able to provide him with at least the basic outlines of the public pronouncements he must make; a secretariat which cannot perform a good deal of the "ghost writing" a president requires on so immense a scale is, by definition almost, an ineffective secretariat. It must be able so selectively to deal with his massive correspondence that he sees its meaning in its relevant proportions; and it must give him that relation to it which so remarkably enabled Lincoln to make thousands of humble folk feel that their private problems were, in the public eye, a matter of presidential concern. It must have the faculty of self-suppression; and yet its members must, as persons, be significant enough to talk with authority in the president's name. They must not only know how to negotiate on his behalf; they must know what are the matters upon which they can suitably negotiate on his behalf. Without a secretariat capable of this function and at this level, it is pretty certain that the task of the modern president is infinitely more complicated and burdensome than it needs to be.

I think it is clear that no modern president has had a secretariat of this kind. Those whom they have chosen have, for the most part, been minor party hacks picked for their acquaintance with the party machine, or journalists who had not reached pre-eminence in their profession. John Hay was, indeed, for a time one of Lincoln's personal secretaries, and he appears to have played his part well. But such evidence as we have suggests that few presidents have really thought out at all seriously either the kind of secretaries they require or the function they ought to perform. The nearest approach I know to this effort has been that of President Franklin Roosevelt in the use he has made of Mr. Corcoran and Mr. Benjamin V. Cohen;[16] and it is interesting that a not inconsiderable part of the remarkable work they have done has aroused resentment rather than understanding. That resentment, perhaps, is not unconnected with the recommendation of the president's Committee on Administrative Reorganization that the members of the secretariat which they propose should have a "passion for anonymity." That is not, I fear, a possible ideal. Anyone today who is in the continuous service of the White House is, in the nature of things, news; their problem is less the "passion for anonymity" than the very different one of being able at one and the same time to deflect a reasonable amount of thunder and lightning away from the president without ceasing to be "available" for his purposes. If they succeed in doing that with skill and insight no one can say, granted the delicacy of the task, that they have failed.

The "passion for anonymity," indeed, deserves a separate word. If it is intended to connote the desirability of a secretariat whose ambition cannot be distinguished from the ends of the president, so that their own careers are subordinate to his purposes, it is, I

[16] For some account of their work see Joseph Alsop and R. Kintner, *Men Around the President* (1939).

think, an unexceptionable demand. If it is intended to mean that they should deliberately screen themselves from the public view, I believe that the end called for is not attainable, and possibly not even desirable. A dictatorship can afford, is even built upon, the *éminence grise*; and the history of Lord Esher reminds us that it is even compatible with constitutional monarchy.[17] But, in a democracy, I suggest that the more we know of the men who actually assist in the shaping of policy, the more honest that policy is likely to be. Those who do in fact shape it are pretty certain to be discovered; and it is better that they should be responsibly discovered than vaguely suspected. From the spring of 1938, for example, the rule of anonymity in the British civil service has helped to make of Sir Horace Wilson an omnipresent Machiavelli exercising an evil influence in every direction. I do not know what policies he has recommended, still less whether they have been wise or unwise. What, however, is clear is that the responsibility for action upon them is that of the British prime minister and his colleagues, and that Sir Horace Wilson has been fulfilling the role that is historically assigned to a civil servant of eminence in his country. That this role, and its performer, should be fully known is, I suggest, far better than that he should be the victim of every malicious quidnunc who can find a place for the deposit of his poison. In the end, that kind of speculation is bound to be injurious to the utility of any official who is its

[17] See his *Journals and Letters* (1934), 3 vols.; and my *Parliamentary Government in England* (1939), pp. 337 f.

subject. It prevents him from performing adequately those tasks that, under any circumstances, someone must perform. It offers the largest possible front to any intrigue against him, especially to illegitimate intrigue. So, certainly, it has been with Sir Horace Wilson. So, I think, it has been also with Mr. Corcoran and Mr. Cohen. Their only reward can be the confidence of the man they serve. But the way to preserve that confidence is by the public definition of their function. It can rarely be maintained if they are visualized as, so to speak, a class of administrative "G" men.

Such a secretariat as I have described is, I believe, an urgent necessity at the White House. It ought to act as a liaison between the president and the departments, between the president and the legislature, and, to some extent at least, between the president, the press, and the public. Its members will require ideas and imagination and discretion. Normally, they will need a good deal of experience in the ways of an administration; and this suggests at least the probability that a good deal of their value will be lost if they change with each president who comes into office. For I should judge from the available evidence that so far, most presidential secretaries have become really valuable to their chiefs just about the time when their term of office was drawing to a close. A man of extraordinary capacity can, no doubt, pick up the threads of this delicate task with exceptional rapidity. In general, its very range and multiformity makes it unlikely that this will be the case. It follows from this, I think, that an unchanging personnel in such a secretariat is undesirable. Men who have become habituated to a dozen years of Republican rule like those from 1920 to 1932 will not easily accommodate themselves to the exciting adventurousness of the New Deal. If they are to work usefully, accommodation to the presidential purpose, to its mood and atmosphere not less than to its ideas, is fundamental. This seems to me to involve a core of permanence in the secretariat; the tradition and experience must be handed on from generation to generation. But it seems to me, also, to involve a need in each president to supplement that core of permanence with a small group of men whom he has himself chosen because he feels that they are, in a special sense, his own men. So organized, and working as a team—a vital element in the whole situation—such a secretariat ought to be invaluable to a president. It could see with his eyes and hear with his ears. It could perform a good deal of that incubation of ideas which enables him to take up the threads of a problem midway to its solution. No secretariat can ever make the load of a president anything but grim and heavy; that is the inherent price of being the president of the United States. But, on these conditions, such a secretariat could do a good deal to make the load less intolerable than it now is.

4

Yet, after all, the main problem for the president is his relation to that queer, shifting, labyrinthine amalgam we call public opinion. An average president is

[263]

likely to be a man in early middle age; Theodore Roosevelt, who became president accidentally at forty-three, is the only man, so far, to have attained the office under the age of forty-five.[18] He ought, therefore, to be at the height of his powers, old enough to have the maturity of experience, still young enough to bring energy to its interpretation. But, as he sets about his task, there are certain things he is constrained to remember. Most of the problems he will encounter are, in their ultimate foundations, shaped for him by the great, impersonal forces of past history; he will be able, proportionately, whatever his ability and energy and good will, to affect them in but a small way. He will be dealing with people who, on any showing, are mainly wrapped up in their private lives. They will find the bridge from their particular to his universal through the special interests of the environment in which those lives are enfolded. He will be dealing, too, with a people which is still externally, rather than internally, conscious of its unity, which can still be made only through a gigantic effort to think upon a national plane. Perhaps only two peoples, the Greeks and the British, have been more politically minded than the American; yet, to most of them, the drama of politics is compelling in an interstitial, rather than in a wholesale, way. Indeed, it is almost true to say of them that they are interested rather because things go wrong than because things go right. The harvest is so abundant that

[18] Pierce, Grant, and Cleveland were all under fifty on accession to office; the average age on accession is fifty-five.

prices fall; and the farmer looks suspiciously to know what the government proposes to do. The Stock Exchange is sluggish; and its votaries look around for presidential measures they may blame. The miners have gone on strike, and the winter coal supply is in danger; all eyes are turned on the White House to see how the president will tackle the threatened scarcity. The war clouds lower in Europe; what action will the president take to dispel them? Somehow, he has to transcend the hundred forces, the thousand voices, which compete to turn attention away from, or against, his central purposes. He has to seek the means of making men think his way, rather than another way. How far is it a possible task?

How far, moreover, is it a possible task in the light of certain facts that the observer is too prone to forget? He is president of the United States; but, in all probability, something like 40 per cent of the voting electorate has thought he ought not to be president, is ready, therefore, even eager, to be convinced that the case against him has been decisively made.[19] He is president of the United States; but a very considerable portion of those who voted for him feel that it is an essential part of his function not to compel them again to an interest in politics until the next time they have to vote. Thinking government always provokes a maximum resentment against itself, since the first thing upon which men economize is thought. He faces, too, on any showing, an opposition which will

[19] Cf. Holcomb in Logan, *The American Political Scene* (1938), Chap. 1 for statistics of voting in recent presidential elections.

exhaust all the resources ingenuity can invent, and money can buy, to represent all he does, and most of the things he does not do, in the worst possible light. He is president of the United States; but more people know intimately the habits of their favorite movie star, or the record of the outstanding baseball player of the season, than know the content of his policies. He is dealing all the time with those forces of tradition it is so difficult to move and so troublesome indirectly to circumvent. He is asking all the time, also, for an attention that demands effort, and often action, from people whose instinct it is to remain spectators, even aloof spectators, of the drama in which he is principal actor. "I am not interested in politics": is there any phrase more common in the discussions of our time? He has to deal with indifferent people and angry people, with the ambitious and the disappointed, with the cynical and the corrupt, as well as with those who are genuinely affected with a disinterested zeal for the public good. Only too often, he finds himself the victim of events he cannot control; the purpose he meant to be central becomes peripheral; the side issue becomes the fundamental theme. If he is always in a position to influence events, he cannot but remember that he is never in a position to dominate them.

Yet he starts with advantages that are important, if he knows now to capitalize them. For five months before his election he has been the central figure in the public attention. He has the opportunity to create expectancies. He has the power to compel discussion.

What he has to say, the very minutiae of his personality, will be the theme of talk in twenty million homes. Around him and his plans are a myriad hopes and fears. His problem is to maintain all he can of the tempo of those months. The answer to his problem lies in his having continuously something real to say, something positive and significant to do. The experience of the New Deal has shown, I think, decisively what an immense impact the personality of a president can make when he is able to arouse and retain the conviction that something of real importance is afoot. Whatever his effect upon Congress, a president who can get to the multitude will seize the attention of the multitude. His ideas, his policies, his purposes, will shape the mental climate as will those of no other man in America. He must, of course, be persistent in keeping them to the fore. He must see to it that they are not forgotten. He must persist; but he must never so persist that the public becomes fatigued with the debate in which he is engaged. He must convey the sense that the victory of his purposes is really of importance; and the best way to convey that sense is to fight battles in which both his supporters and his opponents alike feel that his victory really is important. That, it may be noted, has been the secret of much of the hold President Franklin Roosevelt has maintained over his electorate. He has gone for the big things; he has dramatized the issues upon which men know that their lives depend. He has communicated his own eagerness to those upon whose interest he has to rely. The enthusiasm of his supporters, the hate, even, of his opponents, have given a color to his term of office that has influenced millions to whom the spectacle is rarely of itself arresting. He has known how to prick men into thought, not least to prick the younger generation into thought. Because he has himself cared so much, he has made others care too.

That quality, it is important to note, has been characteristic of every significant president in the record. It is true of Jefferson, of Jackson, of Lincoln, of Theodore Roosevelt, of Woodrow Wilson. They were all positive presidents. They had a policy to recommend which seemed to their generation a challenge. Their supporters were, because of this, something more than the little regiment of professional politicians to whom the battle is significant for its spoils. They were, as in a war, an army of enthusiastic volunteers whose public interest in the outcome transcended their private inclination to aloofness. The leader's passion has communicated itself to his followers. He has aroused the dynamic of democracy, an energy, when it is aroused, more powerful and more pervasive than the dynamic of any other form of state.

This is, I think, the answer to the problem I have put. The president who can arouse this dynamic will make his policies a central thread in the life of the electorate. To do so, his effort must be a challenge. It must look forward and not backward. It must arouse a quality of interest that is essentially moral and positive in its nature. To end slavery, to curb the money-power, to build the "New Freedom," to establish, beyond peradventure, the foundations of the

"New Deal"—these make their appeal to the impulse of the crusader in man. The president who can do this penetrates within and beyond the little private life of the individual and links him, through himself, to purposes felt as great. There is an exhilaration in the atmosphere, a sense of big things on foot, which lifts the individual out of himself. Anyone who compares the fierce tempo of American politics under Jackson with that of his successors up to Lincoln, or of the age of Coolidge and Harding with that of Franklin Roosevelt, will, I think, have some sense of what this dynamic of democracy can imply. With the wisdom or unwisdom of the objects to which it is devoted, I am not, of course, here concerned. What alone is important is to emphasize this reservoir of energy to which an appeal is possible, the certainty, when it is aroused, that it will give to the president an authority over public opinion sufficient to make his purposes compete successfully with all other elements in the national life.

The challenge he makes must, of course, be one that is related to and expressive of vital human aspirations; without that relationship, it will rapidly run into the ground. Normally, it must be sufficiently within the framework of what the national tradition is seeking as to express purposes the common man is prepared to accept as a natural part of that tradition. A president so far ahead of his time as to voice aspirations the common man is not yet ready to understand is inevitably doomed to failure. The kind of challenge, this is to say, that he must make is one for which history has already prepared a wide and secure foundation. It must seem immediately and recognizably desirable to a wide area of interests. It must, preferably, evoke attack from those who are widely felt to have been responsible for the need to make the challenge. From this angle, it is easy to see the significance of President Franklin Roosevelt's attack on Wall Street. Therein was implied not only a definite program of reform, the necessary emphasis, that is, upon positive aims; there was also implied the punishment of the men who were largely deemed responsible for the necessity of those reforms. In the first days of the New Deal, Wall Street could only have answered the challenge of the president had it been able, by the classic mechanisms of the free market, to overcome the gravity of the crisis. It would have had to establish recovery in order to stave off reform. Lacking the ability to do so, it transformed the reforming purpose into something akin to a religious crusade. It provided, the more it opposed reform, all the emotions of a drama in which each spectator felt himself associated with the fortunes of the actors involved. At its height, war and revolution provide that drama in its extreme form. In more normal times, the task of the democratic statesman is to elicit sufficient of the emotion to give the feel of great purpose in play, with sufficient of restraint to prevent the precipitation of conflict.

What I am seeking to say may perhaps be stated from a different angle. As soon as the American democracy moved into the epoch of the positive state, it could not afford the luxury of dull government.[20] For it is the inherent implication of dull government that the dynamic of the national life is not profoundly affected by its operations; and it is to the inherent dynamic of the positive state that the operations of government are profoundly important. From this it follows that the government of a positive state must, if it is to be successful, necessarily be a thinking government. It cannot function adequately either if, as with Harding and Coolidge, it has presidents with no ideas at all, or if, as with Mr. Hoover, it has a president whose fundamental philosophy is at variance with its implications. The party struggle in the positive state can safely afford to be built upon a difference of opinion about the rate of change; it cannot afford to be built upon a difference of opinion about the direction of change. Once it is so built over any considerable period of time the conflict between the interests that are battling for power becomes too intense to be compatible with the democratic process. The established expectations of men cannot then be satisfied within the framework of reasoned discussion, because one group will reject the assumptions upon which the other builds. We have seen in our own generation the outcome of such a rejection in Russia in 1917, in Italy in 1922, in Germany in 1933, in Spain in 1936. The positive state demands positive parties; and positive parties demand positive pres-

[20] For the distinction between "dull" and "thinking" government I am indebted to Bagehot, *Collected Works*, Vol. IX; but I fear he would not have approved the use to which I have put it.

[271]

idents. That is the only way in which a democracy can be enabled to affirm its own essence; and a democracy that cannot affirm its own essence is compelled to the loss of its dynamic principle. When that period arrives, its downfall is always imminent.

Now what I have called thinking government is a far more difficult thing than dull government for two reasons. It is not only against more things in the past history of the nation—things, often enough, which tradition has made semi-sacred—it is also for more things in its future history. By the ambit of its affirmations, it provokes more denial than dull government is likely to do. It exacerbates public feeling; it arouses far more vivid emotions than ordinary men have known themselves to possess. Thereby also, it should be remarked, it is a far more educative process than its opposite; and, from this angle, it is far more in accord with the implied logic of democracy. But the inference I am anxious to draw from the fact that thinking government is a difficult process is that, the more urgently it is required, the less valid it makes that doctrine of "availability" which, so far, has played too considerable a part in the choice of presidential candidates. For if a man is to be selected on the principle of least offensiveness, he is likely, above all, to lack the positive qualities the modern president requires. A happy phrase of Mr. Robert Jackson, the attorney-general of the United States, puts with some precision what I have in mind. "I do not know," he told the Commonwealth Club of San Francisco,[21] "whether President Roosevelt is to have a third term; I do know that there must be a third term for the New Deal." Presidential candidates, in other words, must, increasingly, be capable of the kind of leadership the positive state and its problems require. "Availability," however charming, does not produce that kind of leadership. It destroys the possibility of thinking government. It makes for acquiescence in the given *status quo* of any epoch. It closes the avenues to significant change. It is, by its nature, against the future; and, because it is against the future, it is bound to dissatisfy the established expectations of the present. As the new America unfolds its possibilities, the party which stands by the doctrine of "availability" may win an occasional victory; but it will condemn itself, I think inevitably, to long periods in which it is eagerly excluded from power.

For the "available" president will have offered too many hostages to fortune before election to strike out a strong line of his own; his power effectively to lead will have been stricken into impotence before it has got under way. That will mean that while he is president the effective center of policy will be in Congress and not in the White House. That means, as I have sought to show, not merely that there will be no creative central direction of purpose; it means, also, by the nature of what Congress is, the service of sectional interest rather than the service—so urgently required —of national need. For, as I have argued, nothing but strong leadership from the president can give to Con-

[21] Speech of July 6, 1939.

gress the coherence and the responsibility it requires if it is to have that organic unity fit for the needs of the positive state. An "available" president means a weak president; and a weak president means a strong Congress. But a strong Congress does not mean a Congress united in determination of its direction. It means a Congress led in many directions by men whose particular purposes have never been fused into one strong and central purpose. A weak president, in a word, is a gift to the forces of reaction in the United States. It enables them to manipulate and maneuver between every difference that is provoked by the absence of a strong hand at the helm. It arrests the power to transcend the negativism which the scheme of American government so easily erects into a principle of action. A weak presidency prevents that transcendence of the limitations of 1787 which the compulsions of our generation demand.

It is not, I think, an answer to this argument to say that, if emergency requires it, the strong man will be forthcoming. The question rather is whether he will be forthcoming for purposes that are valid in democratic terms. No doubt there is a real measure of truth in Bagehot's well-known aphorism that "the men of Massachusetts could work any constitution." When he wrote, his aphorism had far more truth in it than it has today, simply because the level of expectation from governmental action is so much higher than at any previous time. A constitution works well when men are in large agreement over the ends it should achieve; but their minds must be directed to the definition of those ends. And that there may be clarity in the direction, it is essential that there be leadership of a kind that no one but the president is in a position to supply. If he has the gift of leadership, if he has imagination, if, not least, he has the power, so supremely possessed by Lincoln, of understanding his fellow-men, he speaks in America from an unchallengeable eminence. Whatever voice is drowned amid the babel of tongues, his, granted these qualities, can always be heard. Even today there are phrases of Washington and Jefferson that remain a constant part of the national tradition; and some of the more vital of their gestures shape the habits to which all Americans must conform. Lincoln's brief utterance at Gettysburg has transcended all national boundaries; and wherever a civilized tradition remains, its echo still lives in the minds and hearts of men.

So, with great leadership in the president, it can continue to be with the American nation. If their problems are immense, so also is their promise. Their resources are still vast. There is absent from their lives the weight of that feudal tradition which still bears down so heavily upon Europe and Asia. They are an experimental people, restless, alert, energetic, in a degree that is rich with hope. They confront, no doubt, new issues in a setting far different from any that could have been conceived by the fifty-five men who gathered together in that summer of 1787 in Philadelphia. Science and technology have annihilated their isolation from the Old World. Their freedom is jeopardized, as so much of our freedom in England

[275]

is jeopardized, by their servitude to the past, by the tribute they pay to a privilege which, there as elsewhere, exacts its full meed of claim. But in America, as in no country save one in the world today, there are the two supreme possibilities of exhilaration and hope. With them, too, has come a new maturity and a new seriousness. More people are aware than ever before that institutions are made by men for the service of men, that they live as they are adapted to larger ends. More people, too, realize that the form of a constitution is a dead and inert thing save as it is inhabited by the quick spirit of men eager to make it serve planned purposes of a nobler design. A nation that wills to be free must, as it is there increasingly understood, see its traditions not as chains but as opportunities. To live creatively, it must discipline itself to trust, in the grand manner, the leaders of its choice.

No office in the world today carries with it greater responsibilities than the presidency of the United States; its holder needs the confidence of those who have elected him in full measure if he is to fulfil those responsibilities. He needs criticism, too; the knowledge that comes only through the expression of criticism of the grievances that are felt, the needs to which he must respond. But above all he requires, in a fuller measure than ever before, the chance to lead his people forward. If he has a duty to his people, not less is its duty to him. From it he must expect the renovation of faith in his purpose, the demand that he does not falter in setting that purpose high. Above all, for the refreshment of that faith, he must look to the common man. For it was the central purpose of the American dream to assuage his sufferings and to enlarge his prospects; it was its central purpose to make possible a genuine freedom for the many and not a privileged license for the few. As no man in the Western democracies, the president of the United States can lead in the task of giving reality to that dream. To do so he requires courage and ideas; to do so, too, he must be given the power adequate to his responsibilities. He is waging a war, as he fulfils his purpose, against those who, as Franklin Roosevelt has said, "have conceded that political freedom was the business of the government, but . . . . have maintained that economic slavery was no one's business. They granted that the government could protect the citizen in his right to vote, but they denied that the government could do anything to protect the citizen in his right to work and his right to live."[22] As a people permits the power of a propertied class to insist upon that denial, it embarks upon the road that leads, in the end, to tyranny.

Power, no doubt, is always a dangerous thing; and the temptation to its abuse, as no generation has learned more surely than our own, the subtlest poison to which a man may succumb. Yet power is also opportunity, and to face danger with confidence is the price of its fulfilment. That is why I end with the emphasis that the president of the United States

[22] *Public Papers and Addresses* (1936), V, 233. Speech on the acceptance of the renomination for the presidency.

must be given the power commensurate to the function he has to perform. It must be given democratically; it must be exercised democratically; but, if he is to be a great president, let us be clear that it must be given. With all its risks, its conference is the condition upon which the American adventure may continue in that form of which its supreme exponents have most greatly dreamed. To withhold it, or to frustrate its ample operation, is to jeopardize that adventure. For great power alone makes great leadership possible; it provides the unique chance of restoring America to its people.